Oracle Modernization Solutions

A practical guide to planning and implementing SOA
Integration and Re-architecting to an Oracle platform

Tom Laszewski

Jason Williamson

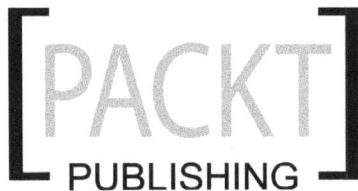

[PACKT] PUBLISHING

BIRMINGHAM - MUMBAI

Oracle Modernization Solutions

First published: September 2008

Production Reference: 2031008

Published by Packt Publishing Ltd.
32 Lincoln Road
Olton
Birmingham, B27 6PA, UK.

ISBN 978-1-847194-64-0

www.packtpub.com

Cover Image by Vinayak Chittar (vinayak.chittar@gmail.com)

Credit

Authors

Tom Laszewski

Jason Williamson

Co-Authors

Mark Rakhmilevich

Michael Oara

Prakash Nauduri

Reviewers

Bob Mackowiak

Marc Connolly

Mike Ballyntine

Senior Acquisition Editor

Louay Fatoohi

Development Editor

Nikhil Bangera

Technical Editor

Bhupali Khule

Copy Editor

Sumathi Sridhar

Editorial Team Leader

Akshara Aware

Project Manager

Abhijeet Deobhakta

Project Coordinator

Lata Basantani

Indexer

Monica Ajmera

Proofreaders

Claire Lane

Camille Guy

Production Coordinator

Shantanu Zagade

Cover Work

Shantanu Zagade

About the Authors

Tom Laszewski has over 20 years experience in databases, middleware, software development, management, and building strong technical partnerships. He is currently the Director of the Oracle Modernization Solutions team. He established the initial business and technical relationships with Oracle's modernization Systems Integrators and tools partners (the Oracle Modernization Ecosystem). His main responsibility is successful completion of all modernization projects initiated through the partner ecosystem. Tom works on a daily basis with EDS and HP alliances, technical architectures and account managers to ensure the success of joint modernization projects. He is also responsible for Oracle Modernization customer assessments and workshops, modernization reference architectures and modernization best practices.

Before Oracle, Tom held technical and project management positions at Sybase and EDS. He has provided strategic and technical advice to several starts up companies in the Database, Blade, XML, and storage areas. Tom holds a Master of Science in Computer Information Systems from Boston University.

I would like to thank my wife for being my voice of reason and helping me to be a better person. For my two boys (Slade and Logan), who make life worth living. Thanks to Marc Connolly and Bob Mackowiak of Oracle, and Mike Ballantyne of EDS for their technical advice and ideas to make the book better. To my current and best manager I have ever worked for, Lance Knowlton, for always being supportive of my career aspirations. To my previous manager, John Gawkowski, for giving me the initial opportunity to work in the exciting world of legacy modernization. Lastly, to Jay Peretz and Prakash Balebail for giving "my first big break" at Oracle.

As Product Manager of Modernization Solutions at Oracle, **Mr. Williamson** is part of the team responsible for developing and implementing Oracle's Modernization strategy, cultivating a partner ecosystem for implementing solutions that modernize to Oracle products. Mr. Williamson works with product management within Oracle and its partners to drive integration, innovation and adoption for modernization to open-systems.

Mr. Williamson has over 14 years experience in the software industry and has extensive knowledge in legacy modernization techniques and commercial software development. Prior to joining Oracle, Mr. Williamson was Global Product Management for BluePhoenix Solutions, where he was responsible for providing technical leadership and new product development within the legacy modernization space. Mr. Williamson also worked for Relativity Technologies assisting the modernization efforts of companies around the world. He has also successfully founded and launched a commercial software company, leveraging emerging technologies as well as creating and managing strategic partnerships key to the company's success. In addition his work within the technology sector Mr. Williamson also served in the United State Marine Corps. He lives with his wife Susan and four small children.

Mr. Williamson has a BSc MIS from the Virginia Commonwealth University.

I would like to thank my wife for her love and support in all of my efforts. God could not have given me a better partner! Thanks very much to all of the Oracle folks who helped me out and our partners. Thanks to the best boss I've ever had, Lance Knowlton, for encouraging me to do great things.

About the Co-Authors

Mark Rakhmilevich is a Director of Product Management for Mainframe Re-hosting and Modernization at Oracle. In this role he focuses on bringing together Oracle and partner solutions that help customers cut costs and modernize legacy applications by migrating mainframe applications to Oracle Database and Oracle's Tuxedo and WebLogic middleware platforms and extending them to SOA and XTP with ESB, BPM, and Business Rules solutions. Mark works with Oracle engineering to address the needs of extreme transaction processing for mainframe-class applications, and to provide mainframe extension and integration capabilities as part of Oracle Fusion Middleware. He supports marketing and sales, delivers customer seminars on Mainframe Modernization, and works closely with customers in US, Europe, and Asia. Mark has worked with platform vendors, global and regional SIs, banking and insurance ISVs, and key technology vendors to provide a complete solution that helps mainframe customers cut loose from the mainframes and/or extend their mainframe applications to SOA.

Prior to Oracle, Mark held senior engineering, management, product management and marketing roles at IBM, Compuware, Tandem, Valicert, Tumbleweed, Chordiant, and BEA. He has extensive experience in system design, software and systems architecture, program and product management, marketing and business development. Mark worked extensively with banks, insurers, payment networks, healthcare, and government organizations focusing on enterprise middleware and SOA platforms, mainframe application modernization, Web services security, financial messaging, PKI, B2B integration, and BPM-driven CRM solutions for customer servicing and selling across multiple channels. His early work at IBM on mainframe operating systems architecture for VM and MVS led to a patent award for "Logical Resource Partitioning of a Data Processing System" — the basis of the IBM LPAR technology for partitioning mainframes and UNIX servers into multiple virtual machines. He also led development and product management for several versions of IBM mainframe UNIX OSes and their clustering capabilities.

Mark has an MS in Computer Science from State University of New York at Albany, and BS in Computer Science from Lehigh University where he was elected to Phi Beta Kappa.

Michael Oara is a Co-founder and Chief Technology Officer at Relativity Technology Inc.

Michael Oara has 28 years of experience in enterprise software and is an acknowledged expert in automation methodologies for modernization and transformation of legacy applications.

Michael has written multiple articles on the subject of legacy modernization and is the author of a number of patents. He is an active member of the Architecture Driven Modernization Task force of the Object Management Group.

Prior to Relativity Technologies, Michael was Director of Development for Seer Technologies, a pioneer in technology for building large-scale client/server systems and legacy modernization software. He has also worked for a number of banks in New York, where he has established an IT consulting company.

Michael has a MS in Mathematics from the University of Bucharest in 1979 and pursued graduate studies at the Courant Institute of New York University. As a teenager, he received the 1st prize in the Mathematical Olympiad in Romania.

Prakash Nauduri has over 16 years experience in databases, middleware, software development, and maintaining partnerships with SI's and ISVs. Prakash possess the unique ability to work on technologies from Java EE to Oracle Warehouse Builder, and from mainframe CICS adapters to Oracle BPEL Manager. His strong technical aptitude along with customer relationship skills has helped him become very successful in his roles throughout his career.

Prakash Nauduri is currently the Technical Director of the Oracle Modernization Solutions team. He played a major role in creating initial technical relationships with Oracle's modernization SIs and tools partners (the Oracle Modernization Ecosystem). He was instrumental in defining Modernization Framework as well as promoting Oracle technology stack as the foundation for target platforms. Prakash works with strategic SIs like EDS, HP and Unisys on a regular basis to bring fruition to customer projects/POCs. Prakash is also responsible for technical architectures and project leadership to ensure the success of joint partner and customer modernization projects. He is also responsible for Oracle Modernization Workshops, modernization reference architectures and modernization best practices.

At Oracle, Prakash formerly was a Principal Technologist in Oracle's Partner Technology Group (PTS). Since joining Oracle in 1998, Prakash has engaged with hundred's of ISVs in various industry verticals like healthcare, financial services, retail, public sector, education etc enabling partner solutions on latest Oracle technology providing wide range of services including Architecture Reviews, Performance Benchmarks, Training etc.

Prakash previously worked as a Sr. Systems Analyst at auto major Hero Group in India handling system design, development, implementation roles.

Prakash holds a Bachelor of Science from India.

Table of Contents

Preface

Much has been written about legacy modernization in the past few years. Most of the books, analyst reports and white papers focus on why you should modernize and theorize at a high level regarding the different approaches and possible outcomes. This book intends to get to the heart of the matter very quickly and into the details of two very well known modernization approaches—SOA Integration and Re-architecturing.

The book is agnostic in terms of hardware and operating systems as most of these have proven to be able to handle the reliability, scalability, and performance of a mainframe system.

What This Book Covers

Chapter 1 gives an overview of the legacy modernization space. Here, we look at the different options for modernization and some of the drivers of modernization.

Chapter 2 Here, we will present an overview of modernization through SOA Integration. We will explore three strategies for SOA Enablement and when these options make sense.

Chapter 3 The focus of this chapter is to place SOA in the context of Modernization. SOA Legacy Modernizaton will bring you legacy IT infrastructure into the world of World Wide Web, Web 2.0, and all the other latest Internet-based IT architectures.

Within days, a legacy system can be accessed via a web browser. Your time-to-market using the Legacy SOA Integration approach is weeks, instead of months or years for some other modernization options.

Chapter 4 is an SOA Integration hands-on example using web enablement of mainframe COBOL/VSAM. We will use Java Server Pages (JSP), Java Database Connectivity (JDBC), the Oracle Legacy Adapter, Oracle Application Server, Java EE Connector API, and XA transaction processing to show a two-phase commit across an Oracle database and VSAM on the mainframe.

Chapter 5 takes a deep dive into what re-architecture is, how to approach re-architecture and strategies for execution. This will enable you to gain an understanding of this modernization option and prepare you for hands-on examples in the next chapters.

Chapter 6 Re-architecture is a multidimensional set of technologies and business drivers, similar to a Rubik's cube. In this chapter, we will simplify the target architecture variable, by making a move to Oracle. Even as we do this, we will find a wide selection of Oracle products and technologies, which we will narrow down for you. We end the chapter with a mapping of re-architecture business drivers to Oracle products, and finally a bit about modernization re-architecture and IBM.

Chapter 7 There are probably some legacy systems out there without batch, but it is most likely that batch processing is a key component of your mainframe legacy system. Business information processing in today's world is workload automation centered, event focused, and business-centric. However, we learn in this chapter that there are many reasons—both technical and business—why nightly batch jobs will be with us for some time. New technologies such as BPEL could potentially replace classic mainframe job scheduling software in the distant future.

Chapter 8 The online technical architecture has the potential to be much more complex than the batch open system architecture because the possible combination of products and technologies are endless. The combinations of target products and technologies include everything from cell phone access, to ERP application integration, to business intelligence, and transactions across multiple databases from different vendors. The same can be said of the source legacy system: multitudes of end user devices, languages, transactions processors, and databases. What we will immediately do is simplify the target architecture to three layers: presentation, transaction, business logic processing and database.

Chapter 9 The purpose of the scenario is to reinforce that re-architecture is not "rip and replace", but leveraging existing mainframe artifacts and forward engineering these artifacts into an Oracle/Java EE architecture using Relativity, and Oracle tools and products. The focus in this example will be on Relativity tools because the most complex and important aspects of re-architecture are discovery, recovery, capture of legacy artifacts, and creating a source model. The source application is a classic mainframe COBOL/CICS/VSAM/DB2 order entry system.

Chapter 10 Re-host based modernization approach is focused on migrating the application off the mainframe to a compatible software stack on an open-systems platform, preserving the language and middleware services on which the application has been built. It preserves legacy investment by relying on a mainframe-compatible software stack to minimize changes in the core application, and preserve the application's business logic intact, while running it on an open-system OS using more flexible and less expensive system infrastructure. It keeps open the customer's options for SOA enablement and re-architecture, by using an SOA-ready middleware stack to support Web services and ESB interfaces for re-hosted components.

Chapter 11 will let us examine trends in computing, where the modern data center is going and how this affects modernization choices today. We will see where the industry is trending with respect to tools, software and infrastructure. We'll examine concepts such as cloud computing, model driven modernization and green computing.

Appendix A gives an overview of the technological terms and legacy acronyms used throughout the book.

What You Need for This Book

- Application Server 10g Release 3–Version 10.1.3.3
  http://www.oracle.com/technology/software/products/
  ias/index.html

- Application Server Adapters for Legacy Applications with Oracle Connect Mainframe component, Oracle Studio for Legacy Adapters, Legacy adapters for CICS, IMS/TM, IMS/DB, and VSAM
  http://www.oracle.com/technology/software/products/ias/
  htdocs/101310.html

- Oracle Business Process Analysis Suite — Version 10.1.3.4
  http://www.oracle.com/technology/software/products/
  bpa/index.html

- Oracle JDeveloper — Version 10.1.3.3
  http://www.oracle.com/technology/software/products/
  jdev/index.html

- Oracle SQL Developer — Version 1.5.1
  http://www.oracle.com/technology/software/products/
  sql/index.html

Who is This Book For

Legacy system architects, project managers, program managers, developers, database architects and Cx0 technology decision makers tasked with modernization will all find this book useful.

The book assumes some knowledge of mainframes, J2EE, SOA, and Oracle technologies. The reader should have some background in programming and database design.

Conventions

In this book, you will find a number of styles of text that distinguish between different kinds of information. Here are some examples of these styles, and an explanation of their meaning.

Code words in text are shown as follows: " This is not sufficient, as ERROR-CODE value 15 does not tell me anything about the real expectation about the shipping date."

A block of code will be set as follows:

```
MOVE INPUT-DATE TO DATE1
MOVE CURRENT-DATE TO DATE2
PERFORM DATE-INTERVAL-COMPUTATION
IF DATE-INTERVAL < 3 THEN
    MOVE 15 TO ERROR-CODE
```

When we wish to draw your attention to a particular part of a code block, the relevant lines or items will be made bold:

```
<center>
    <div style="position:absolute;top:625;left:0;width=1200">
    <input type="button" onclick="window.location=
        'ORDSET1.ORDMAP1.html'" value="Update" style="background-
        color:while;color:blue;border:1px solid black">
    <input type="button" onclick="window.location=
        'MENSET1.MENMAP1.html'" value="Return" style="background-
        color:while;color:blue;border:1px solid black"></div>
</center>
```

New terms and **important words** are introduced in a bold-type font. Words that you see on the screen, in menus or dialog boxes for example, appear in our text like this: " So we will name it the **inventory_by_state** ruleset ".

> Important notes appear in a box like this.

> Tips and tricks appear like this.

Reader Feedback

Feedback from our readers is always welcome. Let us know what you think about this book, what you liked or may have disliked. Reader feedback is important for us to develop titles that you really get the most out of.

To send us general feedback, simply drop an email to feedback@packtpub.com, making sure to mention the book title in the subject of your message.

If there is a book that you need and would like to see us publish, please send us a note in the **SUGGEST A TITLE** form on www.packtpub.com or email suggest@packtpub.com.

If there is a topic that you have expertise in and you are interested in either writing or contributing to a book, see our author guide on www.packtpub.com/authors.

Customer Support

Now that you are the proud owner of a Packt book, we have a number of things to help you to get the most from your purchase.

Downloading the Example Code for the Book

Visit http://www.packtpub.com/files/code/4640_Code.zip to directly download the example code.

The downloadable files contain instructions on how to use them.

Errata

Although we have taken every care to ensure the accuracy of our contents, mistakes do happen. If you find a mistake in one of our books—maybe a mistake in text or code—we would be grateful if you would report this to us. By doing this you can save other readers from frustration, and help to improve subsequent versions of this book. If you find any errata, report them by visiting http://www.packtpub.com/support, selecting your book, clicking on the **let us know** link, and entering the details of your errata. Once your errata are verified, your submission will be accepted and the errata added to the list of existing errata. The existing errata can be viewed by selecting your title from http://www.packtpub.com/support.

Piracy

Piracy of copyright material on the Internet is an ongoing problem across all media. At Packt, we take the protection of our copyright and licenses very seriously. If you come across any illegal copies of our works in any form on the Internet, please provide the location address or website name immediately so we can pursue a remedy.

Please contact us at copyright@packtpub.com with a link to the suspected pirated material.

We appreciate your help in protecting our authors, and our ability to bring you valuable content.

Questions

You can contact us at questions@packtpub.com if you are having a problem with some aspect of the book, and we will do our best to address it.

1
Introduction to Legacy Modernization

A lot has been written on legacy modernization in the past few years. Most of the books, analyst reports, and white papers discuss at a high level why one should modernize and theorize, and the different approaches to, and possible outcomes of modernization. Instead of going into modernization theory, we will quickly dive into the details of two very well known modernization approaches: **SOA Enablement** and **Re-architect**. There will be a specific focus on modernization to Open Systems taking advantage of the Oracle technology stack, which can provide mainframe quality of service while delivering the agility of a modern architecture simultaneously. We will uncover a specific set of tools and show the process from end-to-end.

We will take an agnostic perspective of hardware and operating systems as most of these have proven to be capable of handling the reliability, scalability, and performance of a mainframe system. In fact, at the time of this writing, the current records for transactions per second have been delivered with Oracle on Intel-based servers.

For most organizations, the ideal solution would be to re-architect everything since re-architecting yields the **most modernized** environment—the environment that makes the best use of modern technology, is the most agile when it comes to change, and relies no longer on legacy skill sets.

Although such a **big bang** scenario is technically feasible, in reality, it is difficult and risky for any organization to accomplish this in a single re-architecting step—no matter how desirable the outcome. Most organizations would view such a big bang approach as putting their entire organization at risk. As a result, they take several intermediate steps. The following chapters show several options that could be considered in order to **break down** the modernization problem into byte-sized chunks—all the while delivering the final goal of achieving a process-driven SOA architecture based on J2EE. Additionally, these intermediate steps of SOA enablement will yield measurable ROI and benefit.

What We Won't Cover

Before we begin our path to modernization, let's take some time to talk about the things that we will not cover in this book. The main focus of this book is a practical application of how to modernize a legacy application using two specific techniques. We won't cover topics such as marketplace, methodologies, and estimation techniques.

Methodology and Estimation

Countless books have been written on application development methodology. Every system integrator/programming shop within a large company or technology group has a general development methodology, be it waterfall, agile, or eXtreme programming. The techniques in this book can fit any given protocol.

Estimation is a bit different and varies from system to system and with the choice of the modernization option. It can depend upon factors such as target language, tools, and the level of automation you are employing. If someone tries to sell you a solution based on the line of code or function point counts and complexity, you can pretty much throw that out of the window. Function point analysis is a great tool for understanding the complexity of the source code and can drive estimation, but there is certainly no general formula for how long a modernization will take, or how much it will cost. Another book can be written on this subject.

The Modernization Marketplace and Why Modernize

If you are reading this book, then we will assume that application modernization is a necessity for you. You are looking at "how to modernize" rather than "why modernize". Further, much market research has been done on this subject. Countless presentations, white papers, and events are actively being conducted on this subject.

The largest and best of breed systems integrators of the world have practices built solely around the modernization market. There are several reasons that drive a legacy modernization project. High costs, lack of agility, an aging technology workforce are just some of the reasons for modernization. Sometimes the motivation to modernize is driven from the business, at other times it is pure technology play. The reasons are many, and the final decision to embark on this effort depends on each organization. Again, much material is being developed on this subject and is not the topic of this book.

The **Oracle Modernization Alliance (OMA)** is an effort by Oracle to bring together the best of breed partners and products to enable modernization to open systems. This is truly an emerging field both for companies considering modernization, and for the companies working to provide those technologies. The OMA is a resource to help customers identify the best path to modernization. The following is a table of some key resources that you can have access to from Oracle around modernization. In addition, we will list some key alliances that Oracle has in the modernization space. Here, you will find abundant market research, white papers, and links to key contacts for getting engaged on a modernization initiative.

Oracle Modernization Alliance resources are as follows:

- Oracle Modernization Alliance (`http://www.oracle.com/goto/oma`)
- Oracle Modernization Blog (`http://blogs.oracle.com/jblog`)
- Application Modernization Initiative (AMI) Oracle/HP/Intel (`http://www.hp.com/go/ami`)
- Oracle Migration Technology Center (`http://www.oracle.com/technology/tech/migration`)
- Oracle Migration Knowledgebase (`http://www.oracle.com/technology/tech/migration/kb`)

Oracle works with many global systems integrators who focus on legacy modernization. The following is a list of the current system integrators that are apart of the Oracle Modernization Alliance.

OMA Member System Integrator	Information Link on Modernization
Accenture	`http://www.accenture.com/Global/Technology/Application_Renewal`
Computer Sciences Corporation (CSC)	`http://www.csc.com/industries/government/offerings/938.shtml`
Datamatics Limited	`http://www.datamatics.com/`
Electronic Data Systems (EDS)	`http://www.eds.com/insights/whitepapers/legacy_modernization.aspx`
Hewlett-Packard (HP)	`http://www.hp.com/go/ami`
Hexaware Technologies	`http://www.hexaware.com/`
Oracle Financial Services Consulting	`http://www.iflexsolutions.com`
Perot Systems	`http://www.perotsystems.com/Services/Consulting/EnterpriseConsulting/Oracle`
TaTa Consulting Services (TCS)	`http://www.tcs.com/offerings/itservices/migration`
Unisys Corporation	`http://www.unisys.com/services/outsourcing/application__services`

Deep Dive on Approaches

There are five primary options for modernization, and all are worthy of deep exploration. In the next section, we will review each of these options at a high level. However, this book is a deep technical dive on two approaches for Legacy Modernization, namely SOA enablement and re-architecture. These two options are selected for two reasons. First, it gives a modernization option for staying on the mainframe (SOA enablement) and moving off the mainframe (re-architecture). Second, many organizations around the world are engaged on one of these two paths, or both in many cases. Although either modernization option can be chosen independently, together they provide a smooth and measured path to a modern environment without the risk of a big bang approach. We also cover a rehosting-based approach to modernization, which minimizes the upfront risk and supports SOA enablement and selective re-architecture during or following the automated platform migration. We will cover more of this later.

Overview of the Modernization Options

There are five primary approaches to legacy modernization:

- Re-architecting to a new environment
- SOA integration and enablement
- Replatforming through re-hosting and automated migration
- Replacement with COTS solutions
- Data Modernization

Other organizations may have different nomenclature for what they call each type of modernization, but any of these options can generally fit into one of these five categories. Each of the options can be carried out in concert with the others, or as a standalone effort. They are not mutually exclusive endeavors. Further, in a large modernization project, multiple approaches are often used for parts of the larger modernization initiative. The right mix of approaches is determined by the business needs driving the modernization, organization's risk tolerance and time constraints, the nature of the source environment and legacy applications. Where the applications no longer meet business needs and require significant changes, re-architecture might be the best way forward. On the other hand, for very large applications that mostly meet the business needs, SOA enablement or re-platforming might be lower risk options.

You will notice that the first thing we talk about in this section — the Legacy Understanding phase — isn't listed as one of the modernization options. It is mentioned at this stage because it is a critical step that is done as a precursor to any option your organization chooses.

Legacy Understanding

Once we have identified our business drivers and the first steps in this process, we must understand what we have before we go ahead and modernize it. Legacy environments are very complex and quite often have little or no current documentation. This introduces a concept of analysis and discovery that is valuable for any modernization technique.

Application Portfolio Analysis (APA)

In order to make use of any modernization approach, the first step an organization must take is to carry out an APA of the current applications and their environment. This process has many names. You may hear terms such as Legacy Understanding, Application Re-learn, or Portfolio Understanding. All these activities provide a clear view of the current state of the computing environment. This process equips the organization with the information that it needs to identify the best areas for modernization. For example, this process can reveal process flows, data flows, how screens interact with transactions and programs, program complexity and maintainability metrics and can even generate pseudocode to re-document candidate business rules. Additionally, the physical repositories that are created as a result of the analysis can be used in the next stages of modernization, be it in SOA enablement, re-architecture, or re-platforming. Efforts are currently underway by the **Object Management Group** (**OMG**) to create a standard method to exchange this data between applications. The following screenshot shows the Legacy Portfolio Analysis:

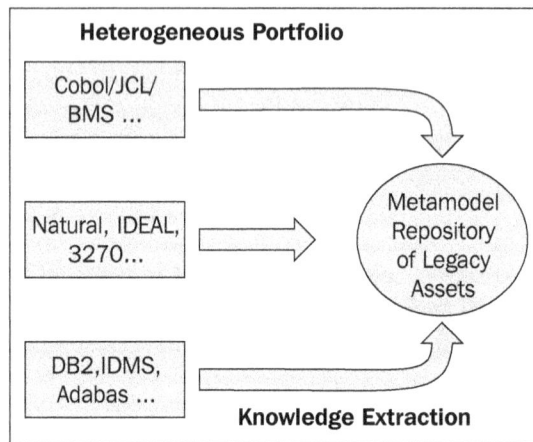

APA Macroanalysis

The first form of APA analysis is a very high-level abstract view of the application environment. This level of analytics looks at the application in the context of the overall IT organization. Systems information is collected at a very high level. The key here is to understand which applications exist, how they interact, and what the identified value of the desired function is. With this type of analysis, organizations can manage overall modernization strategies and identify key applications that are good candidates for SOA integration, re-architecture, or re-platforming versus a replacement with **Commercial Off-the-Shelf** (**COTS**) applications. Data structures, program code, and technical characteristics are not analyzed here.

The following macro-level process flow diagram was automatically generated from Relativity Technologies Modernization Workbench tool. Using this, the user can automatically get a view of the screen flows within a COBOL application. This is used to help identify candidate areas for modernization, areas of complexity, transfer of knowledge, or legacy system documentation. The key thing about these types of reports is that they are dynamic and automatically generated.

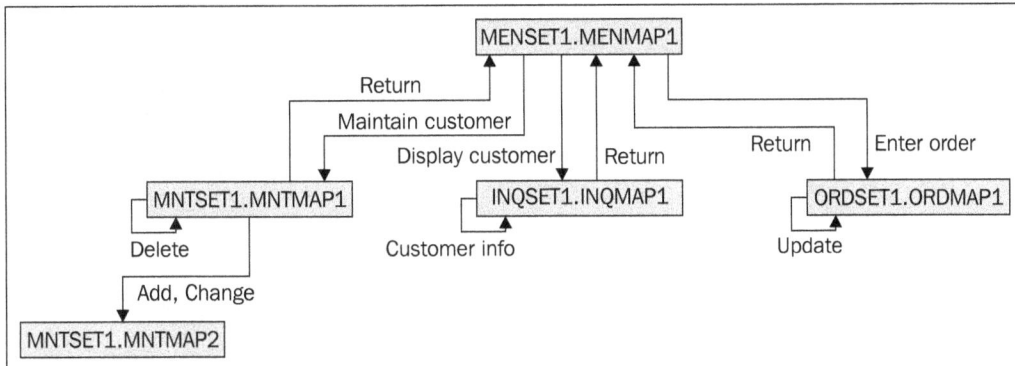

The previous flow diagram illustrates some interesting points about the system that can be understood quickly by the analyst. Remember, this type of diagram is generated automatically, and can provide instant insight into the system with no prior knowledge. For example, we now have some basic information such as:

- **MENSAT1.MENMAP1** is the main driver and is most likely a menu program.
- There are four called programs.
- Two programs have database interfaces.

This is a simplistic view, but if you can imagine hundreds of programs in a visual perspective, we can quickly identify clusters of complexity, define potential subsystems, and do much more, all from an automated tool with visual navigation and powerful cross-referencing capabilities. This type of tool can also help to re-document existing legacy assets.

APA Microanalysis

The second type of portfolio analysis is APA microanalysis. This examines applications at the program level. This level of analysis can be used to understand things like program logic or candidate business rules for enablement, or business rule transformation. This process will also reveal things such as code complexity, data exchange schemas, and specific interaction within a screen flow. These are all critical when considering SOA integration, re-architecture, or a re-platforming project.

The following are more models generated from the Relativity Modernization Technologies Workbench tool. The first is a COBOL transaction taken from a COBOL process. We are able to take a low-level view of a business rule slice taken from a COBOL program, and understand how this process flows. The particulars of this flow map diagram are not important; rather, this model can be automatically generated and is dynamic based on the current state of the code.

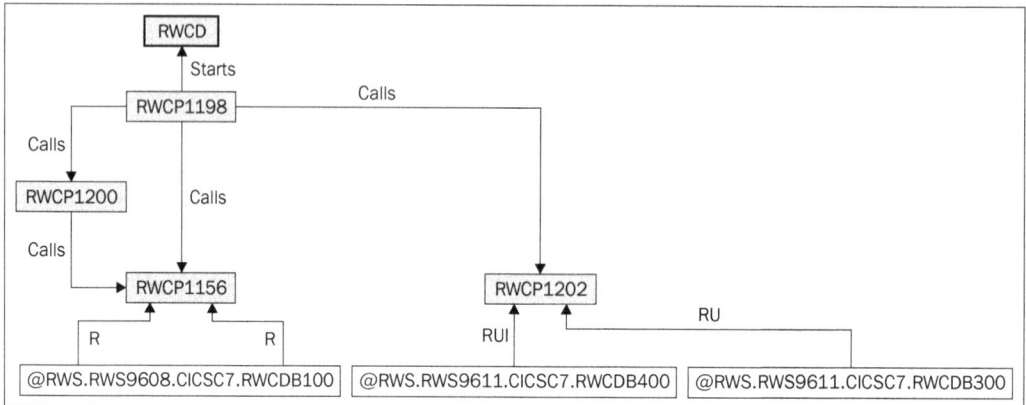

The second model shows how a COBOL program interacts with a screen conversation. In this example, we are able to look at specific paragraphs within a particular program. We can identify specific CICS transaction and understand which paragraphs (or subroutines) are interacting with the database. The models can be used to further refine our drive for a more re-architected system, help us identify business rules and help us populate a rules engine, which we will see in the later chapters.

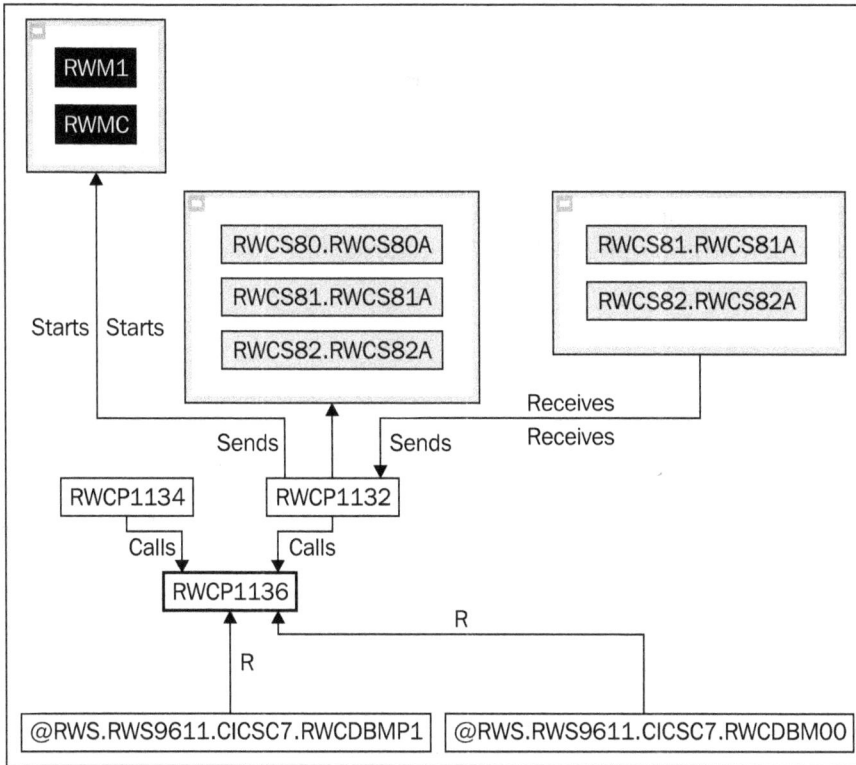

This example is just another example of a COBOL program that interacts with screens — shown in gray, and the paragraphs that execute CICS transactions — shown in white. So with these color coded boxes, we can quickly identify paragraphs, screens, databases, and CICS transactions.

Application Portfolio Management (APM)

APA is only a part of IT approach known as Application Portfolio Management. While APA analysis is critical for any modernization project, APM provides guideposts on how to combine the APA results, business assessment of the applications' strategic value and future needs, and IT infrastructure directions to come up with a long term application portfolio strategy and related technology targets to support it. It is often said that you cannot modernize that which you do not know. With APM, you can effectively manage change within an organization, understand the impact of change, and also manage its compliance.

APM is a constant process, be it part of a modernization project or an organization's portfolio management and change control strategy. All applications are in a constant state of change. During any modernization, things are always in a state of flux. In a modernization project, legacy code is changed, new development is done (often in parallel), and data schemas are changed. When looking into APM tool offerings, consider products that can provide facilities to capture these kinds of changes in information and provide an active repository, rather than a static view. Ideally, these tools must adhere to emerging technical standards, like those being pioneered by the OMG.

Re-Architecturing

Re-architecting is based on the concept that all legacy applications contain invaluable business logic and data relevant to the business, and these assets should be leveraged in the new system, rather than throwing it all out to rebuild from scratch. Since the new modern IT environment elevates a lot of this logic above the code using declarative models supported by BPM tools, ESBs, Business Rules engines, Data integration and access solutions, some of the original technical code can be replaced by these middleware tools to achieve greater agility. The following screenshot shows an example of a system after re-architecture.

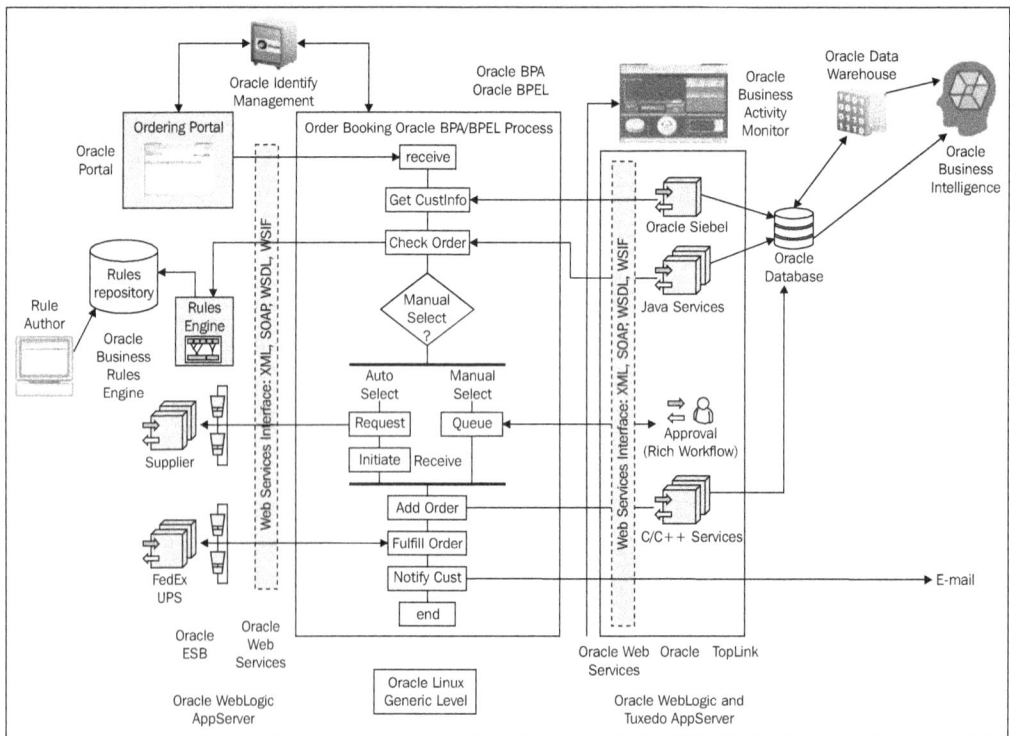

The previous example shows what a system would look like, from a higher level, after re-architecture. We see that this isn't a simple transformation of one code base to another in a one-to-one format. It is also much more than remediation and refactoring of the legacy code to standard java code. It is a system that fully leverages technologies suited for the required task, for example, leveraging Identity Management for security, business rules for core business, and BPEL for process flow.

Thus, re-architecting focuses on recovering and reassembling the process relevant to business from a legacy application, while eliminating the technology-specific code. Here, we want to capture the value of the business process that is independent of the legacy code base, and move it into a different paradigm. Re-architecting is typically used to handle modernizations that involve changes in architecture, such as the introduction of object orientation and process-driven services.

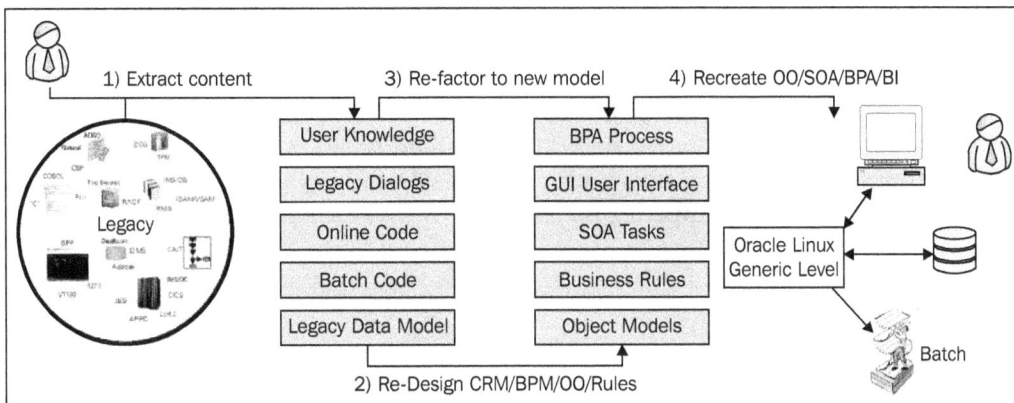

The advantage that re-architecting has over greenfield development is that re-architecting recognizes that there is information in the application code and surrounding artifacts (example, DDLs, COPYBOOKS, user training manuals) that is useful as a source for the re-architecting process, such as application process interaction, data models, and workflow. Re-architecting will usually go outside the source code of the legacy application to incorporate concepts like workflow and new functionality that were never part of the legacy application. However, it also recognized that this legacy application contains key business rules and processes that need to be harvested and brought forward.

Some of the important considerations for maximizing re-use by extracting business rules from legacy applications as part of a re-architecture project include:

- Eliminate dead code, environmental specifics, resolve mutually exclusive logic.
- Identify key input/output data (parameters, screen input, DB and file records, and so on).
- Keep in mind many rules outside of code (for example, screen flow described in a training manual.
- Populate a data dictionary specific to application/industry context.
- Identify and tag rules based on transaction types and key data, policy parameters, key results (output data).
- Isolate rules into tracking repository.
- Combine automation and human review to track relationships, eliminate redundancies, classify and consolidate, add annotation.

A parallel method of extracting knowledge from legacy applications uses modeling techniques, often based on UML. This method attempts to mine UML artifacts from the application code and related materials, and then create full-fledged models representing the complete application. Key considerations for mining models include:

- Convenient code representation helps to quickly filter out technical details.
- Allow user-selected artifacts to be quickly represented in UML entities.
- Allow user to add relationships and annotate the objects to assemble more complete UML model.
- Use external information if possible to refine use cases (screen flows) and activity diagrams—remember that some actors, flows, and so on may not appear in the code.
- Export to XML-based standard notation to facilitate refinement and forward-re-engineering through UML-based tools.

Modernization with this method leverages the years of investment in the legacy code base, it is much less costly and less risky than starting a new application from ground zero. However, since it does involve change, it does have its risks. As a result, a number of other modernization options have been developed that involve less risk. The next set of modernization option provide a different set of benefits with respect to a fully re-architected SOA environment. The important thing is that these other techniques allow an organization to break the process of reaching the optimal modernization target into a series of phases that lower the overall risk of modernization for an organization.

In the following figure, we can see that re-architecture takes a monolithic legacy system and applies technology and process to deliver a highly adaptable modern architecture.

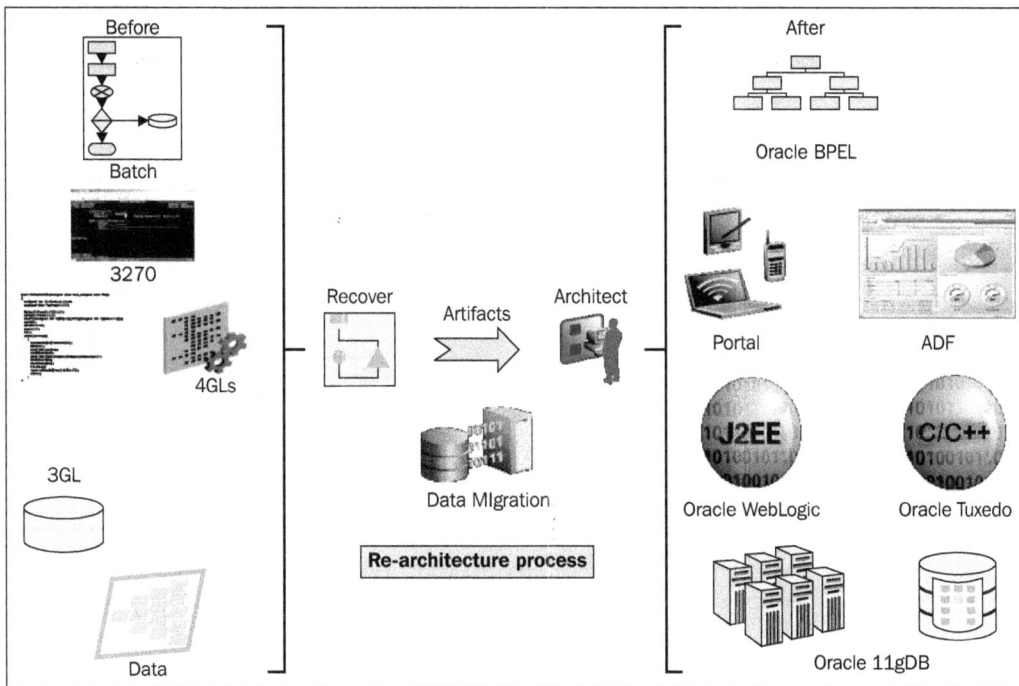

SOA Integration

Since SOA integration is the least invasive approach to legacy application modernization, this technique allows legacy components to be used as part of an SOA infrastructure very quickly and with little risk. Further, it is often the first step in the larger modernization process. In this method, the source code remains mostly unchanged (we will talk more about that later) and the application is wrapped using SOA components, thus creating services that can be exposed and registered to an SOA management facility on a new platform, but are implemented via the exiting legacy code. The exposed services can then be re-used and combined with the results of other more invasive modernization techniques such as re-architecting. Using SOA integration, an organization can begin to make use of SOA concepts, including the orchestration of services into business processes, leaving the legacy application intact.

Of course, the appropriate interfaces into the legacy application must exist and the code behind these interfaces must perform useful functions in a manner that can be packaged as services. SOA readiness assessment involves analysis of service granularity, exception handling, transaction integrity and reliability requirements, considerations of response time, message sizes, and scalability, issues of end-to-end messaging security, and requirements for services orchestration and SLA management. Following an assessment, any issues discovered need to be rectified before exposing components as services, and appropriate run-time and lifecycle governance policies created and implemented.

It is important to note that there are three tiers where integration can be done: Data, Screen, and Code. So, each of the tiers, based upon the state and structure of the code, can be extended with this technique. As mentioned before, this is often the first step in modernization.

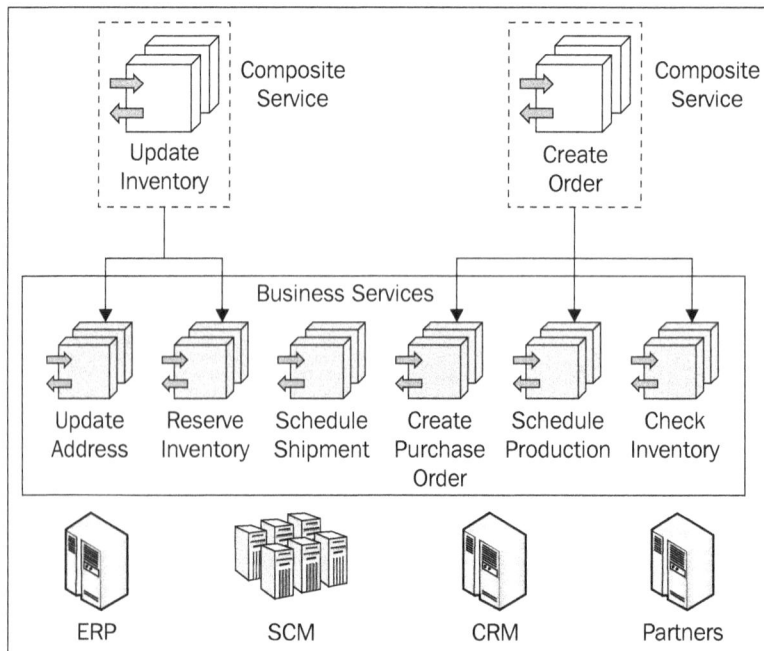

In this example, we can see that the legacy systems still stay on the legacy platform. Here, we isolate and expose this information as a business service using legacy adapters.

The table below lists important considerations in SOA integration and enablement projects.

Criteria for identifying well defined services	**Services integration and orchestration**
• Represent a core enterprise function re-usable by many client applications • Present a coarse-grained interface • Single interaction vs. multi-screen flows • UI, business logic, data access layers • Exception handling — returning results without tranching to another screen	• Wrapping and proxying via middle-tier gate-way vs. mainframe-based services • Who's responsible for input validation? • Orchestrating "composite" MF services • Supporting bidirectional integration
Discovering "Services" beyond screen flows	**Quality of Service (QoS) requirements**
• Conversational vs. sync/async calls • COMMAREA transactions (re-factored to use reasonable message size)	• Response time, throughput, scalability • End-to-end monitoring and SLA management • Transaction integrity and global transaction coordination • End-to-end monitoring and tracing
Security policies and their enforcement	**Services lifecycle governance**
• RACF vs. LDAP-based or SSO mechanism • End-to-end messaging security and Authentication, Authorization, Audition	• Ownership of service interfaces and change control process • Service discovery (respository, tools) • Orchestration, extension • BPM integration

Platform Migration

This area encompasses a few different approaches. They all share a common theme of low risk, predictable migration to an open system platform with a high level of automation to manage this process. With platform migrations, the focus is moving from one technology base to another as fast as possible and with as little change as possible. In Chapter 10, Introduction to Re-hosting Based Modernization using Oracle Tuxedo, we will focus on moving from mainframe platforms to open systems through a combination of re-hosting applications to a compatible environment maintaining the original application language (usually COBOL), and automated migration of applications to a different language when necessary. Each uses a high level of automation and a relative low level of human interaction as compared to other forms of modernization. The best re-platforming tools in the market are rules-based, and can also support automated changes to business logic or data access code when required to address specific business needs through specifically configured rule sets.

Automated Migration

Automated migration is a technique in which software tools are used to translate one language or database technology to another. It is typically used to protect the investment in business logic and data in cases where the source environment is not readily available or supportable (example skills are rare) on the target platform. Such migrations are only considered automated if the scope of conversion handled by the tools is at least 80 percent. Automated migration is very fast and provides a one-to-one functionally equivalent application. However, the degree of the quality of target code is heavily dependent upon what the source is.

There are two primary factors which determine how good the target application is. The first factor being, what is the source paradigm? If you are coming from a procedure-based programming model such as COBOL, then the resulting Java will not be a well-structured object-oriented code. Many vendors will claim pure OO, or 100 percent compliant Java. But in reality, OO languages programs can still be used in a procedural fashion. When the source is a step-by-step COBOL application, then that is what you will end up with after your migration to Java. This solution works quite well when the paradigm shift is not large. For example, going from PL/I to C/C++ is much more attainable with this strategy than converting COBOLto Java. This strategy is often used to migrate from 4GLs, such as Natural or CA Gen (formerly COOL:Gen) to COBOL or Java. Of the two target environments, migration to Java is more complex and typically requires additional manual re-factoring to produce proper OO POJO components or J2EE EJBs that can be easily maintained in the future.

The second factor one needs to consider is the quality of the source. Some re-factoring can be done on the source language, or the meta-language often generated in the transformation. But these usually only address things such as dead code or GOTO statements, not years of spaghetti code.

If your goal is to quickly move from one technology to another, with functional equivalence, then this is a great solution. If the goal is to make major changes to the architecture and take full advantage of the target language, then this type of method usually does not work.

Re-Hosting

Re-hosting involves moving an application to another hardware platform using a compatible software stack (example COBOL containers and compatible OLTP functionality provided by Oracle Tuxedo) so as to leave the source application untouched. This is most commonly used approach to migrate mainframe COBOL CICS to an open systems platform and has been used in hundreds of projects, some as large as 12,000 MIPS.

The fundamental strength of rehosting is that the code base does not change and thus there are no changes to the core application. There are some adaptations involved for certain interfaces, batch jobs, and non-COBOL artifacts that are not inherently native to the target environment. These are usually handled through automated migration. The beauty of this solution is that the target environment using open systems platform, typically UNIX or Linux, has a significantly lower TCO than the original mainframe environment, allowing customers to save 50 to 80 percent compared to their mainframe operations. The budget savings gained from this move can fund more long term, yet beneficial re-architecture effort.

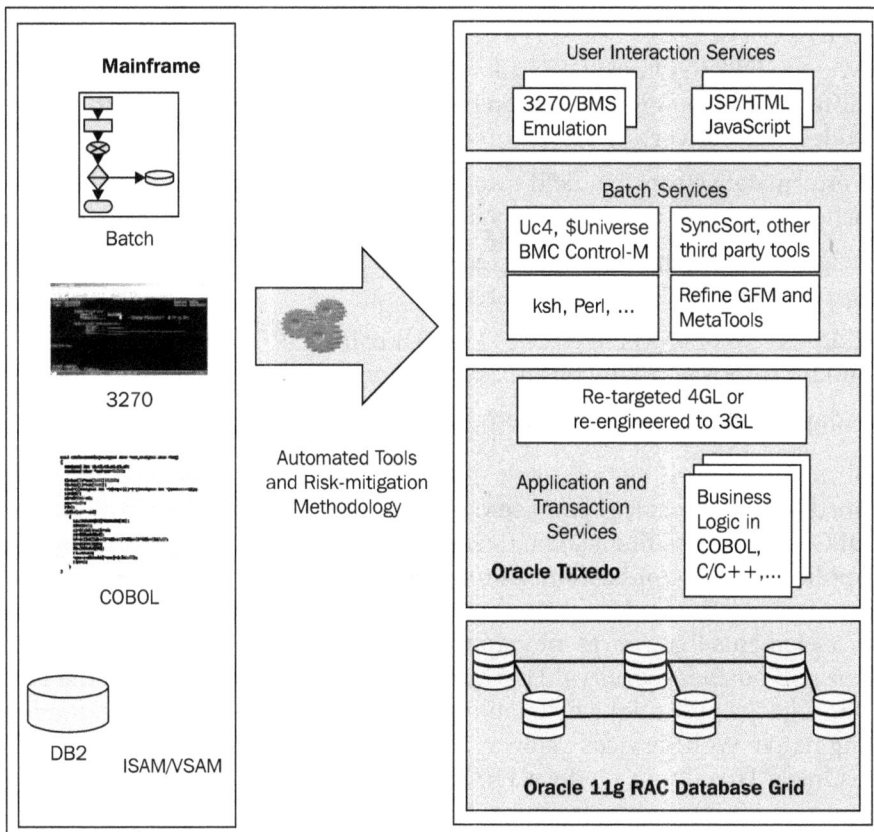

Re-Hosting Based Modernization

Evolving from the core re-hosting approach and leveraging flexible, rules-driven automated conversion tools, this approach goes beyond re-hosting to a functionally-equivalent application. Instead of a pure shift of COBOL code to a target system without any changes to the original code, some of the automated tooling used by Oracle's migration partners to re-host applications and data also enables automated re-engineering and SOA integration during or following migration. For example, Metaware Refine workbench has been used to:

- Automatically migrate COBOL CICS applications to COBOL Tuxedo applications.

- Convert PL/I applications running under IMS TM to C/C++ applications under Tuxedo.

- Identify and remove code duplication and dead code, re-documenting flows and dependencies derived from actual code analysis.

- Migrate VSAM data and COBOL copybooks describing the data schema to Oracle DB DDLs and automatically change related data access code in the application.

- Migrate DB2 to Oracle DB, making appropriate adjustments for data type differences, changing exception handling based on differences in return codes, and converting stored procedures from DB2 to Oracle.

- Perform data cleansing, field extensions, column merges and other data schema changes automatically synchronized across data and data access code.

- Migrate non-relational data to Oracle DB to provide broader access from applications on distributed systems.

- Convert 3270/BMS interface to Web UI using JSP/HTML, enabling modifications and flow optimization in original legacy UI.

- Adapt batch to transactional environment to shorten batch windows.

APA tools for automated business rule discovery can also be used to help identify well defined business services and use Oracle Tuxedo's SOA framework to expose these COBOL services as first class citizens of an enterprise SOA. This approach can also be applied to PL/I applications automatically migrated to C/C++ and hosted in Tuxedo containers. The bulk of the re-hosted code remains unchanged, but certain key service elements that represent valuable re-use opportunities are exposed as Web Services or ESB business services. This approach protects investment in the business logic of the legacy applications by enabling COBOL components to be extended to SOA using native Web Services gateway, ESB integration, MQ integration, and so on of the Oracle Tuxedo—a modern TP/Application Server platform for COBOL, C, and C++.

Thus, we gain a huge advantage by having a well structured, SOA-enabled architecture on a new platform that was delivered with a high degree of automation. Using a proven application platform with built-in SOA capabilities, including native Web Services support, ESB transport, transparent J2EE integration, and integration with meta-data repository for full services lifecycle governance, makes this a low-risk approach. It also helps to address some of the key considerations in SOA integration table above. With this approach we have the ability to extend and integrate the legacy environment easier than a pure re-host, while benefitting from the automation that ensures high speed of delivery and low risk that is comparable to a black-box re-hosting.

The other aspect of this process is identifying components that will benefit from re-architecture — usually code with low maintainability index or code requiring significant changes to meet new business needs — and using re-architecture techniques to re-cast it as a new components, such as business process, declarative rules in a business engine, or re-coded J2EE components. The key is to ensure that the re-architected components remain transparently integrated with the bulk of the re-hosted code, so that the COBOL or C/C++ code out-side of the selected components doesn't have to be changed. With Oracle Tuxedo this is done via transparent bi-directional support for Web Services (using Oracle SALT) and J2EE integration (using WebLogic-Tuxedo Connector). The key guidelines listed for business rules-extraction and model mining apply to the components selected for re-architecture.

Re-hosting based modernization is sometimes referred to as Re-host++. This term highlights its roots in re-hosting applications to a compatible technology stack together with the broad range of re-engineering, SOA integration, and re-architecting options it enables. This unique methodology is supported by a combination of an extensible COBOL, C, and C++ application platform — Oracle Tuxedo, with flexible, rules-driven automated conversion tools from Oracle's modernization partners.

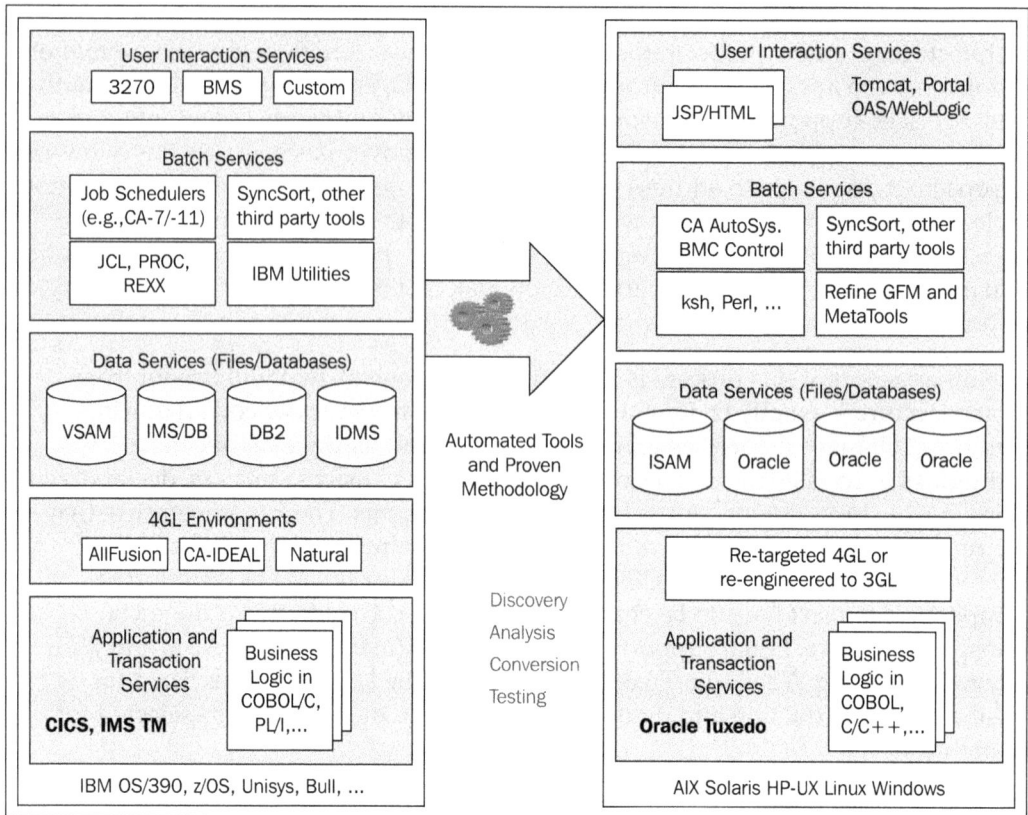

User Interaction Services			
3270	BMS	Custom	

Batch Services

Job Schedulers (e.g.,CA-7/-11)	SyncSort, other third party tools
JCL, PROC, REXX	IBM Utilities

Data Services (Files/Databases)

| VSAM | IMS/DB | DB2 | IDMS |

4GL Environments

| AllFusion | CA-IDEAL | Natural |

| Application and Transaction Services **CICS, IMS TM** | Business Logic in COBOL/C, PL/I,... |

IBM OS/390, z/OS, Unisys, Bull, ...

Automated Tools and Proven Methodology

Discovery
Analysis
Conversion
Testing

User Interaction Services	
JSP/HTML	Tomcat, Portal OAS/WebLogic

Batch Services

| CA AutoSys. BMC Control | SyncSort, other third party tools |
| ksh, Perl, ... | Refine GFM and MetaTools |

Data Services (Files/Databases)

| ISAM | Oracle | Oracle | Oracle |

Re-targeted 4GL or re-engineered to 3GL

| Application and Transaction Services **Oracle Tuxedo** | Business Logic in COBOL, C/C++,... |

AIX Solaris HP-UX Linux Windows

Data Modernization

Here we look at strategies to modernization—a set of data stores that are stored across disparate and heterogeneous sources. We often have problems with accessing and managing legacy data. There is an increase in cost to run batch jobs, which generate reports 24 to 48 hours after they are needed. Further, this legacy data often needs to be integrated with other database systems that are located on different platforms. So, from a business perspective, there is a real problem in getting actionable data in a reasonable amount of time, and at a low cost.

With Data Modernization solutions, we can look at leaving legacy data on the mainframe, pulling it out in near real time, lowering MIPS costs by processing reports outside of the batch winding, and integrating this with heterogeneous data sources. This is leveraged through employing several technologies in concert.

Legacy Adapters

With a collection of legacy adapters provided by Oracle and our partners, we are able to enable the organization to access almost any data store with any environment. Further, many of these technologies can employ bidirectional change data capture so that we can publish data changes to a data warehouse in near real time.

The following is the current list of legacy adapter and change data capture partners that are a part of the Oracle Modernization Alliance. The following is the list of legacy adapter/data migration partners along with their respective URLs:

- Attachmate (http://www.attachmate.com/)
- Attunity (http://www.attunity.com/)
- DateDirect Technologies (Progress Software) (http://www.datadirect.com/)
- GT Software, Inc (http://www.gtsoftware.com/)
- Hostbridge (http://www.hostbridge.com/)
- Micro Focus (http://www.microfocus.com/)
- OpenConnect Systems (http://www.oc.com/)
- SeaGull Software Systems (http://www.seagullsoftware.com/)
- Treehouse Software (http://treehousesoftware.com/)

With legacy data adapters, we can access relational and nonrelational data stores. So, once we have access to this information, we then need to rationalize that to a common data set. This is where we can employ Oracle's ETL Tools.

Using **Oracle Data Integrator (ODI)**, or **Oracle Warehouse Builder**, we can then connect to these data stores to do the data mapping and transformation. With ODI, we can integrate with high volume and event-driven processes. Once this has been transformed to the target database, we then employ **Oracle Business Intelligence**.

With **Business Activity Monitoring**, we can extend the notion of Business Intelligence and gain a real-time view into the business processes of the organization. Managers can now transform their core business from disparate data, expensive, and stale reports to a vision into the discrete business processing that drives the organization. This enables organizations to leverage their legacy assets to deliver not only key business intelligence, but also correlate these processes to key performance indicators (KPIs).

Finally, another important feature of this solution is that it is noninvasive. Many mainframe shops do not go for the large scale modernization efforts due to the perception of high risk involved. With data modernization, an organization can retain the entire legacy infrastructure without changing it. We would rather employ SOA technologies to extend the mainframe, while simultaneously lowering MIPS costs.

From a visual perspective, we can go from this type of latent and expensive static reporting:

To this, leveraging Business Activity Monitoring/Business Intelligent in a fully integrated manner.

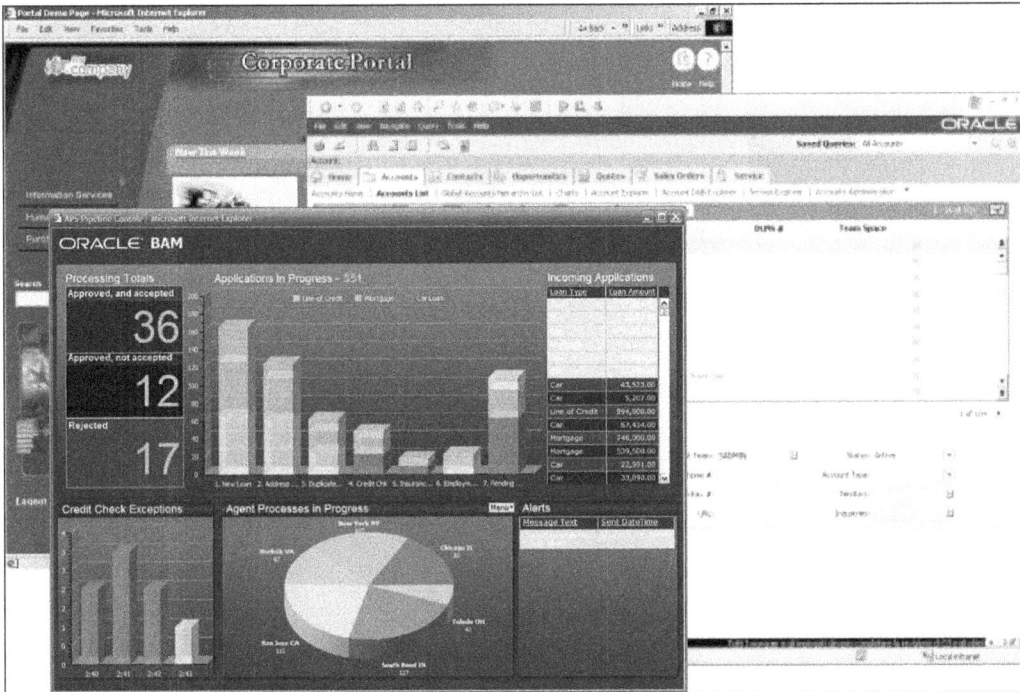

Replacement

Commercial Off-the-Shelf (COTS) products are frequently considered when a modernization project is undertaken. If the target package exists, COTS Replacement can be a highly cost-effective strategy with a significant reduction in risk. This works very well with common applications such as billing, HR, payroll, and other more commonly used applications.

The implementation of a COTS solution assumes that the organization is willing to adapt to the new system paradigm. Therefore, core business processes must be altered and adapted. Another aspect of a COTS Replacement built on a SOA framework is that one can utilize this new architecture for other component orchestration. Oracle Applications are built upon **Fusion Middleware**, which can enable an entire organization to integrate heterogeneous applications and data faster.

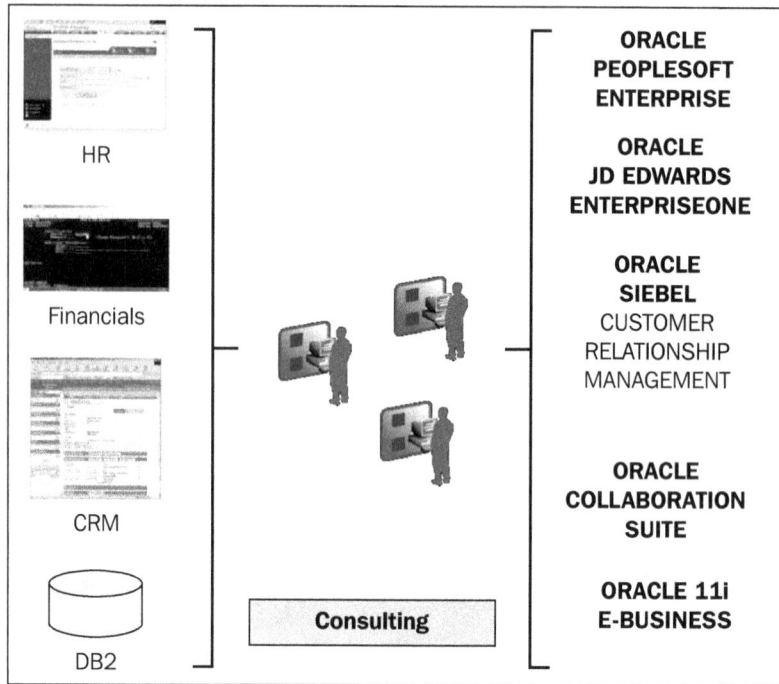

Business Value—What Really Matters?

It is very important to take a holistic view on what the benefits are for legacy modernization. There are, of course, cost savings in hard dollars that are associated with a large-scale modernization. After all, TCO/ROI is often what drives most organizations. However, we have seen an increasing amount of proof points around the soft dollar costs. Those are the benefits that have an indirect impact on costs, but a direct impact on the quality of service, agility, and the ability to service the customer. Remember, not all organizations are driven by profits, for example, the Public sector. So, C-level executives do not just look at the hard dollars, but also consider the soft dollar impact to modernization. The following is a detailed list of some of these hard and soft dollar benefits of legacy modernization. These are all real world examples, though some of the company names have been omitted for the purpose of nondisclosure.

These examples are mapped to specific Oracle products and partner's solutions delivered in a modernization effort.

Soft-Dollar Benefits	Solution Details	Hard Dollar Benefits
Improved access to data	Simplified access to relationally based data, open to self service reporting	Using Oracle BI (Discoverer) a United States federal research agency reduced Compliance with National Nuclear Security Agency regulations and management reporting from 5 weeks to less than an hour.
Ability to enable Business Intelligence	Data harvesting and business analysis enables business agility	A hardware storage vendor increased Sales Productivity 100 percent, sales metrics updated 4 times a day using Oracle BI
Grid enabled infrastructure	Oracle Database and Middleware Grid technology lowers costs, increases uptime, increases performance and allows for capacity 'on demand'.	Public information indicates the average results when moving from SMP to Oracle GRID: 1. ROI over 5 years ($1.7M investment) 150 percent 2. Hardware Savings First Year 55 percent 3. Projected HW Savings in 5 years 73 percent 4. Reduced Labor Requirement 3.75 FTE 5. Improved Computing Performance 10 percent
Reduced time to market for enhancements	Simplified and highly productive development environments enhance developer productivity	1. A sports equipment manufacture implemented a customized B2B portal built and launched in 3 months. 2. A U.S. based insurance company saw a 25 percent savings on process changes to the existing system using Oracle BPEL.
Faster response to regulatory/ legislative changes in health insurance	Migration from mainframe to Tuxedo enabled tighter integration with J2EE components at reduced cost and enabled development organization to immediately start extending existing COBOL application with Java components, transparently to existing COBOL programs	Modules that used to take 6-12 month to develop and deploy, are now completed in 2-3 month. Customer reduced overall TCO of $65M a year for a 12,000 MIPS mainframe environment down to $10M a year for an open systems infrastructure.
Open java based solution with vendor choice	Java based solutions foster greater competition among vendors and avoid vendor lock in	
Ability to use third party open tools	Very rich third party toolset eco-system using open systems	
Ability to create robust internet applications	Open access to end users, remote staffing, and partner eco-systems	

Soft-Dollar Benefits	Solution Details	Hard Dollar Benefits
Improved customer perception	Ability to develop dynamic, new generation applications enabled for emerging markets	An internal customer study (integrated platform running on a single instance) estimated a major U.S. based manufactures' overall investment generating $6.2 million in benefits and an ROI of 222 percent over the life of the project. In addition to capital cost avoidance, savings came from higher staff productivity across several departments, lower inventory carrying costs, and reduced IT management expenses. The investment also yielded significant strategic benefits by lowering 'the manufactures' risk of business disruptions, ensuring compliance with industry standards, and supporting new marketing and other business initiatives.
Improved time to market for enhancements	Ability to avoid IT backlog	US Navy project using a model-driven service framework provided up to 80 percent code generation, dramatically minimizing coding time. The Jacada Integrator product provided about a 90 percent codeless transactional integration solution for its Windows-based PowerBuilder application and its mainframe based financial information system.
Enabled for Business Process Optimization	Ability to optimize systems to capture new markets	
Real time processing vs. batch orientation	Ability to respond immediately to changing business conditions	
Reduced print requirements	Ability to elimate traditional costs of printing via online reporting	
Reduced report writing requirements	User reporting eliminates the need for centralization of reporting and associated costs	A shipping logistics firm on Oracle Fusion Middleware had the following to say after moving to Oracle based reporting: "Our fast-growing system handles the following: – Adds 215,000 new shipments a month – Sends 4,000 to 9,000 shipment milestone notification e-mails a day – Generates 15,000 reports a month (reports are customizable with over 70 possible information fields) – Server generates business critical documents such as bills of lading and invoices for customers"

Soft-Dollar Benefits	Solution Details	Hard Dollar Benefits
Business rules implementation	Ability to compartmentalize business logic for quicker response, lower maintenance costs and higher quality	
Common execution model	Ability to standardize on one model for database, application server and business rules and process environments	1. One study (integrated platform running on a single instance) estimated a major U.S. based manufactures' overall investment generating $6.2 million in benefits and an ROI of 222 percent over the life of the project. In addition to capital cost avoidance, savings came from higher staff productivity across several departments, lower inventory carrying costs, and reduced IT management expenses. The investment also yielded significant strategic benefits by lowering the manufacturers' risk of business disruptions, ensuring compliance with industry standards, and supporting new marketing and other business initiatives. 2. Another study (platform consolidation) estimates a public sector agency will realize cumulative benefits of more than $105 million over the life of their. project, translating into a net present value of $60.2 million. The public sector agency will achieve payback on its investment in about 2.5 years, the study projects, and earn an overall return on investment of about 137 percent. 3. A major university projects that their implementation will yield a savings of 185 percent during the next five years, taking into account the performance and availability of the new systems, and the efficiency gained in managing a single vendor's system.
Centralized systems management	Grid management technolgoy reduces systems management staff	Public information on Oracle Database 10G Grid Management indicates: 1. 46 percent less DBA time than DB2 UDB 8.2 2. 30 percent less DBA time than Microsoft SQL Server 3. Saves up to $50,000 per year per DBA

Soft-Dollar Benefits	Solution Details	Hard Dollar Benefits
Dashboard capabilities	Ability to enable dashboard capabilities for key decision makers	A higher education customer indicated: "Our legacy systems were unable to transform and organize data into the business intelligence the university needed. For example, the schools' management could not effectively analyze and manage the costs of services provided by the university's hospital, which accounted for 70 percent of the medical center's expenses. Without the means to make data available through Web browsers, the universities' users also lacked easy access to vital information." The university projects that the implementation will yield a savings of 185 percent during the next five years
Low cost development production environments	Jdeveloper represents outstanding development environment	"The built-in framework of Oracle JDeveloper makes our Java developers more productive. We can deliver J2EE applications based on the MVC design pattern in less than a month, compared to the many months it would have taken us without such a framework." — IT Manager, US state agency.
Native global language support	Cost avoidance supporting new markets	
Client training cost is reduced	Easy to use tools make training quicker and less expensive	1. A global IT organization tracks $1.5B EUR of projects for 15000 employees in 20 countries without end-user training. 2. A major hardware vendor deployed Oracle Analytics for sales-oriented contact center to 800 users in under 90 days. 3. A large telecom deployed Oracle Sales Analytics to 3000+ users in 3 months. 4. A Global drug maker project implementation cycle is 4 months from decision to live for 1200 users for Oracle Pharma Analytics. 5. A major IT software vendor goes live in 100 days, 6500 users using Oracle Sales and Marketing Analytics.
Client self-service changes, enhancements	Business Analysts, power users able to change rules, do data maintenance, report writing and so on.	

Soft-Dollar Benefits	Solution Details	Hard Dollar Benefits
Stream lined business processes	Reduced number of screens to complete a transaction, less manual workflow	
Open Systems, Distributed Job Scheduler estimated Cost Savings (TCO/ In Production)	A major analyst/research group identified an averaged payback period from deploying an open systems, distributed job scheduling software of 6.4 months, yielding an average return on investment of 342 percent.	
Open Systems, Distributed Job Scheduler estimated IT Productivity (38 percent of overall savings here)	To determine the increase in IT staff productivity from deploying the job scheduling software, a major analyst/ research group-asked questions about staff time needed for various activities related to IT administrative, operational and support functions, before and after the software's implementation.	Time savings on defining job schedules after deploying the software averaged 42.7 percent. On average, the companies also spent 33.6 percent less time on monitoring batch job operations. Additionally, there were average timesavings of 14.3 percent in managing and supporting desktops and other clients.
Open Systems, Distributed Job Scheduler estimated User Productivity (20 percent of overall savings here)	A major Analyst Group asked about the increase in productive time and percentage of users affected after deploying the software. This firm also inquired about the number of downtime incidents and amount of down-time before and after the implementation, as well as the percentage of users affected and their average loaded salary	Based on an average loaded salary for the first year of $32.30 per hour, and annual 5 percent increases, the savings in user productivity averaged close to $1.4 million annually over three years, or $9,023 per 100 users
Open Systems, Distributed Job Scheduler estimated CPU Cost Savings (29 percent of overall savings here)		The added CPU benefit came from an average 18 percent reduction in the length of batch windows. Over the three-year period, the CPU savings averaged more than $2 million annually, or $13,352 per 100 users.

Soft-Dollar Benefits	Solution Details	Hard Dollar Benefits
Open Systems, Distributed Job Scheduler estimated other cost savings (10 percent of overall savings here)	Additional savings came from reductions in IT travel, missed SLAs, and training costs, and from hardware and software savings.	These cost reductions averaged $718,942 a year. Taken together, the savings from improved IT management efficiency and cost reductions yielded an average total savings of $944,487 a year, or $6,196 per 100 users.
Open Systems, Distributed Job Scheduler estimated IT Efficiency (3 percent of overall savings here)	To determine increases in IT efficiency, a major research firm asked questions about the average number of users and jobs supported by each staff member, before and after deploying the job scheduling software. This firm also asked about IT staff salaries.	For the companies surveyed, the average number of users supported by each FTE rose from 552 before deploying the software to 788 afterwards, an increase of 43 percent. The number of jobs supported by each FTE rose by an average of 204 percent, from 424 to 1,287 per day. With an average first-year loaded salary of $98,127, and annual increases of 5 percent, the payroll savings from increased management efficiency averaged $225,545 a year over the three years.
Relativity Technologies' Cost Savings References (Next four rows)	This information is based upon comparing the cost to doing manual or through processes without Relativity tool set.	
Application Portfolio Management	Areas: 1. High level inventory statistics 99.80 percent 2. Dependencies 99.80 percent 3. Boundaries 99.96 percent	Estimated up to 99 percent reduction in cost.
Application Documentation		Estimated up to 75 percent reduction in cost.
Application Analysis Querying		Estimated up to 30 percent reduction in cost.
Business Rule Mining	1. Inventorying rules 2. High-level \ rule mining 3. Documentation of business rules	Estimated up to 74 percent reduction in cost.

Summary

IT organizations are under increasing demand to increase the ability of the business to innovate while controlling and often reducing costs. Legacy modernization is a real opportunity for these goals to be achieved. To attain these goals, the organization needs to take full advantage of emerging advances in platform and software innovations, while leveraging the investment that has been made in the business processes within the legacy environment.

To make good choices for a specific roadmap to modernization, the decision makers should work to have a good understanding of what these modernization options are, and how to get there. We have outlined five methods of modernization: SOA Integration, Re-architecture, Platform Migration, Replacement, and Data Modernization as well as some key factors to be considered for each option. We also explored the imperative that all modernization projects start with a legacy understanding phase.

Finally, this chapter exposed you to the advantages and considerations that need to be made when endeavoring to create a roadmap for modernization. In the following chapters, we will examine two of these methods in detail: SOA enablement and re-architecture, and how you can leverage the Oracle technology stack to achieve these goals. Now that we have built a foundation, let's get into the details.

Overview of SOA Integration

2

Today, there is an increasing drive for organizations to move away from monolithic, static applications to **Service Oriented Architecture (SOA)**. SOA promises to deliver services which are agile, cost-effective, and future-proof. We work with many Fortune 500 companies with legacy applications. Almost all of them have these monolithic systems at the core. What's interesting is that our discussions around new application development initiatives encompasses the notion of services, agility, and portability. We have never gone into an IT planning session with a CIO for the development of linear applications that are not standards-based and do not integrate well with the existing systems. So, the elephant in the room is what to do with these legacy applications. What does SOA mean for organizations that have applications that are years, if not decades old, which are very costly to change and are maintained with a dwindling workforce? These are issues that every IT manager has to deal with. The simple fact is that these systems are at the heart of banking, transportation, and manufacturing sectors around the world. We maintain in the following chapters that there is a methodical way to open these valuable core processing to the future. Organizations do not have to throw the baby out with the bath water when it comes to new initiatives. In the following chapters, we will explore ways to open up our legacy infrastructure. These can enable the integration and extension of the mainframe and even provide a foundation for a full migration, if the business requires it.

It is observed that the term SOA has been used, or I should say, overused, so much in the industry today that it has lost its currency with decision makers. Before we dive into this chapter and examine the drivers for modernization to an SOA architecture, let's define what SOA means in terms of legacy mainframe environment and legacy modernization. Think of SOA as a framework for building applications, rather than a specific set of technologies or protocols. SOA is just a way of providing computing resources by exposing discrete business processes via a standard way for use by consumers. As we had mentioned, it is more than a set of protocols and technologies like SOAP and WSDL or Java/RMI; think of it as a blueprint for building applications. Web services may be one of the ways to implement this framework. Other technologies which can be leveraged to employ an SOA architecture include, **Business Activity Monitoring (BAM)**, **Business Process Execution Language (BPEL)**, **Enterprise Service Bus (ESB)**, and **Business Process Management (BPM)** engines. Technically, FTP is an SOA interface!

In Chapter 3, we will take a deeper dive into the practical application of Legacy Integration strategies utilizing the concept of **Enterprise Information Integration (EII)** and **Enterprise Application Integration (EAI)**. Using EII/EAI, we can address data and process centric strategies respectively on the legacy platform. To prepare us for a deeper dive into those technologies, let's take some time to cover some more high-level SOA concepts with respect to legacy modernization.

Integrating SOA into a Legacy Framework

The fundamental idea of enabling a legacy application starts with identifying the core building blocks and access points in the mainframe. There are three main points of integration into the legacy mainframe:

1. **Presentation Layer**: The goal here is to provide some level of service to the consumer to improve the user experience and extend access to other applications through the front-end. The following figure shows that we open up the interface to the legacy system via screen adapters. So, we do not change any legacy code and simply drive the old system with a newer looking front-end.

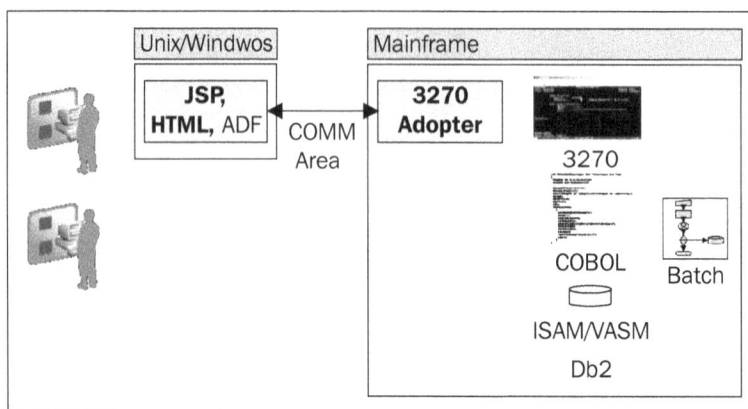

2. **Business Layer**: Simply stated, this is wrapping of a procedure call with an SOA service. As we will see in the hands-on case study, this can really open up a legacy application for re-use and agility. This can be a nontrivial task. As with any legacy application (mainframe or otherwise), business processes are often not discrete, standalone services. After years of development, we usually end up with a code base that resembles a big ball of string. It can be tough to determine where a process starts, and where it ends. Therefore, in some cases, some remediation work needs to be done on the legacy side to create more service procedures. We will cover this aspect later in this chapter where we examine some of the pros and cons of SOA enablement.

In the following figure, we see that the business layer is abstracted and extended. So, we wrap the programs with legacy adapters to expose those programs as business services.

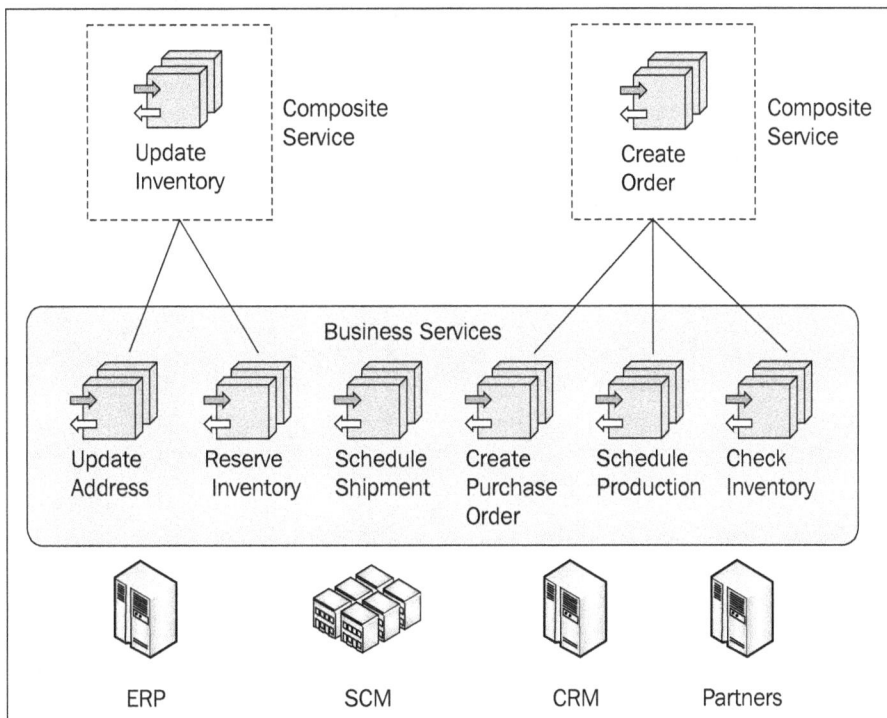

3. **Data Layer**: In this instance, a SOA service or call can be made to a legacy data store or file system. This enables users to use native data calls, yet access relational or nonrelational data stores. With data integration, enterprises can support fully-transactional, bidirectional, and *SQL-based* access to any data store on the mainframe. This can also include change of data capture to facilitate data warehousing, integration, and reporting.

Drivers for SOA Integration

All modernization projects should always begin with a clear understanding of the business drivers of a modernization initiative. It does seem a bit obvious to make this statement, yet many managers embark on technology projects for technology's sake. With respect to SOA integration, we have outlined several different types of methods, none of which is mutually exclusive or without planning, efforts, risks, or costs. So, to understand which path one needs to take, it is important to discover what the drivers are for your business.

In a recent survey by MetaGroup, CIOs were asked about the critical drivers for their modernization initiatives.

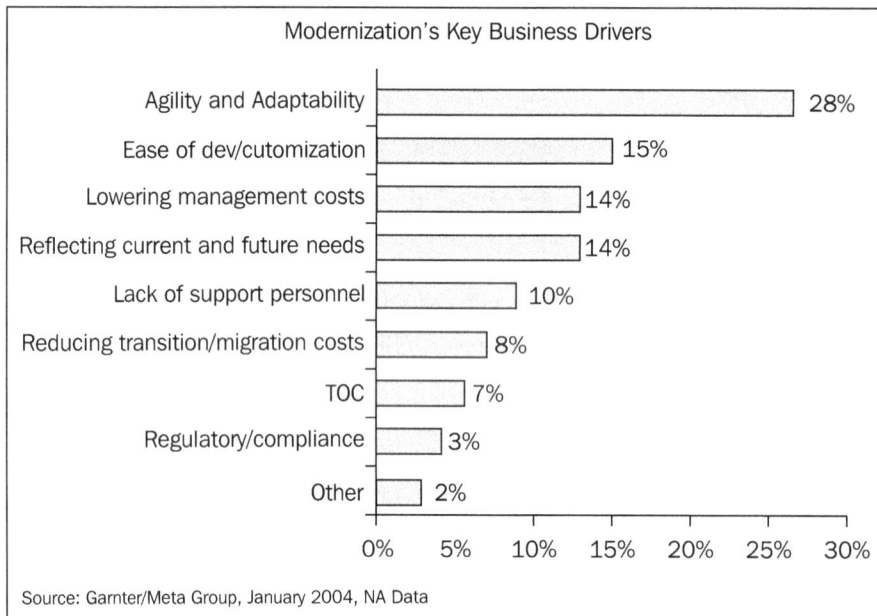

Modernization's Key Business Drivers

Driver	Percentage
Agility and Adaptability	28%
Ease of dev/cutomization	15%
Lowering management costs	14%
Reflecting current and future needs	14%
Lack of support personnel	10%
Reducing transition/migration costs	8%
TOC	7%
Regulatory/compliance	3%
Other	2%

Source: Garnter/Meta Group, January 2004, NA Data

There are several key factors that are currently driving today's legacy modernization efforts. The following is an overview of just some of the driving factors that you should consider when understanding business objectives for any modernization project.

- **Agility** — Enable innovation within the business

  Today, many business CEOs believe that IT is an inhibitor of innovation. A lot of dollars is spent on maintenance and infrastructure. Changes to code take a very long time and can delay a company's need to respond to changes in the market. SOA integration reduces the development cycle and enables change quickly.

- **Value** — Expose and extend business value locked in the legacy system.

  Years of business expertise have been baked into legacy applications. There is much value inside, and enabling these services to be exposed and consumed outside the legacy environment can help streamline applications, help business respond quickly to competition, and also help create new business services quickly.

- **Reduced Cost**

  Time to deliver upgraded applications in the legacy world is usually measured with many months and a large amount of people resources. Changes in these monolithic systems are simply very expensive to make, in terms of both time and money. There is also a high frequency of redundancy in applications. So, eliminating redundant processes and having a component-based SOA architecture reduces the overall cost of maintenance by enabling fewer people to deliver faster.

- **Dwindling Technology Resources**

  There is a steady decline in experienced personnel in the IT industry today. New developers are not learning the older technologies and the subject matter experts are leaving the workforce at an increased pace. A recent Accenture study indicated that 45% of all US Federal Employees will be retired within 6 years* (need to source this). Now is the time to begin with the planning and execution of this large and ongoing transfer of demographics in the workforce.

With the legacy systems taking up a majority of IT budgets today just for maintenance, technology is becoming less of a differentiator and more of a deadweight. In 2006, Forrester surveyed CEOs, and asked if their IT departments enabled innovation, or were a stumbling block for innovation. The survey revealed that a vast majority of the surveyed CEOs said that IT was an inhibitor of innovation. This was predominately attributed to the dedication of a high percentage of IT budget to maintenance rather than to new features, and the lack of (IT's) agility. The good news is that SOA can help organizations become a source of accelerated innovation rather than hold them back. The following is a chart on how SOA can be a value accelerator for the business:

Accelerator	Impact	Metric
Constant Industry Change	SOA minimize the impact of change from frequent changes to business processes	Max. time allowed to respond to process changes
Industry Consolidation	SOA helps to consolidate duplicate functionality across acquired/merged companies	# of mergers and acquisitions
Customizations from Common Base	Shared service platform powers a business model able to deliver "variants" ("repeatable solutions") of a generic platform service	# of customers and customer growth on platform Degree of customer flexibility
Multi-Channel Applications	Multiple channels (agents, online service, distribution through partners) share services platform	# of channels replicating common service capabilities
Multi-Channel Applications	Multiple channels (agents, online service, distribution through partners) share services platform	# of channels replicating common service capabilities
B2B Services Network	SOA allows to flexibly incorporate electronic partner services into a "virtual service offering"	# of partners providing B2B Web services

Considerations for SOA Enablement

We have covered some high-level concepts with respect to SOA and what that means for legacy integration. As with any choice, there are benefits and drawbacks to each option. In the following table, we have outlined some of the key things to consider for SOA integration. Note that the strengths and weakness listed here are defined in terms of both business and technical aspects.

Strengths	Weakness
Relatively short path to SOA	Still incurs cost of the mainframe
Utilizes current workforce	Can increase MIPS
Reduces development cycle	Dependency on legacy personnel resources
Provides business service and enables BPM of legacy environment	High dependence on legacy platform
Can be the initial step in a phased approach to overall re-architecture of legacy system	Often requires third-party software
No need to implicate the legacy mainframe	

Where to Begin—a Word on Application Discovery

Once we have identified our business drivers, and some of the first steps in this process, we must understand what we have before we can modernize it. Legacy environments are very complex and quite often, have little or no documentation. This introduces a concept that is true for any modernization technique to be used — Application Portfolio Analysis (APA). In the introduction chapter, we discussed the importance of APA and mentioned that every modernization project must begin with this stage. Remember, the key to application discovery is leveraging technologies that will provide a repository for leveraging the business logic contained in the core legacy systems. In practical terms, this means that if we are to leverage legacy assets, we will greatly benefit from being able to interact with a repository of the metadata derived from these legacy assets.

In the next chapters, we will explore how we can open up a legacy system for SOA integration, and take the next step to a re-architected system by leveraging this valuable repository. The following figure illustrates the APM process:

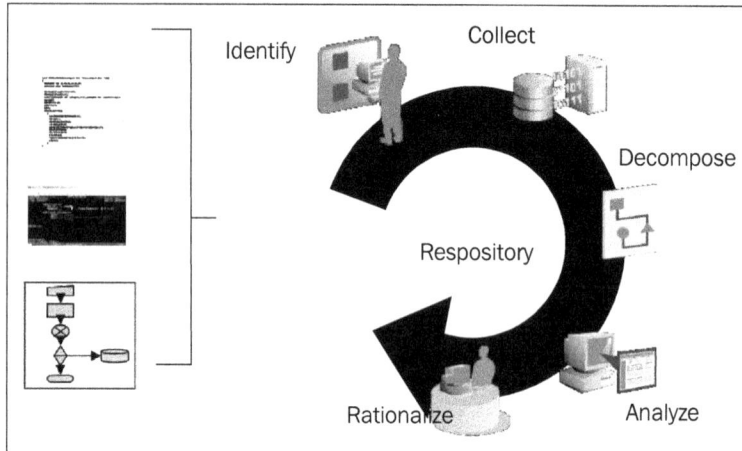

Currently, the Oracle Modernization Alliance has several partners that can enable a repository-based solution for APA.

APM Partner	Resource
Relativity Technologies	http://www.relativity.com
MicroFocus	http://www.microfocus.com
CAST Software	http://www.castsoftware.com
Troux Software	http://www.trouxsoftware.com

Assessment Process: Bringing it together

While it is very important to understand in detail how legacy code such as JCL, COBOL, and Copy Books is parsed, and enabled for SOA services, it is equally important to briefly outline a sample workflow of steps to show how one of these legacy repositories can be leveraged into our overall SOA Strategy. So, as we utilize these technologies to SOA to enable our legacy application, we will outline some key stages that need to be integrated into the development cycle and modernization roadmap. Determine the business case.

We can break this SOA analysis into three stages:

1. Determining the requirements
2. Understanding Legacy
3. Defining Roadmap

The following diagram illustrates the workflow steps involved in the technical assessment of a system using a technology from an APA vendor. Each phase of this scoping will enable you to build a business case for which processes will be good candidates for SOA enablement.

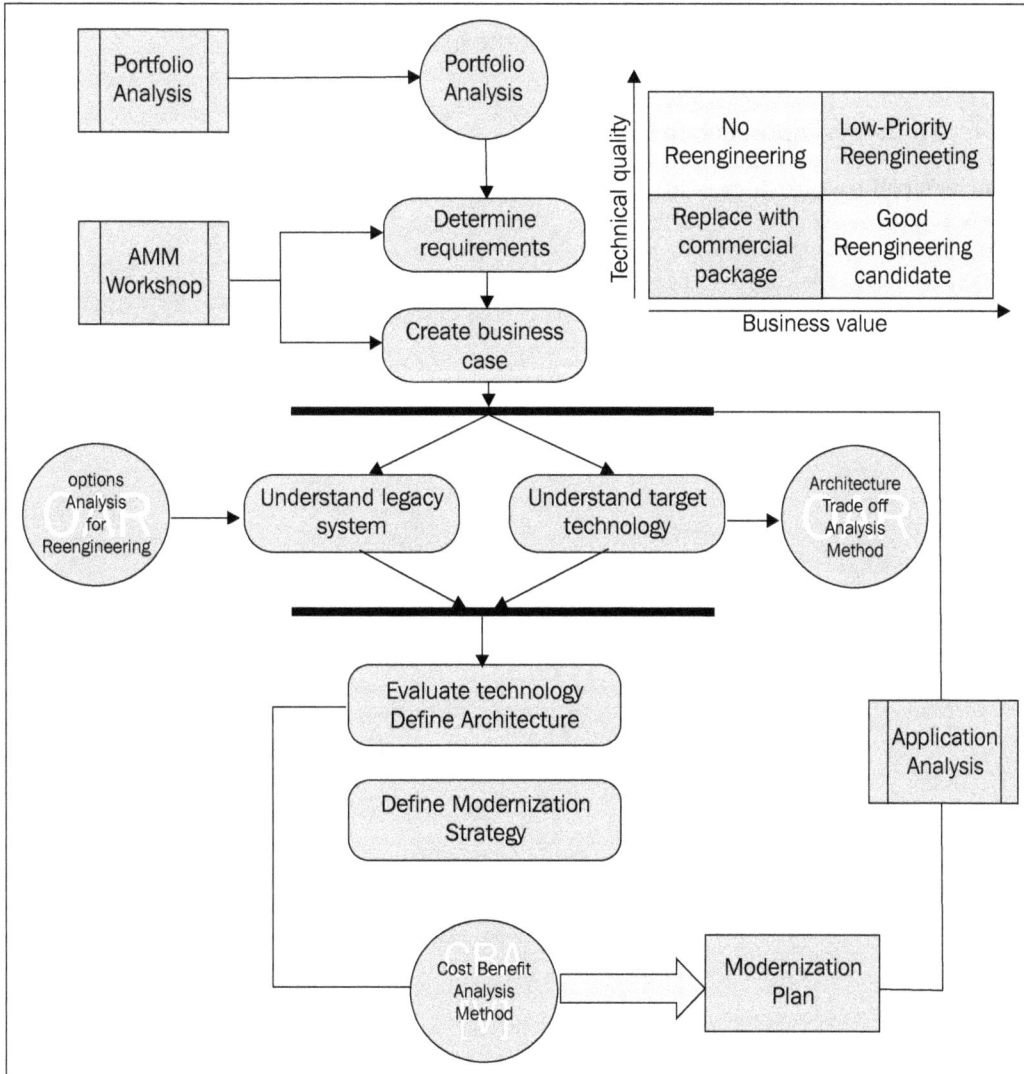

Summary

In this chapter, we laid the foundation for Legacy Modernization through SOA enablement. The key concepts we discussed were:

- SOA context of the legacy
- Techniques for SOA enablement of the mainframe
- Key drivers for SOA enablement
- High-level approach to SOA projects

Now let's roll up our sleeves and get into some technology!

3

SOA Integration—Functional View, Implementation, and Architecture

Let us not expect this chapter to be a primer on Services-Orientated Architecture (SOA). The focus of this chapter is to place SOA in the context of Modernization. SOA can be over hyped and has been, in some cases, exploited by IT vendors as the 'holy grail' of software architecture. However, in the context of Legacy Modernizaton, an SOA Integration architecture can bring your legacy environment into the world of the World Wide Web, Web 2.0, and all the other latest Internet-based IT architectures. Within days, a legacy system can be accessed via a web browser. This is one of the biggest advantages Legacy SOA Integration has over other types of Legacy Modernization. Your time-to-market in weeks, instead of months or years.

Although not a primer, let's first make sure we are all talking the same language when we talk SOA. Though the concepts behind SOA are not new, SOA is also not yet mature. SOA in it current form has really been around only five years now. The concepts of standards-based protocol handlers, pre-defined communication schemas, and remote method invocations have been around for decades. To get a better understanding of SOA, let's see what SOA is, and what SOA is not:

What SOA is	What SOA is not
SOA is an architectural blueprint, a way of developing applications, and a set of best practices. SOA is a journey to a better way of doing business and the technology architecture to support it.	SOA is not an 'out of the box' solution you buy, install, and then have up and running in a matter of months.
SOA architectures can be implemented using Java EE CA, XML file transfer over File Transfer Protocol (FTP), or Remote Procedural Call (RPC) over TCP/IP, Remote Method Invocation (RMI), or other protocols. SOA is a concept and can be implemented in many different ways, some very rudimentary, such as transferring flat files between applications.	SOA is not the same thing as Web services. Web services imply the use of standards such as Java/JAX-RPC, .NET, or REST. Web services also imply the use of a WSDL, SOAP, and/or Java EE Connector Architecture (Java EE CA), and HTTP. In other words, Web services are a very specific set of technologies.
SOA will make your business more agile, increase business visibility, reduce integration costs, and provide better re-use.	SOA will not solve all your IT legacy technology, human, or cultural problems.
SOA is also a broader set of technologies including more then just Web services. Technologies such as an Enterprise Service Bus (ESB), Business Process Execution Language (BPEL), message queues, and Business Activity Monitoring (BAM) all are part of the SOA architecture.	Web services will probably be a part of your SOA architecture, but they are not mandatory. How, when, and where to use the technologies mentioned in the left-hand column is not defined in a manual. You pick and choose the SOA technologies that will be part of your SOA architecture.

Legacy SOA Integration is one aspect of an IT architecture called **Enterprise Information Integration** (**EII**) and **Enterprise Application Integration** (**EAI**). EII is a more data-centric approach to information integration, and EAI is a process or application approach to information integration. EII and EAI include data consolidation, data federation, shared data access, and remote method invocation:

- **Consolidation** — Data consolidation moves all disparate data sources into one central database. This is akin to a data warehouse, and in many ways it can use the same approaches and tools, but with update, insert, and delete capabilities. In many cases, the first stage of data consolidation involves creating a data warehouse, as migrating all the existing applications that access the data can take years or even decades.

- **Federation** — Data federation leaves the data in the individual data source where it is normally maintained and updated, and consolidates it on the fly as needed. In the case of Legacy Modernization, multiple data sources, many of which are non-relational, will appear to be integrated into a single virtual database. The platform will mask the number and different kinds of databases behind the consolidated view.

- **Shared Data**—Shared data integration actually moves data and events from one or more source databases to a consolidated resource, or queue, created to serve one or more new applications. Data can be maintained and exchanged using technologies such as messaging queues and ESBs.

- **Remote method invocation**—The first three options focused on the data side, or EII. The last option is focused on the processes and business logic, or EAI. This is integration at the application layer instead of the data layer.

SOA Integration is a combined data federation and remote method innvocation approach to solve EII/EAI in a Legacy Modernization project. Traditionally, EII has been achieved using Extract, Load, and Transformation (ETL) products. With the advent of SOA technologies such as ESBs, more customers are willing to use ESB products for information integration. ETL vendors have not been standing still and have introduced Web services, and standards-based transformation and workflow engines instead of proprietary software. This means that the differences between ETL and ESB technologies are blurring. In addition, the capabilities of **Business Intelligence (BI)** and **Business Activity Monitoring (BAM)** technologies are converging. BI tools are becoming more real time, and BAM technologies are offering reporting capabilities.

A major component of an EII/EAI infrastructure is **Master Data Management (MDM)**. MDM is a single version-of-truth for your information, which is maintained in a central repository. MDM is all about sharing, reusing, and enabling maximum interoperability of your core master reference data. This allows your applications to access the data through a common object or model and a common set of access schemas. Therefore, it does not matter where that data might reside. Your application can access the data through a virtualized access layer. As you can see, MDM is very important in an SOA Integration environment. MDM is a large topic and a lot has been written in this area. Therefore, we are not going cover MDM in this book.

Now we know what Legacy SOA Integration is, and why we are going to do it. We must now embark on the journey of how we are going to get from a monolithic mainframe to a SOA-enabled mainframe. Before we can just start calling our mainframe or midrange systems, we must first understand the following from a technical perspective:

- What does our business community really want to see?
- How are they going to see it?
- When and where do they want to get the information?
- What should my first project be?
- What will our architecture look like?

We will answer all these questions in this chapter.

The fundamental question many business people ask today is, "Why can't enterprise IT architectures be as straight forward and easy to use as Google, MySpace and other web sites?". This is a valid question, to which the answer is, "IT systems don't have to be and should not be".

As any good IT architect knows, you must balance the combination of cool products, time-to-market, maintainability, ease of use, and cost of the technology. We have not even begun to build the architecture and we are talking of costs for a very good reason. Cost, as in **total cost of ownership** (**TCO**), is something every IT decision maker must consider. TCO is not just the upfront cost of the product, but also the cost to maintain, enhance, and manage the environment.

Just placing Web services on an already unwieldy mainfame architecture that does not scale when interfacing to other systems is not the answer. The SOA Integration architecture must be fully secure (in terms of access and data), capable of replication, scalable, and performant. The architecture must also take into account the legacy system that will need to be both a source, and a consumer of Web services.

Unfortunately, most companies with systems older then ten years are starting with an architecture that is appropriately called the Accidental Architecture. This architecture probably looks something like this:

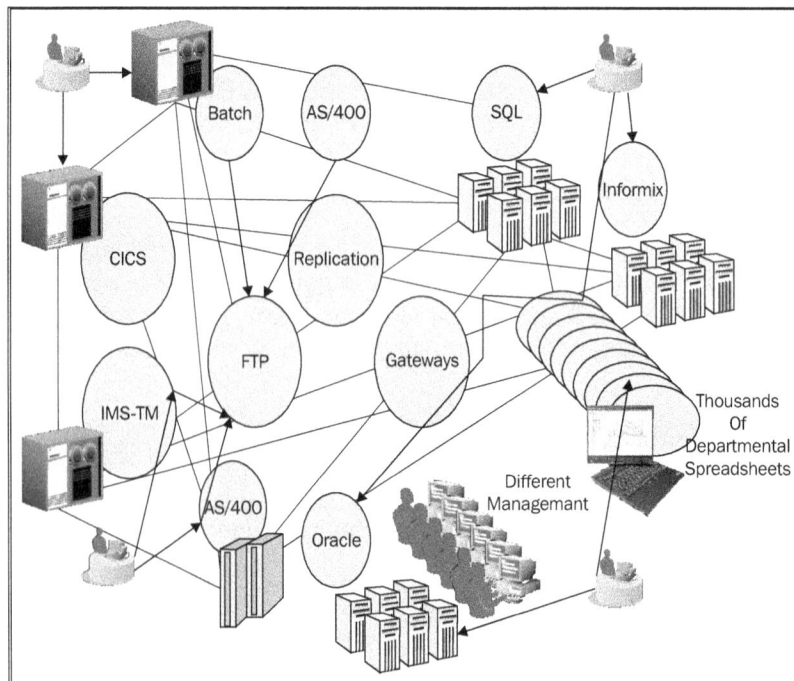

These lines should cross, go every way, and make a complete mess. The accidental architecture diagram above shows a simplistic view of the integration points in the mainframe systems. Most mainframe systems have far more complex infrastructures with more database vendors, more hardware systems, and systems communicating with each other. As the real diagram would most likely be complex to follow, we have used a simpler version here.

The idea in modern SOA architectures is to eliminate this complex IT architecture. Back in the old days, business IT infrastructures were rigid and complex because memory was expensive, the mainframe disk was small, few people knew about technology, not many technologies or vendors existed, and most IT infrastructures had to be custom coded.

The other thing to consider when developing a Legacy SOA Integration Architecture is that in most cases business processes and workflow are likely to change. Changed business processes entail mapping business services, while taking into account the current business flows, to the new business use cases and creating a business process workflow to implement these use cases.

SOA cannot be discussed without discussing the topic of accessing internal and external Web services. When Web services and SOA were first conceived, the grand idea of developers and users dynamically discovering and using Web services from all over the Internet was at the forefront of the discussion. In reality, this idea was way ahead of its time. Although, almost all SOA implementations leverage internal services, they do so on a very limited basis. Therefore, this chapter will focus on the internal legacy services.

According to the Aberdeen Group: "Organizations that are SOA-enabling their legacy applications on the legacy platform are outperforming those that are using any other approach. They report better productivity, higher agility, and lower costs for legacy integration projects". This is one IT analyst's perspective but it does highlight the importance of SOA integration in any company's legacy modernization strategy.

Keeping It Real: The most difficult aspect of building a new architecture that is completely SOA-enabled is the vast amount of business logic that exists on the mainframe, mostly in COBOL code. A Legacy SOA Integration architecture preserves that legacy business logic but incorporates it into the new world of relational databases, SOA, and Web 2.0.

SOA Integration: Functional View

The business community is not concerned with IMS, VSAM, CICS, IMS-TM, 3270, and other legacy technologies. Business users think in terms of the applications they use, the business processes they execute, and the information they need access to. Their view of the world looks like this:

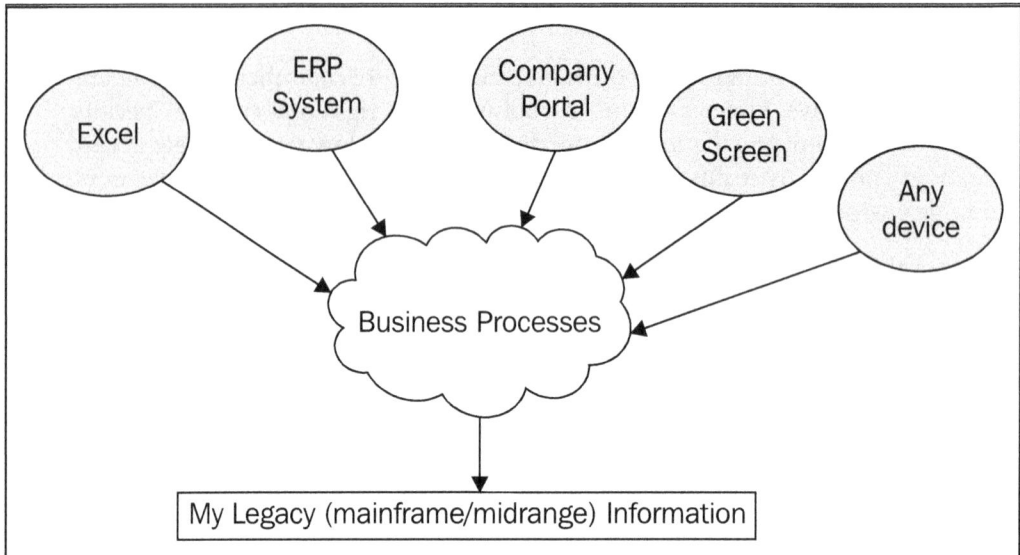

The business community sees the business processes/services as a cloud, something they can see but is far from their world, and not something they can touch or feel. The information they need is like a mysterious 'black box'. It resides somewhere in a dark corner of the IT department.

The business community's functional view of the world consists of four things:

- Applications—This is their interface with the legacy systems. These applications are typically accessed via archaic 3270 (IBM mainframe), 7561 (Fujitsu mainframe), UTS, T27 (Unisys mainframe), and 5250 (IBM iSeries/AS400) 'green screen' terminals. The users don't necessarily like these interfaces, but this is what they deal with today. They would prefer to get access to information like they do at home, through web browsers and cell phones. They wonder why they can do online banking at home from a nice browser interface, but when they go to work they must use a 'green screen' to look up account information for a client.

- Legacy business processes/services they access — Create new account, check account status, check payment information, submit purchase order, and so on. These are some of the business processes and services the user community executes every day. Most of these transactions ultimately take place on a legacy system.

- Legacy information they need — The user does not care where the information resides. It may be in relational databases on mainframes, hierarchical database, network database, flat files, and so forth. They just want access to the data now and in a fashion that is flexible, adaptable, and easy.

- To an IT person, the business community's view of the world is way too abstract. The IT community will look at SOA Integration in a more technical context and include things like transformation services, legacy connectors/adapters, and types of legacy artifacts. The functional view from the technical perspective looks like this:

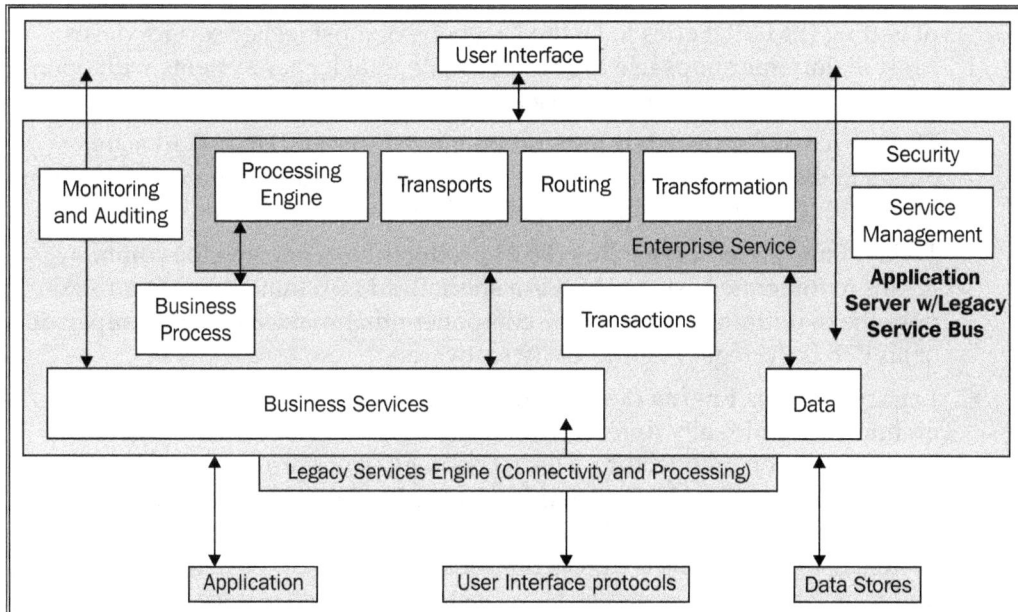

The view consists of four basic components:

- **User Interface** — In the legacy world, these are most likely to be CICS transactions that are executed from COBOL applications and rendered on character-based 'green screens'. The most widely used mainframe 'green screen' is a 3270 device that was manufactured by IBM. These devices have long gone the way of the dinosaur. However, there are many software packages that emulate the 3270 device protocol on modern hardware such as the PCs.

  In the modern world of IT, the user interface could be a PC-based web browser, Java, or .NET application, a browser enabled PDA or cell phone, or any device that understands HTTP.

- **Legacy Service Bus (LSB)** — LSBs have existed for decades. Traditionally, they have taken the form of FTP, mainframe CICS to CICS calls, custom COBOL applications, TCP/IP and/or SNA socket communication, messaging queues, and the list goes on. IBM has done an incredible job of getting IBM MQSeries to be the backbone of most legacy service buses. Most mainframe shops use MQSeries to integrate legacy systems with open systems, internal systems, and packaged applications.

  The world of IT service bus integration moved to RPC, DCE, Corba and others in the late 1980s. Most of the technology has still not become commonplace with FTP and queuing still ruling the legacy world, even today.

  Today, **Enterprise Service Bus (ESB)** products have become the common means to integrate systems. LSB is a specialized ESB that allows you to expose the mainframe artifacts. The component that makes the LSB a superset of an ESB is the legacy connectivity software.

- **Legacy Services Engine (LSE)** — Business users don't see this piece of the architecture and really don't care about it. But it is central to the legacy SOA integration architecture. This technology/software stack is where the magic happens. The magic is making legacy hierarchical and network data stores appear as relational data (and mainframe DB2 accessible from open systems), legacy business transactions look like Java or .NET transactions, and legacy interfaces as accessible as just another Web service. The LSE also provides features such as governance and security that the business users are concerned about. There are other features such as scalability and performance that are transparent to the business user, but are expected to be in the platform. Lastly, features like adaptability, flexibility, auditing, and management are not the domains of business users, but are an IT management concern. Adaptability and flexibility could be argued as transparent business user features, but we put them in IT domain features because business users don't care how rigid or nonrigid that infrastructure is, they just want what they want right away.

- **Legacy Artifacts**—These are the data, application processes, and the user interface. Application processes could be actual COBOL modules, transactions, stored procedures, or even dynamic SQL. To the user, they just want to see the information that is important to them. To you as the IT person, the decision, which legacy artifacts to base your Legacy SOA Integration platform on, is a very crucial one. In most cases, a hybrid, or a combination of the above is what your architecture will require. Typically, IT will not have a comprehensive or corporate SOA plan, let alone a plan for their LSB. So they will take the 'easy path' and expose legacy 'green screens' as Web services. As we will learn later in this chapter, this may not be the best approach.

> **Keeping It Real**: It is possible to call legacy services directly from a script, Java application, or an HTML page. However, your overall SOA architecture becomes even more chaotic than your legacy 'Accidental Architecture' was earlier. A complete Legacy SOA Integration platform provides services such as orchestration, messaging, presentation and data access services, service management, central control, transformation, security, and monitoring in one easy to use solution stack.

SOA Integration: Technical View

This section will describe all the products and technologies that are available to complete your middleware architecture. This may include an LSB, Java EE application server and security infrastructure. Don't get overwhelmed by all the choices and technologies. Your specific business and technology drivers will quickly narrow down the set of products and technologies in your LSB and Java EE application server to a handful mentioned in this section. However, before you buy anything specific, it is important you understand the entire set of products and technologies that make up the LSB and Java EE application server. Otherwise, you run the risk of solving a specific use case but not building an agile middleware architecture that will meet both tactical and strategic business objectives.

The technical view adds aspects to the architecture that are very important from an implementation perspective: performance, scalability, reliability, security, management, end-to-end testing, and governance. It is not that these attributes are not important to the business community. Business users just assume that the IT infrastructure will be easy to use, will always be on, will run fast, are secure, and will run without errors.

Governance must be considered in terms of both design time (developing, controlling, and managing) and runtime (security, control, monitoring, and managing). Questions that are typically asked are: Who is running my services? How are they being used? What are the impacts to current business processes?

Something else that has not been discussed is the mainframe as both a provider and consumer of Web services. In most situations that we encounter, the requirements are that the legacy system will call a Web service (provider), and will also call Web services that are Java or .Net based on open systems (consumer). Your technical architecture should take into account both inbound and outbound Web services support (the legacy system can act as a Web service server, or a Web service client).

Sometimes, we are asked, "Do I really need an LSB or application server? Can't I just call my legacy Web services from an HTML page?". In other words, is an application server and/or SOA suite of products really needed? You could create a LSB without using a SOA product. However, if you thought your legacy architecture was a 'hair ball' to start with, it will now have more lines and points of entry crossing each other. Remember, the idea is to create an infrastructure that is less rigid and more agile then your current system.

The technical view consists of the four basic components from the functional view. Although this is represented as a two-dimensional model, it is actually a three dimensional model. The third dimension includes the aspects of functionality, performance, and governance that cuts through the three layers represented here. The complete set of technologies (once again, don't panic as you will not need any of these) looks like this:

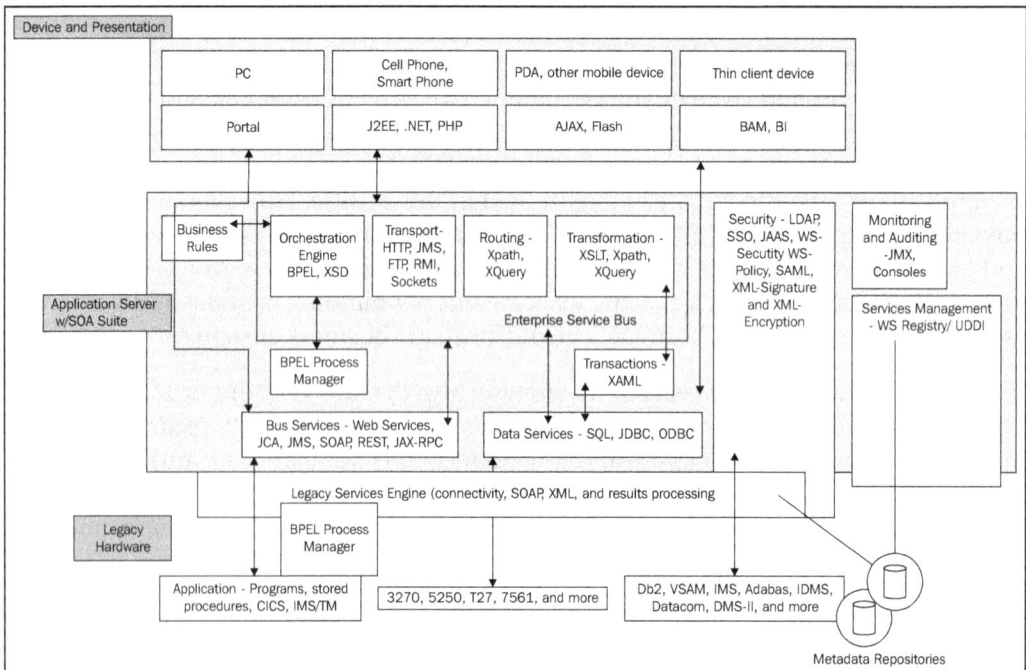

User Interface

In the legacy world, the device and presentation layer are very tightly coupled, for example, a 3270 device displaying a 3270 presentation data stream. In the new world of IT, the user interface device and presentation layer are not tightly coupled, and the devices become much broader. The user device could be a PC, PDA, cell phone, thin client terminal or any device that supports HTTP, and a browser. The presentation layer could be a Java Applet, Java Server Page (JSP), or Java Server Faces (JSF), AJAX, PHP, or .NET application residing in a Portal. Since the device is not fixed, and new devices will emerge that did not exist five years ago (like smart phones and iPhones), the presentation-tier should be capable of display in any channel. This is often called multichannel delivery.

Legacy Service Bus (LSB) and Application Server

The LSB is a component of your middleware stack. Middleware can be anything from a crude, homegrown, internally developed XML data transfer and transformation, to an all-inclusive SOA Suite. Middleware in the open systems realm has advanced from HTTP servers, Java applications, Portals, data integration servers to a complete integrated stack of application server and SOA software. The term SOA Suite has become commonplace in the IT industry. An SOA Suite consists of the following components:

Functionality	Description
Enterprise Service Bus	A multiprotocol server to connect applications and provide a common bus for data integration
BPEL-based Process Manager	An orchestration and workflow engine to compose and execute services within a business process
Business Rules Engine	Capture, centralize and automate business policies and application logic
Business Activity Monitoring	End user graphical dashboard to gain real-time visibility into the operation, and the performance of business processes and services
Web Service Management	A security solution to enforce authentication, authorization and runtime policies on services
Connectivity	Adapters to connect to virtually any data source including applications, databases, queues, RFID and other physical devices
SOA Data Integration	A high-volume, high-performance SOA data integration server
Event processing	A message based system that applications subscribe to which they use to send and receive event alerts and messages

The interesting aspect of SOA Suites in the Legacy SOA Integration space is that some of the components can either reside on the open systems middle-tier, or on the mainframe-tier or on both. These components (as shown in the above picture) include BPEL, Security, Management, and the ESB (normally the queue). This is important because in some cases, it may make sense to do the BPEL process orchestration on the mainframe. So the processing is closer to the application and data. This will reduce network traffic and boost services response time. However, it could increase the MIPS usage of your mainframe, which is typically what you try to reduce.

Legacy Services Engine (LSE)

Talk to any of the legacy connectivity vendor and they will quickly avoid the conversation of gateways and screen scraping, and for good reason. Screen scraping is an old method of exposing the legacy presentation-tier as Web services. It relied on the field position (row/column), and the type of terminal stream. Both these restrictions make it very inflexible. A big problem occurs when a screen map changes. The application that receives the screen scraped stream is most likely to fail. Gateways are taboo because they imply heavy weight, and are difficult to manage products. Most legacy SOA companies will refer to their products as adapters or servers. We will use the term Legacy Services Engine (LSE) believing it incorporates everything that this engine does, all the way from mainframe connectivity to results processing.

The LSE is where the real action happens. This is where the bridge between the legacy system and the middle-tiers takes place. This engine also has features such as security, monitoring, caching, and management. As this is such an important and broad area, we will break this into LSE components, development, and implementation/deployment areas. We will start with the LSE Components.

LSE Components

We will cover the key LSE components in this section – the connectivity and processing engine for mainframe connectivity and information processing of mainframe screens, logic, and data.

Connectivity and Processing Engine

The processing engine has a protocol server, SQL engine, XML parser, and transformation processer. The typical protocols supported are SOAP (HTTP and XML), JMS and Java EE Connector Architecture (Java EE CA). SOAP requires neither an adapter, nor a process on the middle-tier to handle the results on the client. When Java EE CA is used, you hear the term adapter being used. An adapter implies that there is a piece of software on the middle-tier to handle the processing of the results. The Java EE CA adapter will communicate through SOAP messages. JMS is not typically used in a synchronous online transaction environment.

This engine is where the results are processed, and the request sent back to the client. The client could be an HTML page, a BPEL process, or a Java application or some other process residing on the middle or client-tiers. As mentioned earlier, the engine needs to be both a provider and consumer of services. For a provider of Web services, the standard processes are as follows:

- Receive a service request from the client—The LSE has a protocol and request handler to receive the request from the client.

- Map the request to the appropriate legacy artifact—The request is then processed using the metadata repository to map the call to the correct mainframe call and do any data type conversion. If the request is a database call, the SQL engine will transform the call into the appropriate legacy data store access scheme.

- Call the appropriate legacy artifact—The application, transaction, program, stored procedure, 3270 screen, or a data store is called.

- Process the results—The results are returned to the processing engine. The metadata repository is used once again to perform any data transformations, data type mapping, or cleansing. The results are formatted into a SOAP response.

- Send the request back—The results are put back on the communication network and sent back to the client.

SQL Engine

The SQL Engine is required for data-enabled services. The SQL engine will evaluate subqueries, joins, and aggregate functions when possible. It is best for these operations to happen closest to where the data is stored, so the engines will typically do this type of processing before sending the results set back to the client. The SQL engine has minimal work to do when a request is made via SQL, and the database source is an SQL compliant database engine such as IBM DB2. However, differences do exist despite vendor's compliance with industry standards such as SQL. Data type translation is typically more intensive as there are no industry standards on how data is stored. The situation gets exponentially more complicated when you bring non-relational data stores (such as, VSAM, IMS, IDMS, Adabas) into the mix. These databases do not support SQL natively and the database calls in the application are not likely to be SQL. The automated transformations required to solve this problem are fourfold:

- **SQL translations**—SQL translation takes into account the differences between Oracle's implementation of SQL and each participating non-Oracle databases data store call interfaces. In the case of DB2, the differences are minimal, and easy to discover. For nonrelational data stores, SQL is not the native calling method. So SQL will need to be translated into the native call. The SQL statement passed to the engine will look like this:

```
Exec :Bind-variable := value;
Select column1 from table-name where id = :bind-variable;
```

The corresponding VSAM read statements looks like this:

```
MOVE value TO key1.
        READ file-name RECORD [INTO ws-field]
            INVALID KEY do something
            NOT INVALID KEY do something else
        END-READ.
```

- **Data Dictionary translations**—The data dictionary holds the information to map the source tables to the native files or record sets, the column/field mappings, the data type mappings, and other information necessary to transform the calling SQL to the native call interface. IT developers must have the capability to query the metadata of the remote, non-Oracle database in order to diagnose problems. In Oracle, the data dictionary is stored in an Oracle table. The data dictionary translation information on the mainframe is typically in a flat file, sequential file, or in a relational database.

- **Indexing**—Anyone who has done relational database SQL coding knows the importance of indexes. Have the right ones, and your application runs fast; don't have the right ones or have too many wrong ones, then performance suffers. Indexing must include the ability to create indexes on legacy non-relational sequential data sets such as the VSAM files. This means you can have direct indexed access, even to data that does not have a native index. Where native indexes exist, they should automatically be used to optimize query performance. This support becomes more important as you get more sophisticated with your SOA data sets and start joining relational and non-relational data sets. Joining data sets without indexes becomes painfully slow.

- **Data type translation**—Legacy data types must often be converted when viewing the data in a relational format. These data types need to be translated transparently. There are many data type translations that need to happen for date and time, floating point, pic x, and pic n fields. These data types map easily to relational data types. Three common data types in legacy environments that do not map easily to relational databases are: Comp-3 (packed decimal), redefines, and occurs. In COBOL, these data types look like this:

- ° Packed decimal

  ```
  05   BALANCE-DUE    PIC S9(6)V99 COMP-3.
  ```

- ° Redefines

  ```
  05 a pic s9(4) comp-5.
    05 a1 redefines a pic x(2).
  ```

- ° Occurs

  ```
  05   MONTHLY-SALES OCCURS 12 TIMES    PIC
       S9(5)V99.
  ```

The corresponding Oracle data types looks like this:

- ° Packed decimal

  ```
  BALANCE-DUE       DECIMAL(8,2);
  ```

- ° Redefines

  ```
  a BINARY;
  a1 CHAR(2);
  ```

  The redefines becomes two separate columns in the relational table.

- ° Occurs

  ```
  MONTHLY-SALES-JAN NUMBER(7,2);
  
  .  .  .
  
  MONTHLY-SALES-DEC NUMBER(7,2);
  ```

  The relational table has 12 columns, one for each month in the year. You will have 12 separate columns coming back in the resulting SOAP message.

We don't want to turn this into an XML parsing and transformation book, but it is important to mention this briefly. XML processing—parsing and transformation—is both a memory-intensive and a processor-intensive activity. It is an important part of the LSE, as all service requests will come as XML streams, and all responses will go out as XML streams. Therefore, it is critical that the LSE has a highly performant XML engine.

Optional LSE Components

The next components of the LSE we will discuss are often part of (although they don't need to be) the LSE. They can be separate processes that reside on in the middle-tier, on mainframe, one or the other, or even both. There are pros and cons to each of these configurations that we will discuss in the implementation/deployment section of this chapter. For now, we will review each of these components:

Orchestration

Orchestration supports execution of a business process. The business process can consist of a number of steps, transactions, decision points, and other business processes. Orchestration is really just a fancy word for traditional workflow. What is different is that orchestration engines have a common, standardized execution language and run time engine. Most workflow engines are built upon proprietary languages (T-SQL, PL/SQL, VB Script), and run in proprietary runtime engines. The execution language for orchestration is BPEL, and the runtime engine is Java. BPEL supports both human and automated orchestration. In Legacy SOA, BPEL is important because in many instances, the legacy services will be integrated with other Java, .NET, or REST based services that reside on open systems. For example, a web based shopping cart is mostly open systems based, but it needs to communicate with a mainframe based inventory management system to fulfill the order.

Security

Security is a broad topic and includes everything from basic authentication and authorization, data encryption on the network to repudiation (you are who you say you are) and integration with mainframe security. Mainframe security includes, amongst others, **Resource Access Control Facility (RACF)** and **Access Control Facility 2 (ACF2)**. Everyone thinks technologies such as RACF and ACF2 make mainframes secure, but in reality, they are secure because of their physical nature — the hardware is in one location and hosted in a locked, physically secure location, and all communication happens over a private network. RACF or ACF2 don't do anything to enhance this locked down hardware environment. In open systems, as the infrastructure and user community is geographically dispersed and public networks are used, the LSE should consider including these technologies:

- **Java Authenticate and Authorization Service (JAAS)**: As the name implies, JAAS is for determining whether the user or device is authorized to access the service and has the correct privileges. The authentication and authorization information is typically stored in a **Lightweight Directory Access Protocol (LDAP)** server.
- **Secure Sockets Layer (SSL)** — SSL has become the defacto standard for securing HTTP traffic over the Internet. SSL is very simple to deploy, and all application server vendors support SSL traffic. In most cases, SSL as the security mechanism will do just fine.

- **WS-Security** — WS-Security is a set of standards for ensuring the integrity and confidentiality of data transmitted via Web services. The specific standards that are most important to your LSB are: WS-Policy, Security Assertion Markup Language (SAML), XML-Signature, and XML-Encryption. These standards are constantly evolving and changing, so the best place to find more information is OASIS (`http://www.oasis-open.org/`); the standards board responsible for WS-Security.

  LSEs will also typically integrate with RACF and ACF2 since the services reside on the mainframe. Check with your LSE vendor to see what type of 'out of the box' mainframe security integration they provide.

Caching

Caching may seem like it should be discussed along with performance. Perhaps, but performance is a broad topic while caching is a specific technology that most LSE vendors use to increase end-to-end response time. Caching basically involves storing data in memory. The data may be from a database, a screen, a transaction or any other legacy artifact. An LSE that does not have some type of caching is not going to perform as well.

LSE Development

Just like end user interfaces, the latest trend in development environments is thin client, web-based. There is also a trend towards power users (tech savvy business users) being able to use the design tool on their own. A combination of these two methods would involves the end user using a web-based application to define his or her own Web services. It is up for you to decide which is the best LSE design/development environment for your company:

- Thick or thin — Thick clients (high powered PCs with heavy graphics) have more 'bells and whistles', and are usually much more graphic intensive. However, they require a more expensive workstation for the developer. Obviously, with thin (web-based) client tools, the development environment can be accessed from anywhere. To use the thick client, the user needs to have the PC or laptop with them, or have the PC software installed on all the machines they use. This can lead to a maintenance nightmare, as all workstations need to have the latest development software loaded on them.

- COBOL/Legacy or Java EE/open systems centric — This choice comes down whether you have more COBOL developers or more Java EE developers. Some tools emphasize that a COBOL developer can easily develop and deploy mainframe-based Web services. However, if all your developers know Java EE, or if the groups responsible for the middlware platform are all open systems developers, this may not be the best choice.

- Power users or developers—You may want your business users to define Web services on their own. They are ultimately the customers, and know what they want. However, they don't know the entire ramifications of the services they are creating, and the load they will put on the IT infrastructure. I am sure we have all heard of the horror stories when power users are allowed to write their own ad hoc database queries.

LSE Implementation/Deployment

LSE implementation and deployment must take into consideration the LSE server location, the legacy artifacts, and the metadata repository. LSEs can all be run on the mainframe, run off the mainframe, or in some cases run with part of the server on the mainframe and part off the mainframe. In cases where the LSE is part of the CICS region, it will of course run on the mainframe. The legacy artifacts are the components on the mainframe that we are going to expose as services. The metadata repository contains the mapping and transformation information.

LSE Server Location

It is not just a matter of deciding to run the LSE on the mainframe or off the mainframe but also whether to run the process on the mainframe in a CICS region or not. For the most part, the vendor will decide this for you. Most vendors run outside the CICS region, but a few run in the CICS region.

- **Within CICS region**—The most obvious limitation here is that you must be accessing artifacts (CICS transactions, BMS maps) that are CICS-based. The advantages are that you are closer to where the processing is happening, and the process takes up less memory.
- **Outside CICS**—Outside the CICS region, you can perform any type of screen, transaction/application, or data SOA integration that you want.
- **Off mainframe server**—In some cases, it is not practical, or it is not allowed to run any new processes on the mainframe. **Distributed Relational Database Architecture (DRDA)** servers are processes that run off the mainframe and access DB2 on a mainframe server. Some LSE vendors architect their solution to be able to run off the mainframe.

- **Hybrid**—This is dependent on the vendor. Some of the LSE processes, which make sense running closer to the legacy artifacts, run on the mainframe and other LSE components run on open systems if most processing takes place there. BPEL is an example wherein it makes sense to run some of the processing—orchestration of CICS transactions—on the mainframe and then run it on open systems when integrating to Java EE or .NET Web services. Oracle has built in middleware JCA adapters for CICS, IMS/TM, IMS/DB, and VSAM. These adapters are actually OEMed technolgy from Attunity. Oracle also offers DRDA servers for access to DB2 on mainframes and iSeries/AS400. As they are DRDA servers, no footprint is required on the mainframe or the midrange server. Oracle partners with companies that offer LSE solutions: Attachmate, DataDirect, GT Software, Hostbridge, Seagull Software, Micro Focus, and Treehouse. These companies have solutions that either compliment what Oracle offers out of the box, or provides support for presentation or data-tier not offered directly by Oracle such as 3270, 5250, Natural, Adabas, Datacom, and others.

Legacy Artifacts

Legacy artifacts are the actual pieces of logic, screen, or data that reside on, and are processed on the mainframe. The legacy artifact is what the business users want to get to. Since these artifacts were already described in detail earlier in the chapter, we will focus on why you would chose one Legacy artifact/access method over another:

- **Presentation-tier**—This refers to mainframe 3270 or VT220 (DEC) transmissions, iSeries transmissions (5250), and others. Remember, this is not terminal emulation and screen scraping. These techniques were inflexible and tightly coupled to the device. This solution uses the actual field name in the screen map.

  Why choose presentation-tier over applications, data, and others? The simple answer is that none of the application source is available. Other reasons may be that the data stores cannot be accessed directly because of security or privacy restrictions, or that no stored procedures or SQL exist in the application. SOA enablement of the mainframe application is as simple as running and capturing the screens, menus, and fields you want to expose as services. This is fast, simple, and for the most part, easy.

- **Application**—Application service enablement is more than wrapping transactions as Web services. This is all about service enabling the behavior of the system, and includes CICS/IMS transactions, Natural transactions, IDMS and ADS/O dialogs, COBOL programs, and batch processes. This also includes the business rules, data validation logic, and other business processing that are part of the transaction.

Why application based legacy SOA? The application is at the core of most systems. The application contains the screens that are run, the business logic, business rules, workflow, security and the overall behavior of the legacy systems. Transactions on mainframe systems are the way that IT users interact with the system. So using the application layer makes the most sense when you want to replicate the functionality that the legacy system is currently using. This approach allows you to leverage all the behaviors (rules, transaction flow, logic, and security) of the application without having to re-invent it on open systems.

- **Data** — The data can be relational or nonrelational on the legacy system. In most cases, the legacy system will have a nonrelational data store such as a keyed file, network database, or a hierarchical file system. While accessing data in a legacy system, the SOA Integration layer will use SQL to provide a single, well-understood method to access any data source. This is important as some customers will prefer to have SQL-based integration as opposed to SOA-based data integration. The IT architect may decide that having a SQL statement in an open systems database is easier than putting in place an entire SOA infrastructure.

  Why data? This is ultimately the source of the truth. This is where the information that you want is stored. If you are using any of the other three artifacts, these methods will ultimately call the data store. So, it seems very reasonable that most of your services act directly against the data. Sometimes, security and privacy concerns will not make this possible. Sometimes, the data needs to have business logic, business rules, or transformation applied before it is valid. However, if these things are not applicable, going right to the data source is a nice way to proceed.

- **Other** — Stored procedures and SQL are the way most distributed applications get results from a data store. Stored procedures also provide major benefits in the areas of application performance, code re-use, application logic encapsulation, security, and integrity. Why stored procedures and SQL? You are making a move to distributed, open systems, and relational databases so you should use technologies that work well in this environment. There is also the people and skills aspect. Your open systems developers will be very familiar with stored procedures, and will find them easy to develop.

Keeping It Real: An architect who is well experienced in SQL access and relational databases may be tempted to perform Legacy SOA Integration using direct access (SQL instead of Web services) to the mainframe data. There are a couple of fundamental flaws with this approach:

In some cases, the programs may not be available, and the legacy system owners may not allow direct access to the data, or the data does not exist in a clean format.

In many instances, mainframe data is not readily usable until the appropriate business logic or business rule transforms it into meaningful information. On a mainframe, the business rules and business logic are frequently implemented as a program, or as part of a transaction.

In these cases, the user interface or application approach is the one to take for your SOA architecture.

Metadata Repositories

The various combinations of products being used will result in multiple repositories. The objective is to have the least amount possible, and the ones you do should be able to share information with each other. We could have one for LSE, BPEL, ESB, application server, security, services management, and other products that are part of the middleware will have their own repositories. At a minimum, you will have two repositories, one for the application server and one for the LSE. If the best-of-breed approach is taken, you could end up with a handful of repositories.

Other Technical and Business Aspects

The third dimension mentioned earlier will be discussed across all of the components just covered. This dimension is a combination of technical, business, and human nature—yes, human nature in a technical book.

Scalability

Scability is important because legacy personnel are accustomed to mainframe technologies such as Sysplex and CICSplex, which provide scalability on the mainframe. Some questions to ask an LSE vendor are: Does the engine take advantage of Sysplex and/or CICSplex? Can the engine be distributed across multiple mainframe LPRs?

Performance

Usually, performance is determined by the developer's application code. You can tune the operating system, network, and database, but the performance issues will usually come down to an SQL statement, or a poorly written piece of Java code. In the case of SOA Legacy Integration, the biggest areas of concern are not just the developer's application code, but also the performance of the LSE. On the developer side, the results coming back (is there a qualifier – where clause – on data results set) and the number of requests to the legacy system to get all data required are the biggest areas of concern. Having course grained legacy services, instead of fined grained services, can control the number of requests. Course grained (service bundled together) services will eliminate unnecessary network traffic, and back and forth 'chatter' with the legacy system. The performance of the LSE can be addressed through caching, SQL optimization, and high-speed XML processing. These are questions you will need to ask of your potential LSE vendors. Workload Management (WLM) and load balancing can also help.

Failover

If your application server and/or LSE goes down, this can cost you large sums of lost revenue, lost credibility with your business users, negative impact on your entire IT operation, and more. Therefore, application server and LSE failover is key to the success of your SOA Legacy Integration architecture. The simple approach, and actually the one most commonly used in mainframe environments, is to have a duplicate system configured at another location. However, this can be expensive, difficult to manage, and take hours to bring the remote site online. This is an area where open systems have made advances because Internet-based applications are 24X7. Most LSB vendors offer the capability to automatically and transparently fail over to another configuration. The vendors also offer the capability to do **active-passive** or **active-active**. In active-passive, the failover configuration will do a cold failover. In this case, the environment will need to start-up at the time of failover, and the transactions in process will be required to return. In active-active, a hot failover to a configuration that is up-to-date with all the transactions in progress will be made. Therefore, the transactions will automatically be restarted, and in some cases, picked up where they were left off.

Transaction Processing

When you first embark on your journey to Legacy SOA Integration, it is quite likely that most services will not require transactions processing (insert, update, and delete). They will be query or read only. As Legacy SOA matures, we will begin to see more OLTP-based legacy SOA environments. The next phase of SOA Legacy architecture requires high-speed transaction processing across multiple systems, mainframes, mid-range, and open system environments.

While Web services can be based on any transport, they typically use stateless HTTP communication. In addition, not all data sources can support the common commit procedures. For example, an Adabas data source is capable of supporting only one-phase commit, and cannot participate in a two-phase commit coordinated infrastructure. While these would seem to limit transaction support in a SOA integration environment, they are not really a concern as long as the underlying application server and LSE have transactions support. One method of transactions support is the use of the industry standard XA (eXtended Architecture). XA is a very mature distributed transaction manager. Some would argue, just because it is mature does not make it the right technology to use. They see OASIS **Web Services Transaction (WS-TX)** or vendor-lead WS-Transaction as better because they are Web services centric. However, as of today, XA is supported in all transaction processors (CICS, Tuxedo), application servers (Oracle, BEA, IBM), and database servers (Oracle, IBM, Microsoft). As we will see in the next chapter, XA transactions can be used to support the transaction needs of your SOA Integration architecture.

Governance

SOA governance is about managing the portfolio of services, planning development of new services and updating current services, managing the service lifecycle, using policies to restrict behavior, and monitoring performance. SOA Governance is spoken about by industry pundit as being very important to SOA architecture. In reality, when you are just starting off and creating internal Web services, or read-only external services, the need for governance is limited. You will have less then twenty services, so there is no need for a sophisticated service management tool. When you create a new version, or release an existing service, you will probably just delete the old service and put the new service into production. No need for a crazy scheme to make sure all existing transactions use the old service, and new requests use the new services. When you get more services and many consumers of your legacy Web services, something like version or change management control will be important. What if all your customers (Web services consumers) cannot upgrade to the latest release of your Web services? You will need SOA Governance products to handle requests for different versions of the same services from different clients. Monitoring performance is something that should be implemented immediately.

Human Factors

The human factor is a mix of the type of resources, company culture, and adaptability. What type of resources do you have? Are they mostly proficient at Java/.Net, COBOL, JCL, or some other language? Do they work on UNIX, Linux, Windows, or z/OS? These variables play a heavy role in the implementation process and target Oracle architecture.

People don't like change. Don't think your older COBOL programmers have a corner on the "I don't like change market". I have been involved in BEA to Oracle Application Server, and Sybase to Oracle Database migrations, with younger developers and DBAs that resist change. They say, "I am a Sybase DBA", and not "I am a DBA". Well, any form of Legacy Modernization involves change, and in most cases big time change. Both the company culture and the adaptability of the people involved can make or break a project. Over the years of managing IT projects, it has become obvious that technology does not make or break an IT project, but people and company culture do.

Agility and Adaptability of Architecture

We saw how systems developed over 30 years became fragile with different people, and constantly changing business initiatives, technologies and people. With limited resources of money, time, and people, we end up developing an architecture that is not agile. What staggers me is the number of companies that, given a chance to start fresh with modern technologies, develop Legacy SOA Integration architecture that are not flexible, are cobbled together with nonintegrated components, use proprietary technologies, and are different across organizations within the same company or division.

Host Support

It is important to understand the extent of support that the LSE vendor has for operating systems, presentation-tiers, transactions, languages and databases that are supported. Common operating systems support includes IBM zSeries (S/390), IBM iSeries (AS/400), UNIX, and Unisys. Not so commonly supported operating systems include IBM VSE, HP OpenVMS, and HP e3000. Before you choose an LSE product, you must make sure it supports the legacy presentation-tier, data, transactions, and/ or languages that you have. Some may support only the presentation-tier, or only the CICS transactions. Keep in mind all the different combinations of host support as we decide on the implementation options in the next section.

SOA Integration

Decisions! You had made some in the last chapter, and now you will be presented with some more. This time, decisions will have to be made on how we move from a rigid, fragile architecture to a more flexible, 'business ready' architecture. In other words, how do we get from source to target? You may think that the quickest and the most flexible option is to build it yourself. Although this is an option many consultants love as they can charge endless hours for doing just that. The products and technologies available today make it much easier and quicker than having to 'reinvent the wheel'.

Implementation Options

Let's have a look at your options. There are basically three options for the implementation of your Legacy SOA Integration solution. You can build it all yourself, buy products from different vendors, and 'glue' everything together, or purchase an end-to-end solution from one vendor. Each option has its strengths and weakness, and your company culture will definitely play a role in the option or options you chose. One of the options can be to choose a mix of the different options. The end goal is to choose an option that is easy to implement, is adaptable and maintainable, and has the lowest cost of total ownership.

Roll My Own

Architects and developers hear about things such as REST, XML, Java messaging, TCP/IP connects to mainframes, and MQSeries. Why can't we just build something? That would be very cool. Using Java EE CA, JAX-PRC, and other APIs, we can build a connector to the mainframe that calls a COBOL program and gets XML results back. We can then process these results, and return the results back to a web page that we develop in JSP. There are many drawbacks to this solution. You have to hand-code the solution while taking into account security, performance, reliability, governance, scalability, and service management. You also need to code and maintain low-level infrastructure software such as a data and SQL translation engine and a high-speed XML parsing and transformation engine.

Buy a Bunch of Products and become an Integrator

You or someone you hire becomes the 'general contractor'. Have you ever tried to be the general contractor for a house project such as finishing a basement, or putting an addition onto your house? You end up doing most of the work. You have to find an electrician, plumber, framer/drywall installer, painter, and research all the materials you will need, and also go out and buy them. It is the same thing here; you have to research all the products, negotiate contacts with each of the vendors, then buy, install, and configure the products. You then get the job of integrating the solution. Chances are that they use different repositories (with different RDBMS as there data store), different caching mechanisms, and different APIs. You also don't know who to go to if the end-to-end process does not work. It could be the fault of the application server, mainframe adapter, security provider, or someone else. This makes it difficult to do 'root cause analysis'.

One Pre-Integrated Stack

SOA Suites have become the latest IT technology rage in the last few years. SOA Suites are for the middleware industry what ERP systems are for the business applications world. They take a number of related but loosely coupled products, and make them tightly integrated but maintain the loose coupling. This gives you the best of both worlds, an integrated solution that does not rely on the other components but shares a common platform across all SOA Suite components. Not only are the SOA Suite components tightly integrated, the LSE is also integrated with the application server. This gives you end-to-end SOA Legacy Integration.

Keeping It Real: You can build your own TCP/IP and/or HTTP communication to the mainframe with custom Java (Java EE CA) adapters that talk to custom code on the mainframe. You can even create your own message queuing system that resides on the mainframe or open systems. But why would you do this? There are many products from Oracle and its partners that bring you bundled, 'out of the box' Legacy SOA Integration solutions to you.

Implementation Approach

Not surprising, the approach we are going to take is pre-integrated stack using as many tools as possible in the development, deployment, and management of the solution. We want the target architecture to be as 'out of the box' as possible, and the development environment to be as much of a 'drag-and–drop' as possible. In this chapter, we will also introduce you to Oracle products and technologies for development and run time/production. We will use the Oracle products to get from Accidental Architecture to SOA Integration architecture. The transformation from Accidental Architecture to an agile architecture looks like this:

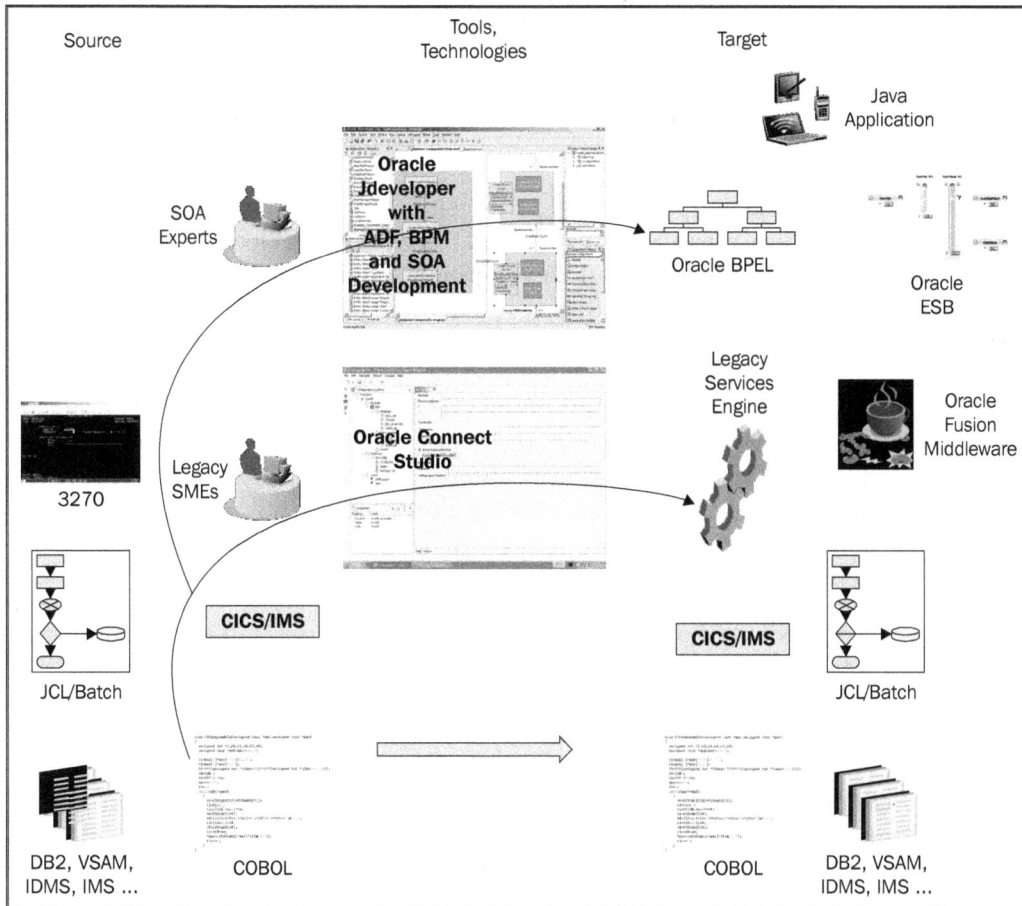

The diagram does not explain the steps or sequence of events. It is not intended to do so as we will cover them next. First, let's examine the overall approach, the tools, products, and technologies used. We will start from the bottom as this follows the high level approach that will be taken.

The big red arrow indicates the COBOL and other legacy languages. JCL/Batch, data stores, and transaction monitors stay as they are today. SOA Integration does not change anything that exists on the legacy system. If you are on the mainframe, you stay on the mainframe running COBOL, Pl/1,JCL, VSAM, IDMS, and other legacy artifacts.

The next level up on the diagram is the LSE development tool. This tool will allow the person responsible for exposing legacy artifacts as Web services to do this in a GUI, drag-and-drop based **Integrated Development Environment (IDE)**. These tools will typically make it very easy to expose presentation, transactions, or data as Web services. In the case of presentation and transactions Web services, the tool will allow the developer to view the actual legacy interface, and choose the screens, menus, transactions, and fields that will be part of the Web service. The reason for the Legacy Subject Matter Expert(s) listed, as the person(s) doing the work, is that they are best suited to identify, design, develop, and deploy legacy SOA-enabled artifacts. Although these are GUI tools, it is important to have a person adept in legacy technologies performing this process. In this step, we will actually deploy services to the legacy system and/or the open systems platform.

The highest level is where the legacy Web services are incorporated into the SOA Suite and/or open systems presentation tier. In some cases, you may just want to access the services from a Java Server Page, Java Server Faces, or AJAX presentation-tier application. In other cases, you may integrate the services with other services using Oracle BPEL, or you may want to use an ESB when some of the legacy services need to be transformed or passed onto another application. Any of these application types can be monitored using Oracle BAM. The tool used for this development is Oracle JDeveloper. Oracle JDeveloper is Oracle's Java Model Driven Development Environment. The tool contains a Business Process Analysis Suite (BPA Suite) from IDS Sheer. This provides you with the option to start modeling the SOA architecture with business users, and Legacy SMEs using the Unified Modeling Language (UML) and other user-friendly diagrams. The modeling done in the BPA Suite can then be used by Oracle JDeveloper/BPEL Designer to fill in the missing details or incorporate additional elements such as service definition, monitoring elements etc. in the business process (BPEL). Oracle JDeveloper also includes Oracle's Application Development Framework (ADF) to develop standard Java-based Java Server Faces, Struts, and EJB 3.0/Toplink-based applications. ADF is a GUI drag-and-drop based environment to create Java/Java EE-based applications rapidly.

Keeping It Real: Having worked with Independent Software Vendors (ISVs) for years, I can tell you that it is less costly and easier to manage a complete integrated stack of products than a custom-built solution or the best-of-breed architecture. Legacy architectures contain custom developed messaging, integration, interface, rules engines, workflow, and even business applications (inventory, order entry, accounting) for a reason. These pre-packaged solutions did not exist years ago. The great thing about being a Modernization architect is that legacy IT groups get to take advantage of SOA, and the 'out of the box' messaging, workflow, security, integration, management, and even the business application it brings to the table.

Phases in the Implementation Cycle

The implementation lifecycle to create your modern Legacy SOA Integration architecture looks like this:

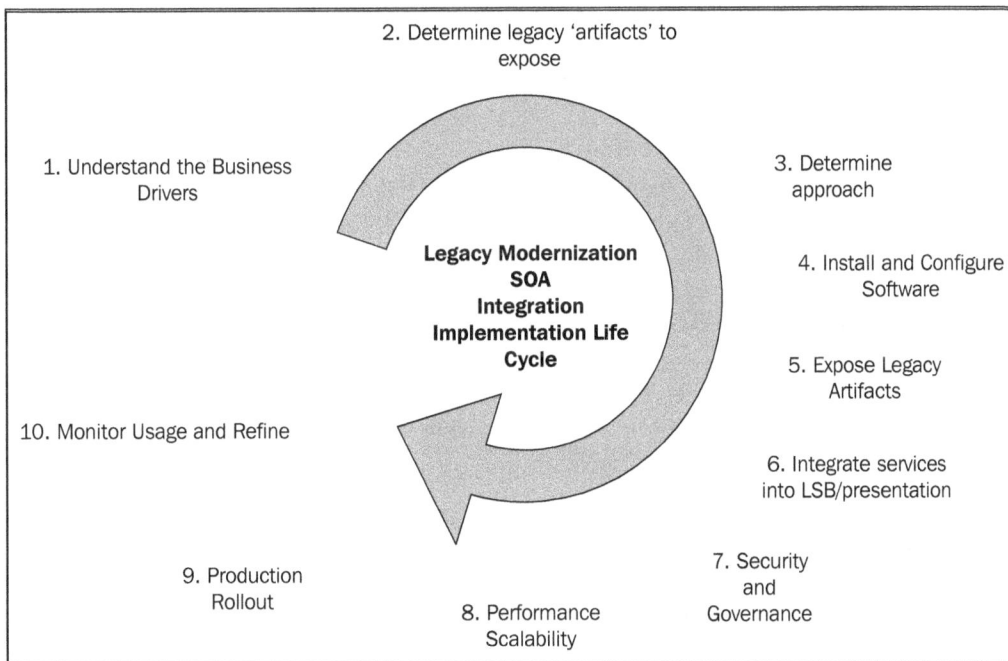

The implementation life cycle is an iterative approach. There will be multiple iterations of the same or similar process. Let's dive down into each of the phases or steps in the implementation life cycle:

Understanding the Business Drivers

Understanding business drivers is an overused mantra. I have seen entire chapters in books dedicated to the importance of business drivers. In the end, we all know that you must understand the business drivers, as technology for technologies sake doesn't make sense. A few of the common business drivers for Legacy SOA are:

- Web enabled applications for internal customer service — In today's 'flat world', many of your customer service agents work either from a home in Idaho, or in a call center in India or Philippines. Imagine trying to put a 3270 terminal at someone's home office or in offices around the world. No way! The answer is a thin application that runs in a browser.

- Customer self-service applications — Fedex was one of the trendsetters in this area. First they gave you the ability to track your packages online. Then, they allowed customers to create their own shipping manifests. What a great way to reduce your customer support costs– get the customer to do it and feel good about it! Today not only do we have the ability to check into our flights from home, but also make our own hotel, airline, and car reservations online using the Web. Believe me, most of these self-service airline reservations are communicating with a mainframe somewhere in the booking process. Online banking is another great example of Legacy SOA integration.

- Alignment with the corporate SOA strategy — This is the grand daddy of them all. This is big because you are operating at a strategic level. If you have a corporate SOA strategy, chances are very good that legacy systems integration will be a part of the architecture.

Products and Technologies Used in this Phase

The choice here is to use a repository based modeling tool, or a simple word processing document. The advantage of the modeling tool (Oracle BPA Suite) is that multiple users can contribute and information in the repository can be used to actually generate code for the implementation.

- Oracle BPA Suite — Oracle Business Process Architect (a component of the Oracle BPA Suite) using an Event or Business Process (BPMN) diagram.

  And/or

- Open Office Writer or PDF document — Business drivers can also be simply captured in a document. It is more difficult to show business requirements in a picture or a diagram format, but text may do just fine.

Determine Business Processes to Expose

Get this phase correct, and you are in good shape. Get it wrong, and you have technology for technology's sake. During this phase, you need to align the business drivers with those legacy technology artifacts. This means finding the correct transaction, screen/fields, or data store in an application that was written over 30 years back containing millions of lines of application code. This can be a daunting task without a tool that can help you identify and document the code or data that is important. Modernization vendors, OpenConnect and Relativity have technologies that discover legacy artifacts to expose. Relativity does static analysis of code and discovers the legacy processes to wrap as services. OpenConnect does real time analysis to do the same thing. These tools also provide additional functionality:

- Proactive performance identified — A focused, automated analysis reveals where the application's existing architecture could lead to a failure of the service or performance issues. The tool will also tell you how you can eliminate these potential performance or service issues.

- Artifact classification — Classification of artifacts makes the next step much easier. Classification also provides you with an application program and/or the screen communication flow and the data stores that the applications access.

- WSDL generation — These tools can even generate the WSDL that can be used in integrating the Web services into the application server or the presentation tier.

Of course, you could always complete this phase using a combination of manual discovery and design using the Oracle BPA suite. This would involve getting the legacy SMEs in a room and doing whiteboarding, modeling in Oracle BPA Suite, and writing the technical specifications.

Products and Technologies Used in this Phase

The choice of tools to use for discovering business processes is really a choice between a tool specifically built (Relativity or OpenConnect) to handle legacy SOA artifact discovery or a generic BPA tool (Oracle BAP Suite).

- Oracle BPA Suite — Oracle Business Process Architect UML Use Case or Activity diagrams.

  And/or

- Relativity — Parses the application sources and performs understanding of the application source code. The information from this analysis is used to determine the application and the data flow. We will use the Relativity RMW Analyst tool in the next chapter to complete this phase of the modernization project.

OR

- OpenConnect Comprehend—Combines real-time interaction with process execution static data from existing system interfaces (logs, batch job output, CICS transaction logs), so a full end-to-end business process can be determined.

- Determine the approach—I believe we covered this sufficiently earlier in the chapter. Now you know what the process is, you need to decide if presentation, application, data, and/or stored procedures are the best approach. The approach identifies the specific use cases/scenarios that you will be implementing. As the integration points in the system may vary with the use cases, you may have a combination of these approaches.

Install/Configure the Software

Remember, this is where you need to be nice to the legacy system data center team. Installing and configuring software on a mainframe is not like doing it on a local Linux box. You also probably need to give them plenty of time to get the appropriate approvals, software and hardware upgrades, and legacy system configured. You will also need to install and configure the Oracle software required for your application server and presentation-tier. We discussed the LSE configuration in the previous section. As I mentioned, the LSE configuration depends upon the vendor. In the case of the Oracle LSE, it is a hybrid configuration where some of the processing takes place on the middle-tier, and some on the mainframe.

Products and Technologies Used in this Phase

These products and technologies are not choices but the products you will need to use. It includes the application server and LSE.

- Oracle SOA Suite—The Oracle SOA Suite is bundled with the Oracle Application Server. The Oracle Application contains the Java EE runtime, Web services support, and HTTP Server among other components.

- Oracle Internet Directory (OID)—Oracle has a number of identity management products, and OID is one of the products in the suite. OID is an industry standard, Lightweight Directory Access Protocol (LDAP) repository. We are going to keep it simple and use LDAP for authentication and authorization.

- Oracle Integration Adapters—This is your LSE from Oracle. You must first install the Oracle SOA Suite. Then, you can install the Oracle Legacy Integration Adapters.

Expose Legacy Artifacts

The GUI development tools from LSE vendors make it easy to expose legacy artifacts as Web services. They will generate the corresponding WSDL, so the legacy Web service can be integrated into the Oracle Application Server. The three most common types of legacy Web services are generated in the following manner:

- Presentation-Tier—Most screen integrations can be done by executing the application using the transaction ID on the mainframe in the LSE development tool, and capturing the screens and fields you want to expose. Developers gather application metadata (screens and fields) from the existing host application, and in most cases, modify the legacy metadata to be more user-friendly.

- Application—Web services access to business rules and business logic can be administered through a simple three to four step process:
   ◦ Specify the name of the program to be invoked
   ◦ Specify the region where the program is to be executed
   ◦ Specify the interface to the program using the COMMAREA of the COBOL module
   ◦ An optional fourth step is available, to handle the transformation from legacy standards to modern SOA standards. The limitations of mainframe naming conventions generated standards that are incompatible with the flexibility offered today.
   ◦ Most tools supports the ability to transform element names in COMMAREAs to comply with the Web services naming standards, and make them more readable.

- Data access—Data access integration is all about exposing relational and nonrelational data stores as SQL, and then publishing the SQL interface through a WSDL. The steps to do this are:
   1. Select the type of data source you will be exposing
   2. Connect to the legacy data source
   3. Select the legacy files or tables you will be accessing
   4. Write the SQL for the queries you will be making
   5. Expose the SQL as a Web service

- Products and technologies used in this phase—Oracle provides a tool in order to expose your legacy transactions and data as Web services.
- Oracle Studio—Oracle Studio comes bundled with the Oracle Integration Adapters you installed and configured earlier. It is a GUI tool that is based on IBM Eclipse. The tool has support for introspecting the metadata in COBOL copybooks, and SQL modeling of IMS/DM and VSAM, and automatically generating the XSD and WSDL schemas.

Integrate Services into the application server

This is a key phase as it makes the Web services we expose on the mainframe accessible to the end users. The end goal of Legacy SOA Integration is to get the mainframe to be part of your SOA infrastructure. We will achieve this goal in this phase. In many cases, the services are exposed in the presentation-tier. The presentation-tier may be a simple JSP or JSF application, Oracle WebCenter (portal framework) or Oracle BAM. It is also common to see these services integrated into an Oracle ESB, Oracle BPEL, or Oracle Data Integrator (ODI) process.

Products and Technologies Used in this Phase

Oracle JDeveloper is the development tool for Java EE and most of the Oracle SOA products. Oracle BAM and Oracle Data Integrator are not required.

- Oracle JDeveloper—A great thing about Oracle JDeveloper is that it can be used for Java EE (JSP, JSF, or ADF), ESB, BPEL, and Oracle WebCenter development.

- Oracle BAM—Developing a BAM dashboard can be done using the Oracle BAM development tool.

- Oracle Data Integrator—Oracle Data Integrator will be used if you are going to include your mainframe Web services as part of your Enterprise Information Integration architecture.

Security and Governance

As we are just getting started, we will be adequately secure using Oracle Internet Directory for authentication and authorization, and SSL for securing the Web services network traffic. For now, we are not going to implement a full-blown governance solution. The auditing and tracking capabilities built into the Oracle Application Server and Oracle Enterprise Manager products should be adequate for your first implementation.

Products and Technologies Used in this Phase

Security and management will become more sophisticated as the Web service number of legacy Web services grow. The products listed below are adequate as you first start Web service enabling your mainframe:

- Oracle Internet Directory(OID) — Autherization and authenticate can be provided through username/passwords and Access Control Lists (ACL) using OID.

- Oracle Application Server — Auditing and logging of Web service usage is automatically done by the Oracle Application Server.

- Oracle Enterprise Manager — Monitoring of Web services can be done using the Oracle Enterprise Manager web-based console.

Performance and Scalability

Just because I have placed this in the latter part of the process, it does not mean you don't take the performance and scalability into account earlier. It means that it is the first opportunity to do real performance and tuning work. Not until the complete environment is installed, configured, and deployed can you determine where your bottlenecks reside.

Products and Technologies Used in this Phase

The Oracle BPA Suite allows you to proactively manage your systems performance and scalability. The Oracle Enterprise Manager Diagnostic pack allows you to manage application performance during production.

- Oracle Business Process Simulator — This technology is part of the Oracle BPA Suite. The tool simulates the process models based on a set of discrete events to do 'what if' analysis.

- Oracle Enterprise Manager (OEM) with Diagnostics Pack — OEM is an end-to-end system management and performance monitoring tool for your database, application server, and the supporting infrastructure. Oracle Application Diagnostics For Java (Oracle AD4J) is a monitoring solution to improve the availability and performance of Java EE application.

Production Rollout

Production rollout is a large and complex area. Production rollouts also tend to vary across company to company. Since most companies already have detailed production rollout plans in place, I will not try to cover different aspects of production rollout here. This will depend on an organization's IT governance standards and culture, which is unique to each company and each department within a company.

Products and Technologies Used in this Phase

Keeping all of your hardware platforms running the same release and patches of software is done through provisioning software.

- Oracle OEM with Provisioning Pack — This tool makes it easier to rollout your application to the production environment. It also assists with new software releases.

Monitor Usage and Refine

Monitor the legacy Web services that your users are taking advantage of. Legacy SOA Integration is not 'build it, and they will' come. People don't like to change. You may have built the best Legacy SOA Integration solution ever, but if business users are still logging into their 'green screens', it does not matter. The general area of business process identification and optimization has become so important to companies that OpenConnect has created a product to not only identify services to wrap, but also to understand how services are being used. In addition, Gartner has created a new concept called **Business Optimization Support System (BOSS)** that is focused on just this area.

Products and Technologies Used in this Phase

OpenConnect is uniquely positioned as one of the few companies that provides the software to monitor the usage of your newly web enabled mainframe.

- OpenConnect Comprehend — Comprehend can be used to tell you who is using the new interface and how often, and the usage pattern. This tool graphically displays the usage of the new Web service interface, as compared to the number of people who are still using the old 'green screen' interface.

Keeping It Real: I am a big believer in the 80/20 rule. It applies to your job: 80 percent of the success of an organization is attributed to 20 percent of the people. It applies to life: 80 percent of your happiness is dependent upon the 20 percent of the things you do each day. More importantly, for this book, it applies to Legacy SOA Integration: 80 percent of the business benefits you will derive from Legacy SOA Integration will come from 20 percent of all the possible services you can create from legacy artifacts. Keep this in mind, and you will find that you just need to focus on a small set of services once you identify the top 20 percent.

SOA Integration—Top Four Scenarios and Oracle Solutions

This section is not really about the final product. How can it be, when we have no idea what your environment looks like, what your business drivers are, what your strategic direction is, what tactical solutions you have already thought about, or what your biggest pain point with your current legacy system is today. It has been said a number of times in the technical journals and by IT analysts that SOA is not a product or solution but a journey. If SOA is a journey, then modernization is a journey where you 'pack extra clothes'. This is because your modernization journey will take unexpected twists and turns, and you may go to unexpected places as business objectives, key personnel, and technologies change during the journey. By the end of this section, if we have done our jobs, you will have answers to the questions, when, where, and how to start.

SOA Integration has been chosen for our first book and as the first approach, because it is often the first approach in your modernization journey. It gives you the ability to deliver something tangible quickly. This will make you happy, your bosses happy, and more importantly your IT users and customers happy. SOA projects typically last three to four months and deliver high customer value. This is far from the legacy project of yesterday that involved three to five year efforts. We now live in a world of short attention spans, and instant gratification; we don't read the morning newspaper but get it on the Internet. So our modernization journey needs to reflect these changing times.

In this section we will focus on why specific products and technologies, as opposed to what they are. We will also use a set of common situations we have come across, as we help customers and partners on their journey to a modern IT platform. These situations will be put in the context of a scenario. We will then use a design pattern that we have found successful in that scenario. Design patterns have been around for decades, but have gained a lot of popularity recently and are commonly used in the world of OO and Java. The term design pattern can be overloaded, overused, and be made overly complex. For our purposes, a design pattern should provide an effectively implemented solution to address a recurring problem (in legacy systems).

Oracle Products Included in the Solution

Before we get started, let's cover why these particular products make the most sense, and explain why other products were left out. The Oracle Fusion Middleware family of products contains all the necessary components for your SOA Integration architecture.

- Why Web services?

  Web services are the foundation of our communication and results processing of the mainframe artifacts. Without Web services, you really don't have a Legacy SOA Integration. Enough said.

- Why Oracle Legacy Adapters?

  The Oracle Legacy Adapters are what we have been referring to as your Legacy Service Engine. You need this as it makes the flow of information from your legacy environment to your open systems environment happen in a seamless fashion.

- Why Oracle BPEL Process Manager?

  Business process orchestration and human workflow are key to communicating with your mainframe, internal services, and external services. To align business with IT, applications must become more process-driven. In today's world, users do not have to remember all the activities that need to be done. Instead, workflow engines place tasks that need their attention in workflow inboxes.

  Oracle BPEL Process Manager allows SOA service implementations, human interaction, and system workflow to be orchestrated quickly and easily using graphical 'drag-and-drop' techniques that allow users to be involved in orchestrating their own systems, thereby reducing the amount of custom code required, and increasing an application's agility by allowing users a more direct interaction with their systems.

- Why Oracle Enterprise Service Bus?

  BPEL will provide you with business and human workflow for your business services. However, there are also a number of services that are generic to many applications. A service bus provides these generic services by implementing standard facilities such as messaging or integration capabilities often by encapsulating different existing technologies that implement the generic services and making them appear as one.

  Oracle ESB provides a messaging and integration layer for directly connecting applications and Web services through a common infrastructure. Oracle ESB combines an asynchronous messaging backbone with intelligent message transformation and routing, to ensure messages are passed reliably. Using Oracle ESB, integrating applications becomes a drag-and-drop exercise using prepackaged ESB adapters for file, database, message queue, and COTS access. The mainframe is known for its quality of service and reliability. Oracle ESB makes use of Oracle Application Server's grid capabilities to allow the formation of an ESB grid that crosses multiple platforms.

- Why Oracle Enterprise Manager (OEM)?

  As discussed earlier in this chapter, you don't need a specialized Web Services Manager or Web Services Registry at this point in your journey. However, it does make sense to make use of the technology in the Oracle Enterprise Manager product that your company is going to use, to manage your SOA middle-tier and perhaps at some point your Oracle Database Grid. The Oracle Enterprise Manager 10g SOA Management pack integrates with Oracle BPEL Process Manager Console and Oracle BAM. This allows administrators to view service levels for key business processes, and SOA infrastructure components. The SOA Management Pack also provides a means to monitor Web services both from an end user perspective as well as request based monitoring. Administrators can define SOAP tests for one or more partner links of a BPEL process, any hosted Web service, or an external service.

  The OEM plugin Application Diagnostics for Java has interactive transaction tracing feature for the web transactions (legacy Web services) defined as part of web applications. Application Web Transactions can be easily created using a simple, intuitive transaction recorder. Once an application performance problem is identified, Web Transactions can be executed on demand to immediately trace problems to specific application tiers. Transactions are played back interactively, and in-depth breakdowns of response times across all tiers of your application server provide for quick problem diagnosis.

- Why Oracle Identity Management?

  Any IT environment would need some form of security. We will start our SOA Legacy Integration journey with security that is strong but not overwhelming to implement and maintain. Identity Management is a very broad topic when it comes to Oracle. This includes everything from single sign on to provisioning, federated identity, directory services, certificate authority, and more. In the immediate term, we will use Oracle Internet Directory (remember this is called OID and is an LDAP compliant directory) and Oracle Enterprise Single Sign-On so that all applications (Web services) can be logged at once.

- Why Oracle WebCenter Portal?

  A portal provides a single web-based entry point into a variety of applications. Using a portal allows an organization to create a unique user experience that combines many of the functional components of the SOA applications into a single point of access.

The introduction of the Internet and web-based computing is one instance where even users will agree that technology has changed business in a positive fashion. The ability of the users around the world to easily access systems via web-based thin client technology has eliminated the need to have applications executed on a client machine, thus opening the door to self-service applications that have clearly changed the way business is done. Incorporating the use of the Web is fundamental to any modern application using Oracle WebCenter Portal.

- Why Oracle Data Integrator?

Oracle Data Integrator (ODI) allows users to extract data from many legacy and nonlegacy sources – including those on the mainframe – using web services that are part of your application server and load and transform the data into a number of data sources. Often we times find that flat file information sharing is a corner stone of legacy information integration. Replacing this custom processing with a product such as ODI makes the processing of the flat files more centralized, agile, and adaptable. Also, enhancing the system for new flat file types or changes to current structures is much easier.

- Why Oracle Business Activity Monitoring (BAM)?

Modern systems do not require you to wait until a report, query, or lengthy batch process is complete before you can get information on business activity. Instead, real-time information is viewed via graphical dashboards that can send out alerts through a variety of communication mechanisms when user-defined 'thresholds of importance' are met. Oracle (BAM) will be used to provide this real time feedback for our Web services, BPEL, and ESB processes.

- Why Oracle Business Intelligence?

Instead of relying on hard copy reports, real-time business intelligence and data mining tools can be used to "slice and dice" data to determine key performance indicators and discover data trends without having to wait for IT. This increases the overall agility of the organization, allowing end users to react more quickly to ongoing business changes.

Oracle Products Not Included in the Solution

What is equally important is identifying the components that may apply but will not be included in this architecture. The components mentioned here will play a significant role in re-architecture. The following section discusses the products not included and why they are not part of the architecture.

- Why not Oracle Business Rules?

  Business Rules Engines can be used to store business logic and business rules for BPEL processing. For example, what is the credit limit based upon the customer's credit rating? Since business rules play a more significant role in re-architecturing COBOL to Java/Java EE, we will wait until Chapter 6 to show the power of business rules engines in legacy modernization. For SOA enablement, a majority of the business rules will continue to be embedded in the legacy COBOL application.

- Why not Oracle Web Services Manager?

  Oracle Web Services Manager (WSM) is a comprehensive solution for securing and managing service-oriented architectures (SOA). It allows IT managers to centrally define policies that govern Web service operations such as access control (authentication, authorization), logging, and content validation, and then attach these policies to one or multiple Web services, with no modifications required for existing Web services. In addition, Oracle WSM collects runtime data to monitor access control, message integrity, message confidentiality, quality of service (defined in service-level agreements—SLAs) and displays that information on graphical charts. Oracle WSM brings better enterprise control and visibility over their SOA deployments. As discussed earlier, a combination of SSL, OID, Oracle Single Sign On, and OEM can provide you the security, governance and monitoring that is required for this phase of our modernization journey.

- Why not Oracle Web Services Registry?

  Oracle Web Services Registry is an industry-standard UDDI-compliant Web services registry. As mentioned earlier, the limited number of services and the fact that these will mostly be consumed internally make the use of a Web Services Registry something of an 'over kill' at this time.

- Why not Oracle ADF?

  Oracle JDeveloper is packaged with Oracle Application Development Framework (ADF), which provides a rich set of templates for developing business applications. For example, using Oracle ADF Faces—a set of user interface components based on industry standards—a developer can quickly develop web-based presentation layers from legacy screens with limited coding. We will use JDeveloper in the next chapter as we develop our Web services. But we will not utilize the complete functionality of Oracle ADF until the re-architecture chapters. Re-architecting is the best place to implement the full features of ADF.

Each scenario defines a situation or situations that we have encountered while working directly with our customers. For each scenario, we define the problem, context of the problem, forces (business, human, and technology) and the Oracle product solution set. The design pattern is a combination of the scenario and the recommended Oracle architecture.

Before we get started with the scenarios, a few disclaimers are in order:

- The scenarios are not in any particular order or sequence
- The scenarios described next are not phases, but could be put into any order that fits your technical and business drivers
- The scenarios may not fit your particular situation exactly, but you are most likely to find a fit in one of the four scenarios listed here.

Scenario One—Enterprise Information Integration

Also known as: Data Integration, file sharing, file messaging

Problem

My current Infrastructure for information integration is fragile, expensive, and hard to maintain.

The problem is often characterized by issues with no common work-flow approach, lack of data quality, and data profiling capabilities, customized transformation logic unique to each data feed, lack of real time monitoring capability, and inability to quickly add new data feeds.

Context

Data needs to be shared with new systems developed on open systems and other mainframe systems, both internal and external to the company/organization we work for.

Almost all legacy systems (I have not seen one that doesn't, so I would like to say all, but once you say all, someone will find the exception) have data feeds coming into them or going out of them.

Forces

Applications and organizations were standalone in the past. Now there is a big need to share information between application and businesses.

Solution

The solution includes Oracle ESB, Oracle BPEL, Oracle Legacy Adapters, Oracle Ebusiness Suite Adapters, and Oracle OEM as depicted here:

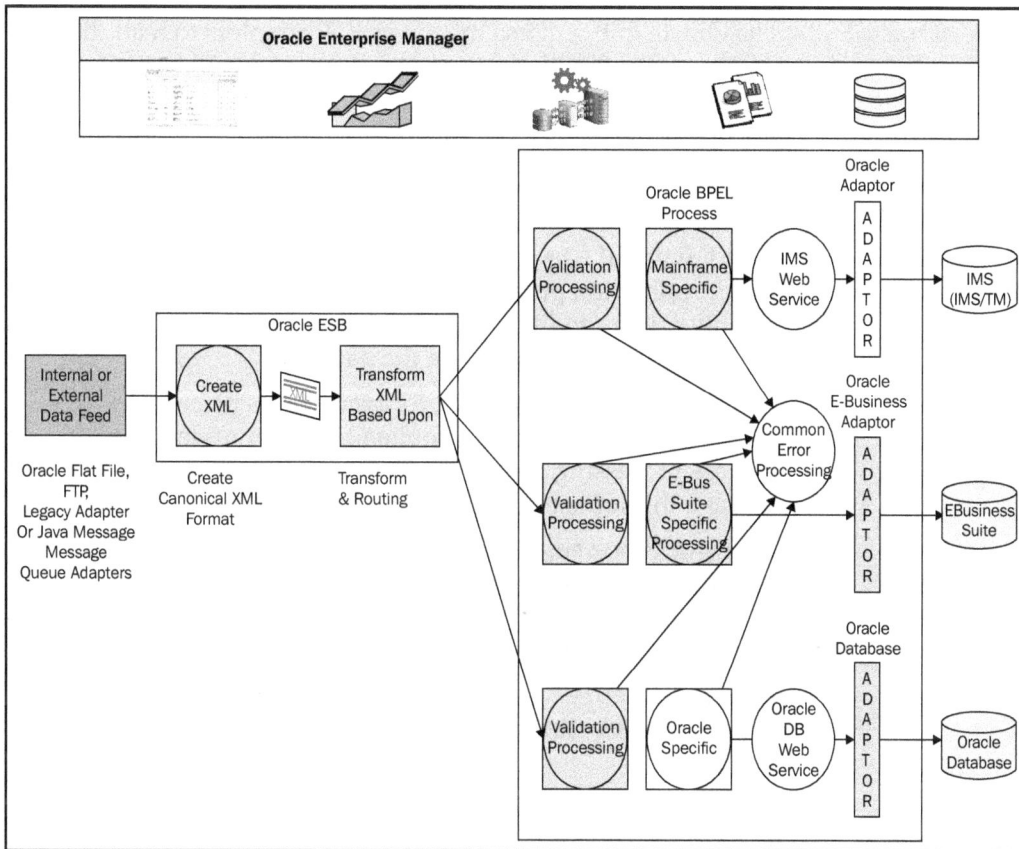

Scenario One Summary

The objective of Legacy SOA Integration is not to disrupt the current business processing and legacy system. We hold this to be true by keeping the same data feed the same. Attempting to perform even minor changes to data feeds are near impossible because:

- If a third party or even an internal organization outside your control is involved, the ability to get the change completed can take months.
- Even internally owned data feeds impact the source systems, current processing, and target systems so that even a small change has a ripple effect that causes the change to take months.

The current data feed will remain and download FTP to a directory and will most likely remain batched. The diagram shows technologies such as Legacy Adapters and Oracle Messaging as these can be adopted when changes to business processes are made.

- Oracle ESB – The Oracle ESB will use the file or FTP adapters to read the flat file and then transform the flat file to a common (canonical) XML file format. Based on the source of the data feed, the message will be routed to the appropriate Oracle BPEL process.
- Oracle BPEL – This is where the workflow and processing that we discussed earlier comes in:
  - Oracle BPEL will call a Java or Web service process to perform any validation processing. This validation processing will probably call out to the Oracle database to validate information based upon the data in the database.
  - After validation, file type specific processing takes place. This is basically 'business rules' being applied to the input data file. This business processing could call the Oracle Rules engine (we will leave this topic to Chapter 5).
  - Common Error Processing – Validation and/or business rule processing errors will be passed to an error-handling route. The BPEL worklist will be populated, so a human may correct the problem file or records.
  - Data persistence Web service – The data will be persisted in the Oracle database, IMS database, and/or the Oracle Ebusiness Suite.

Scenario Two—Web Enablement

This is also known as Screen Scraping, or Re-interfacing.

Problem

My customer support people, sales representatives, customers, and partners would like to access our system through the Web. Why can't I have one interface to update both my legacy system and the Oracle system?

Old 'green screen' technologies have many limitations. A big one is that they are not very intuitive. You have to access several screens or systems to get the information you need, and there is no 'point and click'. In addition, many times, users may have to go to multiple systems to either query or update the same or similar data.

Context

Users want their data now, wherever they are, and at any time of the day or night. Users also want their legacy systems and new Oracle environments to work together.

A business process that requires a user to have to query multiple systems, and then update multiple systems makes everything move slower, and in many cases may cause data inconsistencies.

Forces

We are seeing the ranks of users who were online and on the web at a very young age. Technologies providing better application interfaces have been in the market place for years.

Solution

The solution includes Oracle WebCenter and/or JSF/JSP, Oracle Legacy Adapters and Oracle OEM as depicted below:

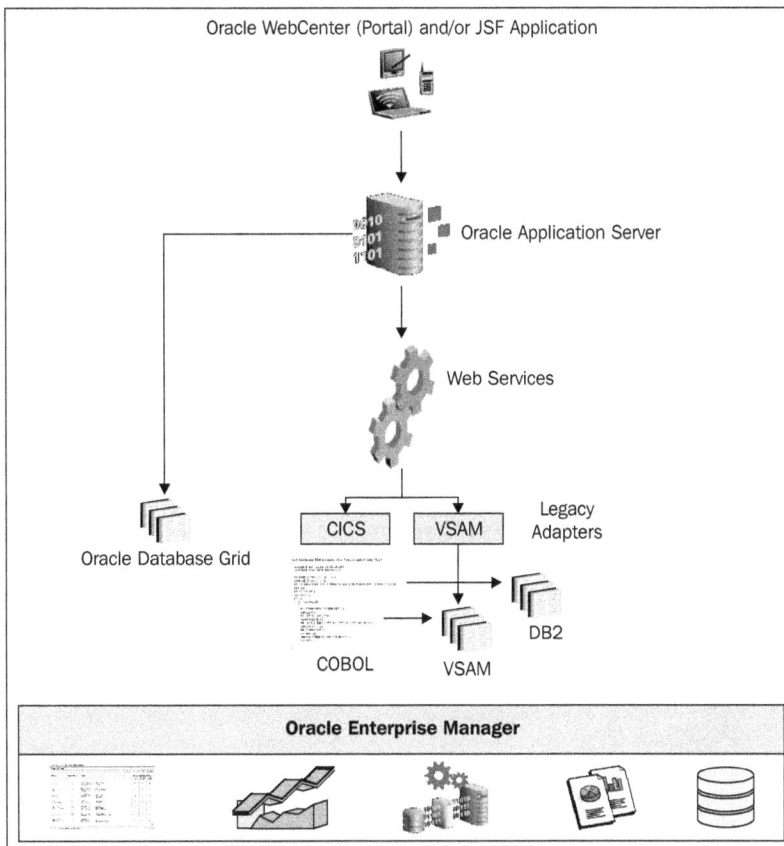

Scenario: Two Summary

The key to this scenario is the interface. Therefore, Oracle WebCenter and/or JSP/JSF will be used. For the first iteration of this scenario, JSP and/or JSF can be used to keep development simple and deployment quicker. A more sophisticated interface would be to use JSF to develop JSR-168 portlets, and deploy them using Oracle WebCenter.

Scenario Three—Report Off-Load Using Data Migration

This is also known as Data migration, Legacy Operational Data Store, or Reporting Modernization

Problem

IT Perspective—My legacy reporting infrastructure is costing me millions to run and I have a six month back log of report requests.

User perspective—I already have 100 green bar reports but I still cannot make business decisions with the information I have.

Context

Users need access to information in a variety of formats and dimensions. They also need to be able to easily do 'ad hoc' and 'what if' scenarios.

It is not uncommon for a mainframe-centric organization to have strategic sales forecasting to be done on all spreadsheets.

Forces

Reporting on the mainframe is expensive, and business users cannot access the information they need to make decisions. So a typical organization will find that users have created their own reports using Excel, SQL, and other desktop tools. Data then gets duplicated throughout the enterprise.

Solution

The final solution includes Oracle Data Integrator, Oracle BPEL, Oracle Legacy Adapters, Oracle BAM, Oracle BI Suite and Oracle OEM as depicted here:

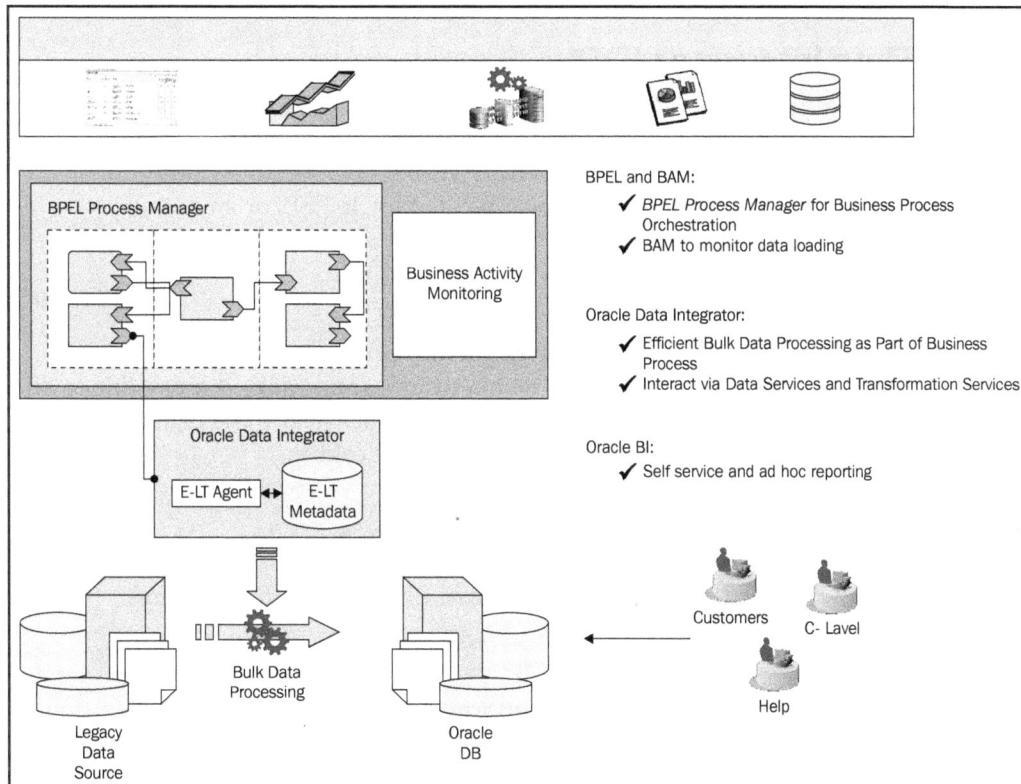

Scenario Three: Summary

In the summary of this scenario, we will discuss why we choose certain Oracle products.

Oracle BAM

In Oracle BAM, both the end user decision makers and IT management see the real time flow of information into the reporting system. End user decision makers can make real-time decisions based upon the most current information. IT management can get immediate alerts if a data load is running slow, alerts on the amount of data being loaded each minute, or the average response time of user ad hoc reports.

Oracle BPEL

Oracle BPEL is used to orchestrate the flow of information into the Oracle database. Oracle BPEL can be used to schedule data loads based upon the time of arrival, or the arrival of a specific file or by constantly looking for the data extracts to load.

Oracle Data Integrator (ODI)

Oracle Data Integrator provides a fast method to bulk load data into the Oracle reporting database. It provides access to data transformation, data cleansing, and data management services. As ODI is fully Web service-enabled, any ODI component can be consumed by Oracle BPEL, Oracle ESB, or any other Web service-enabled tool or product.

Oracle BI

The products we just discussed are all infrastructure products to support the end objective that was to move reporting off the mainframe, and make it accessible to all users. Using Oracle BI tools will hopefully reduce or at least stop the proliferation of Excel spreadsheets and customer SQL reports on user desktops.

Scenario Four: End-to-End SOA

This is also known as Software as a Service, or Legacy SOA Integration

Problem

My legacy system is a 'black box'. Getting information into it is painful and getting information out is worse. I also have no idea of the business processes that run my business.

Context

Your mainframe system does not reflect how business is done today. The legacy system is difficult to maintain, enhance, or rollout new services (product offerings) to internal and external customers.

Forces

The user community demands information to be processed in real time and results to be available immediately. Information integration interfaces into the system are changing every week, and new trading partners wish to interface with you business in days, not months. The system interface needs to be personalized, so that internal power users can see all the information, internal sale people see only sales data pertinent to them, customers only see their data and orders, and company executives have a real time insight into the business as it stands right now, and not what it looked liked three weeks ago.

Solution

The final solution includes Oracle WebCenter, Oracle PBM, Oracle BPEL, Oracle Legacy Adapters, Oracle BAM, Oracle ESB, Oracle OID and SSO, and Oracle OEM as depicted here:

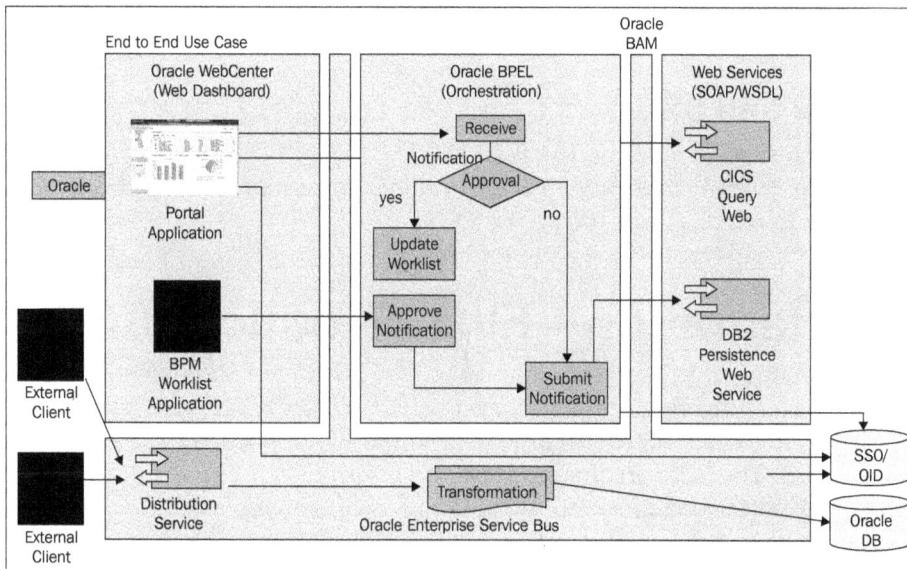

Scenario Four: Summary

As we did with scenario three, we will discuss why we chose certain Oracle products for this scenario.

Oracle WebCenter

Since we want to offer user-personalized views into the system, Oracle WebCenter is the easiest and quickest way to do this. Also, WebCenter provides integration to OID and SSO for user authentication and authorization as well as the ability to verify security to all parts of the system the user will be accessing with one login. Gone are the days of logging into multiple systems. Also, gone are the days of looking between two 'green screens' to verify data. Now all the data is in one web dashboard.

Oracle BAM

BAM plays a big role here, as the amount of processing increases. BAM will make it much easier to monitor all these business process and services in one screen.

Oracle ESB

Just as the ESB was used to help migrate data from other systems and provide an integration bus earlier, ESB is used here to accept two different input file formats and process them in a single workflow.

Oracle OID and SSO

OID is used across all of SOA products (BAM, ESB, and BPEL) to provide a common security repository. SSO makes life easier by allowing access to all applications with a single log on to which a user has access to.

SOA Integration—Final Product Summary

The implementation of SOA in this chapter will be leveraged and extended upon as we look at re-architecting our legacy system in Chapter 6. The idea is what you are building in this chapter will become the foundation of your SOA environment moving forward. The SOA architecture you are building is not 'throw away technology' but a quick and hopefully painless way to get you started on the modernization journey.

Keeping It Real: It may seem like 'everything plus the kitchen sink' was thrown in. In a way, it was. SOA is a broad architecture and each scenario is a bit different. The idea here was to show some of the options available. At a minimum, you will require the Oracle Legacy Adapters and a Java-based interface to call the legacy artifacts. Oracle Enterprise Grid Control, Oracle BAM, Oracle BPEL, and Oracle ESB are the next most common components. Next in line comes Oracle Web Services Manager and WS-Security. Most Legacy SOA Integration solutions don't require a Web Services Registry (UDDI register) like Oracle Service Registry as there are not enough services to merit this, and no one really does dymanic/runtime look up of Web services today.

IBM and Legacy SOA Integration

No chapter on Legacy SOA Integration can be written without considering the IBM mainframe hardware and software that have an impact on Legacy SOA integration. In fact, most independent vendors in this space view IBM as their biggest competitor, as well as one of their biggest partners. IBM hardware and software have six capabilities. There are more, but we will focus on those that have an impact on Legacy SOA integration:

- Native IBM Mainframe Integration—WebSphere **Host Access Transformation Server (HATS)** can be used to transform existing 3270 and 5250 screens into a Web-browser interface. This is presentation layer SOA integration.

- CICS Transaction Gateway—A user of CICS Transformation Server, Version 3 or greater, has the option of using CICS COMMAREA to expose transactions as Web services. The CICS Transaction Gateway is part of IBM CICS and uses Java EE Connector Architecture (JCA) Version 1.5 to allow CICS transactions to be exposed as Web services.

- IMS SOA Integration Suite—This provides direct access to IMS data stores and IMS transactions from open systems. IMS TM resource adapter and IMS Connect (data services) are part of this bundled suite of middleware, adapters, and mainframe components.

- DB2 Connect—This provides direct access to DB2 data from client/server or web-based applications. This access layer can be exposed as Web services.

- Enterprise Generation Language (EGL) — EGL is a 4GL that has been around for years under various names: Cross System Product (CSP), VisualGen, and VisualAge. IBM promotes 3270 and 5250 SOA enablement using EGL, as EGL includes the notion of a service. EGL is integrated with IBM Rational Business Developer Extension for defining, testing, and deploying the service to all supported platforms, including automated services generation from models.

- zIIP and zAAP processors — Basically, a licensing/pricing configurations to reduce the cost of running Java and DB2 workloads off traditional z/OS partitions on the mainframe. The zIIP and zAAP processor releases followed the release of another specialty processor in 2000, Integrated Facility for Linux (IFL). zAAP is intended for Java and XML. zIIP is intended for DB2 processing. This difference is IFLs are used under z/Linux, and zIIP and zAAP under z/OS. These processors provide significant cost savings over traditional z/OS workloads. The Legacy SOA Integration vendor DataDirect has taken advantage of these processors in the latest release of their product.

IBM's offerings, although complete, continue to be complex. Its Host Access Transformation Server, IMS Connect, and Customer Information Control System (CICS) Transaction Gateway offer a variety of solutions, with or without WebSphere. In addition, IMS, and CICS offer integration capabilities in the form of support for WebSphere MQ, IIOP and Web services. The limitations with the IBM Legacy SOA options are:

- No off host solution — All these products have a footprint on the legacy system. It is not possible to run part of the infrastructure in open systems.

- Limited legacy language and database support — These solutions offer no support for the Natural language or the Adabas database. There is also no support for CA data stores such as the Datacom and IDMS.

- Complex to configure and manage — IBM SOA is really a bunch of point solutions–some for free, such as the CICS with built-in SOA support, and most that are priced separately.

- Different products for screen, transaction, and data access — In order to accomplish SOA legacy across different artifacts and different languages and data stores, you must use a number of different products.

- Need to upgrade to the latest releases of operating systems and CICS — Most of these products require that are on a fairly current release of IBM operating system or transaction monitor.

- More MIPS needed on mainframe — CICS SOA, DB2 Connect, HATS, and IMS SOA Suite require a process on the mainframe and consume more of your MIPS.

Summary

You now have a complete understanding of the source, target, and source to target technical architecture, products and tools involved in Legacy SOA Integration. We learned about some new technologies called the Legacy Service Bus (LSB) and Legacy Services Engine (LSE). We concluded the chapter by applying the product and process knowledge we gained by covering four of the top scenarios. In the next chapter, we will complete an end-to-end, hands-on example for Scenario Two, Web Enablement.

4
SOA Integraton—Scenario in Detail

We are now going to show an example in detail for Scenario Two—Web Enablement, which we have discussed in Chapter 3. We will use JSP, JDBC, the Oracle Legacy Adapter, Oracle Application Server, Java EE Connector API, and XA transaction processing to show a two-phase commit across an Oracle database and VSAM on the mainframe.

Why access legacy data instead of CICS, or presentation-tier integration? Remember in Chapter 3, I had said, "This is ultimately the source of the truth. This is where the data you want is contained. If you are using any of the other three artifacts, these methods will ultimately call the data store". We have access to the COBOL copybooks and actual VSAM file so there is no need to perform presentation tier integration.

Another reason for choosing VSAM with Java EE is that there is a tutorial on Oracle BPEL using CICS. The Oracle CICS BPEL Legacy SOA integration tutorial can be found here: `http://www.oracle.com/technology/products/integration/adapters/pdf/adapter-Tutorial2-InvokingCICSTransaction.pdf`. This tutorial integrates the BPEL Process Manager with CICS through the Oracle Application Server Legacy Adapter. The Adapter uses **EXCI** (**EXternal Call Interface**) to invoke CICS transactions and uses COMMAREA transactions to exchange message buffers. The Adapter creates a metadata schema for CICS by importing COBOL copybooks and transforming them into mapping definitions for Oracle Connect for CICS on the z/OS machine, and then associating the metadata structures with specific physical files. You may find a review of this tutorial beneficial. Remember that we are using JSP/JDBC/VSAM instead of BPEL/CICS.

Assumptions:

- Oracle software is downloaded and installed using the instructions from Oracle.
- No tutorials on Oracle Application Server and Oracle JDeveloper are included in this chapter because there are many of them on `otn.oracle.com`.
- There is no duplication of Oracle Legacy Adapter tutorials that already exist.

Prior to this release, 10.1.3 Oracle Containers for Java (OC4J's) transaction manager required an Oracle database to perform the two-phase commit protocol when using global transactions that span work in multiple databases. The 10.1.3 release includes a two-phase commit coordinator embedded in OC4J that can perform recovery, and no longer requires the database commit coordinator. The new coordinator may be used with resource managers from any vendor that exposes an XA resource as defined in the JTA specification. More information on JTA can be found here:

- `http://www.oracle.com/technology/tech/java/oc4j/1003/how_to/how-to-midtier-2pc.html`
- `http://java.sun.com/products/jta`

The challenging part here is to configure your mainframe environment with Oracle Connect. As mentioned in Chapter 3, data center folks do not like new products on their mainframe. The most challenging part for us, therefore, is the two-phase commit because Oracle Connect will be installed on the mainframe for us. The remaining work — of exposing legacy VSAM data services via Oracle Legacy Studio, Oracle database access objects, and JSP user interface — is simpler.

We believe that this example has never been demonstrated before. Someone may have done it, but we are sure that there are no documented examples of a Java EE application doing a two-phase commit across Oracle and VSAM using the Oracle Legacy Adapters. So we hope you enjoy getting your 'hands dirty' with a fresh look at SOA Legacy Integration.

We cannot possibly take you through all the steps and show you all the code in this chapter. Therefore, we have posted the Oracle JDeveloper project file including all documentation, source code, and diagrams here: `http://www.packtpub.com/files/code/4060_Code.zip`.

> **Keepin It Real**: The objective of this chapter is to show you how to get started with a two-phase commit Legacy SOA Integration project. We don't want to re-invent what is already available at the **Oracle technology Network** (**OTN**) website `otn.oracle.com`. So, when information and instructions already exist, we will point you to the appropriate location on OTN.

Oracle Software Required

The software required is often referred to as the bill of materials. The bill of materials for this Legacy SOA Integration scenario is listed here. As URLs change, and the software is constantly updated and re-packaged, you may want to check the Oracle web site to make sure you have the correct software to complete this use case on your own.

- Application Server 10*g* Release 3–Version 10.1.3.3 `http://www.oracle.com/technology/software/products/ias/index.html`

- Application Server Adapters for Legacy Applications with Oracle Connect Mainframe component `http://www.oracle.com/technology/software/products/ias/htdocs/101310.html`

  - ° Oracle Applications Adapter 10g
    - Installs Application Explorer.
    - Oracle Studio for Legacy Adapters on Windows for the design-time.
    - Runtime components—deploy the following runtime components automatically:
      - J2CA deployment for packaged applications.
      - BSE deployment for packaged applications.
      - Legacy adapters for CICS, IMS/TM, IMS/DB, and VSAM.
      - Java EE Connector Legacy Adapter for connecting with Oracle Connect engine running on legacy platforms.
      - Oracle Connect—The mainframe Legacy Service Engine component, called Oracle Connect, comes with adapter software. It is under the "Oracle_Connect" directory under the staging area of the Legacy Adapter software. There are a couple of files that need to be **ftp**'d to the mainframe, and you will need to follow the installation guide for completing the mainframe configuration steps.

- Oracle JDeveloper—Version 10.1.3.3 `http://www.oracle.com/technology/software/products/jdev/index.html`

- Oracle Business Process Analysis Suite—Version 10.1.3.4 `http://www.oracle.com/technology/software/products/bpa/index.html`

- Oracle pre-packaged tutorials to download and use. We don't want to create material that is already available on the Web:

    ○ Oracle database invoice schema creation using SQL Developer: `http://www.oracle.com/technology/pub/articles/luttikhuizen-esbcase-setup.html`

    ○ Oracle Studio step by step to create CICS adapter: `http://www.oracle.com/technology/products/integration/adapters/pdf/adapter-Tutorial2-InvokingCICSTransaction.pdf`

> More information on creating VSAM adapters can be found here: `http://download.oracle.com/docs/cd/B31017_01/integrate.1013/b31002/toc.htm`

The legacy and mainframe adapters (CICS Adapter, VSAM Adapter, IMS/TM Adapter, IMS/DB Adapter, and Tuxedo Adapter) have a design-time component—Oracle Studio for Legacy Adapters that can be installed on Windows and Linux.

The **Legacy Services Engine** (**LSE**) from Oracle has two run-time components:

1. Oracle Connect that gets installed on the mainframe.
2. Java EE Connector Legacy Adapter component that gets deployed on the Oracle Application Server.

There are different flavors for Oracle Connect depending on the mainframe application that you are connecting to:

- Oracle Connect for CICS
- Oracle Connect for IMS/TM
- Oracle Connect for VSAM (The one we are using in this example)
- Oracle Connect for IMS/DB
- Oracle Connect for Tuxedo

The Java EE Connector Legacy Adapter component that gets deployed on the Oracle Application Server is the same for all flavors of Oracle Connect.

> **Keeping It Real**: Modern software change rapidly. In order to ensure that this example will work in your environment, be sure to use the mentioned versions.

UML and Database Diagrams

UML is often the language used to describe configurations, process flows, and event sequences in an SOA-based development. So we will use UML deployment, use case, activity, and sequence diagrams to describe the scenario being implemented in this chapter. We will use a database diagram to illustrate the Oracle Database and mainframe data stores.

Deployment Diagram

The UML deployment diagram depicts a static view of the run-time configuration of processing nodes and the components that run on those nodes. The diagram shows the hardware for your system, the software that is installed on that hardware, and the middleware used to connect the disparate machines to one another. The following UML deployment diagram was created in Oracle BPA Suite using the Oracle Business Process Architect:

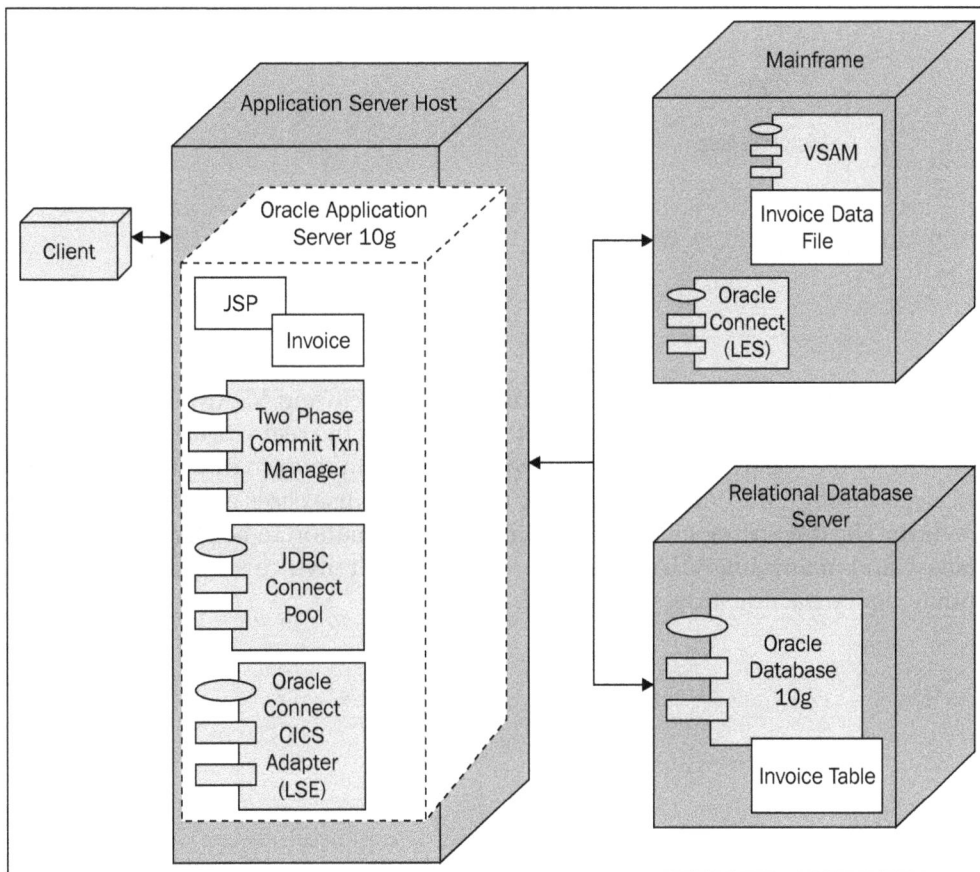

Use Case Diagram

UML use cases are fundamentally in text form. We see the stick figures and oval shaped entities and assume this to be the core of a use case. What many people don't understand is that a 'fully-dressed' use case includes a form at the backend that contains all the important information. This includes scope, stakeholders, primary actors, conditions, scenario, and other detailed information. Our use case, as illustrated in the following figure, is very simple:

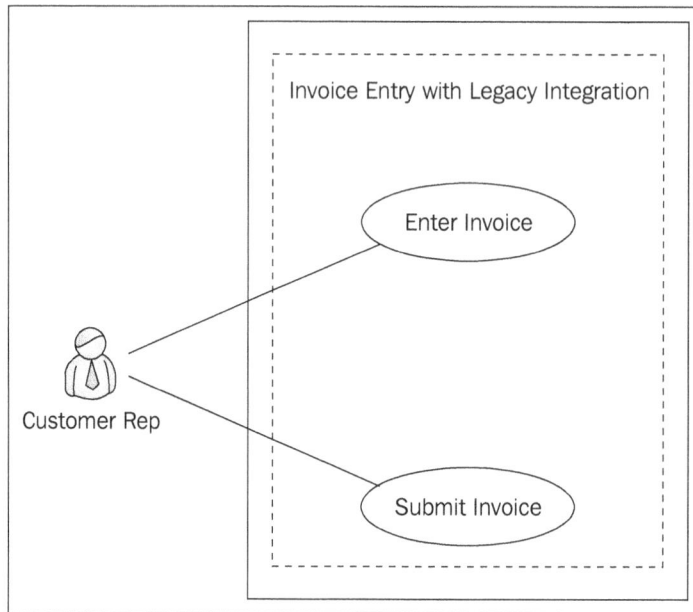

The focus will be on the two-phase commit across Oracle and VSAM. The use case itself is a simple example of an invoice entry screen. In the real world, the invoice is generated by the order. But in our case, we will enter an invoice directly as we don't want to go through the entire order entry process. The use cases are data entries via a Web form. The data being entered is the invoice information to be stored in an Oracle Database and mainframe VSAM data store. The submit invoice use case will then commit one transaction across both databases.

Activity Diagram

The following activity diagram shows, in a top to bottom flow, the state of each database persistence object for the Oracle Database (Invoice), the VSAM database (Legacy Service), and the two-phase commit transaction object in the Oracle Application Server:

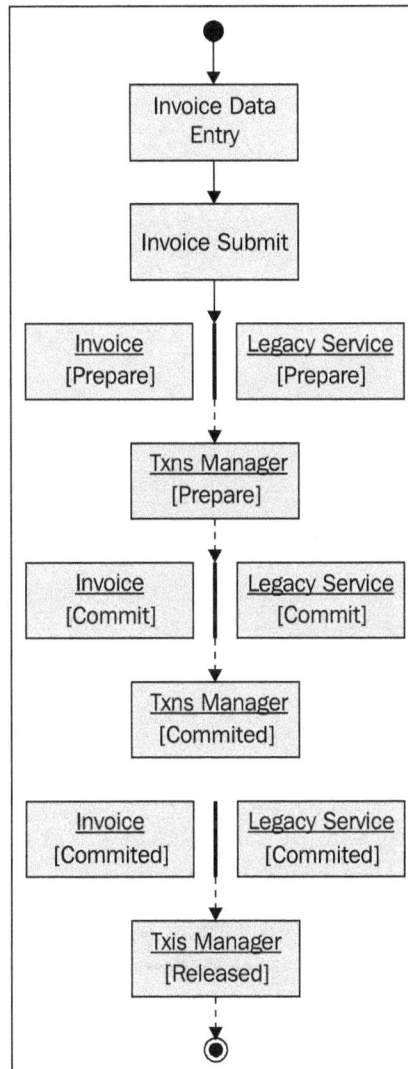

All user activity happens in the first part of the process. The remaining activities are related to coordinating the database persistence objects with the transaction manager, and insuring a successful two-phase commit.

Sequence Diagram

The sequence diagram will focus on the sequence of the two-phase commit as this is the core of your example.

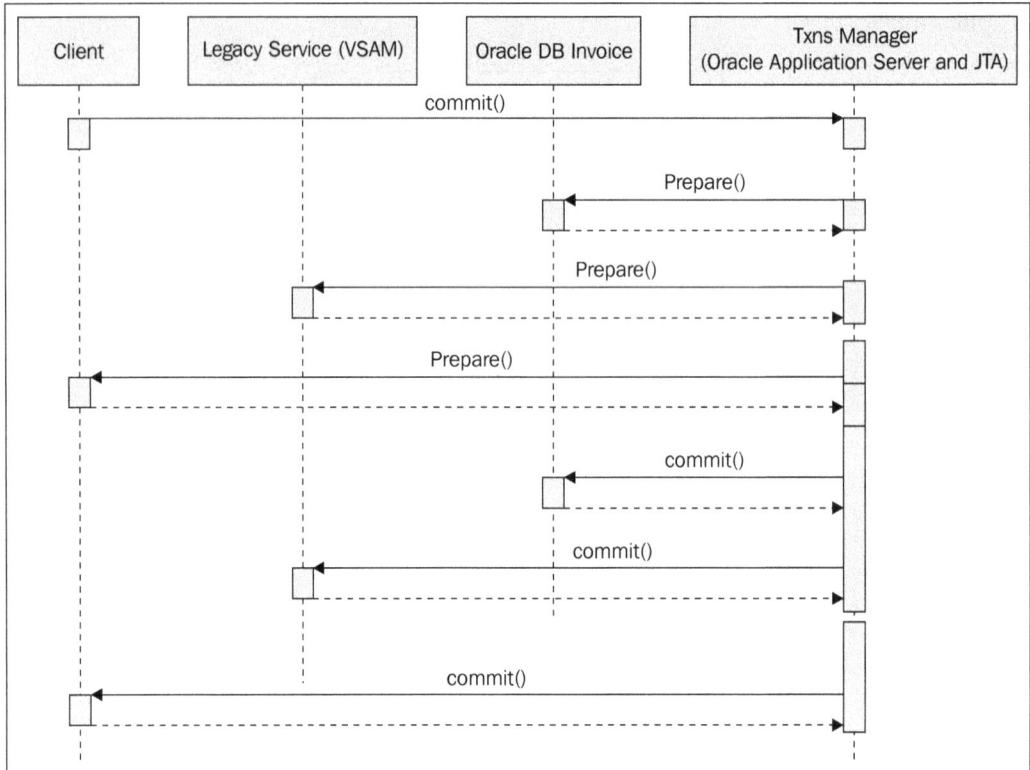

This sequence diagram is representative of any two-phase commit scenario. The only difference is in the object lifelines (client, legacy service, invoice, and transaction manager). The client, invoice, and transaction manager are typical of any two-phase commit sequence diagram. The Legacy Service object lifeline is the only difference here. Typically, in the open systems environment, this would be a data access object that would commit a row to an Oracle or other relational database. In our Legacy SOA Integration example, it is a service that commits a record to the VSAM database.

Data Model Diagram

Let's also take a look at the data model for this application. Remember, we have a table on the open systems Oracle Database 10g instance and on the mainframe in VSAM. As this is a logical data model, it appears as though these two entities are tightly coupled and are on the same Oracle database. As we know, they are on separate databases, and even on separate machines, possibly hosted miles apart. The Oracle Invoice table (INVOICES) and mainframe invoice file (`MF_INVOICE_DATA`) are also loosely-coupled as there is no **foreign** key relationship for the physical implementation of this data model.

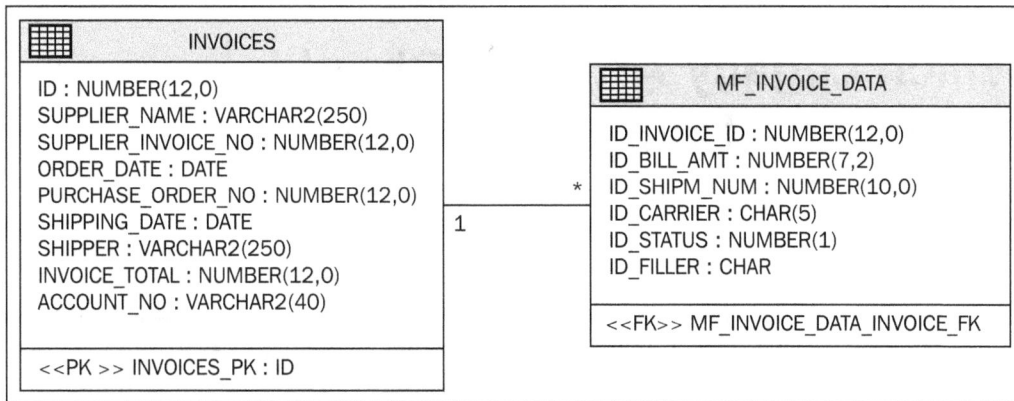

Some interesting things to note when you look at this simple data model:

- Duplication of data—It is not uncommon to find duplication of data when you begin to SOA enable your legacy systems across both the open system Oracle Database and mainframe data store. In this case, invoice total (bill amount), shipper (carrier), and of course invoice ID are present in both the systems. Depending on whether the Oracle or VSAM database is the master database for this information, there may be replication between the two (Oracle Database and VSAM) to keep them in sync. This is typically called **Change Data Capture (CDC)**. If both of them can be updated, then there needs to be bi-directional replication (some times called write-back).

- Some data in Oracle and some on mainframe—The other case is where some of the data is in Oracle and some in the VSAM file on the mainframe. This happens very often, and is the reason why some users have to go to several systems to get the information they need before Legacy SOA Integration modernization is done.

- Data type mismatches—The data types between the two systems may not match identically.

We discussed these anomalies in the previous chapter, but think it really hits home when you see it in an example.

> **Keeping It Real**: Although developers and 'techies' often like to use the "So let's code" (SLC) development methodology, it is best to start with UML and data model diagramming to get a clear picture of the final deliverable. Even for this simple example, the diagrams shown previously can help the developer, IT architects, managers, and even business people have a clear understanding of the solution set.

Which Legacy Artifacts Should I Expose?—Using the Relativity Product Set

In Chapter 3, we covered the concepts of SOA Integration and how to discover the legacy artifacts to expose services. Without repeating from this chapter, the SOA Integration Scenario starts with a detailed technical example on how to discover the VSAM file to be expose, as well as the components that facilitate access to them. Before we do that, we must get introduced to the Relativity tool set, terminology definitions, and tools overview. The Relativity tool set is used heavily in our example.

The complexity of existing legacy applications makes the task of identifying potential services for exposure in an SOA architecture quite difficult. The difficulty varies based on the **layering** degree of the application. We will discuss layering in more detail shortly. It is simpler to identify and expose legacy artifacts as Web services for a well-layered application and more difficult for a non-layered application. It is simpler to identify and expose legacy artifacts as Web services when programs use simple communication areas, and more difficult when these communication areas are complex and consist of a large number of unused fields.

To expose a service, we must solve a number of problems:

- Which programs are suitable for exposure?
- Which programs contain the desired functionality?
- What is the best level of granularity for the service exposure?
- How to proceed when the desired functionality is intermixed with other functionality?
- How to select the essential fields in the communication areas?
- How to perform minimum intrusive changes to the application code, if such changes are needed for service exposure?

To solve these problems, we will use a number of specialized tools:

- RMW Application Analyzer (`http://www.relativity.com/pages/applicationanalyzer.asp`) will be used to parse the application sources and perform some initial understanding of the application

- RMW SOA Analyzer (`http://www.relativity.com/pages/soaanalyzer.asp`) will be used to discover potential services and define them

- RMW Architect (`http://www.relativity.com/pages/applicationarchitect.asp`) will be used to perform certain remedies on some programs so that they can be exposed as services

- RMW Business Rule Manager (`http://www.relativity.com/pages/businessrulemanager.asp`) will be used to discover validation rules relevant in an SOA enablement project

We will start with a discussion of the application layers, which is relevant for all subsequent points.

Application Layers—Understanding Relativity Terminology

Building an application with distinct layers is not a new concept. Even for old applications, architects have understood the benefits of placing the artifacts in well-defined layers (referred to as tiers in Chapter 3). In a perfectly layered application one may distinguish the following layers:

- Layer 0 – User interface layer
  This layer consists of screens which would be visible to the users. This is the user interface.

- Layer 1 – Client layer
  This layer consists of all programs that communicate directly with the screens. This is the presentation tier and/or the navigation tier.

  Such programs would contain all the logic for capturing users' requests, validating the input data, invoking the appropriate "service" programs from the lower layers and formatting the output that responds to the user's request.

  In this layer, the execution moves to the lower layers via CALL or LINK operations, and moves to other programs of the same layer via exclusive transfer of control, which in CICS could be accomplished by XCTL or RETURN TRANID statements.

In fact, this layer may contain two types of programs:

- ° "Client programs" that receive and send screens
- ° "Transitional programs" that make navigation decisions

Transitional programs are sometimes used as traffic dispatchers. A program CPROG1 may receive a screen, SCREEN1 and pass exclusive control to a program TPROG that analyzes the user request in order to decide the next screen to be presented to the user. TPROG may pass exclusive control back to CPROG1, which in turn may present the same screen, SCREEN1, with additional data that satisfies the request. TPROG may also decide to transfer control to a program CPROG2, which in turn may present the screen SCREEN2.

The benefit of transitional programs is that they encapsulate the navigation logic. The client programs are confined to screen logic, while the transitional programs are confined to navigation logic.

- Layer 2 – Service layer

This layer consists of all programs that satisfy a request, without any screen communication or regard to screen logic. Most programs in this layer interact in one way or another with application's persistent data, but they may also perform certain pure logic related to computation, or formatting. As an example, one "service" program may retrieve invoice information based on an invoice number, or it may simply compute the number of business days between two dates.

Service layer programs may be also classified based on their position in the calling hierarchy, resulting in three categories:

- ° Layer 2A: Frontier programs that are called directly by Layer 1 programs
- ° Layer 2B: Indirect data access programs, which access data through some other called service programs, or perform computations or formatting
- ° Layer 2C: Direct data access programs, which access the persistent data from VSAM files, or from databases

- Layer 3 – The database persistence tier.

A classification of assets in a perfectly layered application is illustrated in the following hierarchy, as displayed by the Relativity's SOA Analyzer tool:

```
□··□ SOA Classification
   □··□ User interface
      ⊞··□ Transaction
      □··□ Screens
         ⊞··□ Screens without access to data
         ⊞··□ Screens with access to data
   □··□ Programs
      □··□ Client
         ⊞··□ Client with direct access to data
            ··□ Client with indirect access to data
         ⊞··□ Client without access to data
      □··□ Transitional
         ⊞··□ Transitional with direct access to data
            ··□ Transitional with indirect access to data
         ⊞··□ Transitional without access to data
      □··□ Frontier
         ⊞··□ Frontier with direct access to data
            ··□ Frontier with indirect access to data
         ⊞··□ Frontier without access to data
      □··□ Sub Frontier
            ··□ Sub Frontier with direct access to data
            ··□ Sub Frontier with indirect access to data
            ··□ Sub Frontier without access to data
      □··□ Batch
         ⊞··□ Batch with direct access to data
            ··□ Batch with indirect access to data
         ⊞··□ Batch without access to data
   □··□ Persistent data
         ··□ Persistent data read only
      ⊞··□ Persistent data modified
```

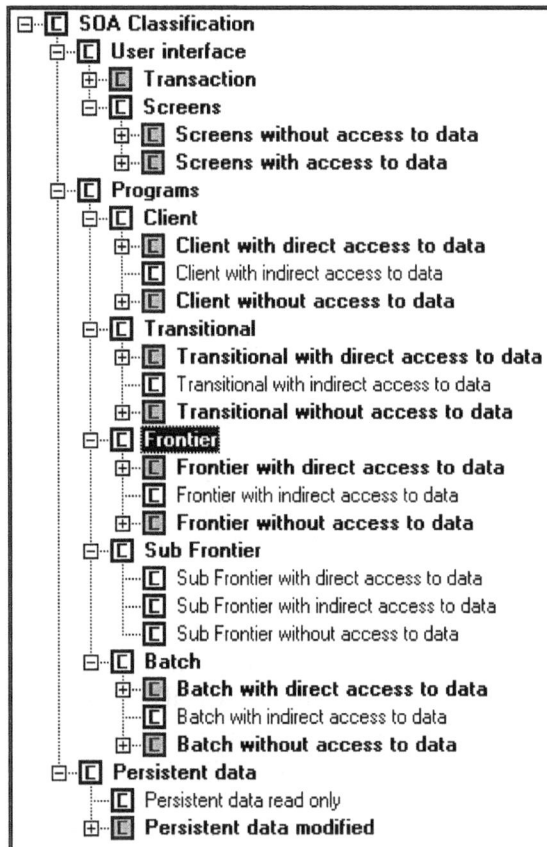

In the case of a well-layered application, programs in each layer will have well-designated business functions:

- Client programs contain screen logic

- Transitional programs contain navigation logic

- Frontier programs contain business level data manipulation logic

- Sub-frontier programs contain both business logic and technical data manipulation logic

The layering of the application is of immediate importance in an SOA enablement project. As we try to expose services that execute discrete requests, we will look at the client and transitional programs only for the purpose of identifying the location of potential services. In themselves, they do not offer services, as they do not execute any server type logic. Their functionality will be replaced in an SOA architecture with new technical artifacts that are "end-user facing", and implemented practically on an application or web server.

The service programs are the ones offering "service" capability, and we can create Web services based on their functionality.

> **Keeping It Real**: Classification and layering of your application assets is valuable in itself. For many organizations, it is the first time they take a complete inventory of their applications, including a classification of all their application artifacts.

Understanding an Artifact's Place in the Architecture

The simple classification of application artifacts does not give us a full understanding of how they are used. The SOA Analyzer provides a more detailed picture when we ask for 'vertical' and 'horizontal' slices that show the context in which the artifact is used. Such 'slices' are very useful, as a complete diagram of the application may be exceedingly complex and hard to understand.

A vertical slice shows "usages", that is, how an artifact is used (for instance via a call or a file access), and how it uses other artifacts. Vertical slicing is the method used to determine the modules that access data files. Vertical slicing is also used to determine 'frontier programs', programs that contain business logic. Both these modules make great candidates for enabling as services. A 'horizontal' slice shows how the control passes between artifacts, usually through exclusive change of control, or through screen navigation. Horizontal slicing is a great way to determine the modules that can be exposed from your presentation-tier (client layer).

Vertical Slices

We can obtain the vertical and horizontal slices by a right-click on an artifact in the **Classification** pane, followed by the selection of the **Show vertical slice** or **Show horizontal slice** menus. Now, let us look at certain examples.

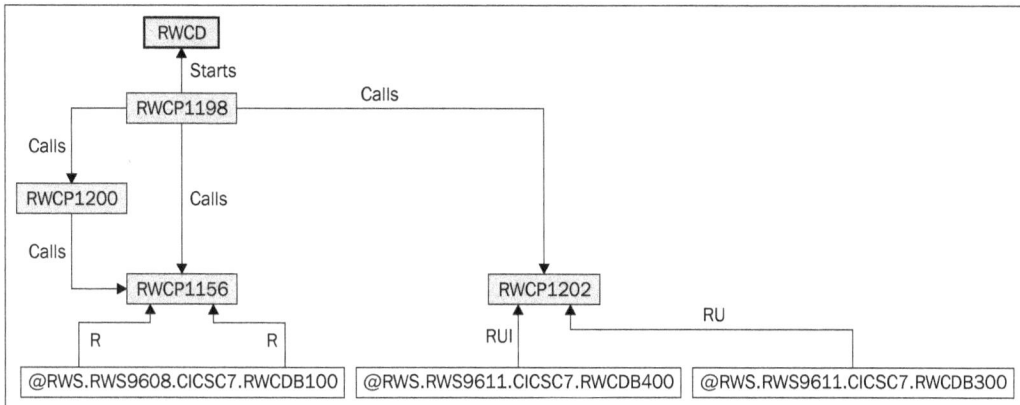

As a CICS transaction appears in the highest layer of the architecture, it is not itself "used" by any another artifact. In the above figure, we can see that transaction RWCD is started by program RWCP1198, which calls RWCP1200, RWCP116, and RWCP1202. In turn, the last two programs access certain files (shown at the very bottom of the diagram) in read mode (R), Read/Update (RU), or Read/Update/Insert mode.

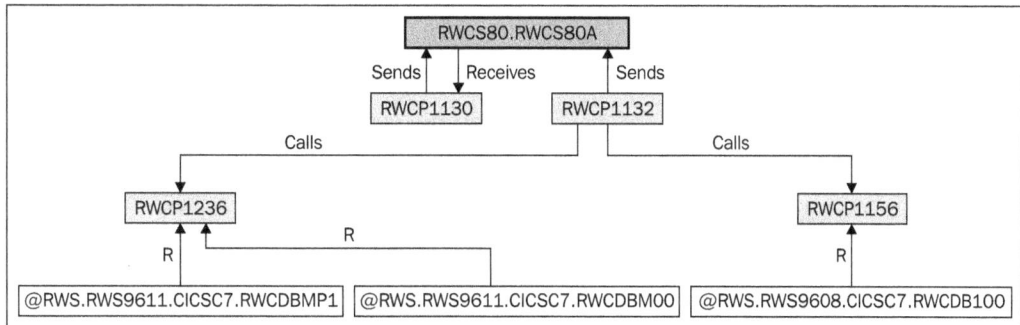

The preceding figure shows a vertical slice of the screen RWCS80A, which is sent and received by the program RWCP110, and sent only by program RWCP1132. These programs then call programs RWCP1138 and RWCP1156 to read data sets.

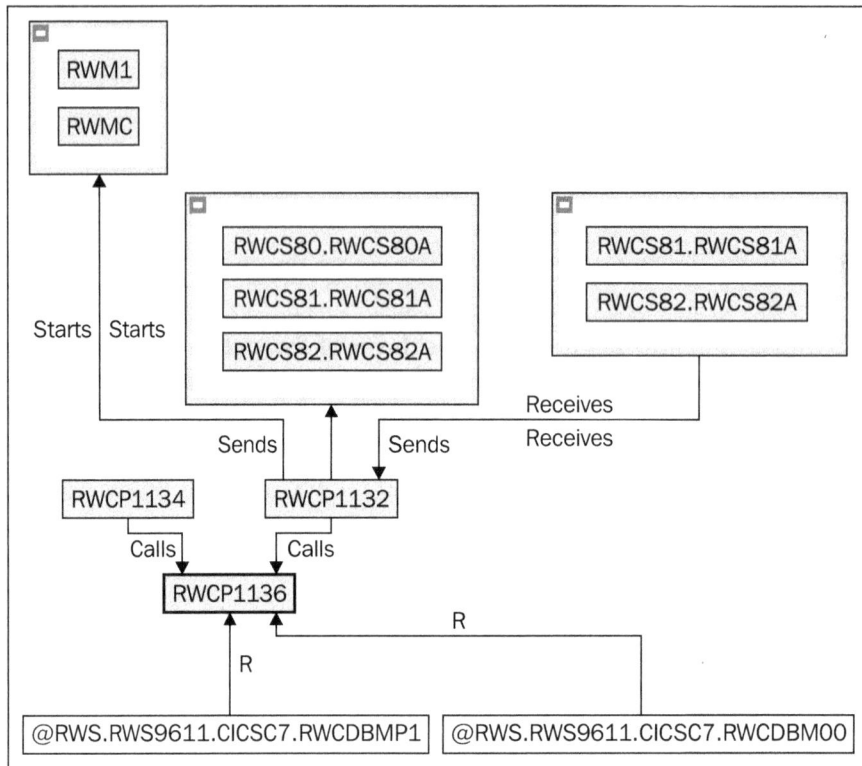

The above figure shows a vertical slice of program RWCP1136. We can immediately notice that this happens to be a 'frontier' program, according to the classification that we have described earlier, as it does not access screens and is called directly by programs that access screens. This special position in the architecture would make it a good candidate for exposure as a Web service.

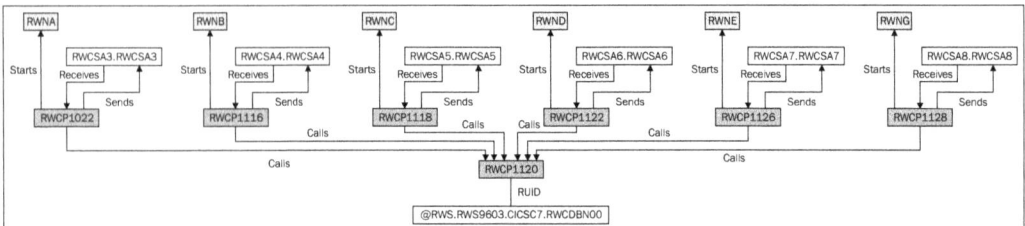

From the preceding figure, we can discover a fact that is relevant in the effort to extract services—all operations against the selected file (seen at the bottom, in a white box) are performed via a single program, RWCP1120. This makes the program ideal as a service, as it certainly contains all the logic needed to access the file from outside.

> **Keeping It Real**: Vertical slicing shows the usage of modules from the presentation-tier through the business logic, down to the data files, and to the modules that access these data files. Vertical slicing is therefore incredibly useful in identifying business logic and data access module to expose as services.

Horizontal Slices

While vertical slices through the application's architecture show usage scenarios, horizontal slices show the processes or workflow performed by the operator. Horizontal slices do not make sense for files or tables of other persistent data artifacts, as they do not represent processes or actions triggered by the user. For programs, horizontal slices show the exclusive change of control from one program to another, as for example via XCTL operations in CICS. For screens, they show the possibilities for the operator to move from one screen to another.

We can look at some examples of horizontal slices.

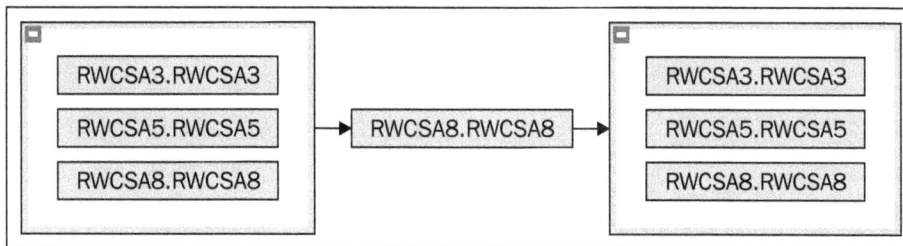

The preceding figure shows a horizontal slice for the screen RWCSA8. The block on the left shows all the screens from which the operator can potentially move to this screen, while the block on the right shows all the screens to which the operator can potentially move from this screen.

I have intentionally used the word "potentially", because not all these transitions may happen at runtime. The simple reason is that the static analysis cannot always discover the exact transitions, due to the fact that they may be controlled deep in a program or even in a file or table. In some legacy applications, the **traffic** between screens is recorded in a table which a **traffic cop** program reads in order to figure out how to process a user request. The preceding figure should be interpreted as "from screen RWCSA8 one can possibly move to screens RWCSA3, RWCSA5 and RWCSA8." In reality, the program that controls RWCSA8 may contain additional restrictions, which prevents, for example, a move to screen RWCSA8.

Keeping It Real: Horizontal slicing shows the modules usage from the perspective of the client and the transitional layers (screens and navigation tiers). Horizontal slicing is therefore incredibly useful in identifying the points or steps in the process where certain services are invoked.

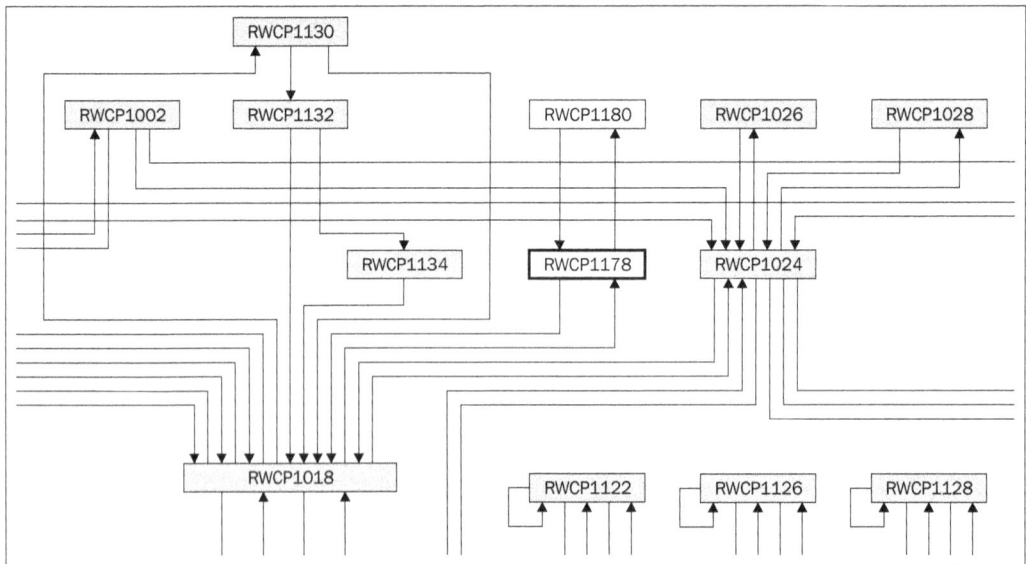

The preceding figure shows a horizontal slice of programs. Every edge in the graph indicates an exclusive change of control from one program to another program.

Together, horizontal slices and vertical slices offer a good picture of the role of a particular artifact in the application architecture.

Understanding Anomalies

In the real world, many legacy applications exhibit various exceptions from the layering scheme described earlier. The SOA Analyzer tool will identify these exceptions, which sometimes need to be addressed in one way or another to allow an SOA enablement by exposing all potential services offered by the legacy application.

We are going to call such exceptions "anomalies", and it is important to notice that they do not represent errors or mistakes. Programs with anomalies (as they are understood here) may function perfectly as they were originally intended, but present difficulties when it comes to a transition towards to an SOA architecture, as you will see.

In all the diagrams presented by the SOA Analyzer, programs with anomalies are shown with a red background. A click on a node for such a program will display the properties pane, where the anomaly is clearly stated, as shown in the following figure:

Name	CUSTINQ1
Type	Program
Layer	Client
Access type	None
Access mode	Direct
Anomaly	Client with data access

There are four types of anomalies that the SOA Analyzer identifies.

Client Programs with Data Access

In a perfect architecture, all programs that belong to the client layer should only deal with screen logic and navigation. Data access should be accomplished through the programs belonging to the frontier and sub-frontier layers, which in turn should be called by the client programs. This is the case in a well-layered application. But in real life, this restriction is not always enforced. In some cases, where no strict architectural discipline is enforced, programmers may take shortcuts and combine the screen access and data access in the same programs, as it is shown in the following vertical slice for program CUSTINQ1:

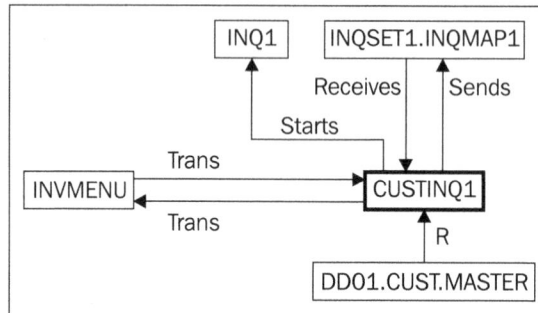

As I have already stated, although a program like CUSTINQ1 may function very well, it may present some limitations when it comes to the mining of services. Let us suppose that this program contains some very special logic that interprets the data read from the Customer Master file. It is possible, for example, that the program reads the date of birth of a customer and calculates the age, which is then displayed on the screen. Many such derivations are possible. We would like to have a service that does not just read a record from the Customer Master file, but also interprets and derives new data items. Unfortunately, while CUSTINQ1 does the interpretation and the derivation, it cannot be simply made into a service, as it is also conversing a screen (by definition, a service cannot do that). We will discuss later what can be done in such a case.

> **Keeping It Real**: Legacy applications are not the only ones that contain database access in client facing modules. Often, Web developers will include JDBC calls directly in JSPs. We will be found guilty of this later on in this chapter. Our example has JDBC calls in a JSP, which is not a recommended practice for production systems, but we will use the excuse that this is just sample/example code!

Calling Client Programs

It is tempting to look at all programs that are called as potential services. In principle, a call is a request to the called program to perform a task, and that is also the nature of a service. However, in real life applications, we will, encounter situations where a called program cannot be made into a service for a simple reason that it also converses a screen, as can be seen in the following figure, with program SYSTEM.PCITN100:

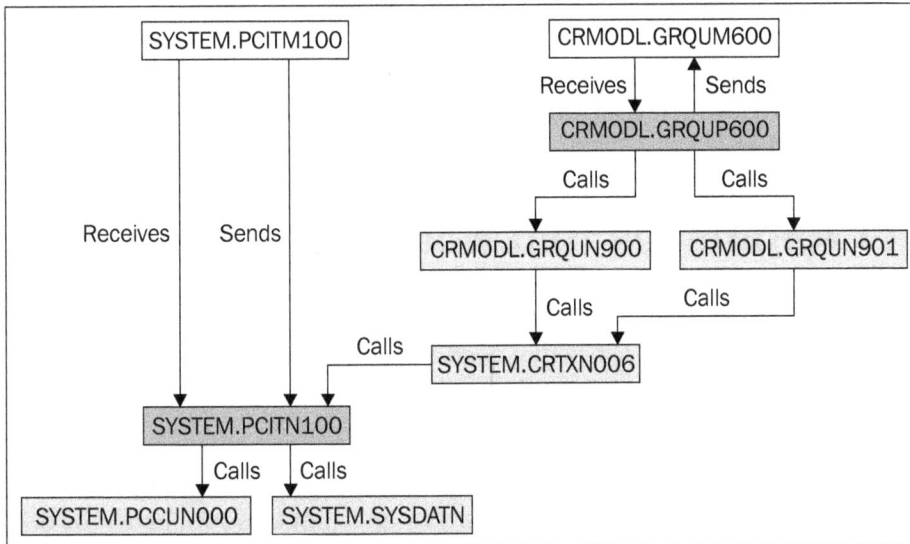

There can be many reasons why the original application included this anomaly. Perhaps the most common reason is that when a "service" program is written the programmer finds it convenient to report an exception immediately to the operator by sending a screen with a message. By writing the program in this style, the programmer simplifies the code, but renders it unfit to become a Web service (which by definition cannot converse with a user interface).

If the program in question is desired as a service, it should be modified such that instead of sending a screen in case of an exception, it should return to its caller with a special return code signaling the same exception.

Calling Transitional Programs

This anomaly is mostly theoretical, as transitional programs are not usually candidates for services. However, it signals a strange situation, in the sense that usually transitional programs (as defined above) are mostly dedicated to directing the screen navigation, and not to the fulfillment of a task (typical for called programs).

Impure Service Programs

This is a generalization of the "Client programs called" anomaly. It happens when a client program calls a "service" program, which in turn calls another client program. Although the one in the middle seems to be a perfect service (because it is called, and does not converse a screen), it is impossible to turn it into a service, as during the execution one of its called programs converses a screen.

In the figure under the heading *Calling Client Programs,* this is the case with the program CRMODL.GRQUN900, which is "almost" a service. This program is called by CRMODL.GRQUN600, but in turn calls SYSTEM.CRTXN06, which calls SYSTEM.PCITN100, which is actually a client program conversing the screen SYSTEM.PCITM100.

Other Anomalies that Need Remedial Action

There are some other challenges we need to overcome in order to expose services from a legacy application. Programs that appear as perfect candidates for services may display certain characteristics that need remedial action.

Data Validation Problem

A perfect CICS service program may not become a perfect Web service due to the fact that it fails to perform data validations. That may not be a problem in its original environment as it relies on its caller program to perform such validations. Let's have a look at the following figure:

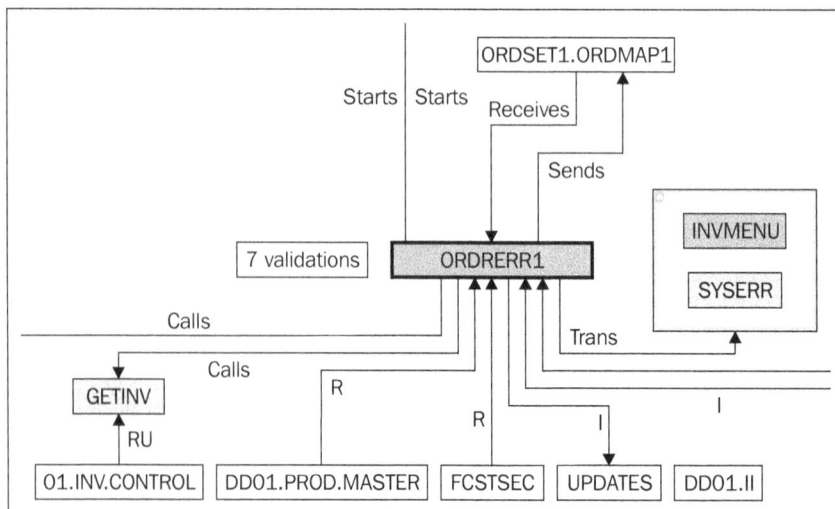

Next to the ORDERR1 program, you can see a label with the text, "7 validations". This label appeared automatically after:

- We used Relativity's Business Rule Manager, where we made a request to automatically detect all screen validations in program ORDERR1.
- We pressed the **Tools | Intersect Validations** menu in the SOA Analyzer.

The "7 validations" label indicates that as ORDERR1 converses the screen ORDMAP1, it performs 7 validations against the data entered by the operator on this screen. Such validations check if the data is numeric, properly formatted, or entered in the mandatory fields. When program GETINV is invoked to perform an operation against the INV.CONTROL file, it assumes that all data is already valid (otherwise ORDERR1 would have issued a warning message to the operator). GETINV can now fulfill the requested tasks without the danger of running into some data that does not make sense.

Although GETINV is otherwise a good candidate for a service, here is the caveat! If this service is invoked from another environment other than its original one, there is no guarantee that the data it receives is valid. What worked perfectly in CICS may not work properly in SOA architecture.

There are various remedies we can apply to resolve this issue. One of them could be that the application server or even the client facing programs in the new architecture perform the validations and ensure that GETINV does not receive anything else other than correct data. Another remedy is to repeat the same validations in GETINV as they exist in its caller, ORDERR1, and have GETINV return with a special return code, should these validations fail.

> **Keeping It Real**: Placing the data validation in your new JSP, JSF, or AJAX application is easily achievable. However, it defeats the purpose of using Legacy SOA Integration as a 'limited coding' modernization approach. However, if your strategic direction is to re-architect your system, you may see writing the data validation in Java EE as your next step toward moving off the mainframe.

The Problem of Transient or Temporary Data Queues

One would usually expect the caller and called programs in a CICS environment to communicate through the CICS COMMAREA. This is the most common way, but not the only way, in which CICS programs pass data. It is also possible that the called program writes the data into a temporary storage queue that the caller reads. As most CICS adapters are equipped to deal only with data passing through COMMAREA, this creates a major difficulty.

We need to discover if such situations exist. It is in fact quite simple. After we display a vertical slice through the architecture (see the description of vertical slices above), we press on the **Tools | Intersect Queues** menu. This will add labels next to the programs that operate with queues, as shown in the following figure:

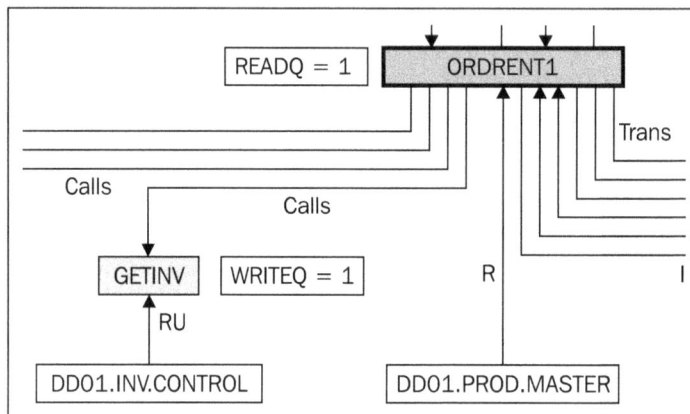

This diagram tells us that GETINV writes to a queue and ORDENT1 reads from a queue. It is just a **red** flag at this point, enough to determine us to investigate. If we really find that the data passes from GETINV to its caller via the queue, then we know that normal service adaptors would not be able to create a good service out of GETINV. When the program is called as a Web service in SOA architecture, the service consumer will expect to collect all the data from the service interface that describes the COMMAREA, while the data actually resides in a queue.

The remedy is to either modify GETINV to pass the data exclusively through the COMMAREA, or to create a special 'service' program that reads the queue and passes it through the COMMAREA. Finally, it is possible that some vendors offer service adapters that are capable of getting the data from CICS queues.

Finding the Service Functionality—Relativity SOA Analyzer Product

As service programs capable of exposure are themselves placed in sublayers, the question is which one to choose. Given that we may look for a particular service function (for example, "retrieve claim"), we need to narrow the search to those that are related to this function, in one way or another. The development team maintaining the application may simply know which are the programs implementing the function. In the absence of such direct knowledge, we can use other methods to find the functionality we want to expose.

Starting from Screens

One such method is to start with the screens that suggest the functionality that we are after. By inspecting the screens, for instance, we may discover that one of them helps the operator perform an **Order Entry** function. Screens may be viewed in the SOA Analyzer by selecting the **View Source** menu visible when we right-click on a screen mode. Our **Order Entry** function will display as follows:

Once we discover the screen that deals with the service function, we can look at its "vertical slice" through the application. The vertical slice, as displayed by the SOA Analyzer, shows a cut through the layers, which includes the screen as well as all the programs that service it, as shown in the following figure:

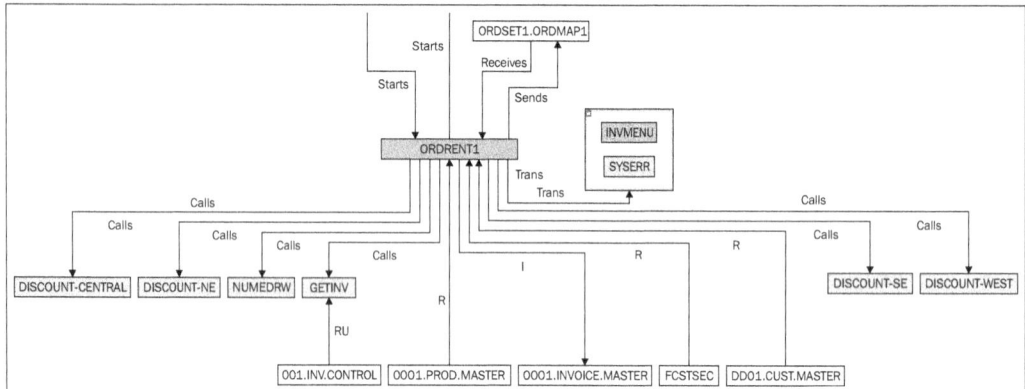

In this diagram, we can see that the screen ORDMAP1 (which appears on the top) is accessed by the program ORDENT1, which in turn calls other programs to fulfill a request. All these called programs are candidates for services. Together, they could become operational in a Web service that would be consumed when one makes a request to create a customer order in the new SOA architecture.

As we look for potential service programs, we should give special attention to the frontier programs. Indeed, they encapsulate the most complete functionality. They not only know which data to access, but also know how to assemble it in a manner consistent with business requirements. If lower-layer programs are selected, then some of the data assembly must be performed on the application server, opening the possibility of erroneous implementations that differ in functionality from the original application. Choosing frontier programs for exposure makes the task simpler and eliminates the possibility for further errors.

Looking for Special Program Constructs

Another method to find the services with a particular functionality is to look for special patterns in the code. This can be accomplished from the Relativity's Application Analyzer with the aid of the so-called clipper queries.

To run a clipper query, we'll go through the following steps:

1. Select a program in the SOA Analyzer, right-click on it, and press the **Show Source** menu. The source of the program appears in a pane of the tool, as shown in the following figure. If you press on the top-right button, a menu appears where you select **Clipper**.

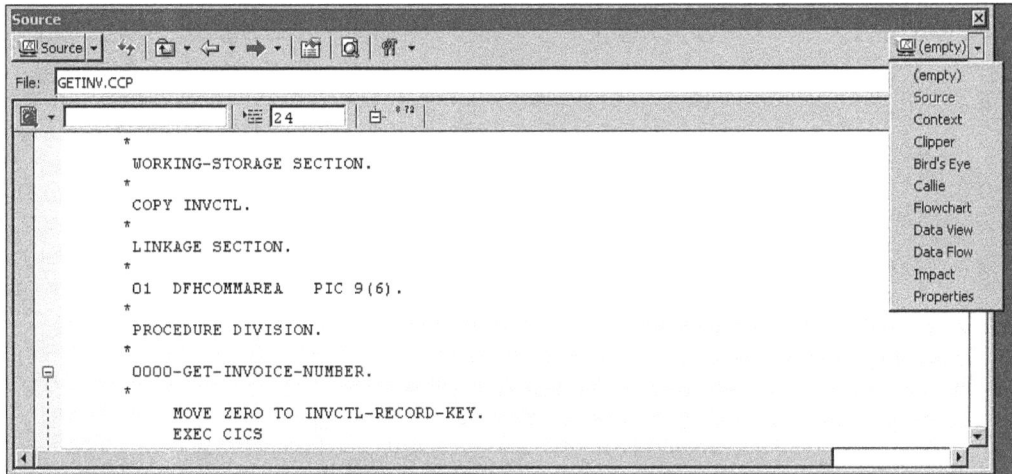

2. A new pane opens up in the **Source** pane. Press the corresponding toolbar button to create a **New list** (this is where the results of the query will be deposited).

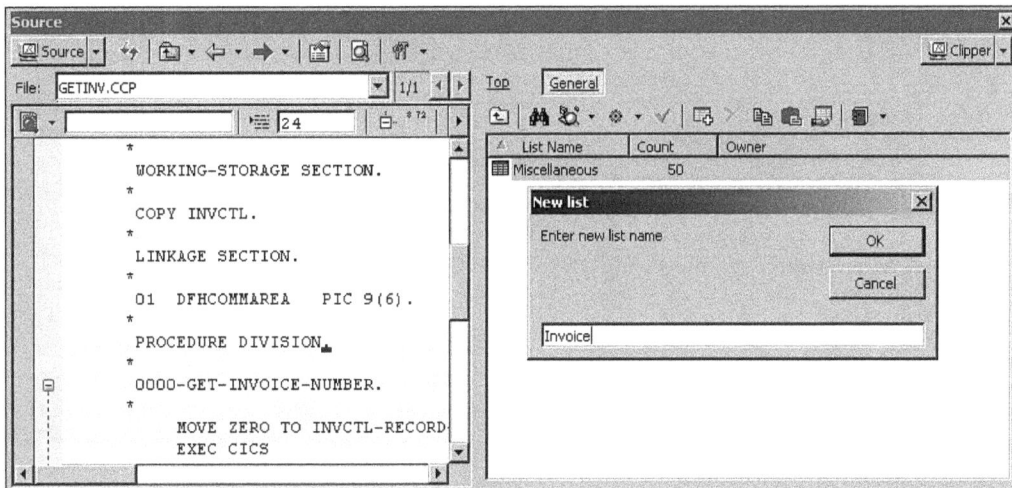

3. A new pane opens up in the source pane, on which you can locate the search button and select **Cobol File** sources as the space where we are going to search, as shown in the following figure :

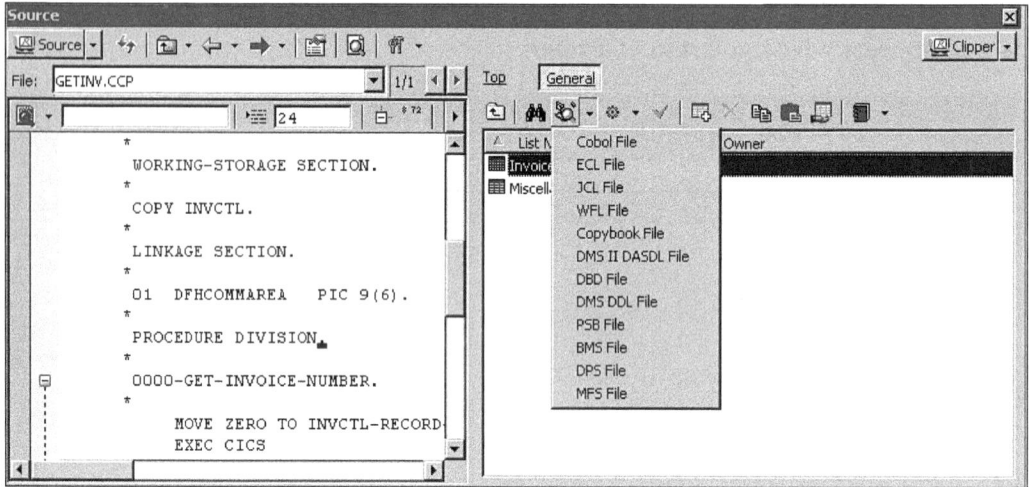

4. We get a new window on which we can build our query. Clipper queries allow us to interrogate any type of program construct as well as combinations of such constructs. In this case, we can build a very simple query that looks for variables containing the string INV, hoping to find the places where an invoice is updated. The intention is to isolate the program that maintains invoice data. The query appears as shown in the following figure:

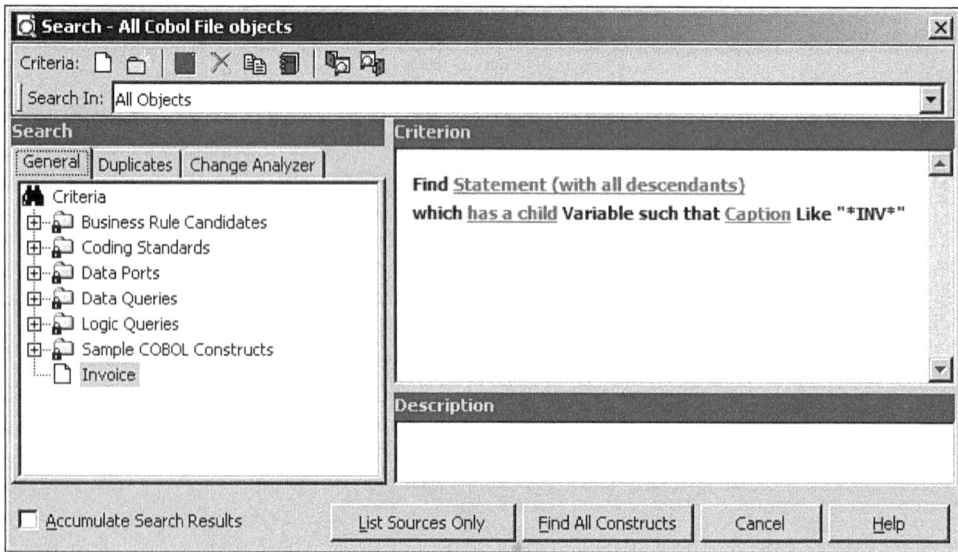

5. After we press the **Find All Constructs** button, a search is performed, and the results are stored in the new list that we have created, called **Invoice**. We can, at any point in time, inspect this list and visit all occurrences of the INV string in a variable name. We can, of course, write down the name of the programs that contain such occurrences, but can also ask the SOA Analyzer to "intersect" any diagram with this list. This will show which programs included in a diagram contain occurrences from the list.

6. In order to intersect a diagram with a list of program constructs obtained from a Clipper query, we first display the diagram, and then select the **Tools | Intersect list** menu. We are prompted with a list of all existing lists, as shown in the following figure, of which we select one (in this case, the one called **Invoice**, which we have just created).

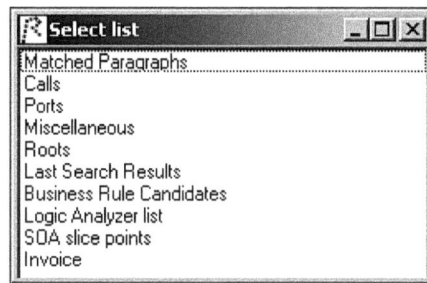

7. As a result of a selection, SOA Analyzer creates labels for all programs in the current diagram that contain items from the list. The text of the label indicates the number of occurrences, as shown in the following figure:

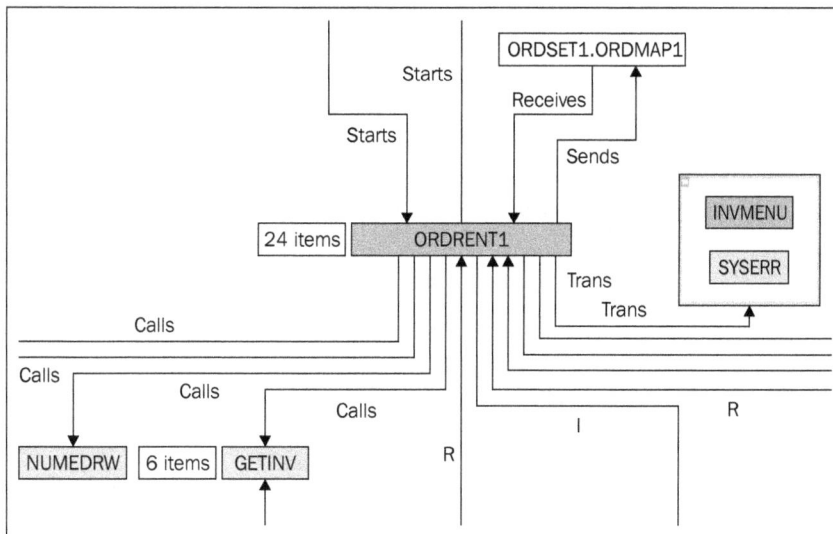

This entire search points to GETINV as a good candidate for the desired service. It performs some operations with the Invoice, and it is a service type program that does not converse any screen.

Keeping It Real: The Clipper query is also very useful while doing a modernization re-architecture project. Often, you will want to determine all the modules that access a particular data element or data file. This is done in order to get an idea of how isolated a particular data element is from access by other systems.

The Case of Mixed Programs—Program 'Slicing'

Sometimes, the functionality we want to expose is found in a client program. Unfortunately, the client program cannot be called as a service as it contains screen communication as well as screen logic that does not make sense in a service call.

There are at least two solutions to this problem:

1. Modify the program by removing all screen interaction and screen logic
2. Split the program into two separate programs, one containing the screen interaction and logic, and the other containing the service function

The first solution has a number of disadvantages:

- It requires a massive modification of the code, which may result in errors
- It results in duplication of code (supposing the original program is kept in production), hence requiring synchronized maintenance of the original and modified versions

The second solution, the one we recommend, avoids the pitfalls of the first. It uses a slicing technique, which could be achieved either manually or by the use of a specialized tool such as Relativity's Application Architect product.

Slicing could be described as follows. Given a program PROG with a paragraph PARA, two programs are created, PROG1 (main) and PROG2 (service), such that:

1. PROG1 calls PROG2
2. Paragraph PARA no longer exists in PROG1, but appears in PROG2
3. PROG1 (which includes the call to PROG2) functions in a manner identical to the original PROG

Program slicing may be employed in order to separate the client functionality from the service functionality. In a simple case, suppose that a program communicates with a screen on which the user requests the content of an invoice with a particular invoice number. The program receives the screen, validates that the invoice number is correctly formatted, determines which program key was pressed by the user, invokes a paragraph GET-INVOICE to obtain the data, formats it, and displays it on the same screen. In this case, paragraph GET-INVOICE may be sliced out of the program. The resulting main program will now contain the screen logic, while the resulting service program will access the persistent storage and return the content of the invoice. Since this second program has the characteristics of a service, it could be exposed to the outside world as a Web service. Furthermore, the application will function just as it used to before the slicing.

If slicing is used to separate screen logic from service logic, the question is, which paragraph should be used as the basis for slicing?

Here, we face a situation similar to the one described earlier, wherein we must decide the level of the granularity offered by the service. If we aim too low in the paragraph **call map,** we risk obtaining services that are too granular and we are losing some of the business logic that prepares the data. If we aim too high, we risk including undesired screen logic. The best choice is to again select a **frontier** paragraph, which sits on the border of the screen and service logic. Such a paragraph would be the highest in the hierarchy of service type paragraphs.

In order to find the best slicing point, and to extract a slice that could be later used as a service, we proceed as follows:

- Once we locate the program that requires slicing, we right-click on a node that represents it, and select the **Show internal** menu. As a result, we can see a new diagram that displays the relationships between paragraphs, as shown in the following figure:

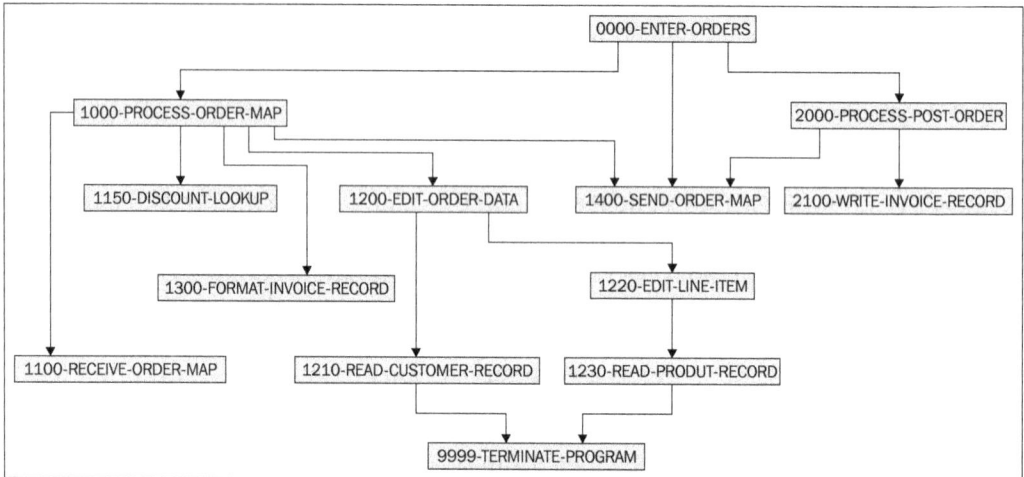

- We must find the paragraphs which can be "sliced out" in the form of separate callable programs. We must select only paragraphs that:
    1. Do not access screens
    2. Do not call other paragraphs that access screens

    In the preceding figure, we can see that 000-ENTER-ORDERS cannot be sliced-out, as it calls 1400-SEND-ORDER-MAP, which contains screen operations. The same is true for other paragraphs, for instance, 2000-PROCESS-POST-ORDER or 1000-PROCESS-ORDER-MAP.

    There are other paragraphs that are good candidates for slicing. It is to our advantage to select one that is as high as possible in this call hierarchy, as that would provide maximum functionality. One such candidate is 1200-EDIT-ORDER-DATA, which accesses both the customer and the product files. Another one is 2100-WRITE-INVOICE-RECORD. If we create slices of these two paragraphs, we obtain two programs, which together offer the functionality needed to create an invoice.

- To mark the selected paragraphs for slicing, we right-click on them and select the **Create slice item** menu. As a result, two things happen:

1. The paragraphs are marked on the diagram indicating that we have selected them as candidates for slicing (as you can see in the figure)

2. A list is created that contains information about these slicing points

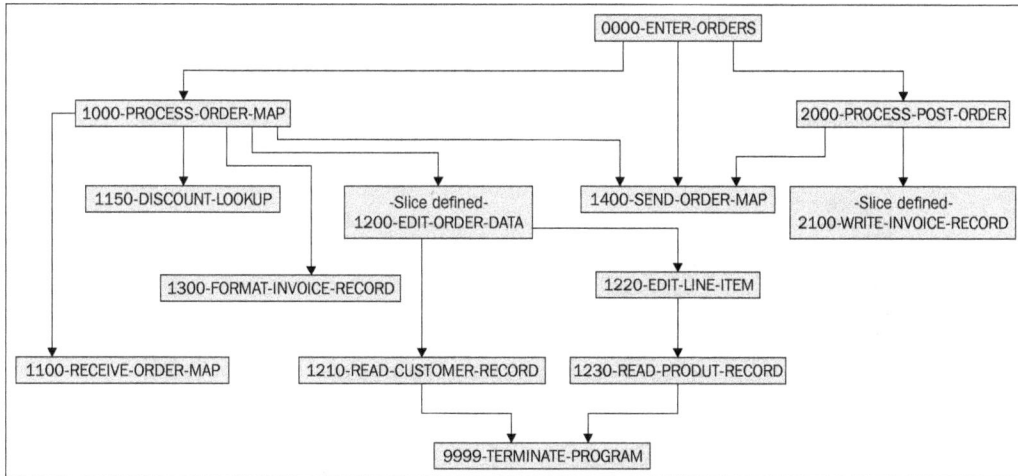

- We switch now to the Application Architect in order to perform the actual slicing operation. We will find two slicing points in a list under the category, **Architect**. As we click on any item in this list, the **Source** pane will automatically select the corresponding paragraph for slicing, as shown in the following figure:

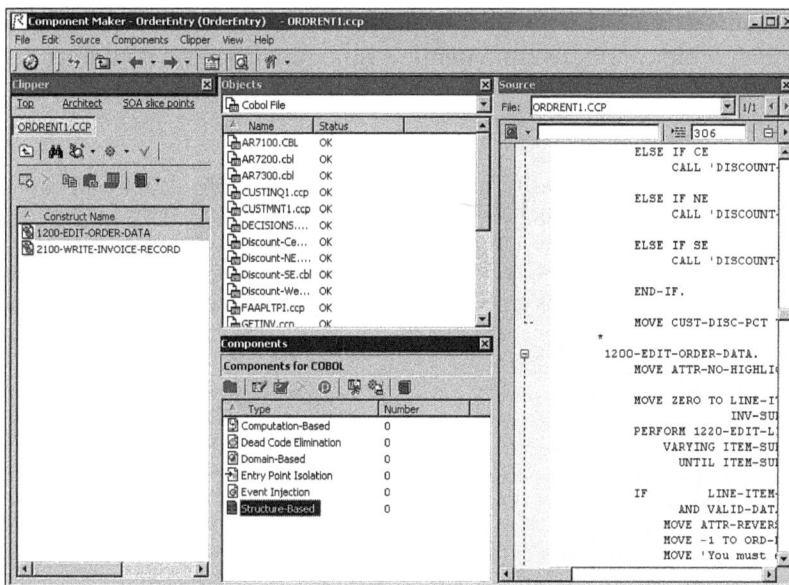

- We right-click **Structure-Based** in the **Components** pane, and then select the **Define new** menu, which opens up another pane, where the parameters of the slice are defined. We only have to point it to the paragraphs in the list created from SOA Analyzer to create a correct slicing definition, as shown in the following figure:

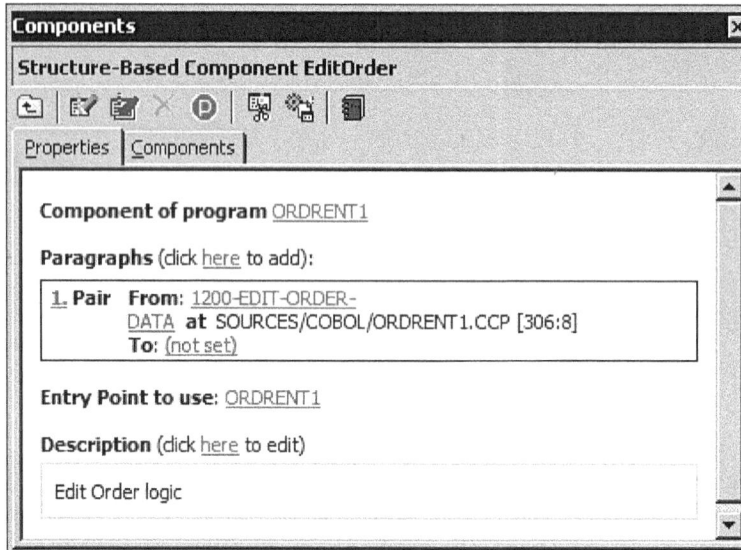

- We press the **Extract** button (represented by an icon showing scissors). We have to specify the number of parameters, say that we want the resulting program to be a CICS callable program. As a result, a new program is created, which contains the intended functionality, and could be exposed as a Web service.

Keeping It Real: Slicing is a technique used by many application portfolio analysis tools. Slicing has been used for years to track back to the source of a problem in code, and was used heavily to help solve the Y2K. Slicing is useful in Legacy SOA Integration as it gives you the capability to look at the legacy artifacts embedded in an application as discrete components that can be exposed as services.

Determining the Data Interface

After we have found the right programs that can be exposed as Web services, we need to define their data interfaces. This is not a trivial task, for a number of reasons.

Let us take the case in which we want to expose the service that retrieves an invoice based on an invoice number. It would be great if:

1. The definition of the COMMAREA of the service program could be stored in a copybook

2. The COMMAREA could have a very simple definition, as in:

```
01 COMMAREA.
        05 INVOICE-NUMBER     PIC 9(7).
        05 INVOICE-CONTENT.
            10 INVOICE-DATE…..
```

In reality, we come across two problems:

1. The definition of the COMMAREA may not reside in a copybook

2. The COMMAREA defined in the LINKAGE section of the program may be very simple, as in:

```
01 COMMAREA PIC X(30000)
```

thus, obscuring the actual fields that appear in another structure to which COMMAREA is moved in the program.

The SOA Analyzer will help us determine the correct interfaces and even create a complete WSDL definition for the service.

We will proceed as follows:

- In SOA Analyzer, we select the **Service | New** menu, and give a name to the service. (We will call it **Invoice**.) This service will appear on a new pane of the tool.

- Having selected this service, we select a proper program (which was found in the previous step), right-click on the node representing it and select the **Add to Service** menu. SOA Analyzer will analyze the program and detect its COMMAREA that will form the basis for the service interface. In the **Service** pane, the SOA Analyzer will display the following:

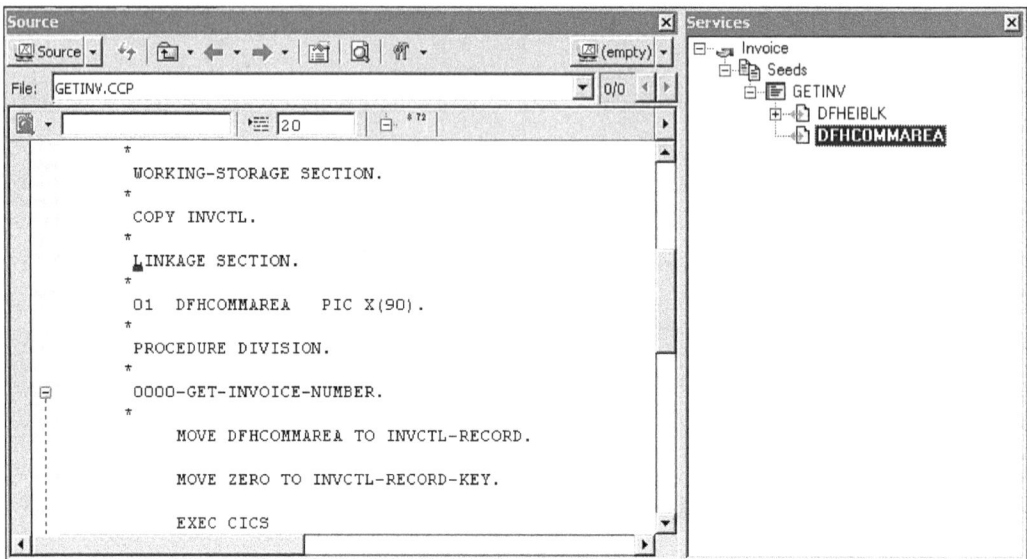

- In the **Service** pane, under the service called **Invoice**, we have a tree with a node called **Seeds**. Under this node, we find the specification for the program that we added to the service, including the COMMAREA that is used as in the interface. However, there is a common problem in that the COMMAREA appears as a single block of 90 bytes, which would not allow us to derive sensible and useful fields for the service interface.

We solve this problem by designating a synonym for **DFHCOMMAREA**. A synonym is another data structure, which either redefines or is moved to DFHCOMMAREA, or DFHCOMMAREA is moved to that structure. Such synonyms are easy to find with the following procedure:

- ° We select the **DFHCOMMAREA** in the **Source** screen and right-click on it

- ° We select the **Instances** menu, which will show a list of all usages of this data structure and whether it is moved, or redefined

- ° As we inspect the list, we select a convenient synonym

- In this example, we notice that **DFHCOMMAREA** is moved to **INVCTL-RECORD**, which may supply a better definition of the interface. We select this data area in the **Source** pane, then select **DFHCOMMAREA** in the **Service** pane, and press the **Import synonym** menu. As a result, the definition of the interface in the **Source** pane changes to what we can see in the following figure:

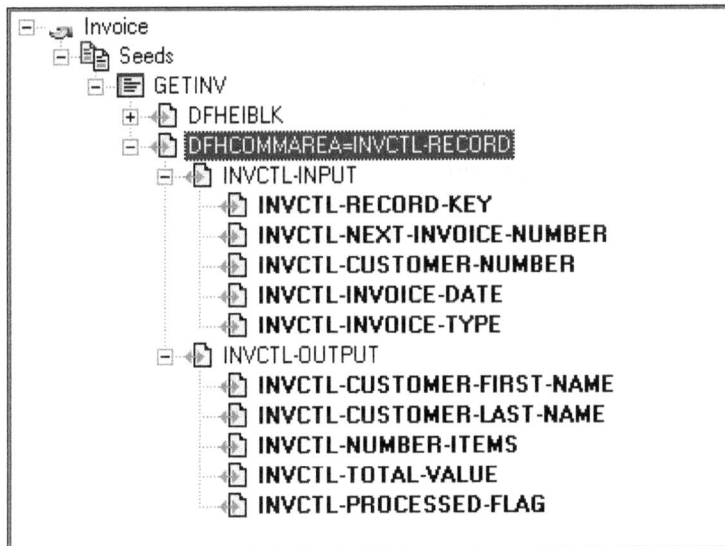

- We now have a detailed specification for the COMMAREA. One last task that we should perform, before creating the WSDL, is to indicate the inputs and outputs of the interface. Although, all fields are both input and output by default, it would be nice to separate them if possible. In this case, it is quite easy, since one substructure contains INPUT and the other contains OUTPUT. We can right-click on **INVCTL-INPUT** and select the **Make Input** menu. In the same way, we select the **INVCTL-OUTPUT** and select the **Make Output** menu. As a result, the specification now looks as shown in the following figure, in which the arrows for the adjacent icons indicate the usage as either input, or output:

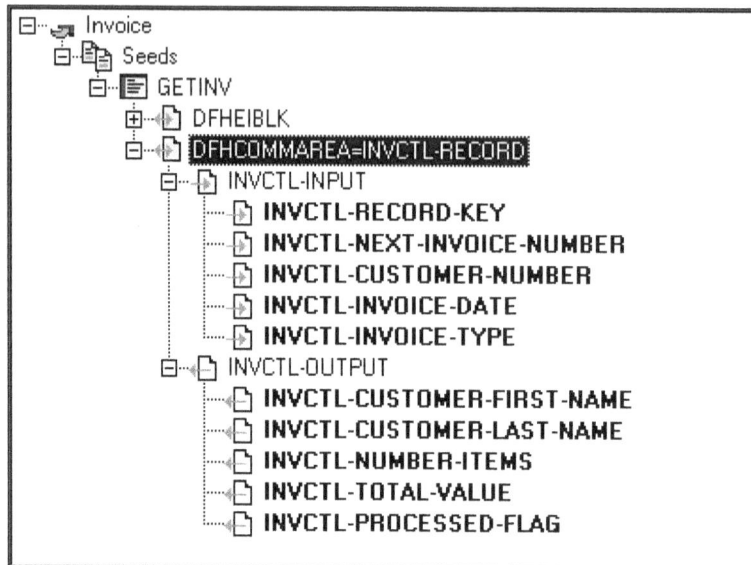

- We have come to the last step, that of creating a service definition. We right-click on the service and press the **Generate WSDL** menu. As a result, a WSDL definition for the service is generated and displayed as shown in the following figure:

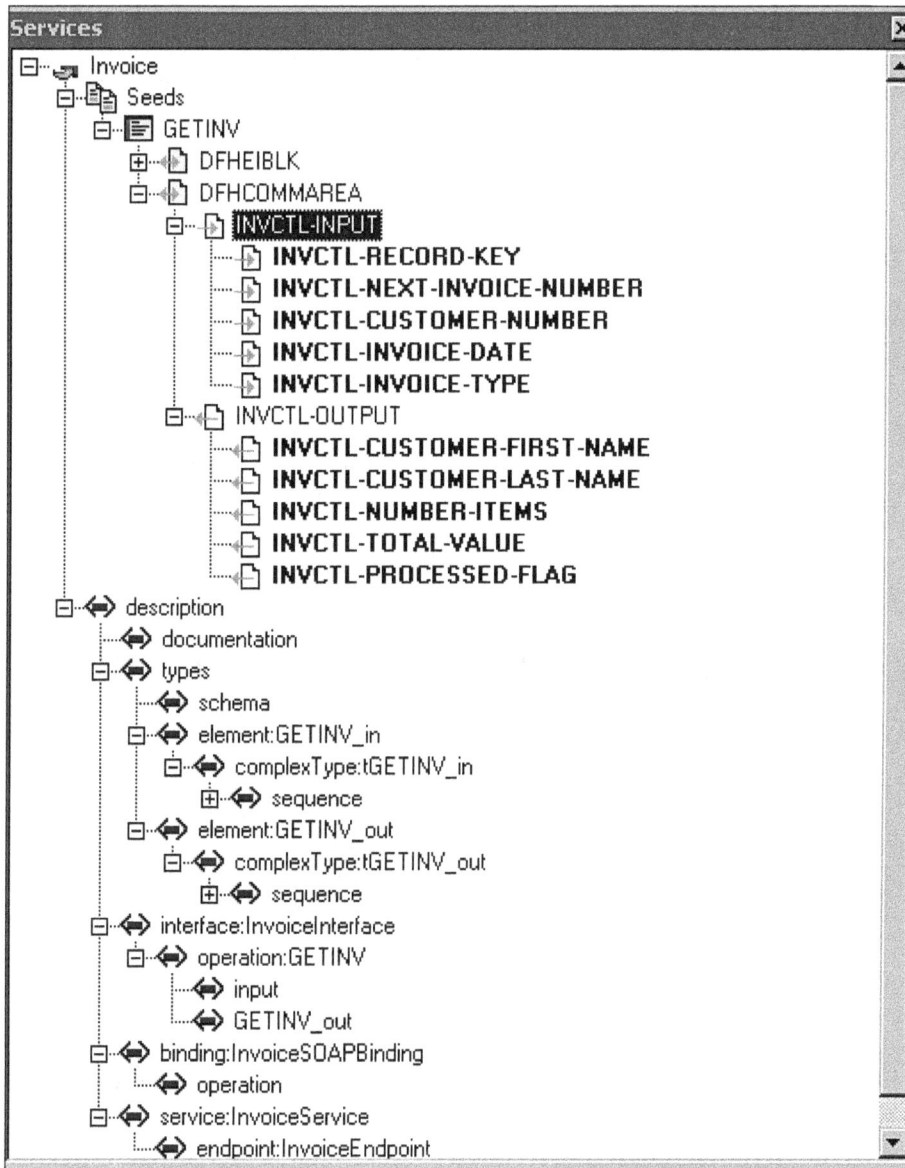

- We can add more then one program to the service. In this case, each program will generate a service operation, while its COMMAREA will define an interface. The resulting WSDL can be exported to an outside file, by using the **File | Export WSDL** menu of the SOA Analyzer tool.

> **Keeping It Real**: In a perfect world, it would be nice to expose a COBOL COMMAREA (that is CICS transaction) area as a service easily. However, in the real world, the COMMAREA definition is not readily available, or it may contain unnecessary fields.

Summary Legacy Artifact Discovery Using Relativity

In the perfect world, you may be able to find the VSAM call to the invoice file that you wish to service enable easily. In reality, you will find that using tools like those offered from Relativity makes the task much easier, especially when faced with millions of lines of code that are poorly documented, or not well understood by your current staff. The last section showed you how to discover the data interface for the service to be exposed. In the next section, we will show how to expose this data access artifact, which we have just discovered.

Exposing the Legacy VSAM File Data Access

Oracle Connect is a component that resides on the mainframe platform. It consists of native adapters for communicating with the mainframe application and data stores. The design-time configuration of Oracle AS Adapter for Legacy and mainframes consists of two steps. The **first step** involves using Oracle Studio for configuring the Oracle Connect engine and the metadata is stored on a file system at the Oracle Connect end. The **second step** consists of exposing the metadata obtained in the first step through a WSIL servlet. Oracle JDeveloper Web service has a WSIL browser which in turn connects to the WSIL servlet. The WSIL servlet communicates with Oracle Connect and exposes the metadata as WSDL with JCA extensions. The WSIL servlet is deployed in the Oracle Application Server Java EE container, and so it needs to be up and running at design time.

Connecting to Oracle Connect on Mainframe and Setting Connection Properties

Before anything is done, you must connect to your mainframe and set the properties for your connection as follows:

1. The Oracle Studio connects to Oracle Connect running on the mainframe. Oracle Connect for VSAM needs to be installed and configured on the OS/390 machine. The steps are detailed in the Adapter User Guide.

    Go to the **Configuration Explorer** view, and select **Machine** folder. Right-click and select **New**. This will bring up the connection panel on the right-hand side. Specify the connection parameters as shown here:

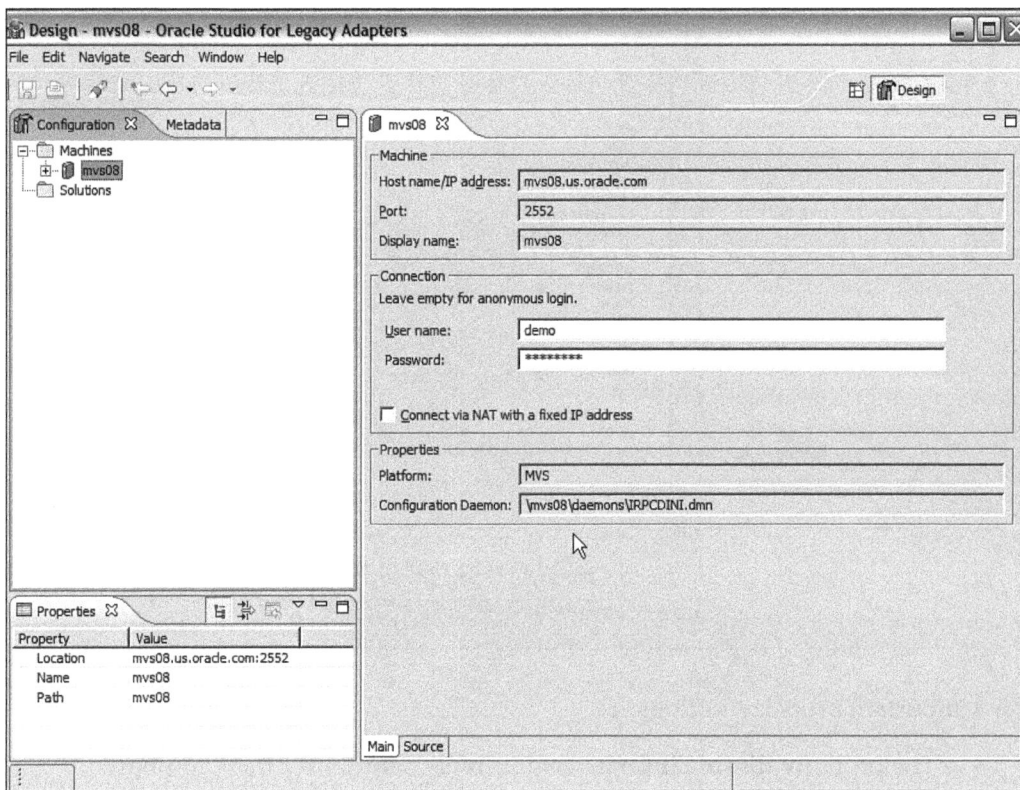

> Your connection parameter will be different based on your mainframe machine name, port number, user name, and password.

2. Expanding the connection object shows a **Bindings** folder for defining workspaces (domains) and a default workspace called **NAV**. Expanding the **Bindings** folder shows an **Adapters** and **Events** folder. The **Adapters** folder is used to define JCA outbound interactions (request-response services), while the **Events** folder is used to define JCA Inbound Interactions (event services).

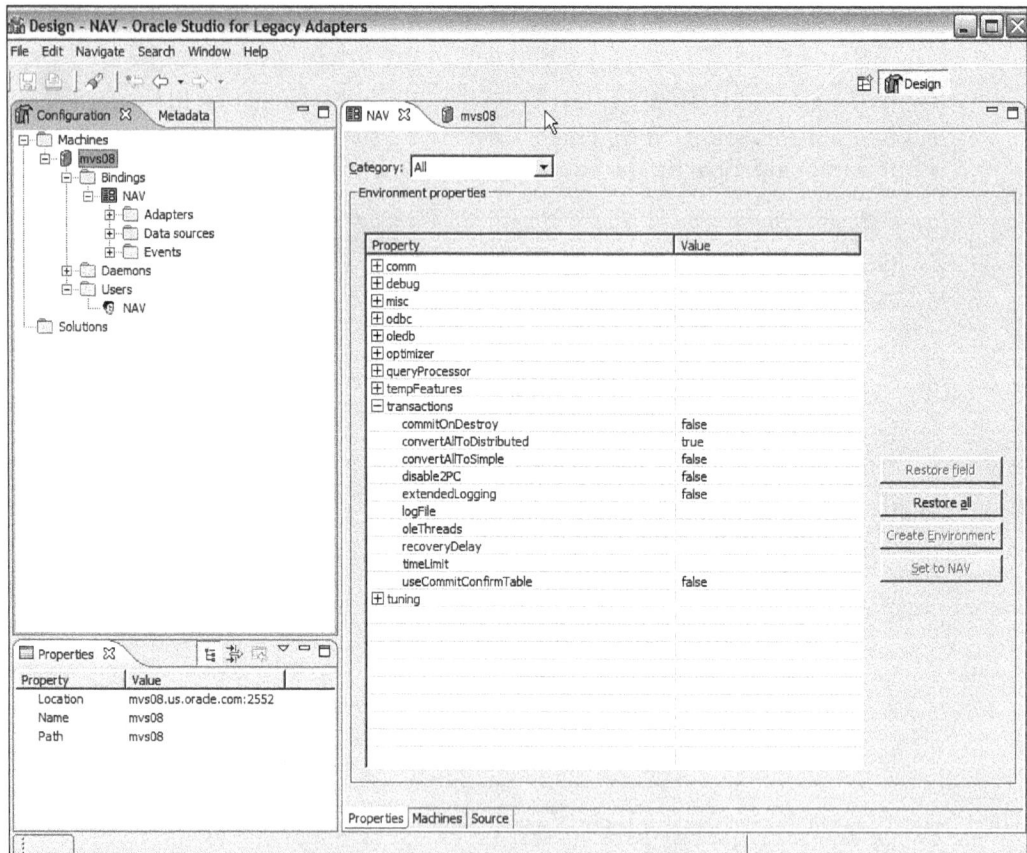

Two important property settings are:

- The property **disable2PC** needs to be **false** in order for the two-phase commit to work.

- To work with global transactions, set the **convertAllToDistributed** transaction environment property to **true**.

More information on the Oracle VSAM Adapter setup in the Legacy Studio can be found here: http://download.oracle.com/docs/cd/B31017_01/ integrate.1013/b31002/vsam_install.htm#i1008132.

> **Keeping It Real**: Once the Oracle Connect mainframe component is installed, connecting to your mainframe system through the Oracle Studio for Legacy Adapters is simple. The difficult task is to install Oracle Connect on the mainframe system because of the processes and procedures, people's resistance – 'not wanting new things on the mainframe', or even a lack of additional mainframe cycles.

Oracle Connect Data Source

Since we have so much to cover in this chapter and we want to focus on aspects such as the adapter, two-phase commit, and calling the adapter from Java, we will not create a new data source. Instead, we will take a look at an existing data source to keep screenshots to the minimum.

1. The **Data sources** folder contains the VSAM data source. We will be using a data source called **DS_VSAM**.

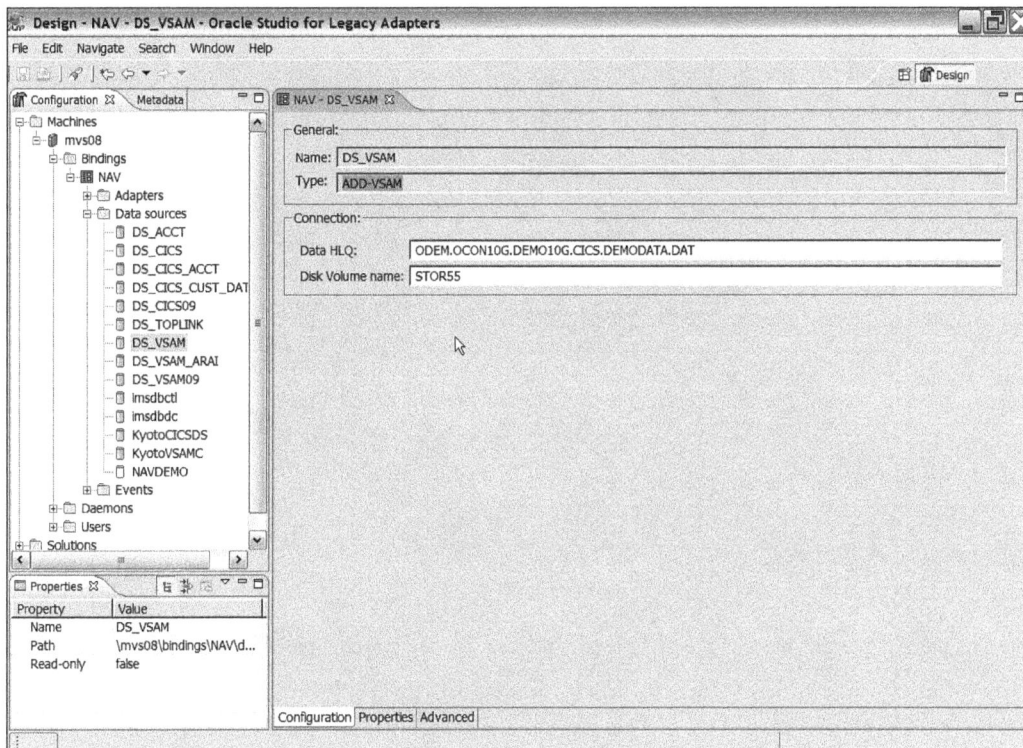

Note that this is a **ADD-VSAM** type of data source.

2. Click on the **Advanced** tab as shown in the screenshot. Click on the drop-down box for the **Transaction type** field. Change the transaction type to **2PC**. This enables two-phase commit for this data source. Your screen should appear as follows:

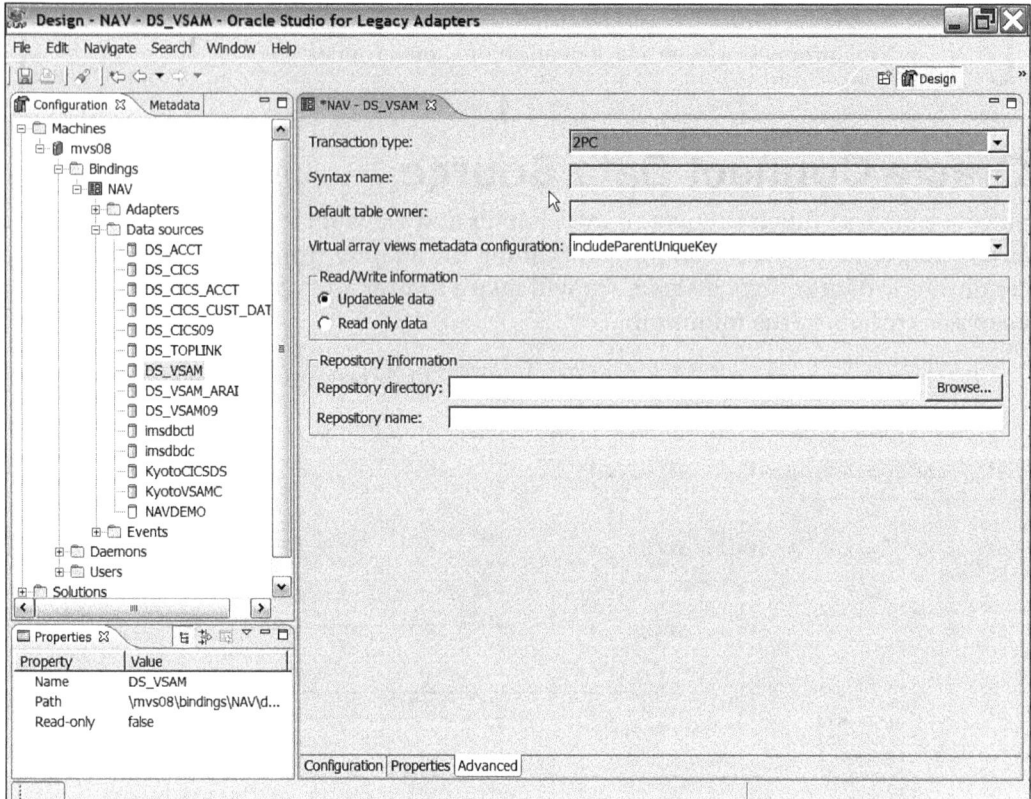

3. Right-click on the **DS_VSAM** data source and select the **Edit Metadata**. Expand the **DS_VSAM** entry (click the + sign) under the **Data sources** folder in the **Metadata** tab. Next, expand the **Tables** folder. Lastly, double-click on the **INVOICE_DATA** table entry. Your screen should appear as follows:

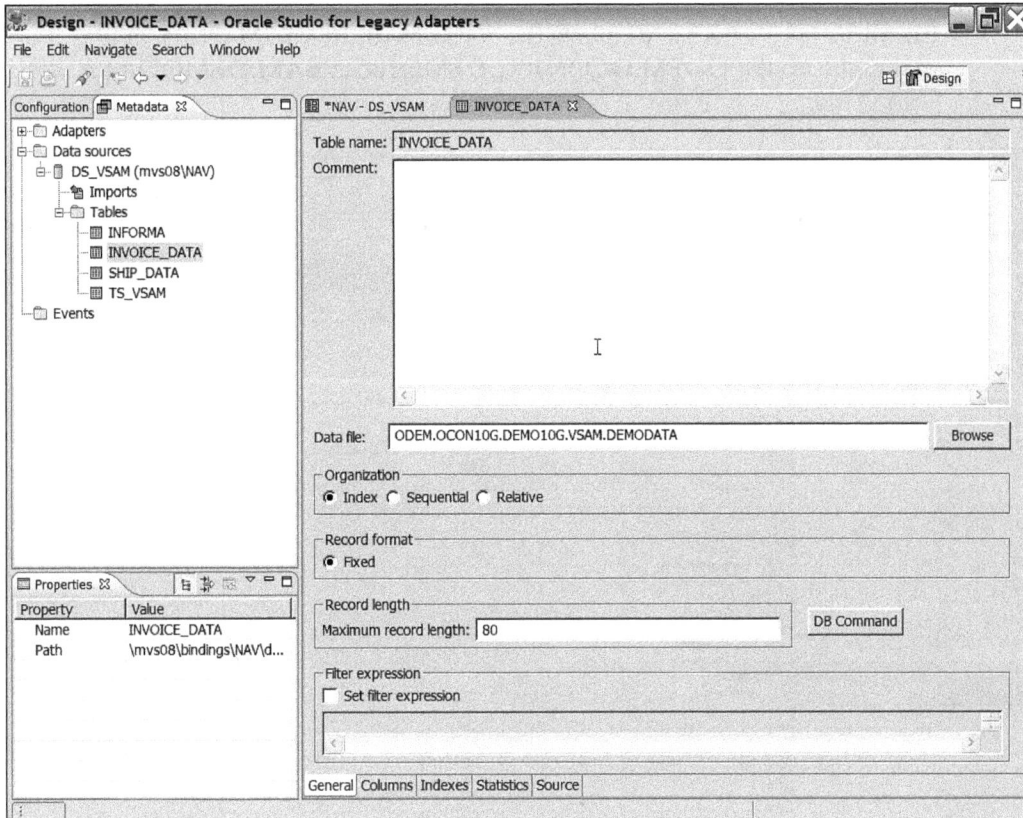

A couple of things to note on this screen:

- **Data file** field — This is the physical location of the VSAM data file on the mainframe.

- **Maximum record length** — The maximum length of each record is **80**.

- **Columns** tab — This tab displays the columns (or in VSAM terms, fields) that make up the **ODEM.OCON10G.DEMO10G.VSAM.DEMODATA** VSAM file.

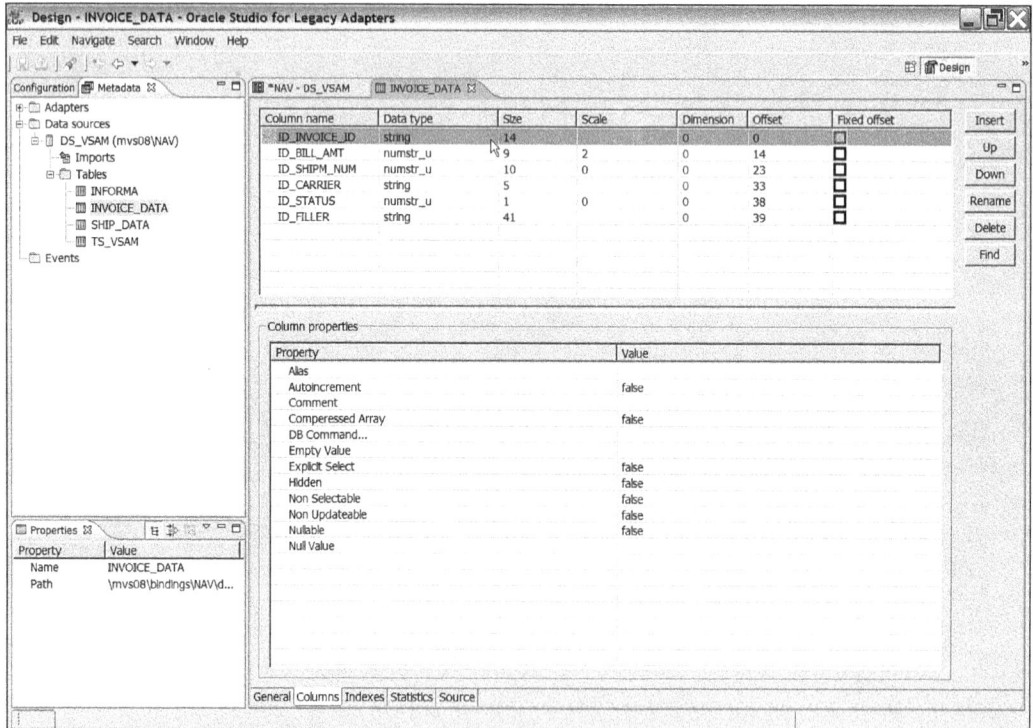

Keeping It Real: Creating the data source is the first step. Most of your legacy services at some point will need to interact with a data source at some point whether they are presentation, transaction, or program-based services. Therefore, exposing the data source as a Web service is a common approach.

Oracle Connect Adapter

The adapter is what you will be talking to from your Java application to insert the VSAM record into the mainframe system using CICS. We will be using an existing adapter called **AD_VSAM**. This adapter uses the **DS_VSAM** data source created in the previous section. The adapter has select, insert, delete, and update interactions associated with it. 'Interactions' are the fundamental methods that Java EE, Oracle BPEL, or other applications interface to the legacy artifacts on the mainframe. Oracle Studio has a test run capability that can be used to test the interactions.

1. The Adapters folder is used to define and modify a VSAM adapter. Right-click on the AD_VASM adapter in the Adapters folder and select Edit Metadata. The Metadata tab appears as follows:

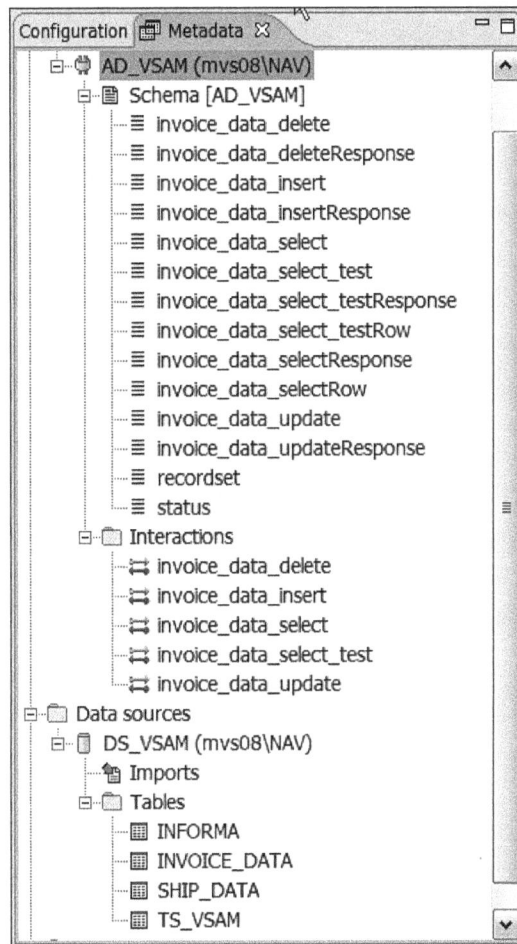

The important thing to note here is that an adapter can have more then one type of interaction. As you can see in the above screenshot, five different interactions are associated with this one adapter.

2. Double-click on the **invoice_data_insert** entry under the **Schema** entry, and you will see the following:

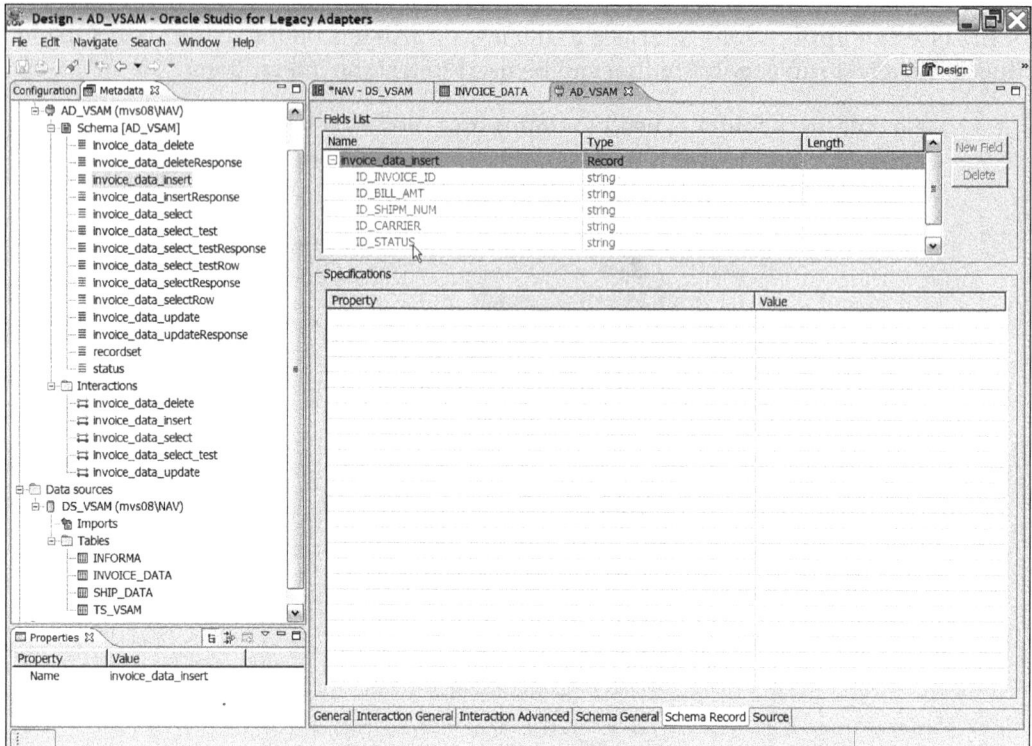

3. The **Schema Record** tab shows the fields that will be passed to the **AD_VSAM** adapter to be inserted into the **INVOICE_DATA** VSAM file using the adapter. The XML payload expects all fields to be character strings so that is why all the fields for INVOICE_DATA_INSERT are string. Double-click on the **invoice_data_insert** entry under the **Interactions** entry, and you will see the following:

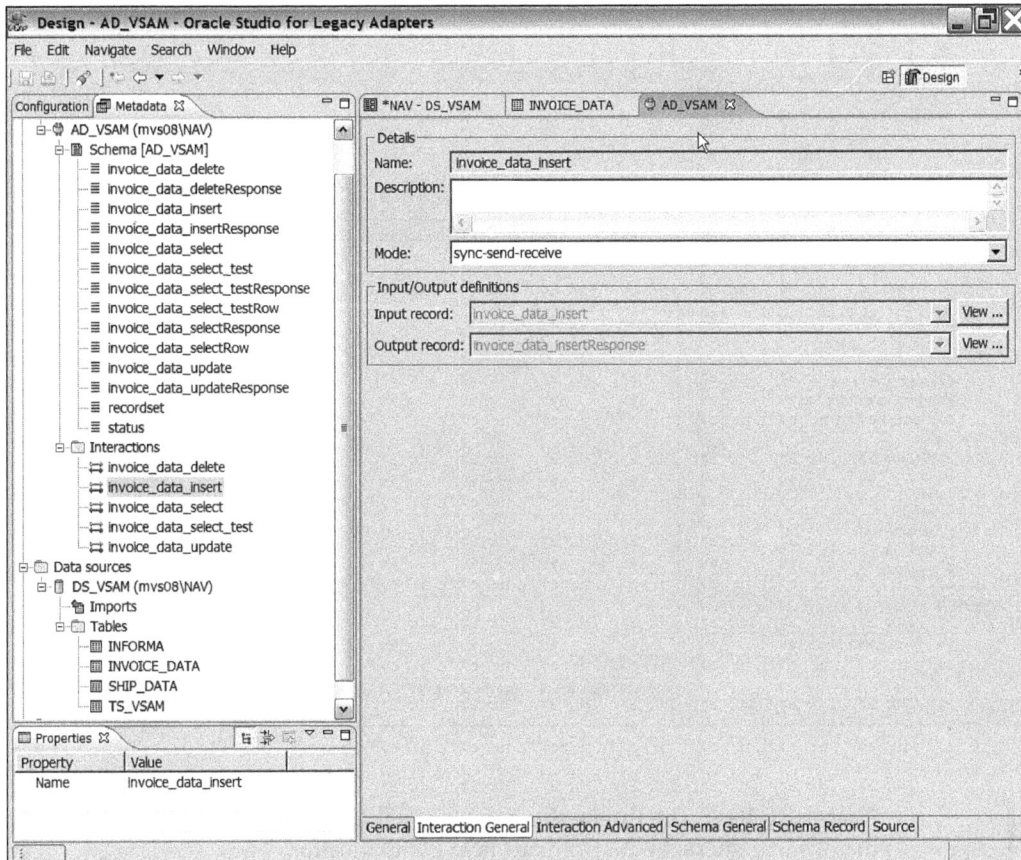

4. The Input record is the **invoice_data_insert** schema we just looked at. The output record is the **invoice_data_insertResponse** schema. The response schema is basically the status of the insert and appears as follows:

Keeping It Real: The **Interactions** created in this step are the services that we will interact with from our Java EE application. These services are different from the standard SOAP/WSDL based Web services. These services will be accessed using the Java EE Connector API.

Development Using Oracle JDeveloper

Oracle JDeveloper will be used for the all Java EE/Java SOA enabled development. JDeveloper is Oracle's free IDE (Integrated Development Environment) for for Java EE, Web services, Oracle WebCenter, Oracle BPEL, Oracle ESB, mobile devices, database persistence, and UML modeling and development. You can write your Java EE code using **code coach** (which will show you the methods and parameters associated with a class), or use many of the **drag-and-drop** capabilities of JDeveloper. JDeveloper has testing, profiling, debugging, and tuning built into the tool. JDeveloper also has an open-standards-based framework called **Application Development Framework** (**ADF**) which is a visual and declarative approach for quickly developing and deploying applications.

JDeveloper is open-source friendly, and includes built-in integration with Struts, Ants, Junit, XDoclets, and CVS. If you have your own tool, or want to extend the functionality of JDeveloper, you can do so by using the Extention SDK.

Our development processes using JDeveloper will flow as follows:

- Inital setting up, which we will call **prework**. This includes creating the database connection, creating the project file, and including the Java EE libraries we will need for our application.
- Creating the presentation-tier and UI navigation modules.
- Writing the code to access our Legacy Java EE Connector Adapters that reside on the mainframe.
- Configuring the Oracle Application Server for the two-phase commit
- Writing the Oracle Database persistence module.

Before we start developing, we will have a look at how to set things up.

Prework

Build the Oracle database schema—Create the Oracle Data Model in JDeveloper (shown above in the UML and Database Diagrams sections and under the Data Model Diagram subsection). This is as simple as using JDeveloper, creating a new database diagram, and dragging and dropping the invoice table on the diagram. The Oracle database schema is a simple two-table invoice schema with invoices and invoice line items. For this example, we will use only the invoice table. Complete preliminary setup by performing Oracle Database (Steps 1 and 2) activities as per the instructions available at this link:

```
http://www.oracle.com/technology/pub/articles/luttikhuizen-esbcase-
setup.html
```

More on creating database diagrams using JDeveloper can be found here:

```
http://www.oracle.com/technology/obe/obe9051jdev/ide1012/dbmodelling/
lesson_dm.htm
```

- Create the workspace and project to hold the application—To start building the application, we can use the **Application Workspace** wizard to generate a new workspace and an empty project, **File | New | General | Application**. Or just create an **empty** project in any existing workspace. We will work with an application named **BookLegacySOAIntegration**. JDeveloper creates a workspace for each application you create. The workspace created on the local files system for this application will be called `BookLegacySOAIntegration.jws`. The project name given for this application will be called `LegacyOracle2PC.jpr`.

  More on getting started with JDeveloper can be found here:

  ```
  http://www.oracle.com/technology/obe/obe9051jdev/ide1012/
  firststep/firststep.htm
  ```

- Include standard Java EE libraries required for the application—Include all the libraries required for this example. The Oracle JDeveloper Project requires these libraries to be added by creating new library entries:

  ○ Attunity libraries for connecting, processing, and executing the services on the mainframe:

  i. Directory: `<OC4J_HOME>\j2ee\home\connectors\jca-legacy-adapter\jca-legacy-adapter`

  ii.Libraries: `attunityCoreResourceAdapter.jar`, `AttunityResourceAdapter.jar`, and `log4j-1.2.8.jar`

  ○ The XA transaction manager library classes for the two-phase commit processing:

  i. Directory: `<OC4J_HOME>\j2ee\home\lib`

  ii.Libraries: `connector.jar`

These libraries are already part of the standard JDeveloper and will simply have to be added to the project:

- JSP Runtime—As we are using JSPs for this application, we will need the JSP runtime libraries

- Java EE—Used for JSPs and Servlets

Perhaps because this is a basic Java EE development task, there is no information on how to do this in JDeveloper. However, we do find that newer Java/Java EE developers can struggle with this task. To locate libraries for JDeveloper projects, right-click on your project file name. Select the **Project Properties** entry. You will then see this screen where you can add and create new library entries:

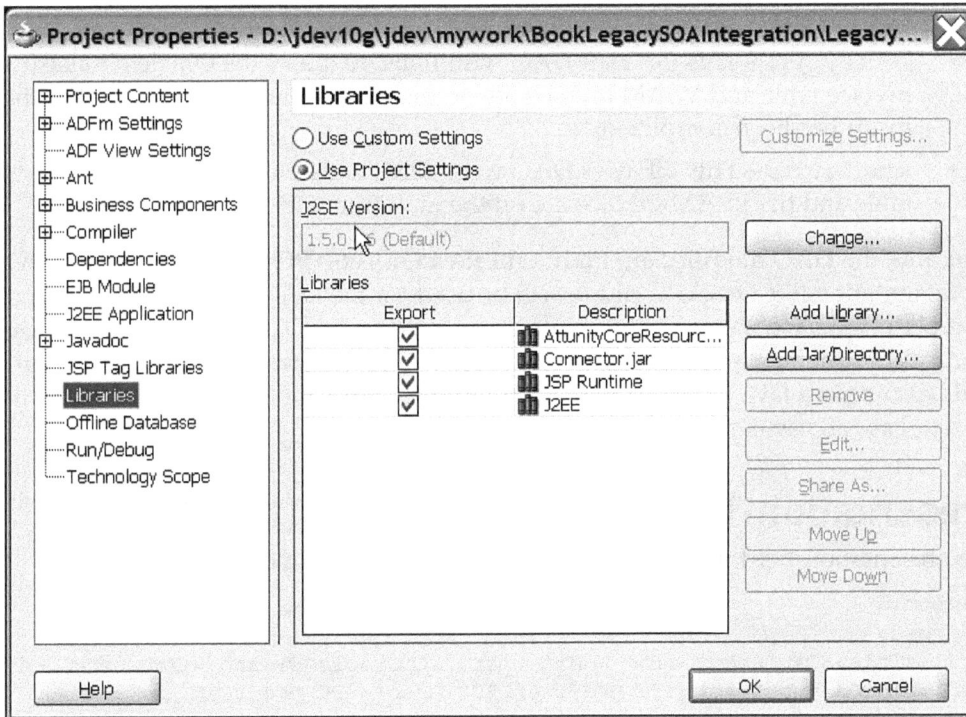

Application Modules

We will demonstrate the separation of the presentation and database access tiers in this example. We will demonstrate the separation of the presentation and database access tiers in this chapter. Further, we will demonstrate business rules and screen navigation separation in the re-architecture example in Chapter 9. There is no business logic in this application since we are doing simple two-phase CRUD against the Oracle and mainframe VSAM data stores. Screen navigation is so basic that it is included in the DAO JSPs.

These are the four application modules that make up this example:

- `Index.html` – This is the presentation-tier for the application. It is a simple HTML form page.

- `Create.jsp` – This JSP is used to create **Database Access Objects** (**DAOs**) that use JDBC to insert a new invoice into the VSAM file on the mainframe. It also has the two-phase commit logic.

- `Verify.jsp` – This JSP uses DAO with JDBC to query the Oracle database invoice table and VSAM invoice file on the mainframe to verify whether the insert has been completed.

- `Remove.jsp` – This JSP uses DAO with JDBC to delete the Oracle invoice table and the VSAM invoice file on the mainframe.

Typically, the DAO modules are **Plain Old Java Objects** (**POJO**s). Perhaps, a POJO implementation like Oracle TopLink will be used for the DAO. In order to keep the example simple, we will use JDBC embedded in JSPs. This is not recommended for production systems. But as this is an example, we are 'cheating' a bit. The JDBC calls could also be in a Java Bean. A Java Bean would separate the presentation-tier from the database access-tier.

Presentation-Tier/User Interface—HTML Page

The presentation-tier for this application is contained within one HTML page:

```
<html>
<head>
  <title>SOA Integration - Mid-tier 2PC Oracle DB and VSAM </title>
  <h1>SOA Integration - Mid-tier 2PC Oracle DB and VSAM </h1>
  <LINK href="../blaf.css" type=text/css rel=stylesheet>
</head>
<body>
      <h3>Create an Invoice in Oracle and also
         create an  invoice in VSAM</h3>
This sample demonstrates two-phase commit scenario involving an Oracle
DB and VSAM. Please enter the invoice details and click on Submit and
the invoice record will either be created in both Oracle and VSAM DBs,
or will be rolled back
              <br>
<FORM ACTION="create.jsp" METHOD="POST" >
    <b>Invoice ID :<INPUT TYPE="text" NAME="invoiceID" SIZE="12"
                          MAXLENGTH="12" >
    <br><br>Supplier Name<b>:</b><INPUT TYPE="text"
                                    NAME="supplierName" SIZE="40"
                                    MAXLENGTH="40" >
    <br><br>Shipper<b>:</b><INPUT TYPE="text" NAME="shipper" SIZE="40"
                          MAXLENGTH="40" >
    <br><br>Invoice Total<b>:</b><INPUT TYPE="text"
```

```
                                    NAME="invoiceTotal" SIZE="12"
                                    MAXLENGTH="12" value="0" >
    <br><br>Purchase Order Number<b>:</b><INPUT TYPE="text"
                                    NAME="purchaseOrderNo"
                                    SIZE="12"
                                    MAXLENGTH="12" >
    <br><br>Account Number<b>:</b><INPUT TYPE="text" NAME="accountNo"
                                    SIZE="12" MAXLENGTH="12" >
    <br><br>Shipment Number<b>:</b><INPUT TYPE="text"
                                    NAME="shipmentNo" SIZE="10"
                                    MAXLENGTH="10" >

    <br><br>

<INPUT TYPE="Submit" VALUE="Submit Invoice">
<INPUT TYPE="reset" VALUE="Clear">
</FORM>
</body>
</html>
```

The user enters all the information required to create the invoices in the Oracle
and VSAM databases. Not the best of practices to show here, but in this example
the navigation logic is in the same module as the presentation code. The embedded
navigation logic is the calling of the JSP `create.jsp` when the **Submit** button
is pressed.

Legacy Web Service—VSAM Adapter Service

As indicated in Chapter 3, the legacy service can be executed as a Web service or
through the Java EE Connector API. The Oracle Legacy Adapters uses Java EE
Connector architecture to access the legacy services. The contract between the OC4J
client application (in this case a JSP) and the resource adapter is defined by the
Common Client Interface (**CCI**). More information on CCI can be found here:

```
http://download.oracle.com/docs/cd/B31017_01/integrate.1013/b31002/
vsam_oc4j.htm
```

Create the Java code using CCI methods to insert into the mainframe VSAM file:

```
Context ic = new InitialContext();
//Legacy Adapter VSAM lookup
AttuManagedConFactory amcf = new AttuManagedConFactory();
amcf.setConnectTimeout("99999999");
AttuConnectionFactory acf;
javax.resource.cci.Connection jcaConnection;
amcf.setEisName("AD_VSAM");
amcf.setServerName("mvs08");
amcf.setPortNumber("2554");
amcf.setUserName("demo");
```

```
amcf.setPassword("use4demo");

acf = (AttuConnectionFactory)amcf.createConnectionFactory();
jcaConnection = acf.getConnection();
        AttuInteraction ix = (AttuInteraction)jcaConnection.
createInteraction();

try {
        // Add an interaction spec
AttuInteractionSpec iSpec              = new
                        AttuInteractionSpec("invoice_data_insert");
        // Create a record via record factory
        out.println("Create a record via record factory.. \n" );
        AttuRecordFactory recordFactory =
                        (AttuRecordFactory)acf.getRecordFactory();
        CoreMappedRecord input = (CoreMappedRecord)recordFactory.
                        createMappedRecord("invoice_data_insert");
        out.println("Created input record of type = " + input);

        // Add data to input record
        out.println("Add Legacy Data to input record..");

        input.put("@ID_INVOICE_ID", invoiceIDString);
        input.put("@ID_BILL_AMT", Double.toString(invoiceTotal));
        input.put("@ID_SHIPM_NUM", Integer.toString(shipmentNo));
        input.put("@ID_CARRIER", shipper);
        input.put("@ID_STATUS", Integer.toString(status));
        input.put("@ID_FILLER", filler );

CoreMappedRecord output     = (CoreMappedRecord)ix.
                        execute(iSpec, input);
        out.println( "Inserted Invoice Data Successfully \n");

        } catch (ResourceException re ) {
            out.println("Error creating an Insert interaction:");
            out.println(re.getMessage());
            re.printStackTrace();
            ut.rollback(); //if there is an error
            return;
        }
```

The VSAM invoice file COBOL copybook file definition looks like this:

```
01   INVOICE-DATA.
     02   ID-INVOICE-ID     PIC X(14).
     02   ID-BILL-AMT       PIC 9(7)V99.
     02   ID-SHIPM-NUM      PIC 9(10).
     02   ID-CARRIER        PIC X(5).
     02   ID-STATUS         PIC 9.
     02   ID-FILLER         PIC X(41).
```

Although the actual data file has character and numeric fields, the CCI code given here uses only string data types. This is because the Oracle Connect on the mainframe receives an XML payload with string data fields.

Two-Phase Commit

The transaction manager in OC4J can coordinate two-phase transactions between any type of XA resources, such as databases Oracle or DB2, Oracle Legacy Adapters, and JMS providers such as MQSeries.

A transaction manager capable of doing recovery in a two-phase commit scenario needs to perform logging at the middle-tier. OC4J provides two ways to log transactions: in the local file system, or in an Oracle database table.

The `server.xml` must contain the following to enable logging by the transaction manager:

```
<transaction-manager-config path="./transaction-manager.xml"/>
```

In this example, we will use file-based logging in the mid-tier. To enable file-based logging, certain changes must be made to the configuration files in OC4J. This includes the type of logging and the location/directory where log files will be stored. We recommend that you use the default location for logging. However, you can modify the location for log files. For example, you have the following in your `transaction-manager.xml`:

```
<transaction-manager
  xmlns:xsi="http://www.w3.org/2001/XMLSchema-instance"
  xsi:noNamespaceSchemaLocation="http://xmlns.oracle.com/ias/schemas/
  file:transaction-manager_1_0.xsd">
<commit-coordinator retry-count="4">
<middle-tier>
<log type="multi-file" location="d:\debu\tpclogs"/>
</middle-tier>
</commit-coordinator>
</transaction-manager>
```

The Java code for the two-phase commit looks like this:

```
Context ic = new InitialContext();
      UserTransaction ut =
            (UserTransaction)ic.lookup("java:comp/UserTransaction");
// Start Transaction
   ut.begin();
```

```
...(code for Oracle database and VSAM insert)
    ut.rollback(); //Issued any time an error is encountered
ut.commit(); //Issued at end if everything is successful in both the
    Oracle and VSAM databases
```

More information on using two-phase commit with the Oracle Application Server can be found here:

```
http://www.oracle.com/technology/tech/java/oc4j/1003/how_to/how-
to-midtier-2pc.html
```

Oracle Database Persistence

We are using a data source that is defined in the Oracle Application Server configuration file called `data-sources.xml`. We will take a closer look at this file in the Oracle Application Server configuration section shown here. For now, the connection string looks like this:

```
DataSource ds1 = (DataSource)ic.lookup("jdbc/OracleInvoiceDB");
Connection conn1 = ds1.getConnection();
```

The close connection command is as simple as:

```
conn1.close();
```

The insert statement (in the `create.jsp` page) uses the values entered in the `Index. html` page to insert the invoice into the Oracle database. As this is a two-phase commit, we need a preparatory step which is in the `prepareCall` method:

```
PreparedStatement  ps1 = conn1.prepareCall("INSERT into invoices(id,
    supplier_name, supplier_invoice_no, order_date, purchase_order_no,
    shipping_date, shipper, invoice_total,account_no) VALUES (?, ?, ?,
    sysdate, ?, sysdate, ?, ?, ?, ?)");
        ps1.setDouble(1,invoiceID );
        ps1.setString(2,supplierName );
        ps1.setString(3,supplierInvoiceNo );
        ps1.setDouble(4,purchaseOrderNo );
        ps1.setString(5,shipper );
        ps1.setDouble(6,invoiceTotal );
        ps1.setString(7,accountNo );
        ret1 =ps1.executeUpdate();
```

> **Keeping It Real**: Relational database access methods such as ODBC and JDBC have been around for years. Therefore, there is no need to go into great detail on how to insert a row into an Oracle database.

Deploying to the Oracle Application Server

The last step before we can run our application is deploying the application to the Oracle Application Server. We will be using Oracle JDeveloper to deploy our application. Before we can do this, we need to add a couple of the Oracle Application Server XML configuration files and the Oracle Application Server connection to JDeveloper. Now, we are set to use the JDeveloper wizards to create the deploy descriptor, and deploy the application to the Oracle Application Server we just created a connection for.

Configuring Oracle Application Server for the Legacy Adapter

The connection factory for the Oracle Legacy Adapter is defined in the `oc4j-ra.xml` configuration file. This file is located in the `<OC4J_HOME>\j2ee\home\application-deployment\default\jca-legacy-adapter\directory`. The entry looks like this:

```
<connector-factory location="eis/legacy/AD_VSAM"
  connector-name="Attunity Connect Legacy Adapter">
      <config-property name="userName" value="demo"/>
      <config-property name="password" value="use4demo"/>
      <config-property name="eisName" value="AD_VSAM"/>
      <config-property name="serverName"
                       value="mvs08.us.oracle.com"/>
      <config-property name="workspace" value="Navigator"/>
      <config-property name="portNumber" value="2552"/>
      <config-property name="persistentConnection" value="true"/>
      <config-property name="keepAlive" value="true"/>
      <config-property name="firewallProtocol" value=""/>
      <config-property name="connectTimeout" value=""/>
      <config-property name="encryptionProtocol" value=""/>
      <config-property name="encryptionKeyName" value=""/>
      <config-property name="encryptionKeyValue" value=""/>
      <config-property name="fakeXa" value="false"/>
      <config-property name="useNamespace" value="true"/>
```

```
        <config-property name="networkXMLProtocol" value="binary"/>
        <config-property name="exposeEventStreamMetadata"
                          value="true"/>
        <connection-pooling use="none">
        </connection-pooling>
        <security-config use="none">
        </security-config>
    </connector-factory>
```

You can also add this adapter using the **Oracle Enterprise Manager**. The Legacy Adapter connection factories in OEM are found in the **OCJ Home | Application: default** area as follows:

Configuring Oracle Application Server Oracle Database Connection

We will use a connection pool for the Oracle Database. The following is an example of the DataSource that can be used for the Oracle Database to access the Invoice table:

```
<managed-data-source connection-pool-name="OracleInvoiceDB"
  jndi-name="jdbc/OracleInvoiceDB" name="OracleInvoiceDB"/>
<connection-pool name="OracleInvoiceDB">
```

```
<connection-factory factory-class="oracle.jdbc.pool.OracleDataSource"
                    user="invoice_demo" password="oracle"
                    url="jdbc:oracle:thin:@localhost:1521:xe"/>
    </connection-pool>
```

From this connection factory configuration, you can see the following:

- Using the Oracle Express Edition Database (XE)
- Running the Oracle database on our local machine
- Connecting to the schema `invoice_demo`
- The JNDI data sources lookup name — `OracleInvoiceDB`

The data sources connections are defined in the `data-sources.xml` configuration file. This file is located in the `<OC4J_HOME>\j2ee\home\config` directory.

Deploying to Oracle Application Server Using JDeveloper

Before you can deploy the application to the Oracle Application Server, you need to create a connection using the **Connections Navigator**. The connection we have set up for this example is as follows:

The name of our connection is **OAS_SOA_Suite_10g**. More on setting up connections can be found here: `http://www.oracle.com/technology/obe/` `obe1013jdev/10131/deployment/deployment.htm`

Next, you create the deployment file in the **Applications Navigator**:

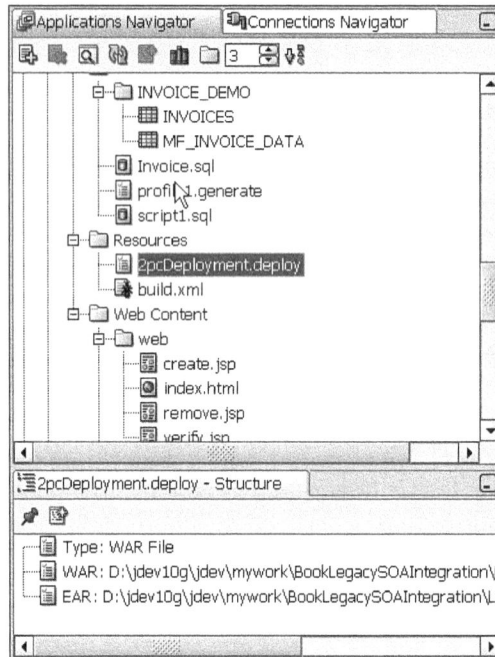

Right-click on the highlighted **2pcDeployment.deploy** file and select **Deploy to OAS_SOA_Suite_10g**. A step-by-step tutorial on setting up JDeveloper Deployment Profiles can be found here: `http://www.oracle.com/technology/obe/` `obe1013jdev/10131/deployment/deployment.htm`

Deploy the application to Oracle Application Server using JDeveloper. You could also use Ants. More on Ants can be found here:

`http://download-west.oracle.com/docs/cd/B32110_01/web.1013/b28951/` `anttasks.htm`

Keeping It Real: Deploying Java EE applications to the Oracle Application Server is easy using JDeveloper. However, in a production environment, you will probably not be deploying applications directly from JDeveloper. In this case, you will probably create scheduled nightly executable batch files that will use Ants to deploy the application to your Oracle Fusion Middleware production environment.

Running the Example

Running the Legacy SOA Integration application in a web browser for the first time in front of users who have been dealing with green screens for years or decades is typically an awe inspiring event. They are usually more than happy to get rid of their difficult to view, bulky 3270 terminal. They also cannot believe the rich graphics and colors presented in the browser. IT personnel, both mainframe and open systems staff, are typically amazed that the mainframe and relational database worlds with so little development effort can co-exist.

Running the application

Test the application by accessing the web app at the URL: `http://localhost:8888/LegacyOracle2PC/web/index.html`

The `index.html` page is displayed where you can enter the invoice information:

> Although the Invoice **ID** is alphanumeric in the VSAM file, it is an integer in the Oracle Invoice table. Therefore, only numeric Invoice IDs are allowed. This slight difference shows you one of the many situations (different data types between legacy and open systems worlds) that you will run into during your Legacy SOA Integration projects.

Click on the **Submit** button, and you will see that the Invoice Oracle Database and VSAM file have been successfully processed:

Oracle SQL Developer will be used to verify the row that has been inserted into the Oracle **INVOICES** database table:

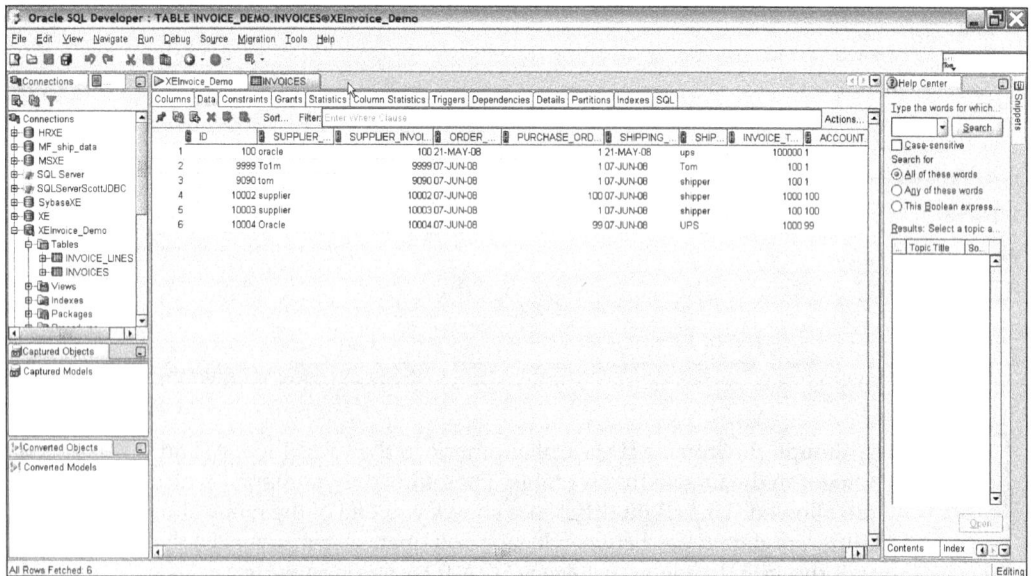

You can see that the row with the Invoice **ID** of 10004 has been added to the **INVOICES** table.

To verify the insert into the mainframe VSAM file, we will use the Oracle Studio for Legacy Adapters. Right-click on the **AD_VASM** adapter in the **Adapters** folder and select **Edit Metadata**. Right-click on the **invoice_data_select** interaction and choose **Test**. In the **Test Wizard**, enter the invoice number, **10004**. We can see that the VSAM file was populated with the same information:

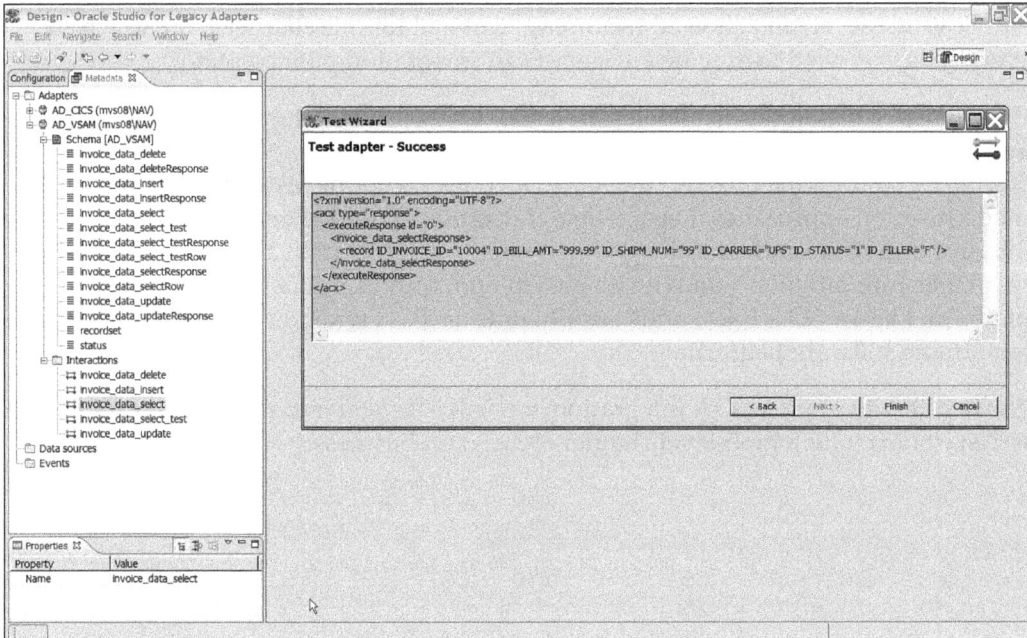

[
Keeping It Real: What you accomplished was one small step in your Legacy SOA Integration journey, but one giant step forward in your first tactical project. By seeing an example that is not just a basic query from a DB2 or VSAM database, we believe you are now much better prepared when you do this for real. We have also given you an example that is not based on BPEL, as enough of those exist already.
]

Summary

We covered significant ground in this chapter. Starting with a sample legacy COBOL/CICS/VSAM application, we went on to discover the legacy artifact that is the best candidate for enabling SOA using the Relativity tools set. Then we used Oracle Studio for Legacy Adapters to expose the legacy VSAM artifact. We used Oracle JDeveloper to create the web-based Java EE frontend for our application. Next, we created the Java module to invoke the Oracle Connect Legacy adapter on the mainframe using the Java EE Connector standard. We deployed our application to the Oracle Application Server, and showed it running. Not bad for one chapter. You now have everything you need to execute a Legacy SOA Integration pilot project.

We will leave the modernization approach of Legacy SOA Integration behind and move on to Legacy re-architecture. This is a significant leap as Legacy SOA Integration is the most noninvasive, less risky, and the fastest among all modernization approaches. Legacy re-architecture, on the other hand, is most invasive and risky, and takes longer then other modernization approaches. However, re-architecture provides you with an end-to-end, fully SOA enabled software platform. Legacy SOA Integration simply puts an SOA wrapper around your legacy mainframe software platform.

As we did with Legacy SOA Integration, we will ease you into re-architecture. So, we will start next with a high-level chapter focused on business.

5

Overview of Re-architecturing

In the Legacy Modernization business, you will get to hear a lot of '**re**' words describing essentially the same concept: re-engineering, redevelopment, renewal, re-architecture, reverse Engineering. In this text, we will refer to the concept of building applications up from the assets of the legacy application as re-architecture, though you may see us interchange these terms a bit.

Since we are defining some common terms, this may be a good time to point out that in the context and examples of this book, we highlight the IBM mainframe running CICS/COBOL DB2/VSAM. Mainframe can be Honeywell, Bull, Unisys, Amdahl, Wang. There are more versions of COBOL, and many more legacy data stores. The concepts covered in the re-architecture sections work not just for IBM CICS/DB2, but any legacy application. Further, one can have a great need to re-architect a legacy Java, VB, or even C#. I often say, 'If it's in production, it's legacy!" Remember the law of entropy, which says that things tend to move from order to disorder? The law applies to this industry in earnest.

The new generation of programmers can snigger at these old COBOL, batch systems with the allegation that they are not sophisticated, and they are poorly architected. Before you bash them up, remember that these systems were developed in days where drag-and-drop was not possible, when things like ETL, work flow, ESBs, business rules, messaging queues, integration, and other tools and products did not exist. The architectures and developer had to develop all these infrastructure and framework technologies on their own. Believe me; I have seen some very sophisticated business rule engines and integration infrastructure systems built from scratch. These code sets also had to deal with limited memory, limited compile opportunities (or waiting till the next day to see the results of their compile), limited storage, and in many cases, low level languages like the **Assembly**.

Most large organizations have systems that have been around for years, and possibly even decades. These applications are often large, cumbersome, hard to change, and yet are running the core of the business. The mainline thinking is that, to modernize these applications, one has to embark on greenfield development in the new target architecture, or in other words, re-write the application from scratch, bottom-up.

Leaders traditionally resist these re-architecture projects for a good many reasons. First, these systems are so large that to understand what they actually do is quite difficult or impossible. Documentation is either old, or non-existent. In our experience, if you sit down in a business process session with users of legacy systems, it would not be uncommon to get several different process flows for what should be a single business process. Going back to the source code is usually an extremely difficult task and until now, has not been a good source for driving future re-development.

What is Re-Architecture?

In re-architecture, the strategy is to reverse engineer legacy applications to preserve business knowledge, then forward engineer applications to modern architectures, which take advantage of open and extensible standards. Characteristics of re-architecture include:

- **Application Discovery** — Understand applications and develop 'as is' models using legacy understanding tools.

- **Mine and Extract** — Mine and extract application business knowledge (business logic / business rules) into a platform-independent model.

- **Forward Engineer** — Forward engineer applications and data to modern architectures using model-based design techniques.

- **Accelerate** — Accelerate application generation for core J2EE application components.

- **SOA** — Develop and integrate application Web services within a service oriented architecture (SOA).

The main point here is that this process is not manual, and it is not fully automated either. With the use of tools and sound process, you can greatly lower the risk, cost, and time to market when re-developing legacy applications.

We will dive into these a bit more later in this chapter, and through a step-by-step example later in the book. Re-architecture is different from greenfield development in that engineers utilize the existing application as the specification, and possibly a framework for future development. The promise of this strategy is the strength found in its ability to identify, untangle, and isolate legacy business rules for future modeling, enhancement and development. Re-architecture is also distinguished from platform-migration, where tools are used at an automation rate of over 80 percent. As mentioned earlier, the platform migration method will often deliver code in a new technology (language), but it:

- Resembles the legacy paradigm.
- Is usually difficult to maintain.
- Is a one-to-one transliteration, and almost impossible to add enhancements during the migration process.

Drivers and Considerations for Re-Architecture

When considering which approach is best for your organization, it is critical to identify what the drivers are for the effort. These can be divided into two general categories, business and technical. We'll review some common drivers for re-architecture with the objective to help identify when it would be appropriate to take this route. Besides mentioning some of the key drivers that make this a good option, we'll also examine some of the considerations that need to be weighed in light of a re-architecture.

Re-architecture starts with learning everything about an existing application (for example, what it does, how it does it, and why it does) and then designing and rewriting the application to take advantage of the new technologies to be more portable, more agile, and more scalable. The following are the key drivers of a re-architect modernization effort:

- High mainframe costs, which continue to escalate.
- Utilization of standard platforms and more off-the-shelf applications.
- Positioning of applications for the next-generation technology.
- An IT infrastructure that is easier to manage, maintain, and upgrade.
- IT's continued increase in criticality to the business.
- Current application architecture not being flexible and adaptable.
- Reduced number of applications & platforms.
- Implementation of application changes in days, and not in months.
- Business functionality.

All good IT organizations want to reduce their cost of ownership, improve their ability to react to business demand, and minimize their reliance on legacy skill sets—all the while ensuring that they are meeting new compliance standards. Forrester reports that 85 percent of the surveyed CEOs view their IT organizations as an inhibitor to innovation. So there is a great drive to allow business to not just sustain, but to react. Technology's promise is innovation, and now it has become lead boots on a marathon runner.

As we stated above, legacy modernization allows the IT organization to leverage the investment made in core IT applications as a springboard for future development, instead of just throwing it out. We can leverage these legacy assets to deliver a lower **Total Cost of Ownership (TCO)** business with an increased level of agility, and ultimately as an agent of innovation for the organization.

Of the different modernization options, re-architecture allows for the **highest** benefits in terms of increased agility, lowest cost, and elimination of the reliance on legacy skill sets.

Platform Agility

What exactly do we mean when we say that re-architecture provides the highest benefits in terms of agility, TCO, and reliance on legacy skills? To understand this better, lets review the modernization options in terms of business benefits. The following chart is a compare and contrast of the legacy modernization options, and how they impact the business with respect to costs, agility, and human resources.

Modernization Option	Agility	Reliance on Legacy HR	TCO*
SOA Enablement	Low-Medium	High	High
COTS	Low-Medium	Medium	Medium
Platform Migration	Low-Medium	High	Medium
Re-Architecture	High	Low	Low

Human Factors to Consider in a Re-Architecture Project

The objective of any successful modernization effort is to add business value. Many organizations begin these efforts for the wrong reasons. The force behind any modernization effort should be driven by the business.

The human factor is also a key business issue that needs to be managed properly for a successful modernization project. Some examples to consider include:

Issue	Description	Mitigation Actions
Job Loss	The technologist of the existing system often sees a modernization project as a path to unemployment. Managers and team members may not have a commitment to the success of the project and can be a hindrance to its overall success.	Utilize team as a critical SME role. (See Technical Considerations later in this chapter) Re-tool personnel in new technology. Job loss is a reality in some business drivers. Prepare ahead of time on personnel attrition. It is important to understand that the value of these individuals is in their business knowledge, not technical skills. They can be taught new technical skills more easily than developing business skills in new employees.
Resistance to Change	With any change, even for the better, comes resistance. (For example, end users may have used a particular screen or set of keystrokes for years and any alteration to this will not be well received.)	Involve user community. They are an integral part of migration testing. Involve end users as early as possible in the modernization process.

How IBM Views Re-Architecture

Much of the messaging put out by IBM in migration and modernization centers around growing the Mainframe footprint. The story centers around application consolidation, open architecture, and virtualization. Further, with Z/Linux, organizations can run their Java applications on the same mainframes that they are running their COBOL/CICS and batch applications. Much of the white papers and strategies of IBM on this topic focus on the reliability of the mainframe, the scalability of Linux on the mainframe, and the TCO of the Z platform. It is important to note that this book it taking an agnostic view of hardware and tries to address the problems centered on applications. While we think it is good for some customers to stay on their Z platforms, we are trying to address what we should do with legacy applications. If an organization is determined to migrate their applications from Z/OS, we want to provide a them road map to get there independent of the selection of hardware.

IT/Technical Drivers and Considerations

When a business considers re-architecting its entire platform there are a common set of drivers that are behind many, if not all modernization projects. Earlier in the book, we examined a few of the modernization options such as SOA enablement and platform modernization. With the re-architecture strategy, there are some key technical drivers that are unique to this method. We will examine a few of those areas here.

Getting Off the Mainframe

There is a large push by organizations to get off the mainframe. This push is more often a function of an actual application that is running on the mainframe rather the inability of the hardware itself to perform. The application costs may be high, hard to maintain or very brittle. Performance of the mainframe is usually not the driver here. As we observed previously, the IBM Z platform can run any open system technology that organizations can deploy on a given white box Unix/Linux system.

The problem exists in COBOL (or other legacy code base) applications. The architects and trusted advisors of the target architectures are not knowledgeable or experienced in the legacy mainframe environment. Combine the cultural shift with the high costs of mainframe hardware, operating system, and third-party applications for things like tape management, monitoring, and integration, and one can see why this trend is continuing in many sectors. If an organization fully eliminates the need for Z/OS by creating a new architecture built upon, say a J2EE architecture, it is much easier to find system administrators who can run non-mainframe system. Moreover, if there are no more legacy applications that need to be maintained, then a build-out approach usually generates a lower TCO.

One of the main hindrances to leaving the mainframe up until this point has been one the quality of the server. Traditionally, nothing could compare to the reliability and throughput of the mainframe. However, times have changed now. From the perspective of availability and reliability, products like Oracle's Real Application Clusters can provide the availability off the mainframe across the computing grid. So, now with the non-mainframe option being able to deliver mainframe quality of service, we are seeing a larger push for this path.

Another push to get off the mainframe is when the organization faces a "burning-platform" situation. The mainframe system they are running is out of support, or coming off support in the near future. So, now we are again confronted with the actual problem of how to migrate off the platform.

Creating a Flexible, Adaptable, and Agile Architecture

The idea of re-architecture implies that the system will be totally different from the original. Just as in any ground up development effort, here we are looking at leveraging the latest technologies and development frameworks. The objective here isn't to refactor, or remediate the legacy code and redeploy it in a polished up mode, but rather totally change the make up of the entire system. The only resemblance to the original is that we've leveraged the original business rules (that we desire) as well as legacy data, which has also probably been restructured as well.

The point to be noted here is that a modernization effort that is only doing a refactoring of legacy structure, but not leveraging any new technologies or delivery platforms is probably not a true re-architecture. For example, let us think about an average COBOL program. Say this program is 50,000 lines long, does some data interaction, screen inputs, program calls, and cleanup. It also probably contains some dead code, and code that was not well written. The idea leveraging new technologies, would take this beyond transforming it simply into Java. I would even argue that cleaning up the dead code, and abstracting data and screen logic isn't enough. A true re-architecture will examine the function of this code base. It will determine things like if it is doing event orchestration, or business rule execution. If so, it would probably not be a good candidate for POJO (Plane Old Java Objects), but rather for BPEL, ESBs, or a business rule engine. Get the picture? This is illustrated in the following figure:

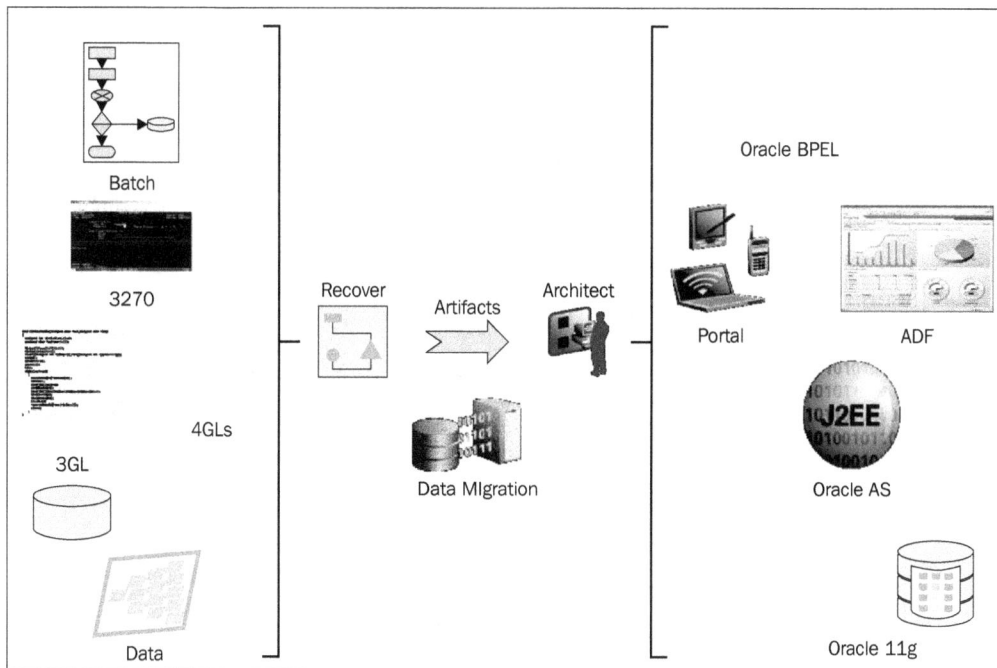

Advanced Development Tools

With the recent push for the open systems movement, a plethora of tools are now available to enable organizations to develop and maintain applications. Users can take advantage of free IDEs, open standard execution languages such as BPEL and modeling languages such as UML. With the pervasive and growing culture of open standards, this gives the organization more choices. With choices comes the competition of products and ideas. So, now, instead of having only one language, one set of tools, and one cost model, we can utilize the growing and more efficient universe of Open Systems. Of course, it is neither more efficient, nor cheaper. We do need to apply thought and intelligence in how we choose to deploy. This is one of the compelling reasons for re-architecture. We can now leverage a host of tools, environments, and standards to take our legacy assets forward into the future.

In this book, we'll be using Oracle's JDeveloper tool. This allows developers to leverage full Oracle ADF framework, and work with transportable models. Moreover, because of it's API, third-party modernization products are able to interface the legacy artifacts into the development environment. The following is a screenshot of JDeveloper in action. You can see that process flows are model-driven, and we can integrate this with other object models and business rule engines.

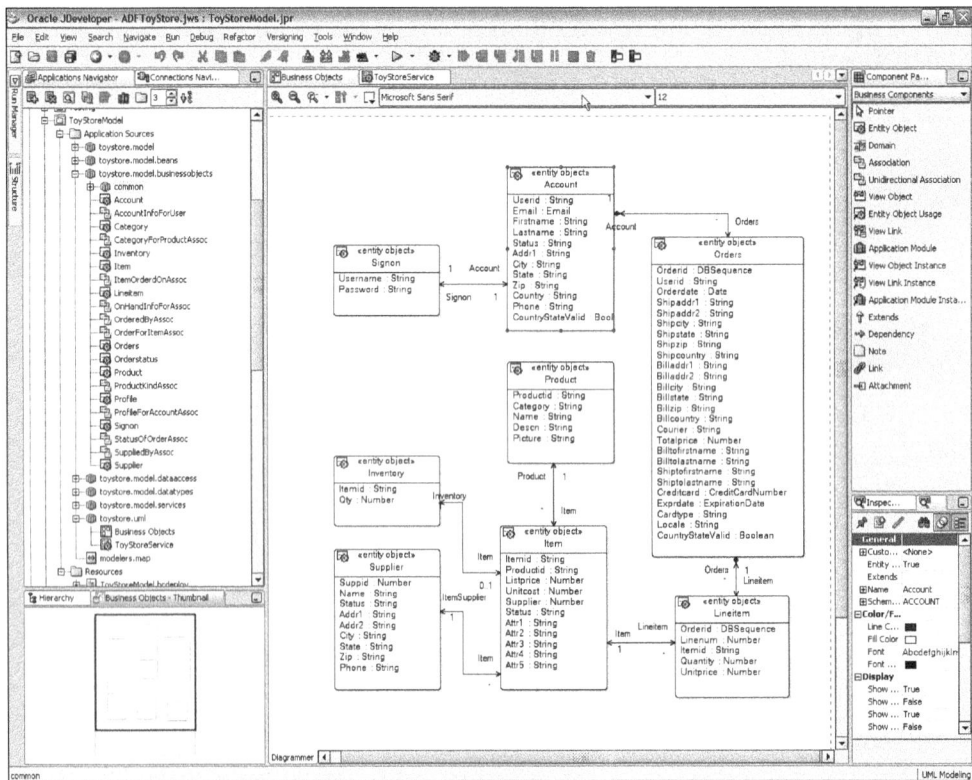

Technical Considerations for a Re-Architecture Effort

As with any project, there are considerations that must be made that drive how the project will be structured and executed. These depend upon the system requirements and the available resources. The following are the key technical considerations for modernization.

Subject Matter Experts (SME)

Access to SMEs, the legacy system can be one of the single largest factors contributing to the success or failure of a modernization project. Many tool vendors provide legacy understanding (see section on Application Porfolio Management in Chapter 1) that can map data and logic, but these tools cannot always reveal the context, manual human processing, business rules, and other intangibles. Often, there is no documentation to assist in the uncovering of the business rules. So the SME can provide valuable insight into where this knowledge is hidden.

If the team does not have access to a Legacy SME, it is critical that test harnesses are carefully crafted so that testing can happen early and often during the modernization process. It is critical to engage end users early and maintain the engagement throughout the development, validation, and deployment processes in order to ensure that the new system being implemented meets the needs.

Risk of Modernization

A key issue in the large scale modernization of a system that is an integral part of the business, is to manage the risk of modernization on the current day-to-day operations. Many businesses that rely on their computing infrastructure for day-to-day operations have very low tolerance for disruptions to business as a result of downtime, data integrity issues, or customer service issues. A rigorous modernization strategy involving validation, insertion, and recovery actions for potential failures is necessary. Key stakeholders within the company, who are impacted by modernization, should be engaged in defining the validation and modernization strategy. For projects involving large scale system modernizations, phased modernization strategies, where business functions are transitioned from the legacy system to the newer system in a phased manner, provide the best risk mitigation strategy. However, this may require some upfront investment in creating insulation middleware such as Web-services-enabled Enterprise Application Integration (EAI) layer to hide the back-end systems from the end user interfaces.

System Performance

A key risk of change is impact on reliability, availability, and performance of the capabilities provided by the system. Modern systems based on mainstream operating systems (Linux/Windows) are designed with distributed component models having an extensible, customizable framework as the core engine, and typically partitioned with three or more tiers (User Interface (UI), Business Logic, Data Base (DB)). Performance of such a system is very dependent on data cardinality (amount of data objects stored in the system) and work load (number of concurrent users, type of usage). A detailed end user usage profile (data cardinality, users, and transaction types) should be analyzed and validated, and the system should be tuned to meet required performance specifications. A successful implementation requires upfront rigor in defining key usage patterns and performance targets **Service Level Agreements** (**SLA**), and ensuring that the system is tuned to meet these targets prior to deployment.

Usability/Training

While a modernization project is usually driven by goals to achieve cost reductions and performance, the end users who interact with the system are the final judges of the success of the implementation. Users who have deep entrenched knowledge of how the current legacy system behaves would need to have upfront training on mapping their usage (how to get the job done) with the new system. In case a system is deployed to a large number of users, upfront usability studies must be done to ensure that the new system user interface meets the efficiency goals of the users (number of mouse clicks, key board touches) to perform a task as compared to the existing system.

Re-Architecture versus Re-Host

There is an ongoing debate within the industry on the merits of re-architecture versus a re-host. Both options should be considered, and later in the book, we will give a brief overview of re-hosting with Tuxedo. The table that follows is a high-level, comparative overview of each approach. It is not meant to weigh one over the other, but to illuminate the merits and issues of each in light of the other.

	Re-Host	Re-Architect
Description	Modernization of legacy mainframe applications to lower cost modern platforms without significantly changing the business features and functions.	Forward engineering applications to the Java J2EE and Windows .NET A3, to achieve true enterprise agility. This approach includes Re-Learn and Re-Platform.

	Re-Host	**Re-Architect**
Benefits	Fast modernization capability.	Application extensibility and additional business functionality.
	In general, shorter return on investment (ROI) as compared to re-architect.	Elimination of unused and "dead code".
	Fairly mature toolset for CICS, COBOL, and DB2 environments.	Ability to re-architect into an SOA using modern toolsets, thereby enabling Best Shore capabilities for ongoing support.
		Conversion from "language and code" to "business rules".
		Ability to architect for use in a shared environment.
		Current technologies that can be supported by more resources in the marketplace today.
Drawbacks	No additional functionality.	Longer modernization timeframe.
	Limited automated assembler conversion tools available.	Lack of automated conversion tools.
	Limited reduction in ongoing support due to one-to-one conversion.	In general, longer ROI as compared to Re-Host.
	No elimination of unused and "dead code".	Overall cost of Re-Architect is not based on traditional metrics (such as lines of code).
	No fundamental change in structure; use of wrappers required to interact with modern software.	
	Re-Architecting of portions of code likely.	
	Potential performance issues due to the requirement to communicate to the operating system through legacy environment.	
	Business Intelligence (BI) and Analysis reporting limited to nonrelational file systems (for example VSAM, IMS).	

	Re-Host	Re-Architect
Target Markets	Large applications consisting of mainly COBOL, CICS, and DB2/VSAM.	Applications that need new or added functionality. Applications for which the existing technology and support structure can no longer be sustained (for example as a result of retirement).

> As a result of this paradigm shift, languages such as the Assembly language (for which at the moment there is no automated conversion in the re-host capability) will have no impact on the overall time frame and cost for re-architect.

There is no single, perfect strategy or approach to modernization. The overall business drivers can help determine the best approach to be used. One needs to evaluate each of the modernization strategies with respect to the business rules. Each has its strengths and weaknesses with regards to costs, time to market, maintainability, and implementation difficulty. There is no **best** modernization strategy. When considering an approach to modernization, one must consider the business drivers. It is possible that some or all of these strategies may be used in any given modernization effort.

When evaluating a re-host strategy, it is important to understand the technology issues that surround this modernization. Re-host implies a simple code shift and recompile. A re-hosting strategy allows modernization of existing business logic and processes to a new environment. It is a much shorter modernization path, and much less costly than re-architecture. When warranted, it also allows application enhancement as a follow on step to the modernization of the current environment.

Although application re-architecture is a more costly and time-consuming effort as compared to re-hosting, there are times when re-architecture of an application can be the correct business approach.

A Gartner report summarizes re-host in this fashion:

> *"Even with the advantages offered by these clones [in reference to re-host vendors Micro Focus, Sun and Fujitsu], the impact of software change related to recreating the mainframe operational environment is significant. Mainframe 4GLs or reporting products such as CA's CA-Easytrieve might be different. Capacity planning tools (such as RMF) must be replaced. Chargeback and accounting solutions (such as CA JARS) must be rebuilt. Except for DB2 or Software AG's Adabas, database migrations are usually required. Sorting software (such as IBM's DFSORT), a key component of most mainframe batch jobs may change. Most mainframe AD tooling for source change (such as IBM's ISPF), source control (such as CA'sEndeavor) and testing products (such as Compuware's Expediter or AbendAid) must be replaced. Job scheduling (such as CA's CA-7) and security products (such as IBM's RACF or CA'sTopSecret) must be changed. The software used to replace these functions is different, depending on whether the destination platform is Windows , Unix or Linux."*

> *Gartner – Publication Date: 10 January 2006/ID Number: G00134326*

Although these concerns can exist, as the Gartner/Meta report points out, in a properly planned and managed modernization, they can all be successfully addressed.

A mitigating factor of the above observations is that the majority of mainframe shops also have a mature Windows or Linux (or both) environment which has already identified these types of concerns. For example, Windows and Linux both have job scheduling systems, tools for source changes and tracking, security, database, and sort products.

These Windows and Linux environments are typically designed, structured and built using the same **Information Technology Infrastructure Library** (ITIL) best practices used in the mainframe environment.

An additional business issue masked as a technical issue that should be pointed out is that it is not the mainframe product that is important, it is the business concerns and rules the product addresses. For example, RACF; although RACF by name does not exist in a Windows or Linux environment, the business functions RACF addresses can be duplicated in a modernization effort.

Re-Architect Deep Dive

Re-architecture can be divided into four phases: recovery, re-factoring, re-specifying, and recreating.

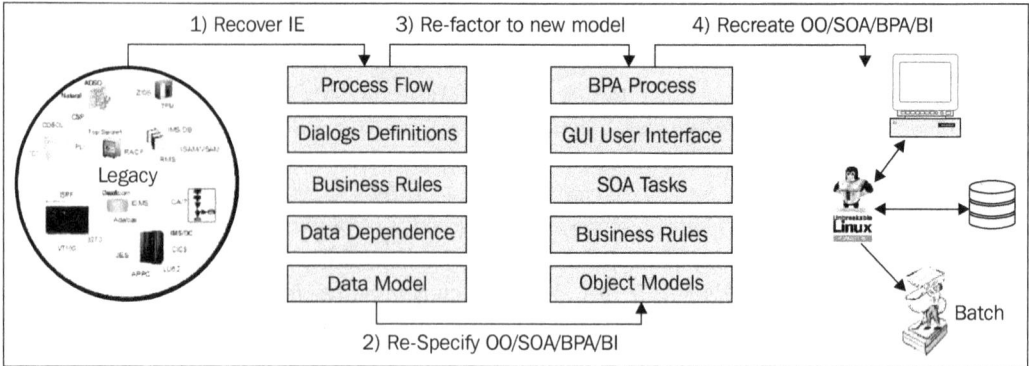

1. Recovery extracts the information from the current application at a detailed level. Things like "business rules mining" and "migration of existing app to UML" fit here. Recovery can be automated to a high degree, since it is mainly concerned with extracting models and model-like information form existing systems.

   The **Object Modeling Group (OMG)** is working in this area via the **ADM (Architecture-Driven Modernization)** group that is setting a **KDM (Knowledge Discovery MetaModel)** standard. This standard is for a common repository metamodel, where existing applications can be "mined". Recognizing that not everything of an existing application can be transformed to a design metamodel, they are also beginning work on an **ASTM (Abstract Syntax Tree MetaModel)** as a common representation for mapping legacy language constructs to a common model/syntax. This allows for transforming platform-dependent languages into platform-independent models.

2. Re-specification phase seeks building a foundation based on new development and design principles such as the SOA. This new stage will help develop new workflow models that are reflective of the future needs of the business. In many cases, this can be mapped to the current state of the system. For example, batch systems may be considered for more online applications in the target case, based on constraints like the CPU or usability. Perhaps the process can only be done in batch, in which case, the current model or case maps to the future state of the system. Another good example is looking at the report paradigm. All the reports in the current case may be mapped to a new specification of a data warehouse. It is important to note that with an advanced methodology and toolset, both current and future cases can be stored in the same model repository.

3. Re-factoring supports changes needed to transform the model information gathered in recovery to a more modern design, for example, a proper OO (object orientated) design, or one that is workflow driven. This process cannot be made 'push button', although tools can help. Deep re-factoring, say for deciding that four CICS programs (add Purchase Order, update Purchase Order, delete Purchase Order, approve Purchase Order) should be pulled apart, or that CICS code should be left behind, or that core logic should be turned into methods on a proper OO Purchase Order object with the screen handling separated and a workflow engine driving everything, takes human intelligence.

4. Re-generation stage is optional, but is included because of what OMG and others are doing. It is possible to re-architect direct to a new platform, but even if that platform is Java, which provides some separation from underlying environment via the Java Virtual Machine, one can do better yet. The latest concepts are that you should re-architect to another abstract, platform-independent model that is "modern" (OO architecture, BPA driven, and so on), and then generate to a platform-specific model that defines what runs where, what AppServer(s) are involved, and what communication mechanisms are being used.

If the approach follows an approach that transforms a recovered model to a "new" model first, then the approach is called Model Driven Modernization (MDM).

No Ripping and Replacing

Legacy SOA Integration was all about keeping the core of the system on the mainframe leveraging the legacy system, and extending it features, functionality, and ultimately its useful life. The next logical and practical step in modernization is considering moving off the mainframe. Re-architecture tools and services vendors can often fall on the ends of two very different spectrums:

- **Glorified green field** — The vendor claims to have tools, technologies, and products to forward engine legacy artifacts into Oracle, SOA, and J2EE. But in reality, it is mostly done manually with some legacy modernization best practices thrown in.

- **100 percent pure automation** — We already discussed this option, and it can really become **garbage in** and **garbage out**. As you can imagine, it is not easy to take the COBOL/CICS code that accesses a VSAM database and generates 100 percent performant, maintainable, Java/J2EE objects running against an Oracle database and an SOA grid.

Neither of these is the best way to move forward, and by the end of this chapter, you will know what it takes to truly re-architecture a legacy system to Oracle. This chapter will drill into how you leverage existing mainframe application artifacts and bring them forward into a flexible, agile, state-of-the-art, Oracle-based architecture. Re-architecting also goes by the names of: re-writing, re-engineering, legacy renewal, forward engineering, and 'rip and replace'. The last of the names (rip and replace) is a bit harsh. As the name implies (rip — to cause something, usually paper, to rapidly become two parts, and replace — to supply or substitute an equivalent), it is often used to belittle re-architecture as a viable alternative. What re-architecture does though is not just create an equivalent, but something much better, new, and improved.

Pros and Cons

With every choice, there are positives and negatives. The following section goes into a few of the pros and cons of both the business and technical perspectives of re-architecture. This is by no means exhaustive, but is based on real world experience.

Pros

The following are the pros:

- SLA management and Load Balancing — With the multinode Oracle database RAC, the workload management can be tailored to meet the specific performance SLAs of all the clients.

- High scalability—The system architecture is fully scalable, depending on the business needs. As the business grows, it can be scaled upward by throwing more machines into the grid to add additional processing power. If the business shrinks, or when the peak season is over, it may be scaled downwards, and the extra machines may be taken out without affecting the processing grid.

- HR—There are many more resources available and coming on to the workforce that has the skills to work within an open system environment. Legacy skills are dying quickly, and the older systems are harder to maintain, not just because of the structure and age, but also because of the lack of knowledge.

- Fast response time—New database design can be geared for high performance, which can yield quicker response time.

- High redundancy and failover—In the multinode Oracle database RAC, the system will continue to function even if three of the machines fail. Similarly, if one of the Application Servers fails, the other one will take over.

- High reliability—Due to the redundancy and failover, the system is very reliable, as much as a mainframe is.

- Built-in disaster recovery—Using Oracle Dataguard, the database is mirrored in real time on to the DR site. Adding an Application Server at the DR site will provide 100 percent application redundancy

- Easy incorporation of the rules engine—The Oracle BPEL Process Manager can easily incorporate any external rules engines.

- Full SOA stack—With re-architecture, a system can evolve from being a static linear application to a full-service-driven system.

- Easier to maintain—Due to its SOA-based framework, changes and new feature are easier to manage, integrate, and test.

Cons

- Cost—The cost of a re-architecture can be higher then an automated migration or a re-hosting, which has a higher level of automation.

- Risk—This strategy is often viewed as being riskier than re-hosting or automated migration. Again as in the previous point, as humans are involved in the technical aspects of the migration, there is a greater opportunity for error.

- Time—The time to deliver these projects can be quite long as compared to automated migrations or re-hosting.

- HR—New resources that understand the target software architecture, the database and the infrastructure must be acquired.

Summary

Every organization may be confronted with the issue of modernization of legacy applications. These applications are expensive to maintain, difficult to change, and are a major stumbling block for innovation. Though it is possible to start over, and develop these applications from scratch, it is a very costly exercise and entails a high degree of risk.

Through re-architecture, organizations can leverage the assets locked into their legacy applications and deliver new functionality. By leveraging specialized tools and processes, the organization can deliver the full promise of an agile system that can be easily maintained, and provide a flexible platform for future growth.

6
Re-Architecture—Functional View, Implementation, and Architecture

Legacy SOA Integration was all about keeping the core of the system on the mainframe while leveraging what the legacy system has, and extending its features, functionality, and ultimately its useful life. The next two most logical and practical steps in modernization are moving off the mainframe and re-hosting the system.

Re-architecture of legacy systems is significantly different from Legacy SOA Integration in a number of ways. You are changing not only the database and application components of your system, but also the entire supporting infrastructure. The infrastructure includes: hardware, management tools, printing and reporting, archiving, disaster recovery, backup and recovery, security, transaction management, debuggers, development tools, database utilities, information integration, application integration, and more. As compared to SOA Integration, re-architecture has a much more wide-open spectrum of possible target architectures and modernization implementation options. Re-architecture is a multidimensional set of technologies and business drivers, similar to a Rubik's cube. In this book, we will simplify the target architecture variable, by making a move to Oracle. Even as we do this, we will find a wide selection of Oracle products and technologies, which we will narrow down for you. Re-architecture involves a revolutionary change to the underlying database, application languages, workflow, presentation-tier, business rules, database access methods, and business processes. We will demonstrate how you can make this revolutionary transformation taking an evolutionary approach.

In Chapter 4, we focused on online systems, because batch SOA enablement is not as popular. However, this is changing as companies are looking to integrate mainframe batch jobs with open-system BPEL engines. This chapter will address batch and online systems because we see customer demand for both in re-architecture modernization. You can choose to modernize both batch and online systems, or perhaps, one, and not the other. It would be great to say all batch goes away, and the code is now all in Java EE, and is real time. This is most often not possible because it involves too many business practice, business processes and cultural changes. Batch is always considered the less fun aspect of mainframe applications. One of the top reasons why mainframe programming positions are unpopular is that programmers get tired of fixing SOC4s and SOC7s all night. However, batch processing is critical to most people's everyday lives as it still processes most of our credit card transactions, makes our daily bank deposits, and processes purchase orders. Batch time windows, the **Million Instructions Per Second** (**MIPS**) that it consumes, and the critical nature of the processing makes batch the first place a customer looks into during a re-architecture.

The approach to the actual modernization project can be top-down, bottom-up, or a combination of both. For our purposes, top-down means starting with the application-tier and generating the database. Top-down also implies the use of a **Business Process Analysis** (**BPA**) Suite to model your business processes. Bottom-up means starting with a new database and developing the application, business processes, and presentation-tier based on the new database schema.

We must also not forget the 'accidental architecture' mentioned in Chapter 4. Accidental architecture means that different systems talk to each other and rely on each other's data. Internal systems over which you have no control, may push or pull data from your system. Or even worse, external systems may communicate with your systems bi-directionally. This situation causes some companies to "freeze" or decide against modernizing their system (which is a decision).

So, given these variables, and the complexity of the situation, why is re-architect such an attractive proposition to companies? Let's look at some customer examples that drive companies to re-architect their systems:

- One customer estimated that 40 percent of the application code and batch processing is unused and no one knows what the other 10 percent does.

- A company must take the system offline for two to three hours a day for batch processing. Or even better, they take the system offline 12 hours a day for batch processing. When I hear this, it really makes me realize that reliability and availability are two very different subjects. A system can be reliable (does not go down unintentionally) but this does not mean it is available. Reliability means your system is up and running when you expect it to be. So, a system can be considered reliable even if it is only up during business hours. Avi/able means that the system can be used during anytime of the day or night.

- An end-user has to go to three different terminals to look up information on an account.

- The accounting department has to wait for days to find out which transactions have errors.

- Integrating a new customer file interface takes months when it should take days.

- Excel spreadsheets rule the company. A four-billion-dollar company does all its sales forecasting on spreadsheets

- A major government institution still processes most of its claims via paper forms, faxing, and mailing letters to claimants.

Recently, some additional drivers for re-architecturing have emerged: preparing for Generation X, paperless world, and going Green. Generation X has started to use technology in its early teens. The Generation X people are often referred to as the digital natives. They are comfortable with the Internet, and have grown up with Sony playstations. The world is also going "green", and businesses have been talking about the "paperless office" for years. Limited resources and an expanding world population have really brought together the worlds of "green technology" and "paperless office". Each of these makes the other one more of a possibility. As screens get bigger and easier to read, government regulations require fewer hard copy versions of checks and legal documents, fewer people will need "something to hold on to" and we will began to see a movement towards a "paperless office".

Technical Advantages of Re-Architecture

A re-architected system provides the IT organization with eight very important technical advantages.

Application Maintenance

Applications are easier to maintain, upgrade, and enhance as the presentation, business logic, workflow, business rules, security, and database persistence layers are separate. This gives you the ability to make changes to any tier of the application at any given time without impacting other layers. This is important as new technologies in different layers of the application become available at different times.

Enterprise Information Integration (EII) and Enterprise Application Integration (EAI)

We hear from customers over and over again about how difficult it is to add a new interface, support a new customer file, and about the amount of custom code, scripts and JCL dedicated to simple integration solutions. The outdated proprietary methods of FTPing flat files, or calling CICS transactions on another mainframe are replaced by EII and EAI products that are based on standards. EII and EAI tools and technologies give you the capability to create new application interfaces in days instead of months.

Architected for the Internet

Technologies used in Legacy SOA Integration can get you on the Web, but this does not mean the core of your application is built for the Internet. In a re-architectured solution, the architecture is built to support the Internet and SOA technologies. Your application architecture inherently includes HTTP, SOAP, Web services, HTML-based reporting, business process flows, portals, and business activity monitoring. In other words, your new open-systems application is built to be truly web enabled.

Scalability

Scalability is not all about being able to handle additional workload without significant degradation in response time. It is also about the ability to handle periodic workload changes such as end-of-year processing, sales traffic, or retailer's experience during the holidays. Database and application server grids are the perfect match for scalability. Not only can you scale out (add more databases, application server processes, storage, and hardware), but you can also provision your workload to utilize your hardware and software based on the current environment. So for the month of December, when your retail sales are higher, more machines can be dynamically configured to handle sales transactions. When December 31 rolls around and you need to close your books for the year, your infrastructure can be changed to handle financial and accounting transactions.

Availability

Mainframe systems can certainly be called reliable, but availability is a whole new subject. In the age of the Internet, clients expect your systems to be up 24X7, all through the year. Legacy systems are typically down anywhere from two to twelve hours a night for batch processing. Much of this has to do with the lack of concurrency built into legacy databases. When the legacy applications were developed, applications were not expected to be available all day. Businesses did not operate on a global scale in what is often a twenty-four-hour day. IT systems were architectured to match the business requirements of the time. These systems, however, do not match the business requirements of today.

With the advent of grid computing, open systems infrastructure and the application and database software that runs on top of it are built to operate 24X7/365. Maximum Availability Architectures are commonplace in open systems as businesses expect the system to be Always on.

Greater Software Options

The major software vendors' product strategies are focused on relational database, SQL, Java, .NET and open-systems hardware platforms. Therefore, the entire ecosystem that exists in software development tools, database and application management tools, ISV applications, COTS applications, and hardware and storage support is in thousands, instead of dozens or maybe hundreds. The combination of more options, more competition, and more standards-based technologies lower the acquisition cost, support and maintenance costs, and increase customer service. It is only logical that the open market creates more choices for you at a lower cost with better service.

On Demand Reporting

One of the main reasons for the proliferation of spreadsheet, Microsoft Access applications, departmental level systems, and "the guy in accounting who took a night class on Crystal Reports" creating dozens of reports which potentially have queries that run for hours, is that in the legacy world it took way too long for the IT department to respond to new reporting and business intelligence requests. So the user community took it upon themselves to solve the problem. Departmental databases and spreadsheet-driven applications became part of the corporate fabric, and many companies rely on these systems for mission critical processing such as sales forecasting, inventory control, budgeting, and purchasing. The information is in the legacy system, but it is too difficult to get to, manipulate, and report on. With hundreds of open systems reporting, querying, data mining, and BI tools in the market place, users can access the re-architected relational database themselves. Or the IT department can easily create the reports or the BI system that the user community is asking for.

Security

Security is often seen as the domain of the mainframe. We hear, "My mainframe is so secure that I am never going to move off". On the other hand, we also hear of companies getting off the mainframe because there is no way to encrypt the data. Relational databases on open systems have built-in security, so IT personnel cannot access data that is not part of their daily job. They also offer transparent data encryption. Remember, most security breaches are made by your own people. This is security of data at rest. Then, there is the security of data on the network, and application-based security. This is where open-system options such as network encryption, single sign, user id provisioning, federated identity management and virtual directories, make sure open systems are more secure than your legacy environment.

Overcoming Barriers to Change

You can always tell the folks in the room who are just waiting for retirement and don't want the mainframe to "retire before they do". Often we can hear them say, "This can't be done", "our system is way to complicated", "only a mainframe can handle this workload", "we have tried this before and it failed". Then you find out that they are running a 300 MIP mainframe with about one million lines of code and about two gigabytes of data. In some cases, you can handle this processing on a two node dual core processor! Or, you may find out that the system is really just a bunch of flat file interfaces that apply 300 business rules and send transactions out to third parties. This can be re-architectured to modern platform, using technologies such as Extract, Transform, and Load (ETL) that did not exist 20 years ago.

You also have to be careful when re-architecting a legacy system, as the business processes and data entry screens, as well as the people who use them, have been around for decades. You have to balance the amount of technology change with the amount of change your business community can digest. You would think that all companies would want an Internet-based web interface to a re-architected system. However, I know of at least one occasion wherein a re-architecture **System Integrator (SI)** had to include a third-party screen emulation vendor that actually turned HTML into 3270 "green screens". So now, the users could have the same look and feel, including PF keys, on the web as they did on their character-based dumb terminals.

One of the most discouraging aspects of my role as a modernization architect is that many companies re-architect legacy systems but continue to custom code application features that can be found in off-the-shelf technology products. This happens often because they don't know the new technologies properly (or even that they exist), developers 'still like to code', or they cannot change their mind set from 'not invented here' (meaning that we know the best way to do this). We discussed this topic in Chapter 4 in the context of how to build a Legacy SOA Integration architecture. We will discuss it again because it is an important topic and one that continues to amaze me.

Custom Integration Applications and Utilities

With all the EII and EAI technologies in the market place, we still see modern-day architects decide that they can write their own, or write it better than a vendor who has spent ten years developing the solution. Initial cost (or sticker shock, some may say) is another reason. The client looks at the initial cost only, and not at the cost of maintenance, adding new interfaces, and of supporting another in-house software application. Looking at the total cost of ownership, in most cases, the advantages of using an EII or EAI product will outweigh the use of FTP and flat files, or some variant of this typical home grown integration application.

Custom Workflow

As indicated previously, workflow in legacy applications is often built into the COBOL/CICS module or is implicitly part of the JCL batch system. You would think companies that run legacy systems would have learned their lesson that this makes maintenance a nightmare and ends up costing large amounts of money, since changes to the COBOL module or JCL disrupt workflow, and vice versa. These new open systems will then have the same problem that exists in legacy code today—the code cannot be changed since no one knows what impact the change will have on processing.

Custom ETL

I once questioned a developer in a large corporation's data warehousing group on why they are not using an "out of the box" ETL/ELT product, to which I got the reply, "we are a development organization, and we like to develop stuff". Someone at the company needs to tell this person they are supporting business users and the business, and if an ETL tool can do the job, then it makes the business happy because it costs less.

Undisciplined Development

Another area where customers are making the same mistakes they did 30 years ago, and creating a new legacy system with modern technologies, is in their random and tactical approach to building applications. I see many modernized systems using a combination of Java, JavaScript, .NET, PERL, CSH, VB, C, C++, PHP, AJAX, and the list goes on. Many applications have hard-coded business rules and presentation-tier validations. When asked why they do this, we are told it is because of their in-house skills, or that they started to modernize but had no modernization governance, and so ended up with pockets of modernized systems using different approaches and development tools. It frightens me to think that we are creating the legacy of tomorrow, today. I hope that the information in this chapter will help other organization not to make the same mistakes when re-architecting their legacy systems.

Decoupling the Application-Tiers

We are going to 'come out swinging' and show you the code right away in this chapter. One of the key principals in re-architecting a legacy application is to decouple the application, business rules, presentation, workflow, and data access logic. This 'future proofs' your application from business and technology changes and advancements. If new technology advances bring out less costly and more productive presentation technologies (or more likely your business users want to support a new device such as an iPhone), you can add this support without impacting other layers of the application. Here are some code "snippets" of presentation, business rules, data access, and workflow all in one COBOL module.

Presentation-Tier

When you see CICS send and/or receive MAP statement, you know you are dealing with the presentation-tier. Here is some code direct from an online CICS-based COBOL module. This code is a simple send of the appropriate CICS screen MAP to the terminal (most likely a 3270 device) when the transaction "INQ3" is executed by the user. In Java EE terms, this would be like an HTML form using HTTP "post" to send the web browser screen to the web server from a URL:

```
1500-SEND-INQUIRY-MAP.

        MOVE 'INQ3' TO CIM-D-TRANID.
        EVALUATE TRUE
            WHEN SEND-ERASE
                EXEC CICS
                    SEND MAP('INQMAP3')
```

```
                          MAPSET('INQSET3')
                          FROM(CUSTOMER-INQUIRY-MAP)
                          ERASE
                  END-EXEC
          WHEN SEND-DATAONLY
              EXEC CICS
                  SEND MAP('INQMAP3')
                          MAPSET('INQSET3')
                          FROM(CUSTOMER-INQUIRY-MAP)
                          DATAONLY
                  END-EXEC
          WHEN SEND-DATAONLY-ALARM
              EXEC CICS
                  SEND MAP('INQMAP3')
                          MAPSET('INQSET3')
                          FROM(CUSTOMER-INQUIRY-MAP)
                          DATAONLY
                          ALARM
                  END-EXEC
          END-EVALUATE.
```

Business Rules

One big IF statement with a lot of branching and decisions tells you that you have found a possible business rule. This code is used to determine the type of customer you are working with and then calls the appropriate COBOL paragraph to do customer-specific processing:

```
S3100-VALIDATE-CB-PARM SECTION.

    MOVE WORK-PARM-BUREAU           TO W-HOLD-WORK-PARM-BUREAU.
    PERFORM S9100-COMMON-TRANSLATION.
    SET CBC-NDX TO +1.
    SEARCH CBC-TABLE-ENTRY VARYING CBC-NDX

    WHEN CBC-CODE-PARM(CBC-NDX) = WORK-PARM-BUREAU
            NEXT SENTENCE
    WHEN CBC-CODE-PARM(CBC-NDX) = W-HOLD-WORK-PARM-BUREAU
            NEXT SENTENCE.

    IF RETRIEVE-STAND-ALONE
            SEARCH W-CUR-PARM-TBL

        AT END MOVE ZERO TO W-LINE-NUMBER
    WHEN W-CUR-PARM-CHAR(PARM-NDX) = C-SLASH
            PERFORM S3150-VALIDATE-LINE-NUM
        WHEN W-CUR-PARM-CHAR(PARM-NDX) = C-COMMA
```

```
        MOVE ZERO      TO W-LINE-NUMBER.

    IF  (ONLINE-TRANS-ID AND (RETRIEVE-STAND-ALONE OR
                             SEND-AND-HOLD-CRED-RPT OR
                             SEND-AND-SCAN-CRED-RPT))
        NEXT SENTENCE
    ELSE
        GO TO S3100-VALIDATE-CB-PARM-EXIT.

    IF  PAGE-COAP
        IF  COAPPLICANT-PRESENT
            NEXT SENTENCE
        ELSE
            MOVE PARMERR TO PCF-ERROR-DATA.


    IF  BUSINESS-APPLICANT OR BUSINESS-COAP-PRESENT
        GO TO P3100-BUSINESS-EDIT
    ELSE
        NEXT SENTENCE.

    IF  PAGE-COAP
        IF WORK-PARM-RPT-NUM = C-P
            IF OLNA-CO-PRE-ZIP-CANADA
                PERFORM S3110-CO-PRE-ZIP-CHECK
            ELSE
                NEXT SENTENCE
        ELSE
            IF OLNA-CO-ZIP-CANADA
                PERFORM S3120-CO-ZIP-CHECK
            ELSE
                NEXT SENTENCE
    ELSE
        IF WORK-PARM-RPT-NUM = C-P
            IF OLNA-PREV-ZIP-CANADA
                PERFORM S3130-PRE-ZIP-CHECK
            ELSE
                NEXT SENTENCE
        ELSE
            IF OLNA-ZIP-CANADA
                PERFORM S3140-ZIP-CHECK
            ELSE
```

Data Access

Data access in COBOL is done through CICS, direct SQL, or READ, WRITE, INSERT, UPDATE, and DELETE statements. Here is a CICS READ in the same COBOL module, which reads the customer information that was entered on a terminal using a CICS transaction, had business rules applied to it, and then written to the VSAM file using a CICS WRITE. Here, we are reading the customer record using a CICS READ:

```
1000-READ-CUSTOMER-FOR-UPDATE.
        EXEC CICS
            READ FILE('CUSTMAS')
                INTO(CUSTOMER-MASTER-RECORD)
                RIDFLD(CM-CUSTOMER-NUMBER)
                UPDATE
                RESP(RESPONSE-CODE)
        END-EXEC.
        IF     RESPONSE-CODE NOT = DFHRESP(NORMAL)
            AND RESPONSE-CODE NOT = DFHRESP(NOTFND)
            PERFORM 9999-TERMINATE-PROGRAM
        END-IF.
```

Workflow/Business Process Flow

Most COBOL modules, like this one, will begin with some type of workflow processing. Workflow in a COBOL module is typically identified by the IF or CASE statements that execute call outs to other programs or subroutines to perform the necessary processing. The code in this case will process the **PF** key pressed by the user on the main customer maintenance screen. Depending on the action the user chooses, the appropriate COBOL program or submodule will be called:

```
0000-PROCESS-CUSTOMER-MAINT.
    *
        IF EIBCALEN > ZERO
            MOVE DFHCOMMAREA TO COMMUNICATION-AREA
        END-IF.
    *
        EVALUATE TRUE
    *
            WHEN EIBCALEN = ZERO
                MOVE LOW-VALUE TO MNTMAP1O
                SET SEND-ERASE TO TRUE
                MOVE -1 TO CUSTNO1L
                PERFORM 1500-SEND-KEY-MAP
                SET PROCESS-KEY-MAP TO TRUE
```

```
      *
                   WHEN EIBAID = DFHPF3
                       EXEC CICS
                           XCTL PROGRAM('INVMENU')
                       END-EXEC
      *
                   WHEN EIBAID = DFHPF12
                       IF PROCESS-KEY-MAP
                           EXEC CICS
                               XCTL PROGRAM('INVMENU')
                           END-EXEC
                       ELSE
                           MOVE LOW-VALUE TO MNTMAP1O
                           MOVE -1 TO CUSTNO1L
                           SET SEND-ERASE TO TRUE
                           PERFORM 1500-SEND-KEY-MAP
                           SET PROCESS-KEY-MAP TO TRUE
                       END-IF
      *
                   WHEN EIBAID = DFHCLEAR
                       IF PROCESS-KEY-MAP
                           MOVE LOW-VALUE TO MNTMAP1O
                           MOVE -1 TO CUSTNO1L
                           SET SEND-ERASE TO TRUE
                           PERFORM 1500-SEND-KEY-MAP
                       ELSE
                           MOVE LOW-VALUE TO MNTMAP2O
                           MOVE CA-CUSTOMER-NUMBER TO CUSTNO2O
                           EVALUATE TRUE
                               WHEN PROCESS-ADD-CUSTOMER
                                   MOVE ADD-INSTRUCTION    TO INSTR2O
                               WHEN PROCESS-CHANGE-CUSTOMER
                                   MOVE CHANGE-INSTRUCTION TO INSTR2O
                               WHEN PROCESS-DELETE-CUSTOMER
                                   MOVE DELETE-INSTRUCTION TO INSTR2O
                           END-EVALUATE
                           MOVE -1 TO LNAMEL
                           SET SEND-ERASE TO TRUE
                           PERFORM 1400-SEND-DATA-MAP
                       END-IF
      *
                   WHEN EIBAID = DFHPA1 OR DFHPA2 OR DFHPA3
                       CONTINUE
      *
```

```
            WHEN EIBAID = DFHENTER
                EVALUATE TRUE
                    WHEN PROCESS-KEY-MAP
                        PERFORM 1000-PROCESS-KEY-MAP
                    WHEN PROCESS-ADD-CUSTOMER
                        PERFORM 2000-PROCESS-ADD-CUSTOMER
                    WHEN PROCESS-CHANGE-CUSTOMER
                        PERFORM 3000-PROCESS-CHANGE-CUSTOMER
                    WHEN PROCESS-DELETE-CUSTOMER
                        PERFORM 4000-PROCESS-DELETE-CUSTOMER
                END-EVALUATE
   *
            WHEN OTHER
                IF PROCESS-KEY-MAP
                    MOVE LOW-VALUE TO MNTMAP1O
                    MOVE 'That key is unassigned.' TO MSG1O
                    MOVE -1 TO CUSTNO1L
                    SET SEND-DATAONLY-ALARM TO TRUE
                    PERFORM 1500-SEND-KEY-MAP
                ELSE
                    MOVE LOW-VALUE TO MNTMAP2O
                    MOVE -1 TO LNAMEL
                    MOVE 'That key is unassigned.' TO MSG2O
                    SET SEND-DATAONLY-ALARM TO TRUE
                    PERFORM 1400-SEND-DATA-MAP
                END-IF
   *
        END-EVALUATE.
   *
        EXEC CICS
            RETURN TRANSID('MNT1')
                    COMMAREA(COMMUNICATION-AREA)
        END-EXEC.
```

Re-Architecture is Happening

If you don't believe me that modernization is a popular trend, just pick up any IT journal or analyst report. CIO/Computerworld Nextgen IT survey: Data Center Consolidation Jul 06, 2006: "Over the next three years, 44 percent of those surveyed plan to eliminate their mainframe environment and 17 percent will reduce the number of installed MIPs. 22 percent will maintain their current level of MIPs and 17 percent will hold steady at their current number of MIPs". Given that, there are an estimated 15,000 mainframes in the world, and many companies eliminating the mainframe are re-architecting, this means a lot of work for us in the next two to ten years.

In this section, we have laid the foundation for what we will focus on in the remainder of this chapter and the next three chapters. This foundation proposes that:

- Re-architecture is a viable approach that companies are using today.

- Re-architecture implies technical advantages over other approaches.

- You should not try to reinvent the wheel by writing your own customer workflow or EII applications.

- We are focused on separating the tiers of the application when we re-architect.

- The separation of the application-tiers (presentation, business, work flow, and data access) is key to implementing a 'future proof' SOA architecture.

> **Keeping It Real**: There is no magic bullet provided by any vendor in the modernization space that will re-architect your system in a model repository-driven automated fashion. Stay clear of any vendor that promises 100 percent code generation — if you know anything about legacy systems, you would never believe that. Also, don't get dazzled by companies that have tools and technologies to forward-engineer your system into Oracle and Java. Most of the tools and technologies are best practices, methodologies, and utilities usable only by the modernization vendor. Re-architecture is very much possible and probably accounts for most of the modernization success stories in the last few years. However, you have to make sure you plan correctly and take an iterative approach with small wins that can be delivered quickly.

Re-architecture—Functional View

In the SOA chapter, we mentioned that the business community does not care to hear about IMS, VSAM, CICS, IMS-TM, 3270, and other legacy technologies. This is true when you are focused on Legacy SOA Integration. When you are talking about the users' entire IT experience, how they view their world expands. Users do care and know about online systems and batch processing. This is because when one of these systems is down, or they did not get their favorite report from the night before they know why this is so. End-users also know the CICS transactions they execute every day to get their job done better than the IT manager know the IDs to these transactions. End-users also know why they cannot log into their online system because batch processing did not complete from the night before. Finally, they know when something has gone wrong with the nightly cycles if the new transactions or reporting files they are expecting cannot be not found. Their more sophisticated and holistic view of the world looks like this:

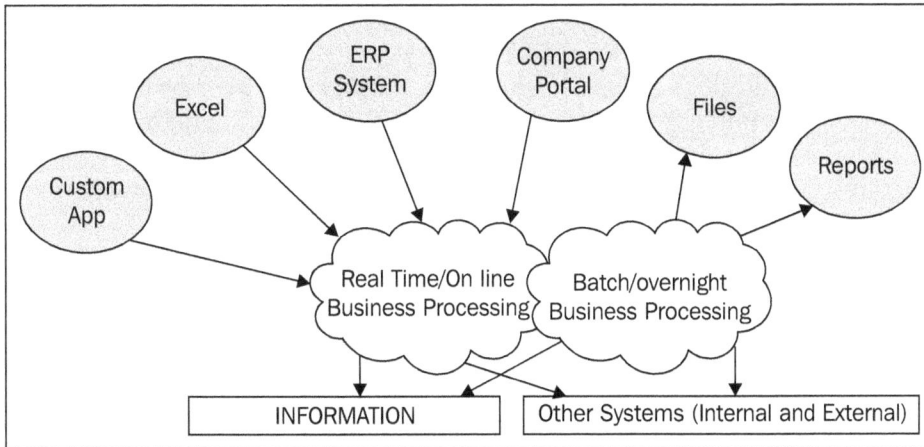

The business community sees the business processes/services as a cloud. It may not be something they can touch but they do understand the pain if the batch or online components of this cloud are not functioning properly. They realize that the information they need comes real time through an online screen or is processed nightly, weekly, monthly, or yearly in something called a batch cycle. The information exists somewhere in a dark corner of the IT department, or maybe on their laptop or in an Excel spreadsheet. Either way, they are going to find ways to get the information when they need it, and in a manner they want. So if we as the IT people don't make the information timely, easy, and flexible, they will do it themselves.

Their functional view of the world consists of five things:

- Applications, reports, and files: Reports and files are two user tools that we have not spoken about yet. The first thing most legacy IT users do in the morning is to check to see if their "green bar" reports have been delivered, and the file outputs from the previous night have been generated correctly. In the words of some users, "This may not seem the most efficient way to do business, but this is the way it has always been done".

- Real Time/Online Business Processes: Create new account, check account status, check payment information, submit purchase order, and the list goes on. These are all the business processes and services the user community executes every day. These are mostly executed through "green screens".

- Batch/overnight Business Processes: These are the processes that get executed every night in the precious, and sometimes precarious, batch cycles. These batch cycles do even more intensive processing during month, quarter, and year end.

- Information (you need): These are the databases and external applications where all the information is stored.

- Other applications (you talk with): Users realize that their system will sometimes talk with other systems during the day and at night. This is because they either find that their information is incorrect, or that a transaction is not getting processed as the helpdesk told them another system was down.

Although "green screen" is the end user's interface, most of the processing and delivery of business community key decision-making information happens in the batch cycle and "green bar" reports.

A Technical Perspective of the Functional View

Re-architecture involves taking a 360 degree view of the legacy system. This means that both the user's functional view and the technical functional view become more sophisticated. From the IT department's technical perspective, the functional view of re-architecture looks like this:

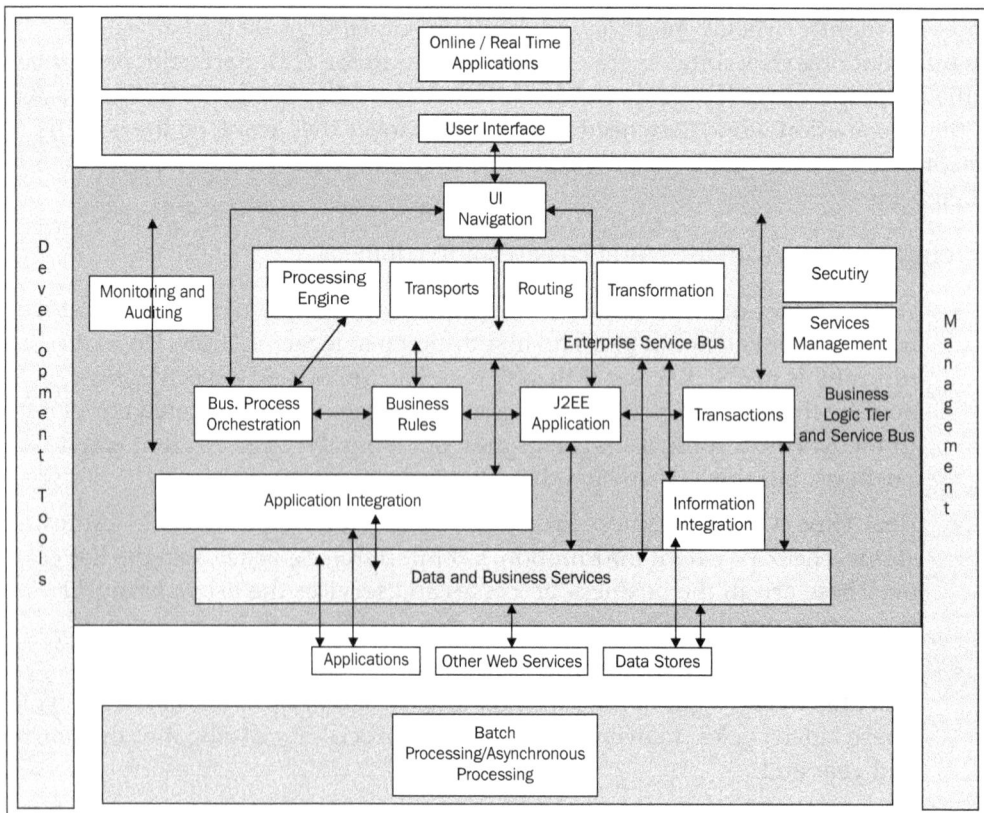

Because re-architecture removes processing from the mainframe, the technical functional view must take into account the entire IT infrastructure from online reporting, to management and development. Let's just take a look at the four components that are at the top, bottom, and sides of this diagram. This functional infrastructure that surrounds our 360 degree view of the IT processing system consists of these four components:

- Online/Real time applications: Online applications get all the glory because they are what the users view most of the day. They are also typically the most pretty to look at (well not in the mainframe world of green screens), when compared to "green bar" reports and batch scheduler output. Online applications are also popular because they give instant response in the form of synchronous request and response fashion.

- Batch Processing: Batch applications in legacy system do most of the heavily lifting and process most of the mission critical data. They also perform many of the functions critical to businesses such as reporting and file generation. Batch is also critical to IT as it is here that all backup and archiving takes place. Batch system processes are managed and monitored through a job scheduler.

- Management: System management in the legacy world includes everything from devices, networks such as SNA, print, database, backup and recovery, operating system, and department usage chargeback.

- Development Tools: We did use some development tools in the Legacy SOA Integration. However, because the code and databases remained on the mainframe, the tools we used were supplemental. For re-architecture, the core development tools are now running on open systems. This includes modeling, application development, business rules maintenance, process flows, testing, database access development, database development, and debugging. Therefore, discussing development tools in this chapter is critical.

Other Components of the Functional Infrastructure

We don't want to cover functional areas that were already covered in the Legacy SOA Integration chapter. The new areas we are introducing in this chapter (and we will map back to in the Legacy SOA Integration chapter when pertinent) consists of four basic components:

- Business Logic Tier: The Business Logic Tier was the **Legacy Business Logic Tier (LBLT)** in the SOA chapter. We drop the word legacy since we are no longer focused on integrating with legacy systems. This is not to say that you won't possibly be doing legacy integration after you're done re-architecturing. You probably will, as some of your systems will still be on the mainframe. However, it just will not be the focal point of your architecture going forward. The Business Logic Tier contains your SOA software and Application Server among other components: security, monitoring, and auditing as discussed in Chapter 4. The components not covered in the Legacy SOA Integration chapter that we will review now include:

  - Business Rules: As we saw in the code example in the introduction section of this chapter, the business rules on the mainframe were embedded in your application code. **Business Rules Engines** (**BRE**) will house all your business rules in the re-architected application. Business rules will be created, updated, and maintained using a BRE UI.

  - Java EE Applications: All your applications on the mainframe which are written in COBOL, REXX, Assembler, JCL, and other languages. Now they are either in JAVA EE, or embedded in an open-system product.

  - Transactions: Mainframe transactions executed in a transaction processor. Transaction processing will now take place in the middle-tier and/or the database. Both these open-system entities provide all the transaction support you need.

  - UI Navigation: The concept of a specific tier for UI/screen navigation did not exist when most mainframe applications were written. As we saw in the code samples earlier, the screen flow was hard-coded into the application. The re-architected application will now have a separate layer for UI navigation.

- Data and Business Services: In SOA, we had a Legacy Services Engine (connectivity and processing) component that is used to connect to, and process information and transactions from and to the mainframe system. In the re-architected system, we now have database persistence and business services tier. The business services tier consists mostly of Web services.

- Data Store: Legacy SOA Integration maintained all the data on the mainframe. The re-architecture process will migrate all this data into a relational database on open systems. This could be an OLTP, OLAP, ROLAP, operational data store, data mart, and/or data warehouse. At this point, the type of database we are moving to is not important.

- Applications and Other Web Services: Applications APIs for Oracle E-Business Suite (PL/SQL, Interface tables) and SAP (BAPI) are commonly used as some applications don't have Web services, or, are not fully Web service enabled.

Re-architecture—Optional Software Components

Individuals familiar with open-systems IT infrastructure are also familiar with caching, or content management. This functionality was intentionally excluded because we needed to be focused on the initial round of re-architecture and did not want to add too many "shiny new objects". "Shiny new objects" are, in the IT department's view, new products or technologies that are nice to have but introduce scope creep. Some of these additional features and functionality include:

- Caching: Web, data, and application caching are all hot technology items. They can help significantly with overall system performance. Caching is something that can be added to the system after it has been re-architectured as most caching technologies are nonintrusive.

- Business Intelligence (BI): Modernization and BI go hand in hand (a big driver for modernization is better, more cost effective BI), and BI is a very extensive topic in the context of modernization. Some of the top reasons customers are undertaking modernization be it through SOA Integration, re-host, re-architecture, COTS, or automated migration are, reducing reporting costs on the mainframe, delivering reports in a more timely fashion, and providing ad hoc and "what if" BI tools to users. Report off-loading with a BI front end has already been discussed in Chapter 4.

- Content Management: Many mainframe processes are still paper based. Forms are manually filled out, faxed, scanned and emailed, and stored in a file system. Document management has come a long way since manual-driven custom mainframe applications were developed years ago. This is another area that is very broad and also specific to the type of system being modernized.

- Radio-frequency identification (RFID): RFID is an emerging technology that has become increasingly important. Since it is so new, RFID support is something to be addressed after the initial re-architecture. It is also something that does not exist in most legacy systems.

- Spatial: Like RFID, spatial support in applications is an emerging technology -even though spatial has been around much longer then RFID. It has been more present in niche applications, and is not yet mainstream.

Keeping It Real: The functional view hopefully gave you an appreciation of what is important to users; that the tools they use to do their job every day are available. When making a transition from mainframe to open systems during re-architecture, the biggest challenge is not technological. The biggest challenge is that business people expect systems to be available and business processes to be predictable. While for IT, the challenge is to create a system that is cost-effective, and can be efficiently managed. You need to be careful about how much change is introduced during the re-architecture process. Change, even for the better, causes real stress on business and IT people. Extensive business processing re-engineering may be the strategic objective, but re-architecture mostly takes a phased approach that slowly introduces change, and "shiny new objects".

Implementation Process: Common Attributes, Approach for Batch, and Online Processes

So if re-architecture provides you with such a great architecture that is flexible, adaptable, less costly, easier to maintain, web enabled, also and mimics your business model, why isn't everyone 'jumping on the bandwagon'? The answer lies in the "holy grail" of **Architecture Driven Modernization (ADM)** that looks like this:

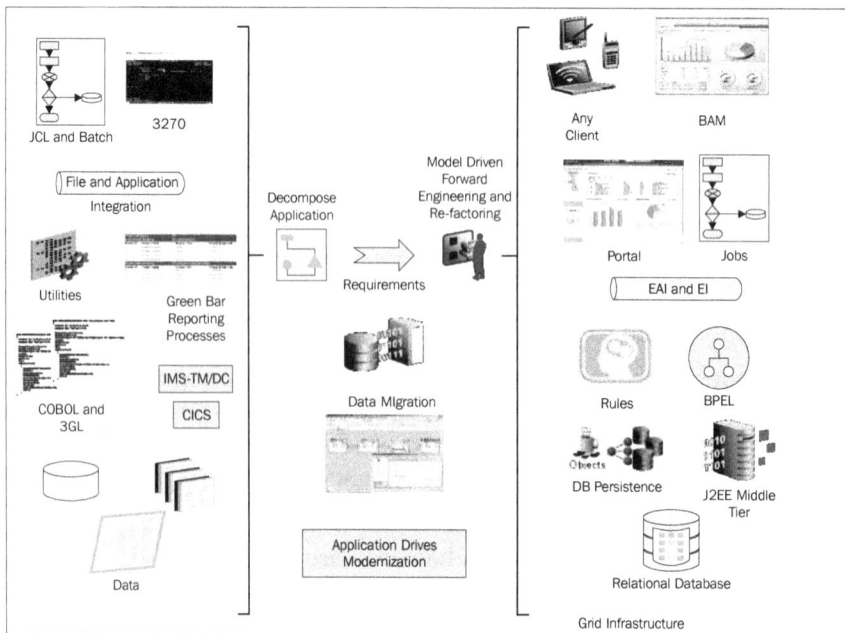

The ADM as shown here has seven steps, which are all tool and model-driven:

1. Discover (understand) all legacy artifacts.
2. Store all the legacy artifacts in a model-based repository.
3. Undertake model-driven forward engineering and re-engineering based on the information in the source repository.
4. Generate the target model.
5. Undertake model-driven forward engineering and re-engineering based on information in the target repository.
6. Generate new database schema and migrate the data.
7. Generate the new application with separate tiers for presentation, UI navigation, business rules, business processing, security, and SOA data services.

The good news is that the IT industry is moving in the direction of ADM. The **Object Management Group (OMG)** created the ADM subcommittee several years ago. This committee is focused on creating UML (with XML and XMI) standards in both the Understanding/Discovery and re-architecturing/forward engineering spaces. In the understanding/discovery space, the Knowledge Discovery Meta-Model (KDM) has been ratified and has created a common UML-based repository for all vendors to use. In the re-architecturing space, the Abstract Syntax Tree MetaModel (ASTM) will provide a standard for all forward re-engineering services and tool vendors to use, so that all language translation tools (that participate) use the same model and are all UML-based. Interestingly enough, many of the modernization vendors mentioned in this document, including Oracle, are part of the OMG ADM subcommittee. The most recent information related to this effort can be found here: `http://adm.omg.org/`.

The second piece of good news is that in most legacy re-architecture modernization projects we have encountered, the mainframe is usually between 400-1000 MIPS. According to industry estimates, this is where about 80 percent of the mainframe applications reside. The amount of application code is usually in the range of one to three million lines of COBOL code. Although not so much about lines of COBOL code, as about integration, interdependencies, number of different databases, utilities, or infrastructure migration. We do find that the number of MIPS and the complexes just mentioned go together — the more the lines of code, the more the chances for different databases, and the more the integration and interdependencies. Systems in the 400-1000 MIPS range are the sweat spots for re-architecture.

Some important things to keep in mind as you start your re-architecture journey are:

- Currently, most aspects of re-architecture modernization are more 'art' then science. Re-architecture is more a process. It is service-driven via methodology supplemented by automation and tooling.

- Even the most advanced modernization system integrators and service providers need "niche" partners to complete a modernization project. These niche partners provide very specific expertise in a legacy application language or database.

- In determining the tools and SI vendors needed, it is often a situation of "it depends" (for example, location, current customer relationships with system integrators, legacy source technologies).

- Moving legacy data such as DB2, VSAM, ISAM, IMS, and IDMS is relatively easier in the context of the entire legacy application and infrastructure. Moving the application that uses this data is more complex. Moving the infrastructure will involve change, as well as extensive training in new products and technologies.

- It is important to limit the number of tools and services vendors involved in a modernization project. However, it is not uncommon to involve several vendors.

- Avoid a "big bang" approach — trying to move all your systems at once, or moving a big application into production over a weekend. The companies that have been successful take a system that is isolated from the "accidental architecture". Remember, the "accidental architecture" includes systems that have multiple integration points. Successful companies use a RAD/Agile approach where small projects with less risks and costs produce quick wins that provide immediate business benefit. It is all about taking the modern agile approach to software development.

Although a "big bang" scenario is technically feasible, in reality, it is very difficult and risky for any organization to accomplish the ideal target architecture in a single re-architecting project. You must "break down" the modernization project into byte-sized chunks/phases, bearing in mind the final goal of achieving a process-driven SOA architecture.

Top Three Re-Architecture Approaches

There are three basic, phased approaches to re-architecture: process, application, and data. The chosen phased approach will depend on a number of factors such as the size of the applications, the degree the application is standalone, the cost savings, and the ROI from moving a particular application. These approaches are not mutually exclusive (you could do all three), and the overall implementation project needs to be both iterative and phased in nature:

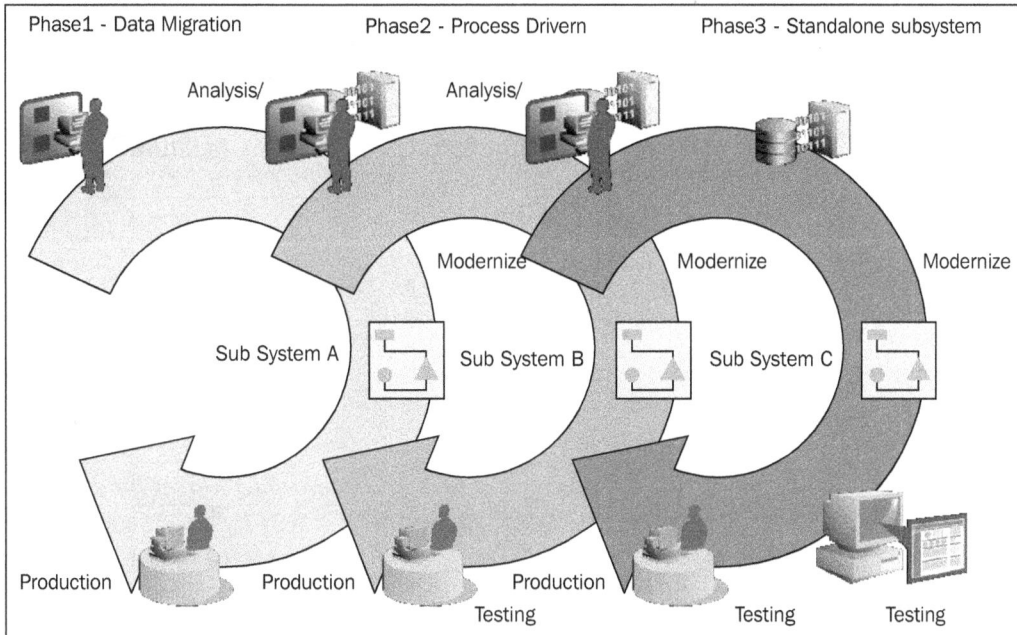

Three "Iterative-Phased" Approaches (IPA)

We are not suggesting you follow the above approaches in the exact order of the phases as shown in the diagram. You could start with a standalone application, or perhaps move business processes off the mainframe. The "iterative-phased" approaches in the order shown in the diagram is typical of how we see customers perform re-architecture. If your most urgent need is to encrypt data, you will probably start with the data migration approach. If you have an application that does not rely on application logic, or data from other applications, you can start by moving a standalone application. Or, if you find that you are already re-aligning business processes and applications to mirror your business processes more closely, start with moving business processes then move small pieces of the actual application code. To help you make the right choice, we will cover each approach in detail.

Data Migration

This phase is very similar to the report off-loading scenario discussed in Chapter 4. It involves moving the data off the mainframe, but keeping the application on the mainframe and "pointing it" to the relational database on open systems. It is a very logical first choice for re-architecture as you effectively 'avoid' the most challenging aspects of the modernization effort: application and infrastructure migration. Oracle Access Manager for CICS is a method to use that allows you to keep the application on the mainframe. It was originally developed to run CICS transactions against an Oracle database on the mainframe. The Oracle Pro Family of embedded SQL language precompilers including Pro*COBOL, Pro*C, and Pro*PL/I can also be used to access an Oracle database from a legacy system when CICS or IMS/TM are not involved. Oracle Access Manager of CICS/IMS and Oracle Pro* products can be configured to talk to an Oracle database running on open systems as follows:

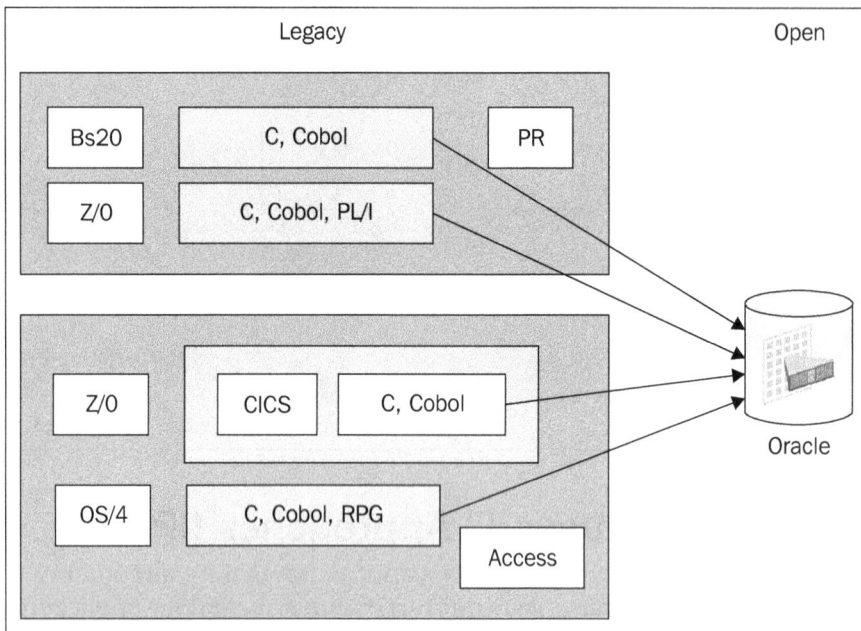

> **Keeping It Real**: Although the option of keeping the application on the mainframe and migrating the data seems very logical, this is not something we have seen in production often. Most customers who use data migration as the first step are using it to offload reporting, data warehousing/BI, and/or building new applications against this data.

Business Processes and Application Logic

In Chapter 4, you have learned how to build the SOA infrastructure while doing Legacy SOA Integration. You also used the Oracle SOA Suite which includes products such as Oracle ESB, BPEL, and BAM that will be further leveraged in this re-architecture phase. Now, you are going to further leverage this infrastructure by moving processing off the mainframe, and eventually moving business logic. This approach allows you to "peel off" select processes and business logic/services, and replace them with identical re-architected equivalents over time. The approach would look something like this:

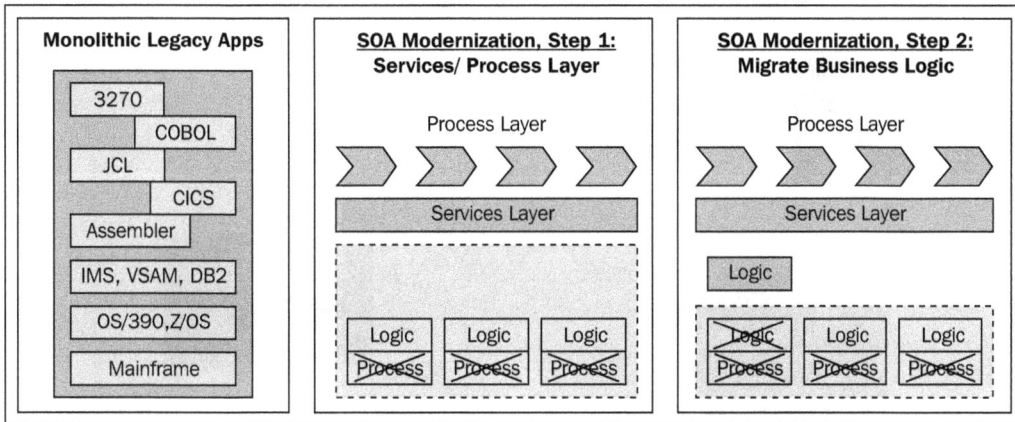

Step One involved moving business processes to a BPEL engine and/or a job scheduler.

Step Two is the beginning of moving selected business logic to Java/Java EE and a business rules engine (BRE).

Move Standalone Application

This system neither uses a lot of different mainframe databases, nor communicates with other systems on the mainframe or external applications. The application was probably developed in the mid to the late 90s, and has not had a chance to get entangled with all the other mainframe applications. Here is an example of a standalone Human Resources (HR) application:

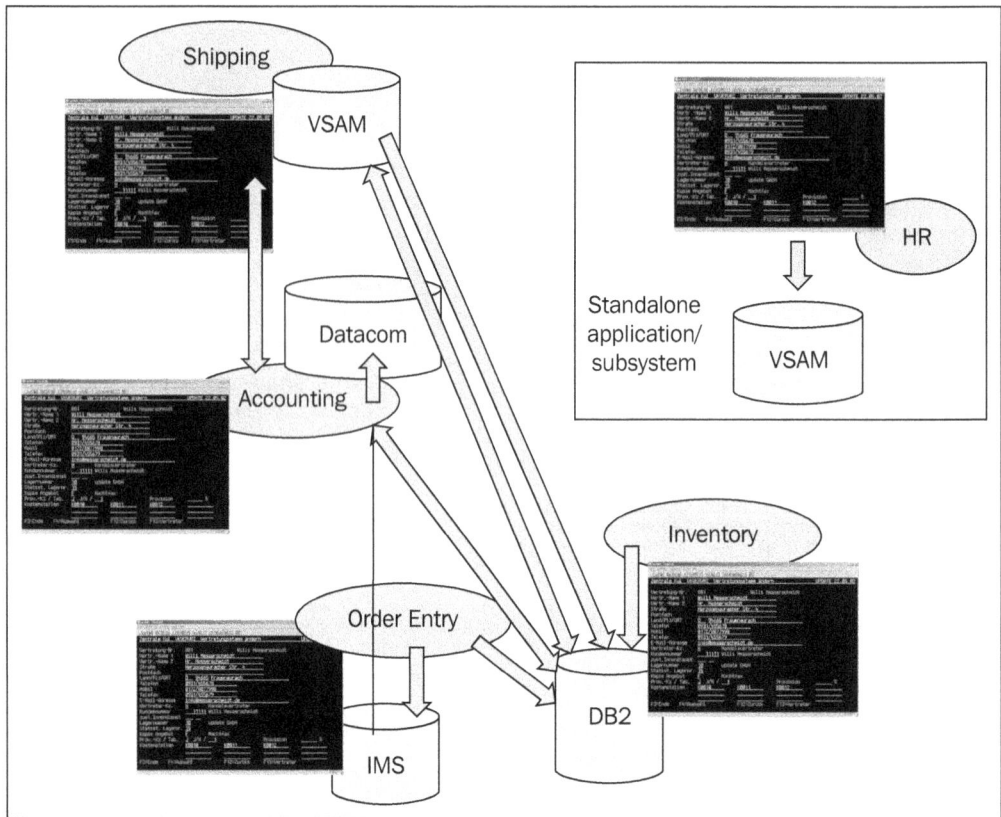

The diagram shows what interrelated inventory, accounting, shipping, and order entry applications are. They share common COBOL application modules, COBOL copy books, CICS transactions, databases, "green screens", and more. The HR application, however, is 95 percent self-contained. No application is an "island onto itself", as it shares some databases or transactions with other applications. However, in the case of HR, it has nothing to do with four other applications. It does take data feeds from external applications, and produces data feeds for internal applications. This is typical of any application and can easily be replicated in a re-architecture system.

Re-archtecture Modernization Life Cycle

No matter which approach, small, manageable projects where success can be shown in increments of six months (or less) is the overall approach to take. The standard implementation approach to re-architecture for batch and online systems is:

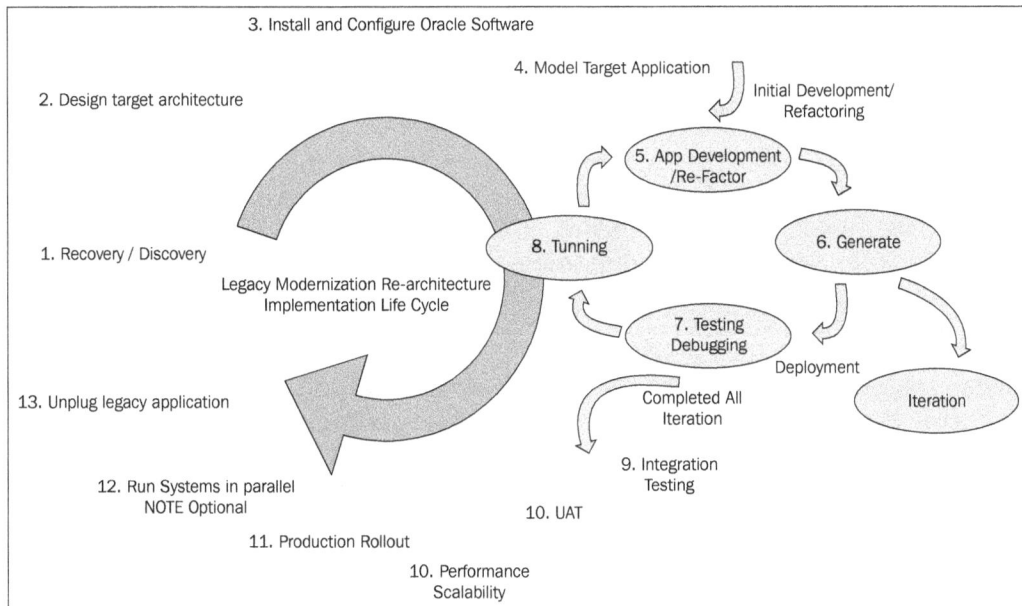

Life-Cycle Caveats

Some things to consider for the re-architecture modernization life cycle:

Application Portfolio Analysis Completed

We don't need to understand business drivers and determine an approach as we have already determined that re-architecture is the modernization choice. The assumption is you have done a complete assessment, portfolio analysis/relearning, and have concluded that re-architecture is the best approach.

Life Cycle compared to Legacy SOA Integration Life Cycle

In the back end, we have added many activities we didn't need in the Legacy SOA Integration approach because we were only enhancing/adding to an existing system. With re-architecture, we need to be concerned with classic "green field" application development activities such as tuning, unit-integration and user acceptance testing, performance scalability testing, running systems in parallel, and unplugging legacy applications.

"Big Bang" and Parallel Production

Don't confuse yourselves over running systems in parallel and doing a big bang. The big bang approach is about trying to move an integrated accidental architecture all at once, instead of moving independent applications or using different approaches (SOA, COTS, Re-Host, Automated Migration, Data Migration) to modernize different parts of the system. The approach to take with moving to production can be done over a weekend, or maybe overnight.

Modernization re-architecture is the perfect time to build an IT foundation for your long-term business and technology strategies. So before beginning, you really have to know what your long-term enterprise IT and business strategy is. Remember, this is not a time to cut corners, and choose short-sighted products and technologies that build the "accidental architecture" of tomorrow, today.

The Human Element

Avoid overdependence on automated migration tools. Tools are only as good as the people using them. The approach, project management, IT culture, team chemistry and business requirements are just as important, or more important, then the tools used. Tools help, but they are not a cure-all.

Training

Coaching and training of both IT and business personnel is important before, during, and after the implementation. I am a big believer in "on the job" training. Many times, staff members start getting trained long before the project starts. So, when the project starts they have forgotten what they learned. Also, since they are going to training with no real world knowledge, they have no idea what questions to ask, and what are the key points in the training. I feel it is important for the staff to start working with the tools and technologies, with the help of a mentor, and then attend formal training. Coaching is important since the technological barriers are small as compared to the changes people have to face on account of moving from legacy to open-systems technologies and product sets.

Re-Architecture Phases

As depicted in the diagram above, these are the common phases in the re-architecture modernization life cycle for both batch and online re-architecture implementation processes.

Discovery/Recovery

This activity is not to be confused with application assessment, or what SI vendors refer to as relearning. First, we discover (understand) all legacy artifacts. Then, they are stored in a model-based repository, which is your source system repository. This model contains the requirements, functional specifications, and the beginnings of the technical specifications for the target system.

In discovery, we mine the current application and its usage to understand what it is about. Although some of the usage information may have to come from external sources (such as users), a great deal of automated mining can also be done by performing macro and micro IT understanding of the application and its environment.

Recovery extracts the information from the current application at a detailed level. Things like "business rules mining" and "migration of existing app to UML" fit here. Recovery can be automated to a high degree, since it is mainly extracting models and model-like information from existing systems. This process creates the information engineering models that should have been in place for the original application, but does not exist for most legacy applications.

The Oracle Modernization partner, Relativity, has several tools that can help with re-architecture. One of these tools is the Relativity Application Analyzer. Application Analyzer abstracts business knowledge from the legacy application. The abstracted artifacts are stored in a standards-based repository. Modernization developers can create and organize entities stored in the repository through a "tagging" architecture based on the function, geography, or other user-defined descriptors.

Design Target Architecture

We must decide the right mix of Oracle products and technologies that are going to comprise the target architecture. You do this when you design, and create the Unified Modeling Language (UML) deployment diagrams and system architecture diagrams to describe the target Oracle architecture. You decide if a web portal makes sense, or if you are going to use JSF or AJAX as the front-end. You also make decisions on whether the Oracle Business Rules Engine, BPEL, BAM, and other Oracle products will be part of the first phase of your re-architecture project.

Install and Configure Oracle Software and Hardware

The Oracle software comprises of your SOA-based architecture. The hardware is implied in this diagram, but not spelled out, as we are not focusing on hardware in this book.

Model Target Application

Model-driven forward engineering and re-engineering are based on information in the source system repository. The meta-data and models are stored in a target repository. The user interface (UI), UI-flow diagrams, and database schema models will be generated in this phase using the information in the target repository. The UML class, use case, sequence, state, activity (process flow) diagrams will also be created during this phase.

Initial refactoring is done here as well. The mined, nontechnical information is matched to the new target platform-independent reference architecture. Re-factoring supports changes needed to transform the model information gathered in recovery to a more modern design, for example, proper OO (object orientated) design and workflow driven. This process cannot be made "push button", although tools can help. For example, deciding that four CICS programs (add PO, update PO, delete PO, approve PO) should really be pulled apart, and core logic turned into methods on a PO object with the screen handling separated and screen navigation driving everything, takes human intelligence.

This is where you start using tools such as Oracle BPA Suite, Oracle BPEL Designer, Oracle Jdeveloper with Application Development Framework (ADF), Oracle Warehouse Builder, and other tools to begin modeling the application that you will generate in the next activity.

The Oracle BPA Suite is a piece of software that has a lot applicability when re-architecting an existing application — taking your legacy code, attempting to decipher the intent of the original code, and then modeling that intent in UML. Then, when the time comes to develop the next generation of the application, the UML becomes the source of your business rules and objects to feed back into the development process. It is a tool to assist in creating and maintaining the target application blueprint of your re-architected system.

Development Iterations

These are the Application Development iterations where code gets produced. Most developers like to jump right into this phase and prefer to manually code the application. We will be using a combination of modeling, drag-and-drop development, and manual coding. For the most part, we will keep manual coding to a minimum. The development iterations have four core activities:

- Generate the target model: Deployment of all target Oracle components including data conversion and capturing, database schema, BPEL processes, business rules, Java/Java EE, and other target components.

- Testing and Debugging: Oracle Jdeveloper with Junit for unit testing. You also perform integration testing and debugging of the iteration in this activity.

- Tuning: Oracle SQL Developer, Oracle Enterprise Manager with performance and diagnostic packs to perform preliminary tuning of the application.

- Model-driven forward engineering and re-engineering based on information in the target repository using Oracle Jdeveloper with ADF, Oracle BPA Suite, Oracle BPEL Designer, Oracle Business Rules, and other tools.

User Acceptance Testing (UAT)

In this phase, you will exercise all the business use cases. This is typically a time-consuming exercise, and is best performed by the customer's acceptance testing organization. UAT is an important phase of the overall re-architecture project. It is recommended you have a comprehsive UAT test plan before the re-architecture project is started.

Performance Scalability

Performance Scalability testing is done using Oracle Enterprise Manager with performance and diagnostic packs to tune the application server, database and storage grids. It is recommended that Oracle experts be involved in this phase of the project.

Production Roll out

It is possible to perform a "big bang" production roll out—moving production from the legacy to Oracle open system platform over a weekend. On Monday morning, when users come back into the office, they start live on the re-architected application. Your "fall back" approach can be to go back to the legacy system on Monday if something goes wrong with the weekend "cut over". Some customers will still do a weekend "cut over", but run the legacy and re-architected systems in parallel.

Before you execute the real production roll out, you will have done a number of mock/test production roll outs. These are done on test systems to ensure that the data is moved correctly, and you don't miss any artifacts during the real move.

Running in Parallel

Running in parallel involves keeping all the mainframe and open system data sources in sync for a period of weeks or months. There are many change-data-capture (CDC) with write-back and bidirectional replication products offered by Oracle and Oracle modernization partners. Oracle modernization partners include: Attunity, DataDirect, Treehouse, and GoldenGate Software.

Unplug the Legacy Application

Once you feel confortable that your re-architected system is giving you the correct results and the performance you expect, you then unplug the mainframe. Most of the time, the mainframe is never turned off completely because other departments in your company are still runnning their applications on it. Or if you are an application hoster, you may still have applications that run on the mainframe. After the modernized system is in production, there will be some post-project activities including continued IT and end-user training, monitoring and tuning the system performance, bug fixes, and enhancements. No matter how much you plan and execute mock production rollovers, there will still be things that you missed.

Keeping It Real: We are years away from truly architecture-driven modernization. This does not mean re-architecture cannot be delivered in a repeatable fashion today. It just takes best practices, methodologies, implementation patterns, and more manual forward engineering than we would like to have to use. As repositories mature and become more standardized, and decomposition tools become more intelligent, we will be on our way towards architecture-driven modernization.

Using a Modernization Factory for Re-Architecture Implementation

Unlike SOA Legacy Integration, where you probably have the skills and experience to complete an SOA project on your own, re-architecture will require the help of a system integrator or a service provider who has done legacy re-architecture before. We find that many customers have already tried to do re-architecture with in-house resources and have not been successful. It was not their fault. Re-architecture of legacy systems, much like implemented ERP systems, is best done by or with the help of a vendor who specializes in the type of project you are undertaking. This is not to say that your in-house resources don't have to be involved. On the contrary, it is critical that a proper mix of in-house open systems delivery resources and mainframe delivery resources are engaged in the project. They are the subject matter experts (SMEs) who know your business, and also know the technical nuisances of the application.

System Integrators and service providers usually employ a factory model. A modernization factory pulls together a proven set of processes, tools, and services that can be offered to customers to modernize their existing solutions. The factory leverages a Systems Integrators experience to make the process more predictable, automated, accessible, and less costly. This scalable, repeatable process enables the re-use of legacy artifacts in a standard development process to accelerate the time to market of customer projects, and also reduces the cost.

Re-architecture service providers typically manage projects using a combination of onsite and offshore resources depending on the needs of the specific project. This approach allows each project to balance the cost effectiveness of offshore staff with the customer interaction and business integration of onsite project management. Most projects typically fall in the range of forty to sixty percent of the work being able to done offshore. It is advisable to choose a service provider or system integrator who specializes in modernization re-architecture projects and the source technologies you are current using. Be wary of vendors who claim to be experts in all categories of modernization (rehost, re-architecture, COTS replacement) and claim they can handle everything from COBOL to RPG, and DB2 to ADABAS.

Final Architecture—Common Oracle Products for Batch and Online

This section covers Oracle products and technologies that are common to both final online and batch Oracle architectures. The following table maps the re-architect business drivers to the the target Oracle product or technology that will satisfy that business driver:

Business Driver	Product
Faster time to Market	Oracle Business Rules Engine, Oracle BPEL Process Manager, Oracle Application Development framework (ADF), Oracle SQL Developer
Web 2.0 presence	Oracle Web Centre
Meet or exceed the RAS (Reliability, Availability and Scalability) requirements	Oracle's Maximum Availability Architecture (MMA) including: Oracle Application Server Grid, Oracle Real Application Clusters (Oracle Database Grid), Oracle Automatic Storage Management (ASM), Proactive Space Management, 'Flashback' human errors
	More on MMA below
High transaction throughput	Oracle Coherence (In memory Java Data Structures), Oracle TimesTen In -Memory Database (In Memory SQL Data Structures)
Reduce cost (FTE) of maintaining the system, and increase efficiency	Oracle Grid, Oracle Database tuning, diagnostic, configuration management and provisioning packs, Oracle Business Rules, Oracle ADF
Provide Mainframe Quality of Service at lower cost	Oracle Grid: Oracle RAC Database, Oracle Application Server
Meet the current Disaster Recovery (DR) requirements	Oracle Data Guard, Oracle Recovery Manager
Monitor business services and correlate KPI's	Oracle Business Activity Monitoring (BAM)
Improve Data Accessibility thru ad-hoc reporting	Oracle Business Intelligence Enterprise Edition (OBI EE)
Meet Payment Card Industry (PCI) Data Security Standard, other industry and government security regulations and standards	Oracle Identity Management, Oracle Database Encryption, Oracle Network Encryption, Oracle Label Security (Designed and used by US Intelligence Agencies and DoD), Oracle Secure Backup Direct back up to tape

Maximum Availability Architecture (MAA) is Oracle's best practices blueprint based on Oracle's proven high availability technologies and recommendations. The goal of MAA is to remove the complexity in designing the optimal high availability architecture. Oracle's MAA provides a simple, redundant, and robust architecture that prevents different types of outages. The best practices embedded in Oracle's MAA transfers Oracle's years of experience in building and managing highly-available systems to suit your own configuration.

The main goal of Oracle's MAA is to handle most outages, so they have little or no impact on availability, and limit catastrophic outages from causing more than 30 minutes of downtime. More on Oracle's MAA can be found here: `http://www.oracle.com/technology/deploy/availability/htdocs/maa.htm`.

End-to-end system and performance management is another area that comes up during a re-architecture discussion. The perception is that open systems cannot provide the management environment that the mainframe has. Oracle Enterprise Manager (OEM) with Grid Control ensures that your Oracle grid-enabled infrastructure is dynamically configurable. All resources are shared and provisioned on demand from shared pools in order to maintain required service levels. OEM continually monitors resource allocations and utilization from the disk to the desktop. It also automatically provides alerts and takes corrective action when the ability to achieve defined service levels are at risk from capacity overload, or from loss of capacity through failure, or when business performance is compromised.

Keeping It Real: Today RAS (Relability + Avialability + Scalability) should not be your inhibitors to modernization. Relational databases are not even close to what they were ten years ago. In the last five years, with the advent of Oracle Grid computing and advances in hardware, and open-system operating and storage, open-system platforms have everything you need in terms of RAS and performance. Security is one of the reasons some people move off the mainframe. Relational database and middle tier applications offer end-to-end network encryption, database encryption down to the column (credit card numbers) level, and even tape encryption.

Hardware, Operating System, and IBM

The Oracle Modernization re-architect platform is designed to be an operating system, hardware, and storage agnostic. We talked a lot about open systems in this chapter. Well, open system has a lot to do with Linux. IBM, like Oracle, has strong Linux support. IBM supports Linux on the z-series mainframe platform. This makes IBM z-series an open-systems platform from an operating system and software perspective. Therefore, one of your options in re-architecture is to modernize to z/Linux on mainframe if that is your preference. All the Oracle products, mentioned in this chapter will run just as well on IBM mainframe running z/Linux.

The Oracle/IBM Joint Solution Center has developed a MAA infrastructure to help educate customers and partner,s and to provide proof-of-concept support. Oracle's MAA on z/Linux which is known as the "Megagrid" looks like this:

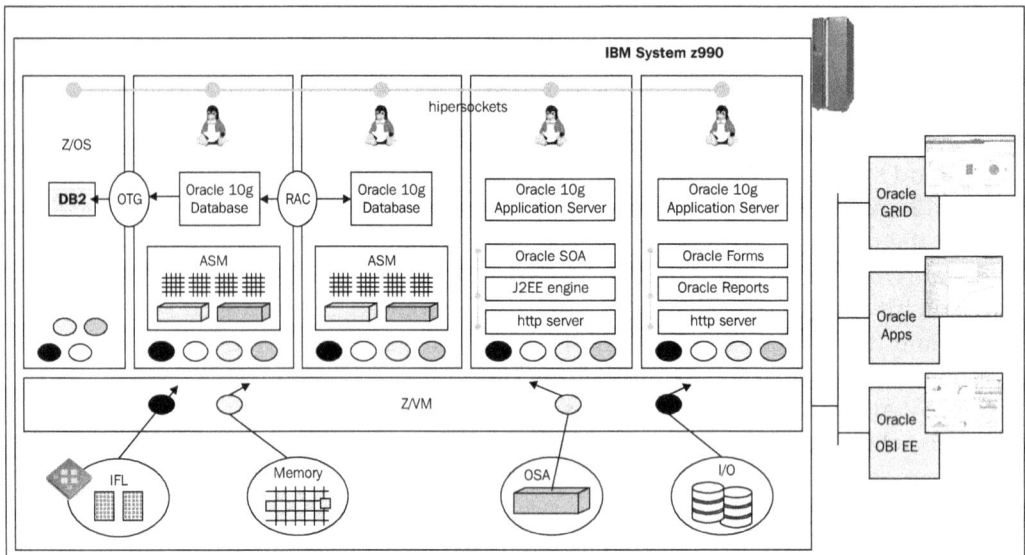

We have covered most of what the Oracle z/Linux modernization stack consists of. A few of the components not discussed previously are:

- OT (Oracle Transparent Gateway for DRDA): The Oracle Transparent Gateway for DRDA enables Oracle users to access mainframe DB2 data without knowing its DB2 characteristics. In fact, users may actually be unaware that the data resides on DB2. The product allows SQL statements executed in the Oracle database to query, insert, update, and delete DB2 tables just like they would Oracle tables. You can also join Oracle and DB2 tables in the same SQL statement.

- Oracle Forms and Reports: We talked about proprietary 4 GL environments from the client/server era of computing. Oracle Forms and Reports are two of the Oracle products from this era. Oracle Forms is for developing GUI-based applications that access an Oracle database. Oracle Reports are for developing standard IT reports similar to legacy 'green bar' reports. Both products have been upgraded to integrate with Web services and Java, and run on the Internet. However, they have for the most part been superseded by Oracle ADF and Oracle BI Publisher.

Another interesting operating system development on the z-series mainframe platform is support for OpenSolaris. This is the open-source version of Sun Solaris, and this new IBM support will allow customers to run Solaris workloads on the mainframe.

IBM also purchased the Platform Solutions Inc. (PSI). PSI offers customers the ability to run z/OS on Intel-based commodity hardware. This opens your doors to modernizing your hardware and software, while retaining the existing operating system, custom software, and all the utilities that run on it.

Summary

This chapter explained the technical advantages, overall implementation approaches, products, technologies, and challenges that are common to both batch and online re-architecture. We now know that there are three most common phased-iterative approaches to re-architecture: the data migration approach, a process-centric approach, or by moving a standalone application. A phased-iterative approach will bring you success, while a "big bang" strategy will bring you headaches and will probably not succeed. We ended the chapter with a mapping of re-architecture business drivers to Oracle products, and finally a bit about re-architecture and IBM. Now that we have eased you into modernization via re-architecture, we will examine batch re-architecture and online re-architecture in the next two chapters.

7
Batch Systems Re-architecture Technical Deep Dive

Legacy environments typically include a batch system. There are probably some legacy systems out there without batch, but it is most likely that batch processing is a key component of your mainframe legacy system. When the 'experts' talk about legacy modernization, they tend to discuss the online part of the application. Batch re-architecting is often left for later. This is why I am choosing to open my technical view re-architecture discussion with batch.

Business information processing in the past was technology-driven, centering around job schedules, involving static workloads. Business information processing in today's world is workload automation centered, event focused, and business-centric. The future of business information processing is in business service automation via the Grid, dynamic business process execution platform, and in processing as a service. However, a dynamic business process execution platform and SaaS (software as a service) cannot happen overnight. First, some things need to change:

- IT infrastructure: IT infrastructure that has grid computing, event-based processing, workload automation, and services enablement, all key components of the architecture.

- Business Process Re-engineering: The way companies do business and business processing needs to change. This is more of a people and processes challenge then a technical challenge. Today, business processes probably don't map to the way business is really being done, but to the way people are accustomed to doing them, and documented to reflect the way things happened in the past.

- Web services ready enterprise: Enterprises need to make the shift to a Service Orientated Architecture (SOA). All IT processing needs to be accessible through services. You will obviously start with a few key business processes and add more every month.

Historical Reasons for Batch

It is easy, and naïve to take a look at a batch system and say 'it is foolish to process the data this way', 'this processing has a lot of redundancies', 'this can all be done in a couple of SQL statements', or better yet 'this should be done through a web page'. It is easy to be critical of batch systems when you have the luxury of knowing where the industry is today. These batch systems have been developed over more than thirty years by different people with different skill sets, and ever changing business and regulator requirements. In addition to these business reasons, there are a number of technical reasons:

- No online access to customer (external): Ten years ago, most homes did not have the capability (computers or network) for customers to interact with businesses via the Internet. Prior to those years, most customer interactions (such as punch cards, 'fill out the circle with a lead-2 pencil'), in fact, could be done only in batch.

- Limited online capability (internal): Even within companies, having terminals and pervasive networks was too costly to make online systems common. The easiest and the fastest way to get processing completed was to send all the 'days work' to the data processing (for new timers, this is what IT organizations were once called) department each night.

- IT infrastructure limitations: The cost of high-speed networks, online disk storage, computer memory, and pre-packaged business applications prevented systems from being online and interactive. The least costly, and the most efficient way to do business was in batch.

- The way business was done: Perhaps, because of IT infrastructure and online limitations, most business processes revolved around the idea of data entry (input), data processing (processing), and reporting/file extraction (output). That is the way business was done, and IT systems reflected this.

- Information integration limitations: Information integration with in-house and third-party systems were required to happen at night using a flat file exchange. The reason it had to be done at night is because batch processing handled a majority of daily transactions. A flat file was used because this was the easiest and the quickest way to exchange information.

- Backup and archiving: Legacy data stores traditionally could not be backed up or archived while the data store was online. Some of these limitations have been lifted, but processing has not changed. Nor is the latest version of the database being used. Therefore, batch systems have a lot of processing that take backups, archive logs, compress data store, and detect data store corruption.

- Report formatting and creation: On account of all the limitations mentioned above, activities such as formatting files for reporting, executing customer programs to generate reports, and print programs to handle high-speed printing and distribution happen in batch.

> **Keeping It Real**: Historically, legacy batch systems were architectured because of technical limitations and 'old ways of doing business', which no longer apply in the global, agile business world. Although business processes have changed, and new technologies have made new ways of processing transactions possible, there are still some fundamental technical requirements a batch system must conform to. Therefore, business process re-engineering of a batch system during the first phase of a re-architecture is not recommended. This means we will continue to have a batch system in the first phase of re-architecture. In the subsequent phases, we will move more of this processing into an online system, or a more real-time environment such as the business process execution engines.

Requirements of a Batch System

Any time a system is modernized, the legacy application source code becomes the functional and technical specifications for the re-architected system. Therefore, the key requirements of the batch system need to be reproduced in the open systems environment. These requirements do not need to be exactly replicated, but the underlying application funcationality must be matched. The core requirements of a batch system include:

- Performance: Most legacy batch systems process tens of thousands of transactions a day. Not only must the new system be able to handle the volume of transactions, but must also do so in a timely fashion.

- Transactional inputs remain in the same format: Batch inputs can come from hundreds of sources/providers. The providers may not necessarily be the aggregators of the input files they send. Due to these reasons, it is not possible to expect file formats to change in the near term.

- Data quality and integrity: The first set of processes that most batch systems perform are business rules and logic such as:
  - The input file is not a duplicate
  - There are no missing records
  - Transactions in the file are in the correct sequence
  - Validation of numeric data types, dates, and other fields such as the social security numbers is done
  - Validation of fields is done by look ups in a master table

  This data quality and validation still needs to take place.

- Reporting: Legacy batch systems drive most legacy systems' reporting infrastructure. It is not necessary for reports to be produced only at night or only in a printed format. However, all report requirements have to be met in the new system.

- External Interfaces: Once again, the reason for external file interfaces generated at night is probably a 'hold over' from the way processing has always happened. File interfaces (known as Enterprise Information Integration—EII) must happen at the end of batch, because all transactions are not processed until the batch is complete.

- Restartability, work flow, based upon calendar: Many of these batch jobs process millions of transactions a night. One small error, even a non-numeric amount field, can bring all processing to a stop. If the processing had to restart from the beginning, it would be impossible to process all the records in one night, or even one day. Therefore, restartability is important to batch processing. Different types of processing needs to happen on weekends, holidays, month end, and year end. It is important that the system be flexible and support these differences.

- Distributed Processing: Legacy systems are a complex web of many systems developed over many years all acting together and reacting with each other. It would not be reasonable to expect all processing to be re-architected to a new platform 'overnight'. Therefore, the batch processing that is moved to open systems will probably need to communicate to batch systems that still reside on the mainframe.

Top Five Batch Patterns

Batch systems do many things, and I am sure that developers have found creative ways to accomplish business objectives using batch that may have been achieved using other means. We cannot possibly document and address all of these batch usage patterns (or some may call them use cases or scenarios). The objective is to take those patterns that occur most often in batch processing systems.

The characteristics of each pattern are listed here to help you identify the pattern. This will help you better understand what that batch pattern is doing. Even though you probably know all of them (assuming your background is legacy systems), it is important that we describe each batch legacy pattern, so we talk the same language.

Multi Record Type Files—Pure Batch File Processing

This is the classic ACH tape, merchant credit card transactions, or daily trades. The file typically has a file header, a bunch of batches, and a number of different types of transactions. The key attribute of this file is that it is one transaction at its core. It cannot be broken into subsets because the batch and file summary records contain transaction total integrity checks. Or, there are dependencies in the records that may not be resolved until all records in the file are processed.

Transaction Processing—Pure Autonomous Transactions

This system is a bank teller application, motor vehicle registration system, or an inventory-tracking package. For a number of reasons, these transactions are logged during the day, and are applied to the master data store in batch. The transactions may contain more then one action, but they are limited in scope, and do not depend on other transactions in the batch (they are autonomous).

Administrative Batch—Backup, Archiving

Even though legacy data stores allow more maintenance activity, database backups, and archiving to happen while the data store is open, many systems continue to operate as though maintenance can only happen when the data store is taken offline. Batch, in effect, is holding back the business from operating 24X7.

Reporting—'Green Bar', Exception Handling, Error Handling

How many temporary files do you see in your batch system? How many sort operations are there? How many COBOL program or utilities are executed to reformat data that has already been reformatted ten times earlier? All these, plus more tell-tale signs indicate that the batch system is doing a lot of end of day business, exception and error reporting. The new questions to ask are: Does it need to be done this way? How can I get information out to my business community in a more economical and timely fashion?

Third-Party Interfaces—Internal and External Information Integration

Just as in reporting, you will probably see a lot of temporary files, sorting, and reformatting. All these happen after all transactions have been applied. The files are then sent via FTP or tape to the receiving party.

Technical View

The technical view that we will focus on in this book will include design patterns one, four, and five. The technical view, along with the eight process flows of these combined design patterns looks like the following:

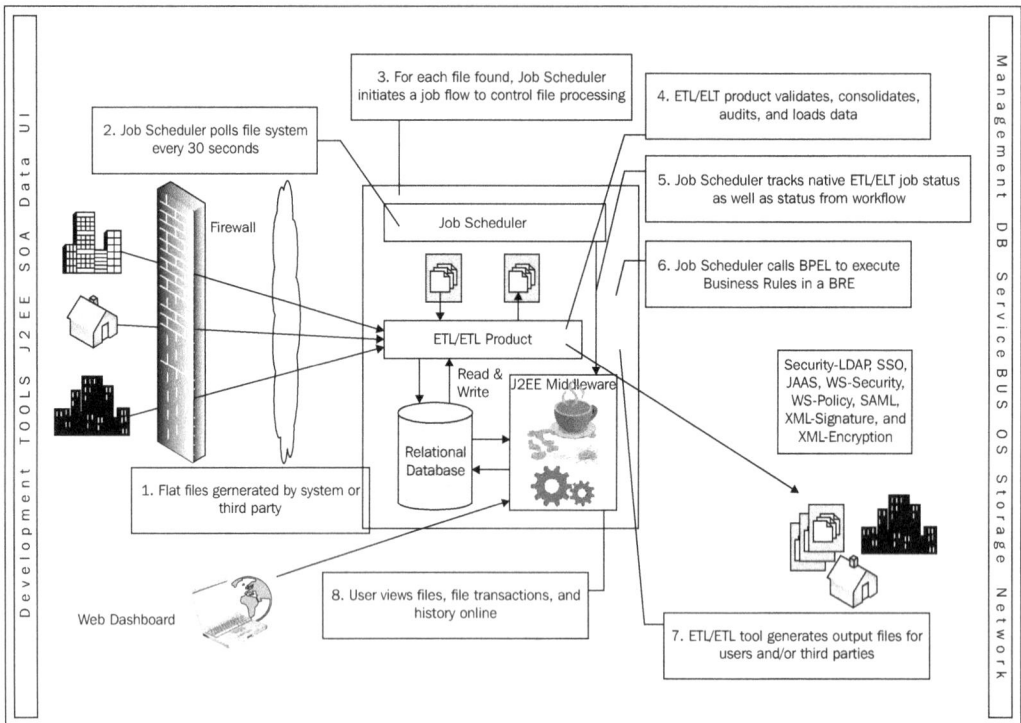

In this technical batch architecture, we have demonstrated the implementation of three batch design patterns: pure batch file processing (pattern one), reporting (pattern four), and information integration (pattern five). The batch file processing pattern is really the entire architecture, and is present in all eight process flow steps. Reporting design pattern is evident in process flow eight. The information integration pattern is part of process flow seven.

Process flow one is really the only process flow where there is not much difference between the mainframe system and the new architecture. In all other process flows, there are sometimes subtle and other times significant differences:

- Job Scheduler polls file system every 30 seconds: In the legacy system, the nightly batch cycle was started at a certain time every day. In the open systems architecture, the ability to process files as they arrive has been added.

- For each file found, the job scheduler initiates a job flow to control file processing: Each file has its own instantiation of an object to work on a different file. You don't need copies of the same job scheduler script. The same job flow can be used for the different vendor files received. Many times, legacy systems will have copies of almost identical JCL to handle the same files from different vendors.

- ETL/ELT product validates, consolidates, audits, and loads data: There is a big change from how files were validated, transformed, processed, and loaded in the batch legacy system. Perhaps, the file was processed by a series of COBOL modules, each of which did a specific set of validations, transforms, or consolidations. Then there was another module that loaded the data. During all this processing, the flat file may have been read, written out with updated fields, read again with more temporary files being produced, and so on. There were most likely SORT utilities run on the interim files as well. Using an Extract, Transform, and Load (ETL) or Extract, Load, and Transform (ELT) product minimizes the temporary files, makes data transformation, data type validations, and load easy, as there are built-in functions for these activities. The combination of an ELT/ETL and a relational database product make validations that require table lookups and auditing much simpler and eliminates the need for multiple passes through the input file, and data sorting.

  During ETL/ELT processing, it is recommended that the input file be inserted into the relational database as soon as preliminary validations such as a duplicate file, invalid file, or key fields are valid. Having the data in the relational database makes all other validations, cross table lookups, data consolidation, and data manipulation happen much faster, and you can take advantage of the built-in features of the database. Their features include standard SQL, built-in functions such as date transformations, parallel query, load balancing, and others.

- Job scheduler tracks native ETL/ELT status, as well as work flow status: Similar to mainframe, job scheduler controls the overall processing, workflow status reporting, monitoring, and notifications. However, open systems job scheduler can monitor the database activity, control ELT/ETL processing, and integrate with Web services based products and Business Process Execution Language (BPEL) engines.

- Job scheduler calls BPEL to execute business rules in BRE: This is significantly different from the way processing happened on the mainframe. Today's systems have BPEL and business rules, instead of COBOL with embedded flow control and business rules. Now, the business rules or the application flow can change without the application having to be changed, re-compiled, re-tested and re-deployed. Even changing one module in a legacy application is a cumbersome process, and it can take days to find the business rule in the module, copy book, or subprogram. With a BRE, the rules are all stored in a central repository, so you know where they are. All of them have a user-friendly name, so they are easy to find. They are also easy to understand as they all follow the same syntax. You could write flow control in Java and call business rules from Java. However, the idea is to automate as much of the modernization process, and keep maintenance of the application simple.

  The usage of business rules in the re-architectured system is very beneficial to the resulting system from the compliance, maintenance, security and privacy stand points. Industries that require strong transparency in the resulting application would benefit a great deal from the use of a business rules engine.

- ETL/ELT product generates output file for users and/or third-parties: This is another area where the difference between the mainframe and the re-architected system is much different. The batch system typically executes custom COBOL modules, or utilities that are in multiple job steps to reformat the flat files for each of the different output files required. Well, now we have no more custom code, and it is as easy as 'point and click' with the visual studio that comes with the ETL/ELT product. In fact, this step could be done with something as simple as SQL statements. However, we want to stay away from using a set of custom developed scripts or code, because as business requirements change, you will need to wrap some scripts, code, or other technologies quickly around the solution that was a 'simple select'. You are then starting to create a legacy environment today. We are already using an ETL/ELT product to transform and load the data, so why not use it for file extraction.

- User views files, file transactions, and history online: The last piece of the architecture is another significant difference not only for IT, but also for customer support, customers, and business trading partners. In the 'old world', if a file did not get processed properly, a transaction was not processed. If a customer wanted to know what happened to his batch of transactions from the night before, the customer service representative had to wade through numerous 'green bar' reports, manually check input and output files, or had to get an IT developer involved. The process of tracking down just one mistake out of millions of transactions processed each night took days.

Using standards-based technology such as Java Server Faces (JSF) for the presentation-tier, Plain Old Java Objects (POJOS) for database access-tier, and a relational database, the user and customer experiences change dramatically for the better. Customer service agents can view the file and the transaction status online; they can look at the input file and compare it to what was processed, or they can go directly to a specific transaction a customer has a question on. Transaction corrections can be made online if the person is authorized to perform this type of activity.

Optional Products

A more sophisticated technical architecture would also include a Portal, Single Sign On, and Business Activity Monitoring (BAM). We didn't want you to experience technology overload. However, here are some quick reasons why and how these technologies could further enhance the new open systems batch technical architecture:

- Portal: Each set of users could have a customized view of the applications and/or application views pertinent to their job responsibilities. There is a self-service portal for the customer that includes transactions processed the night before, how many of which were successful, and how many failed. They can view the transactions, but not change them. The business partner could see the file that was produced for them the night before, and view reports in different portlets. The customer service representative could have the JSF pages talked about early in the portal along with other applications so that all information is available on one portal page. The customer service representative could also have a portlet with update privileges.

- Single Sign On: When there is a portal in the architecture, Single Sign On (SSO) is almost always a must have. This is because multiple applications will be displayed in the portal page. You don't want the end user to have to log in to each application on the page separately. They will log in once, and all the portlets (that is applications) available to the user will be displayed. The privileges they have for these applications will also be validated.

- BAM: Dashboard with the current files processed, total transactions processed that day, number of transactions failed, and number of transactions for specific customers that have failed. All this has to be done real time, so business decision makers can immediately see if, for some reason, an abnormal (set as a key performance indicator) amount of transactions are failing that day for a customer. The dashboard alerts you when a credit card has a large number of high dollar transactions – most likely an indication that the card has been stolen. Oh yes, and the BAM dashboard is all in a graphical format with pie charts, 3-D bar charts, and other UI-based widgets.

[
  Keeping It Real: In the modern world, multiple passes through a file and multiple temporary flat files can be eliminated because transactions are stored in a relational database. In order to avoid major business process re-engineering, and changes to input file formats, the core processing will remain the same.
]

Job Scheduler and BPEL Compared

The job scheduler and the associated runtime are architectural components which, although typically associated with outdated batch processing systems, are very important in the technical architecture of a re-architected legacy system. There is some discussion in the industry that BPEL engines can provide the same type of functionality that a job scheduler provides. This is because fundamentally both job schedulers and BPEL are machine and human workflow engines. However, this greatly simplifies the number of duties performed by job schedulers to provide you with an enterprise-wide, batch load scheduling and management:

- Platform support: You must be able to execute jobs on any popular hardware or OS platform. This also includes integrated scheduling of z/OS, iSeries, Tandem, Unix, Windows, and Linux workloads. This also implies the ability to submit jobs via the job execution engine the customer is using on these different platforms.

- Heterogeneous batch job support: Since batch still rules most of the mainframe world, the ability for job schedules to execute jobs (whether they are CA-7, CA-11, Autosys, UC4, Control-M) and integrate these different jobs into one job stream is necessary.

- Interface with job execution engine: There is a difference between calling a job execution engine and executing a batch job on the mainframe. Job execution engine interface is the ability to interface with the job runtime environment during processing. Job Entry Subsystem (JES) is the IBM mainframe job execution engine. JES2 and JES3 are the two JES execution engines from IBM. Sometimes, it is necessary to call JES2 or JES3 during processing on open systems.

- Sophisticated job monitoring and management: The system manager and developer must be able to set and change job priorities, cancel jobs on the fly, restart jobs, change the frequency of jobs, and more.

- Service classes: Service classes (job priority) are built into JES2 and JES3 from the outset, to provide a mechanism for prioritizing batch processing based on resource requirements and job priority.

- Restart: Job schedulers have workflow restartability in the event of a job, system, or application failure. JCL and the JES engines support multi-step processes with a sophisticated checkpoint and restart capability.

- Calendaring: This is not just a simple system that allows the job to start at a specific time or date. This is a complex calendaring system with the ability to change dependencies and view daily, monthly, quarterly, and yearly job schedules. It is also a calendaring system allowing for easy configuration and maintenance of even the most complex schedules, allowing users to maintain a single job schedule calendar across the enterprise.

- Proactive critical path analysis: Job Schedulers automatically calculate and display job dependencies, as well as analyze the critical path. Proactive notification, in the event it appears, means the timely completion of the critical path is in jeopardy. Also, the ability to analyze the impact of a change in the job schedule before it is put into production.

- Management by Exception: The job scheduler must be able to manage by exception. Management by exception means constantly monitoring the millions of executing jobs, and alerting only on those that fail, run long, or start late.

- User and process-based time limits: The ability to set execution time allocated to a user, number of simultaneous jobs allowed for a user, and the execution time allocated to a process.

- Capturing and storing of historical job data: The job scheduler keeps historical information on jobs, so it can estimate the job execution time. It can also be set to alert you if a job runs over a specific threshold of the estimated time. The job scheduler provides specific details of elapsed execution time of each job and job step.

- Interface to hardware devices: The job scheduler can check on the availability of peripheral devices such as storage and printers before it executes a job that is dependent on a device that is offline, or not functioning properly.

- Dependency checking: Before the next job in a job flow runs, the scheduler checks to make sure all dependences and prescribed events are completed successfully. The next job in the schedule will not 'kick off' unless all the prerequisites of the job flow are completed successfully.

This all being said, job schedulers are adding more BPEL features (SOA, Web services, Java, JMS support) and BPEL products are adding more job scheduler like support (human workflow, critical path calculation, calendaring, execution dependency). Perhaps, someday, we will see the two worlds collide, or merge, depending on your perspective. As of today, it is another five plus years away.

Keeping It Real: Job schedulers in a re-architectured batch system are as important to the technical infrastructure as they were in the legacy system. Open system job schedulers actually become more important and must be more robust as compared to mainframe job schedulers. This is because they must interface with distributed platform ERP, CRM, and other COTS applications. They have to be Web service-ready as they are expected to communicate in a bi-directional manner with SOA technologies such as BPEL and ESBs. Open systems job schedulers will invariably have to execute jobs or talk to job run time engines on the mainframe.

Implementation Process

Batch needs to fundamentally stay a batch process. So for the first iteration of re-architecture we will not add real-time, event based processing. As mentioned earlier, significant business process re-engineering and human resistance to change prevent batch from simply being turned into online or real-time processing. Batch processing will still happen, but there are certain components that will stay, and others that can be eliminated.

Here are the things that stay when re-architecting your system to an Oracle architecture:

- File format: It may be nice, or cool, to have the file come in as XML instead of an ASCII tab or comma-delimited file. It may be desirable for smaller files to come in more frequently. However, the vendors and customers will probably not be able to change that quickly. They may be very small, and lack the technical skills in XML, afford the hardware required to format data into XML, or afford the network required to send XML. They may be very large, and lacking the agility to change business processes quickly.

- Processing the file as a batch: Notice that I did not say 'as one batch of files'. The individual files can be processed as they arrive. This keeps the overall processing the same, but lets us move more towards real-time processing.

- File validations: All the validations done in the old system, will need to stay. These include file duplication checking, data type validation, duplicate record checking, file order checking, and any processing that has exited to make sure we are processing a valid file and a set of transactions.

- Scheduler (batch scheduler in the legacy world): Batch is basically a workflow system with a scheduler. You will still need a scheduler to control the start of the process, the next process to execute, to restart processing, and control the sequencing of processes. Error handling that was part of the legacy batch system will need to be in place, but over time can be re-engineered to be less paper and file intensive, and can be moved to online, real-time.

Here are the things that go away when you move your batch processing to an Oracle architecture:

- Temporary files: There is no need to store information in temporary flat files as the Oracle grid-enabled relational database is the logical choice to store data. Once the data is in relational tables, transformations, validations, updates, and sorting, can be done with SQL through **Oracle Warehouse Builder (OWB)**.

- Multiple passes through the file: The file can be processed once, and then stored in the relational database. As relational databases are great at processing sets of data, a number of validations, transformation, or look ups that require multiple passes of the same data can now be done at the same time on a set of data.

- Custom code: Custom code for validation, transformation, database loading, look-ups, business process flow, and business rules processing can be placed into modern day software products. This code can now be part of a pre-packaged Oracle product that is good at handling this type of file processing. OWB is great at validation, transformation, database loading, and look-ups. BPEL is very good at human and machine business process flows. Business rules are stored in the Oracle Business Rules Engine (BRE).

- Manual, process driven exception handling: No more walking through file print outs, sysout, and using FileAid to see why a file, transaction or batch was rejected. This can all be handled online through a browser in real time.

The end-to-end implementation process for the batch design patterns we choose to demonstrate appear as follows:

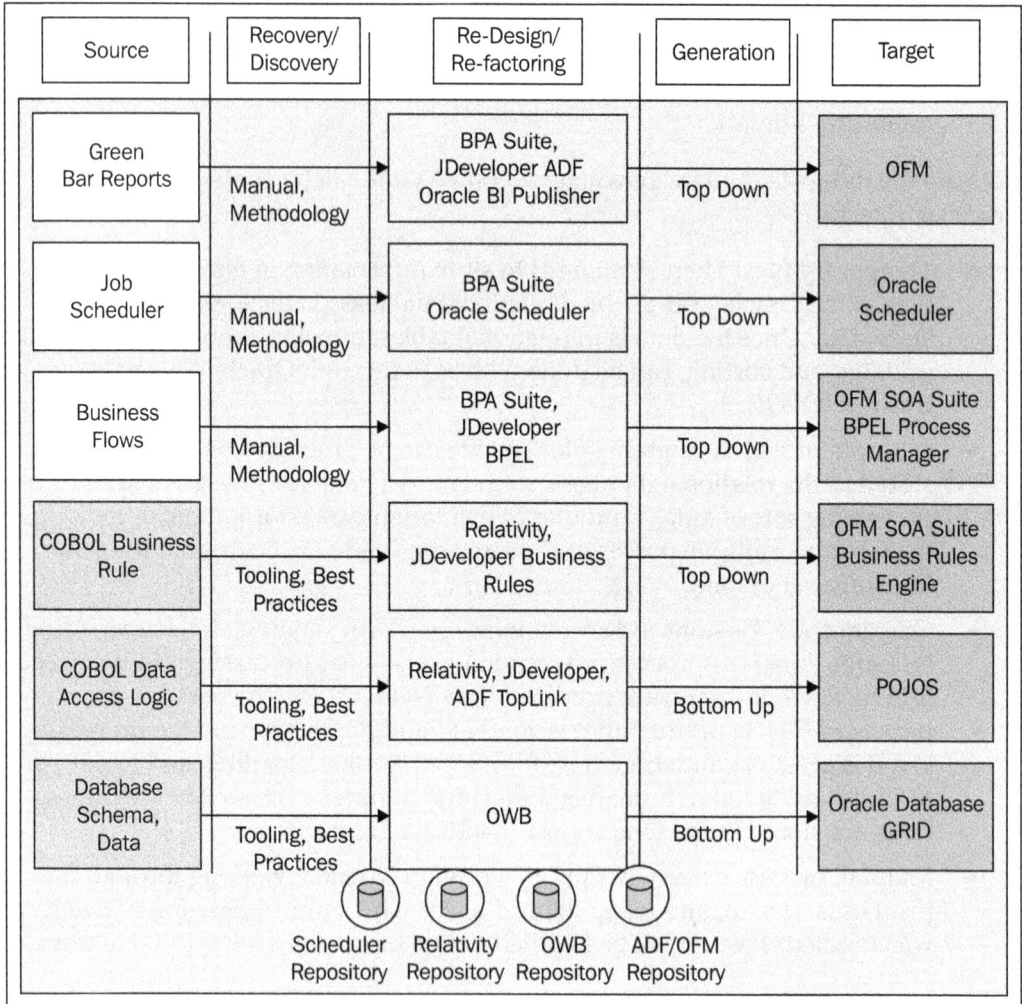

Source	Recovery/ Discovery	Re-Design/ Re-factoring	Generation	Target
Green Bar Reports	Manual, Methodology	BPA Suite, JDeveloper ADF Oracle BI Publisher	Top Down	OFM
Job Scheduler	Manual, Methodology	BPA Suite Oracle Scheduler	Top Down	Oracle Scheduler
Business Flows	Manual, Methodology	BPA Suite, JDeveloper BPEL	Top Down	OFM SOA Suite BPEL Process Manager
COBOL Business Rule	Tooling, Best Practices	Relativity, JDeveloper Business Rules	Top Down	OFM SOA Suite Business Rules Engine
COBOL Data Access Logic	Tooling, Best Practices	Relativity, JDeveloper, ADF TopLink	Bottom Up	POJOS
Database Schema, Data	Tooling, Best Practices	OWB	Bottom Up	Oracle Database GRID

Scheduler Repository   Relativity Repository   OWB Repository   ADF/OFM Repository

Before we get into the details of batch re-architecture implementation, we will first define the terminology and discuss the repositories shown in this picture.

Recovery/Discovery Approaches

This step involves discovering and recovering the artifacts you have on the legacy system. It also defines the process you use to capture and store these artifacts. Recovery/discovery is a tool assisted methodology and best practices driven approach.

Methodology

This refers to anything and everything that can be encapsulated for a discipline or a series of processes, activities, and tasks. This is a specific approach to solve a problem, a particular procedure or a set of procedures, for example, having a Subject Matter Expert (SME) talk with the job scheduler technical expert.

Best practices

I consider best practices one step up from methodology, one step closer to tooling. Best practices imply templates, design patterns, repeatable solutions, and can even include source code examples. For example, a best practice can be a technical specification on how to handle an 'occurs clause' when moving to an Oracle database. The best practice will not only explain the solution but will also show you the DDL that you need to generate.

Tooling

This refers to an actual product you can license and purchase. Some re-architecture system integrators compliment their legacy modernization service offerings with tooling. These tools are usually scripts, Java or .NET applications specific to a client system or a given task, or custom developed tools that are not sold as products. These help speed up the re-architecture process, but if you can't actually buy the tool and use it yourself we do not consider it here.

Re-Design/Re-Factoring Approaches

The top-down, bottom-up, and hybrid approaches have been discussed over the years. Bottom-up is how most legacy systems were developed, and is more of a technical approach. Top-down design is the new approach to developing systems. Both have their merits, which is why a hybrid approach is often times used by companies.

The Top-Down Approach

In a top-down approach, you start with a UML model, process flow diagrams, or some other high-level business process based approach. It is also a more end user and business analyst driven approach. You start with business requirements, functional specifications, and models that represent the high-level view of the system.

The Bottom-up Approach

In a bottom-up approach, you start with something like a piece of code or database schema, and then work your way back to a model or a high-level technical representation such as a logical database model or a screen mock up. Bottom-up doesn't mean you don't use model-based development. It just means the modeling tools are focused on the technology, code and database instead of high-level business artifacts.

The Hybrid Approach

You can also combine the two approaches, top-down and bottom-up. This approach would start with UML and modeling, as well as data schema creation and screen mock-ups. The hybrid approach is often used because you learn new, different things about how the target architecture will unfold by employing both the top-down and bottom-up approaches. These two perspectives can help you develop a system that is both technically sound, and meeting the needs of business community better.

Repositories

It would be great to have just one repository, but re-architecture is not there yet. There are combinations of modernization and modeling tools that need to be leveraged, each with its own repository. We do have a number of repositories, but the great thing is that they store their metadata in an Oracle database, or XML file based database. On legacy systems, you can find multiple repositories in different databases: DB2, VSAM, flat files, and others. More importantly, most aspects of the mainframe such as the presentation-tier, business flow, screen navigation, and database schema do not even have a metadata repository. Instead, the application code, the batch job, or the database contains the only information about the system. This is one of the reasons why legacy recovery/discovery can be so difficult. There is no meta-data, or a set of repositories to query in order to understand the legacy system.

Relativity Repository

The Relativity Modernization Workbench repository is your **Enterprise Application Modernization (EAM)** repository for all information about your legacy system. The EAM contains legacy application analysis, business rule and modeling information, and information regarding SOA readiness. EAM is packaged with a Java SDK, so you can extend and query the repository.

Scheduler Repository

All job definitions, schedules, dependencies, or any other job and schedule information are stored in the Oracle database.

OWB Repository

The OWB repository contains all the information about the source and target databases, transformations, data mappings, data profiling and quality, and other information related to data migration. It can also be used for designing and managing corporate metadata for your enterprise related databases. This functionality can be used for enterprise master data management (MDM).

ADF/OFM Repositories

Legacy systems are known for not having repositories to store metadata about the application and data. Mainframe based **Computer-Aided Software Engineering (CASE)** tools such as Pacbase and Information Engineering Facility (IEF) introduced, repository based design, development, and runtime engines. Today, most design, development, and runtime engines (Java EE, SOA) include repositories.

ADF

The metadata for ADF components (JSF, Toplink) are stored in XML files on the Oracle Fusion Middleware hardware.

OFM SOA Suite for BPEL

All information about your BPEL processes is stored in an Oracle database.

OFM SOA Suite Business Rules

The business rules repository is the exception to the rule, and actually stores the business rules in an XML file based repository.

Re-Design/Re-Factoring for each Legacy Artifact Group

Here, we will drill into the details on how to perform the discovery/recovery, re-designing, and re-factoring. Let us go through each grouping of legacy artifacts. This is different from looking at the batch implementation from the life cycle (discovery through production roll out) approach.

Green Bar Reports

The reporting systems on mainframes will mostly like be custom COBOL application or mainframe tools such as Focus or SAAS. It makes sense to refactor these into Oracle based reporting tools.

Recovery/Discovery

This involves using Legacy SMEs, interviews, Joint Application Development (JAD) sessions, mining current documentation, and reviewing current reports. Use Oracle BPA Suite models to capture this information, and Oracle JDeveloper ADF and Oracle BI Publisher to mock up online web reports and hard copy reports.

Re-Design/ Re-Factor

Use Oracle ADF is one choice to re-design and re-factor the new online reports. Use Oracle BI Publisher templates for Microsoft Word, and Microsoft Excel. Adobe Acrobat is also a good choice to re-design the new online reports and mock up in the reports in the discovery activity. Oracle APEX is also a good choice for simple reporting. APEX is built into the database, and is free.

Job Scheduler—UML Process Flow

A combination of Oracle BPA Suite and Oracle Scheduler can be used for re-architecturing the Job Scheduler. The Oracle BPA Suite is used to create UML diagrams that map the process flow. Oracle Scheduler graphical interface is used to create the new job flow.

Recovery/Discovery

Review the current JCL, job scheduler information (CA7, CA-11, Control-M, Autosys) and job output. If there is no good documentation for the batch system, the current mainframe scheduler or Relativity tool set can be used to recover and discover the mainframe batch system. This information can be placed in the Relativity, Oracle BPA Suite, and/or Oracle Scheduler repository for the re-design/ re-factor phase.

Re-Design/ Re-Factor

Use the Oracle Scheduler to re-design and re-factor the target job schedule. The Oracle Scheduler has a drag-and-drop interface to create job streams.

Business Flows

There is no real 'magic bullet' as business flows are embedded in the current COBOL application, batch schedules, custom work flow systems and other legacy artifacts. It is quite possible that these business flows are not documented, the documentation is out-of-date, or that no one is left in the organization who understands the business flows from end to end. Sometimes business flows are triggered by placing a special value in a 'green screen' field. This special business processing is not documented by users or IT. For example, entering '99999' in the vendor field for the order entry screen indicates that this is a vendor outside the system, and you don't want to keep this vendor permanently.

Recovery/Discovery

This involves using SMEs, interviewing current documentation, and capturing current business flows through **Joint Application Design (JAD)** sessions. The information discovered in these sessions are captured in BPA Suite models and use case, activity flow, state, interaction, and sequence UML diagrams.

Re-Design/ Re-Factor

BPA suite models are generated in BPEL designer, which is part of JDeveloper, to refine business flows. The UML diagrams are also used to re-factor the BPEL processes created from the BPA Suite models.

COBOL Business Rules

The COBOL business rules recovery and discovery is one area where the tools are getting more and more sophisticated. It is also an area that tools vendors continue to invest heavily in. So, you can expect COBOL business rules recovery and discovery to become more automated. For re-designing and re-factoring, automation is constrained by the lack of industry standards for open system rules engine repositories. However, most business rules engines support XML, and have APIs that allow developers to read, write and update the business rules repository.

Recovery/Discovery

Business logic (rules) consists of the core logic for which the system was constructed in the first place. Business logic does not consist of TP monitor calls, logic for system call invocation, or data manipulation. Some understanding tools provide the capability for filtering out this information to provide the analyst with a set of potential rules for further inspection.

A Standish Group study found that less than 30 percent of the code in an application actually contained business logic, and the rest was considered to be related to infrastructure. So business logic extraction via automated tools can significantly reduce the overall size of artifacts to be rationalized.

However, a solid process must be built around the analysis and forward engineering of these candidates, especially in large systems where literally thousands of candidates can be identified for inspection. It is important to consider large-scale, multi-user products having capabilities to logically group and manage these rules.

Relativity Application Analyzer abstracts business knowledge from the legacy application. The abstracted business rules are stored in a standards-based repository. Modernization developers can create and organize business rules stored in the repository through a 'tagging' architecture based on the function, geography, or other user-defined descriptors.

Re-Design/ Re-Factor

The business rules in the Relativity Repository can then be created in the Oracle Business rules engine repository. You will use the Oracle BRE web-based development tool to design and refine the business rules. You can also use the Oracle BRE SDK to programmatically insert the business rules into the business rules engine repository.

COBOL Data Access Logic

COBOL data access logic is another area, business rules being the other, where tools exist to recover and discover legacy data access logic. Discovering data access logic is straight-forward as the tool just needs to look for the 'exec SQL' or data access verb associated with the data store.

Recovery/Discovery

Relativity can mine the application for data access artifacts. However, the approach we are taking here is bottom-up. This is because we already have the database schema. Therefore, it is not necessary to mine the code for all database access. This will probably not be useful for a number of reasons:

- No central location for database access and different types of database access: Database access in legacy applications is spread throughout COBOL, Assembler, and other application modules. It also probably takes the form of direct DB2 or VSAM access as well as access via CICS and IMS transaction managers.

- Database access is being re-engineered any way: The database access will now move to a centralized layer. It will unlikely to resemble the syntax used in the legacy system. If we are re-engineering, it makes sense to start with a new database model instead of attempting to re-engineer the database access from the existing system.

- Oracle makes it easy to generate Database Access Objects (DAO): Once you have your database schema in place, the Oracle ADF TopLink tool makes it easy to create the object to relational mapping layer.

- Service Data Objects (SDO) instead of Database Access Objects (DAO): As we know, database access is the domain of the data, not high-level presentation-tier or business processes. One of the fundamental ideas behind n-tier SOA-based systems is to service enable all the components in your architecture. This includes service-enabled DAO. Since our legacy system was built before SOA, it does not make sense to move our legacy database access layer to an SDO-based architecture.

Re-Design/Re-Factor

This is done bottom-up as once you have the database schema you can generate the Oracle ADF TopLink mappings. Once we have the object to relational mappings in TopLink, the database access tier can be re-factored using JDeveloper.

Database and database schema

The DDL recovered from the mainframe data store can be used to create an Entity Relationship Diagram (ERD) for the existing data store. The ERD is re-factored and a new Oracle ERD is created. This Oracle ERD can then generate the Oracle DDL.

Recovery/Discovery

Static analysis tools are also very useful in conducting data flow and data model analysis. These tools can often derive existing data models present in both DDL and unstructured files, and these models can often be represented in a graphical fashion that enables DBAs to quickly surmise the existing models for the system. These models can then be analyzed for proper normalization, or new models can be defined for unstructured data.

CRUD (Create, Read, Update, Delete) data flow analysis is also another important attribute of some of these tools. This analysis enables the analyst to find all database operations in the system. Once identified, the analyst can choose each operation and identify the CRUD operation as a starting point for analysis. Some tools then trace back from this starting point, allowing the analyst to determine all code interactions that affected the DML operation.

Re-Design/Re-Factor

Once the data model is derived, OWB and JDeveloper database modelers can be used to re-design and re-factor the Oracle database model. OWB also facilitates the extraction, transformation, and load of this data into the target data models. This particular process, schema re-design, and data migration, represents one of the high yielding aspects of forward engineering in re-architecture.

Target Generation

Generation is common to all these activities. We use the re-factored, platform independent representation as a base for creating the final platform dependent application that makes use of platform-specific features.

Oracle Implementation Tools and Source to Target Mapping

In this section, we will take a look at the Oracle implementation tools and at an example of legacy source system artifact count to Oracle target solution artifact count. The Oracle implementation tools table will give you a perspective of Oracle tools by process area. A process area could also be looked at as a high-level modernization implementation activity. For each process area or activity, we will show the Oracle tools that can be used to help expedite forward engineering and development to the Oracle platform. The source to target mapping table will give you an example of the number of Oracle artifacts you can expect to have based on the number of legacy artifacts. Remember, this is only an example; so you may see different results. But we have found this example to be fairly indicative of most re-architecture projects.

Summary of Tools and Frameworks

The following tools/frameworks are utilized for accelerated modeling/development in a batch re-architect project:

Process Area	Oracle Tool
UML, Object Modeling, Class Modeling, Sequence Modeling, Use Case Modeling, Activity Modeling, Java Class Modeling	Oracle JDeveloper, Oracle BPA Suite
Data modeling, Schema generation, forward/reverse engineering	Oracle JDeveloper, Oracle Warehouse Builder
Model, compose and orchestrate Web service process flows	Oracle BPEL Process Manager

Process Area	Oracle Tool
Business Rules Modeling, Business Rules Implementation	Oracle Business Rules
Developer IDE for accelerated development	Oracle JDeveloper
Modeling Java object-to-relational database persistence	Oracle TopLink (POJO)
Service Oriented Development using Re-usable Business Services, Model View controller architecture, Rich set of standard 100+ components, Multiple Channel deployment - Browser, Mobile/PDA/Telnet	Oracle Application Development Framework (ADF)
Batch processing modeling and Batch Scheduling	Oracle Scheduler
File loading into Oracle database, validation, transformation, look-ups and transaction processing	Oracle Warehouse Builder

Source to Target Artifact Mapping

The following is a table that compares the artifact count differences for a re-architecture **Proof of Concept (POC)** when moving a batch system from legacy to an Oracle/Java EE/SOA architecture:

Area	Legacy	Oracle
Batch/JCL	15,000 lines of JCL	A. 500 lines of PL/SQL
		B. OWB – 15 mappings and 4 work flows
Presentation, Business and data access logic	25 +	3
VSAM files/Flat	3 VSAM	56 Oracle tables
	1 Flat File	
	1 rejection file	

The observation and explanation of the numbers in this table are as follows:

- Batch/JCL: The number of lines is reduced by re-use, job object instantiation, and parameter driven processing. What we find in both legacy batch JCL and COBOL code is that, re-use does not take place, but developers 'cut and paste' JCL or COBOL code from other modules. In the case of JCL, instead of parameterizing or making the JCL dynamic so that one set of JCL (or PROCS) can support different vendor input files, the JCL is simply repeated for each vendor. The Oracle Scheduler creates an object from a base job template at run time. This runtime instantiation of a job object makes it possible to have re-use of jobs for different vendor files. This re-use and object-based scheduling greatly reduces the lines of batch code.

- Presentation, business, and data access logic: It is not uncommon to see a 300-400 percent reduction in the lines of code when re-architecting. Some of this has to do with 'dead code' (code no longer executed) and even 'dead modules'. It can also be attributed to the old 'cut and paste' method of coding mentioned earlier. There are probably tens or even hundreds of occurrences of the same leap year calculation. This is repetition of business rules. There are probably many COBOL modules that contain identical reads of the same VSAM data set. This is repetition of data access logic. The same BMS map is duplicated in different COBOL/CICS modules, and is not in a centrally located COBOL copy book. You guessed it! It is repetition of the presentation-tier. The reduction in the amount of code also has to do with the amount of re-use that Java and Oracle ADF has across all these three tiers. As you can imagine, having all business rules in one repository reduces duplication of business rules.

- Temporary flat files: Using the Oracle database to perform the validation and transformation processing greatly reduces the number of temporary flat files. We still have a few temporary tables that the OWB process will use for intermediate processing.

- VSAM files/flat files: In this area, we see an increase in the number of Oracle database artifacts. There are a number of logical explanations for this:

  o One flat file: A batch may contain multiple record types, file and batch headers, three different types of transaction records, and file and batch trailer records. As relational databases require each table to have a predefined structure that supports a common set of data, we need to define tables to store all these different record types.

  o Error handling and processing: Error handling was handled by writing errors to batch error SYSOUT reports, printed reports, and a rejection file. In order to improve efficiency of error processing, we have three different transaction reject tables that store the rejected transactions. We also store all error information in tables instead of storing them in reports or a rejection flat file.

  o VSAM files: VSAM contain redefines which allow one field to store different types of data, and occurs clauses which allow multiple occurrences of the same field. Although, Oracle and other relational database now support occurs clauses, it is not common to store re-defines and occurs data types in one table. So for each occur clause, we will create a separate table to store the information.

> **Keeping It Real**: In the modern world, multiple passes through a file and multiple temporary flat files can be eliminated because transactions are stored in a relational database.

Final Oracle Batch Architecture

This section will put everything we learned about legacy batch systems, legacy batch patterns, methodology, and Oracle products into a real life scenario. The scenario selected should be indicative of a classic mainframe legacy batch system.

Scenario Description

The legacy system is a back-end credit card processing system for large financial institutions and credit card transaction processing companies. The legacy system consists of a large amount of several point-of-sale (POS) terminals collecting credit card payments. Every day, all credit card payments are consolidated into deposit data files and sent in for processing. The service is 40 years old, and runs on a mainframe using CICS, JCL, and COBOL under the control of a CA7 scheduler. The system processes billions of transactions annually while servicing more than one million merchant locations though their electronic information network. Some of these files might contain up to one million payments. These files are currently deposited onto a mainframe VSAM dataset.

In the credit card environment, all the expenses incurred by the credit card processing system (authorization, capture, interchange, assessments, supplies, equipment, accounting statements, customer services.) are recorded and applied against revenue for an accurate reflection of true merchant profitability. It is becoming increasingly difficult to sell this system because it uses mainframe, CICS, and green-screen interface. At the root of the problem is a shortage of people with enough skills to operate in this environment. In addition, credit card issuers mandate new rules for rates calculation in the spring and fall of every year. These changes require ongoing modifications to thousands of lines of COBOL code.

At the end of each day, the batch process creates output files, one file with data for a merchant portal, and a set of files for merchant banks, while the remaining files are sent to corresponding credit card companies. Credit card companies pay merchant banks using data from those files. Output file creation is another high-cost step in operations. The customer pays for MIPS consumed by service software. This daily file creation accounts for the largest part of mainframe MIPS.

New Batch Design Pattern(s) in Oracle

The processing that takes place is very data-centric. So it makes sense for it to be very close to the database. Also, the design pattern here is very much a situation of extract, load, and transform (ETL/ELT). The file is received (or extracted from the source system), initial validation is done using Oracle Warehouse Builder (OWB), loaded into the Oracle database, transformed, validated and reformatted using Oracle Warehouse Builder. The key to modernizing legacy systems is to leverage the new IT infrastructure software that exists in the market place today. One of these 'inventions' is ETL software that is great at performing a specific set of use cases (data loading, transformation, validation), is easy to maintain, and reduces development costs. We should avoid reinventing the wheel when OWB can do the job, and we don't have the added cost of supporting the custom code.

We often ask ourselves, "All this sounds great, but our batch window is six hours. And I heard that things like ETL tools and relational databases are going to run slower than my mainframe?" In other words, "How can the new Oracle open system environment achieve the performance that my nightly cycles demand?" The answer can be found in a number of efficiencies which arise from using the Oracle database, Oracle Warehouse Builder, Oracle BPEL, and Oracle Business Rules:

- Oracle Database Grid gives you the following:
    - Elimination of the sorting process
    - Elimination of writing and rewrite of flat files for each step of the process
    - Parallel processing
    - Grid processing
- Oracle Warehouse Builder (OWB)
    - Data validation and transformation is happening inside the database, close to where the transactional data resides
    - Validation and transformation can be done in parallel
    - No more reformatting of data for different output file formats or reports. A simple SQL select or OWB can be used
- Oracle BPEL and Business Rules
    - Business rules executed in batches instead of one transaction at a time

    °   Oracle's BPEL process manager server provides critical
support for dehydration: This supports the storage of long
running transactions in Oracle's database, so that the features
of security, high availability, and failover are available
for transactions spanning longer periods. Legacy systems
traditionally had to architect and design these types of
behaviors, or develop systems in a pseudo-conversational
approach to handle these types of transactional situations.
Re-architected applications utilizing BPEL will automatically
support these situations without having to write custom code.
As it is part of the BPEL and the service bus, it is typically
more efficient as compared to custom coded solutions.

Overall, the new business flow reduces the number of times the transactions are
read, written, and manipulated.

Exception handling is now written using Oracle JDeveloper with Application
Development Framework (ADF). Oracle ADF also produces Java Server Faces (JSF)
and Oracle TopLink modules. This allows all exception handling to happen in a
browser. As all input file records are stored in the database, they can be edited in the
browser. Other applications such as accounting can be displayed on one web page
using Oracle WebCenter.

Error handling and workflow is built into the Oracle Warehouse Builder and Oracle
Job Scheduler tool sets. Business rules are stored in the Oracle Business Rules
Engines, and execution of these rules is orchestrated using Oracle BPEL. Output files
for the credit card companies and merchant banks can easily be generated in Oracle
Warehouse Builder.

Oracle Scheduler enables users to schedule jobs running inside the database such as
PL/SQL procedures or PL/SQL blocks, as well as jobs running outside the database
such as shell scripts and executables. You can run external executables on the local
system or on remote systems. There are two interfaces for the Oracle Scheduler: a UI
which is part of Enterprise Manager, and a PL/SQL API (DBMS_SCHEDULER package).
Oracle Scheduler is a free feature of the Oracle database. The nice thing about using
Oracle Job Scheduler is that is tightly integrated with OWB and OEM.

Oracle Enterprise Manager Provisioning Pack gives you the ability to manage
gold standard systems and provides new application nodes on demand deploying
them into the Oracle Grid. Gold standard systems are those configurations which
are stable, perform well, and are available 24X7. Oracle Enterprise Manager
Configuration Pack allows you to manage and maintain the deployment of software
throughout the infrastructure. It is not only for software, but also provides centrally
tracking hardware, software installations including patch levels and software
configuration data for every service and system that it manages.

Oracle BI Publisher gives you the ability to create end user reports using standard PC-based software applications such as Microsoft Word and Excel, and Adobe Acrobat. These reports are then stored in XML, and can be published to Microsoft Word, Adobe Acrobat, HTML, and other formats.

The target batch Oracle architecture appears as follows:

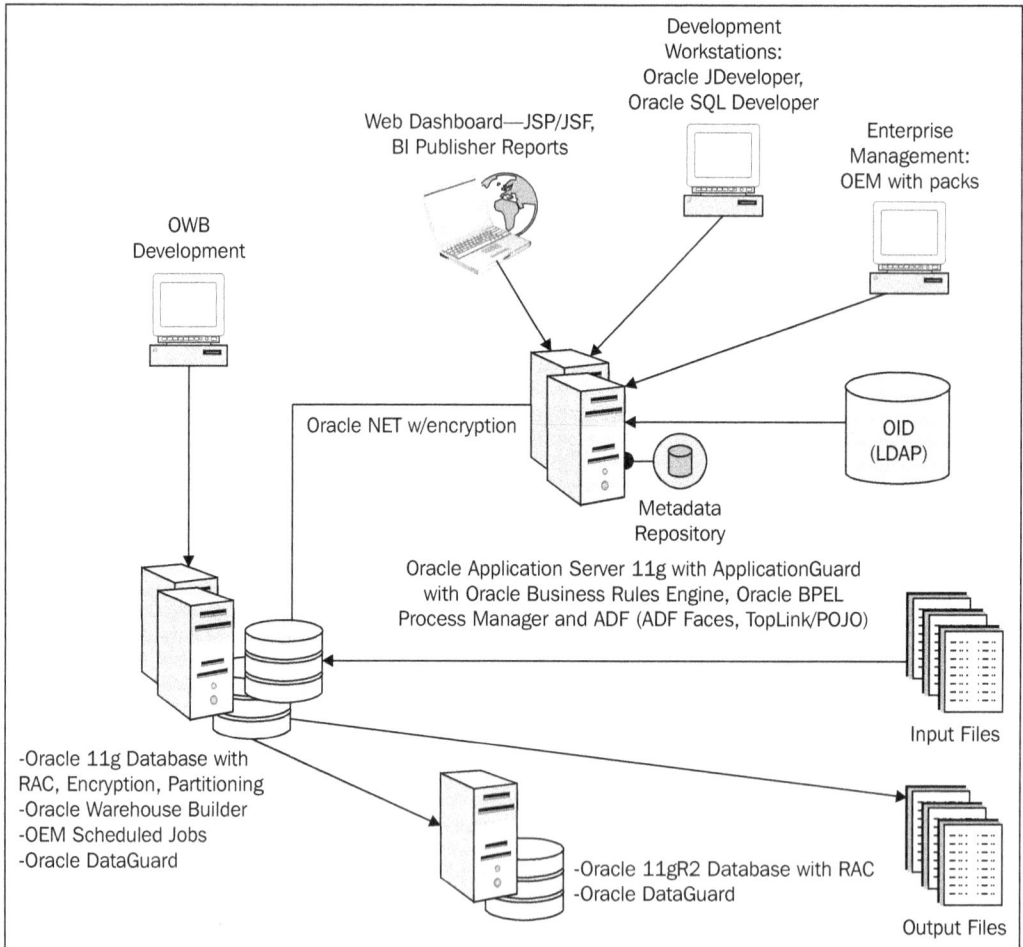

Final Technical Architecture Layers mapped to Oracle Products depicted in diagram

Device/Presentation	Oracle Product
Deposit Header Reject processing	Oracle JDeveloper/ADF
Batch Reject Processing	Provides a presentation tier that adheres to industry standard implementation patterns (JSF) and cleanly separates business services implementation details from the user-interface.
Item Reject Processing	
Modernize current "COBOL code-based" visual presentation to a declarative data transformation and rendering.	
	Oracle WebCenter
Service Bus	Oracle ESB
Merchant fee	Modernized current "COBOL code-based", "table-based" rules to Oracle Business Rules Engine. Processing orchestrated by Oracle BPEL
Reporting	Oracle BI Publisher
Information and Services	Oracle Data Integrator
Record Layout Validation	Oracle Warehouse Builder (OWB)
Duplicate Processing	Oracle Database Grid
Batch record validation	Oracle TopLink (POJOs)
Item Record Cash Advance validation	Oracle DataGuard
Item Record Credit Check validation	Oracle SQL Developer
Threshold validation	
Deposits file awaiting MasterCard File	
Deposits file awaiting Merchant Payment	
Deposits by date range	
Reject List	
Fault tolerance	
SQL and PL/SQL development	
System Management and Job Scheduling	OEM and Oracle Scheduler
System Administration Support: Comprehensive web-based console for administration and real-time performance monitoring	System Administration Support through Oracle OEM and Grid Control with performance and diagnostic packs.
Software change management and provisioning	OEM Provisioning and Change Management Packs
Enterprise Job Scheduling	Oracle Scheduler

> **Keeping It Real**: The design pattern is input file retrieved, or pushed to server, file level validation, data validation, data cleansing and persistence of data to a relational database. It is, at its core, an extract, transform, and load process, also known as ETL or ELT. This is why Oracle Warehouse Builder was used.

Summary

Batch processing may seem archaic from a technical perspective. Technology advances such as databases that can be updated and viewed simultaneously, real time and event-based processing, enterprise information integration solutions, ETL/ELT tools, and other products have made real-time processing a reality. However, batch processing is not going away anytime soon. We learned in this chapter that there are many reasons, both technical and business, why the nightly batch jobs will be with us for some time. New technologies such as BPEL could potentially replace classic mainframe job scheduling software in the distant future. In this chapter, we discussed why BPEL does not include many necessary features that are part of enterprise job schedulers. We discussed the five most common batch system patterns, and we focused on three: multirecord type files—pure batch file processing and reporting—'Green Bar', and exception and error handling. In these patterns, we covered the source to target approach, technology mapping from legacy to Oracle, and the final Oracle architecture, and also discussed why we selected the Oracle solution. In the next chapter, we will discuss legacy online systems in a similar fashion.

8
Online Systems Re-architecture Technical Deep Dive

The online technical architecture has the potential to be much more complex than the batch open system architecture because the possible combination of products and technologies are endless. The combinations of target products and technologies include everything from cell phone access, to ERP application integration, to business intelligence, and transactions across multiple databases from different vendors. We will discuss the five legacy online patterns we typically find in this simplified three-layer architecture. We will then expand the architecture back out to include additional products and technologies that can make up your new online architecture.

History and Evolution of Online Systems

An excellent place to start discussing the technical view of the modernized system is to take a look at where we where thirty years ago with online systems:

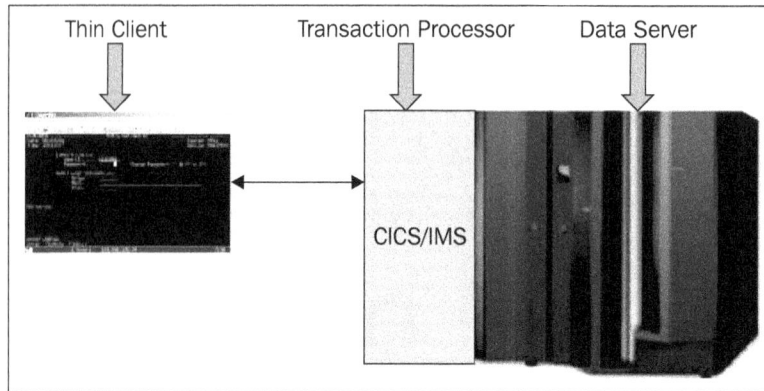

Now, let use take a 50,000 foot view of what modern architecture look like:

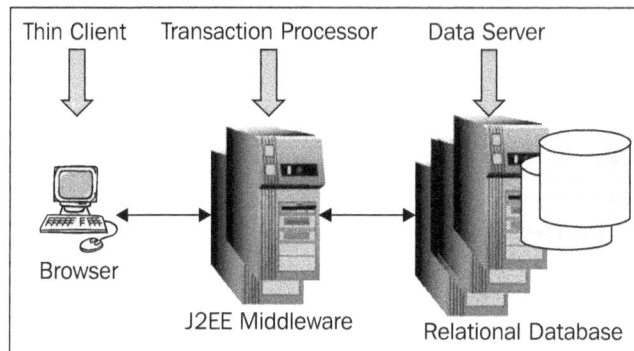

Do these two views look similar? Well, there are good reasons for that. We like to call this 'what is old is new again'. The online processing systems have come full circle from dumb terminals to thin clients. As we all know, thin clients today are much more robust, intuitive, graphical, and 'point and click'. However, they still represent a move back towards a more lightweight client. There is also a big difference in these two pictures when you look at them from a physical perspective. In the legacy picture, all presentation, transaction, business logic, and database processing happened on one tier — the mainframe. In modern architecture, presentation processing happens on the client, business and transaction processing, and business logic on the middle-tier, whereas database processing, along with transaction and business logic processing, happens on the data server. We did not get from the top picture to the bottom picture overnight. We took a detour during the late 1980s when client server technologies were introduced. This IT era that lasted about ten years did not have three tiers but two: the client (presentation tier) and the server (business, transaction and database processing). The client/server era was really initiated by the advent of the relational database.

Between the mainframe and client server eras there was also the midrange system era. These systems were introduced by HP (HP3000), Digital Equipment Corporation (DEC), Tandem, Unisys, IBM, and others to meet the needs of customers who could not afford or didn't need the processing power of the mainframe. DEC was the most important player in the midrange space. DECs' midrange systems, like the other vendors' offerings in this space, were based upon proprietary hardware and software. So, just like the mainframe, they were successful but were inflexible and costly. Midrange systems still exist today (estimates have the number at 400,00 +) but most in the IT industry consider these systems legacy.

Major corporations and IT hosting companies that missed the client/server era may be in better shape than those that embraced it. This is because client/server systems were usually developed at a departmental level. This created hundreds of siloed applications, which IT was probably unaware of. They were also developed using a number of popular, but proprietary, 4GL application development tools that generated very heavy, client-based applications. Therefore, the architectures are very dispersed, dependent on expensive, high-powered PCs, and run proprietary application languages. Client/server was successful from a number of perspectives: offered ease of use, 'point and click' based user interfaces, SQL databases, ad-hoc reporting tools, real-time information, movement away from batch to more real-time processing, and online reporting instead of paper-based reporting.

History of SOA and SaaS

We have now entered into the new IT era of SOA, n-tier, and SaaS (Software as a Service) models of computing. SOA and SaaS are called out as two separate computing models, as they are similar, though not the same:

- SOA is an architecture and does not imply an application or a product.

- SaaS is a means of offering a product that is hosted by a vendor and can be accessed over the Internet.

- They are mutually exclusive. Just because you are offering SaaS does not mean you have SOA or even Web services for that matter. A Saas implementation could be a client/server product being offered over the Internet. Usually, this involves using a technology such as Citrix. However, most SaaS implementations have some level of Web service integration. Also, an SOA environment does not automatically mean you have a SaaS environment.

When you look at the old model of computing, it is more analagous to SaaS. What you are offering with each is a hosted application that can be accessed by clients anywhere in the world. This reminds me of a discussion I had with a 20-something CTO (Chief Technology Officer) of an **Application Server Provider (ASP)** vendor during the dotcom boom. He was touting ASP as a brand new way of computing; 'it was revolutionary', he said. I reminded him that companies such as EDS, CSC, Accenture, ASC, SAIC, Compuware, and IBM have been providing ASP computing for decades. It was just called Application Outsourcing, or Hosted Application Management. He did not understand what I was saying; he really didn't get it. Well, these ASPs, along with hundreds of others, are no longer around. I bring this up because it drives home the point that "what's old is new again". The difference now is (and it is a big difference) that the architecture of today is based upon open standards hardware platforms, operating systems, client devices, network protocols, interfaces, middleware, and databases. Because of open standards, we will continue to see the success of the SOA and the SaaS models of computing.

Open standards and the Java platform have made it possible for concepts such as application re-use, development frameworks, Software Development Kits (SDKs) and design patterns to become mainstream. Design patterns, and Java design patterns in particular, are very relevant when discussing online application modernization via re-architecture. However, we will not debate the merits and demerits of particular Java Design Patterns, or different strategies for modern user interfaces, navigation frameworks, and database persistence options. There are many Java design patterns that can be implemented when designing re-architectured online system: value objects, iterators, facades, singleton, and more. There are also many navigation frameworks such as JSF and Spring. This goes for database persistence as well, where there are a combination of SDKs and frameworks at your disposal: JDBC, SQLJ, Java Entity Beans, Java Data Objects (JDO), Oracle Toplink, and Hibernate. There is enough information on the Web to help you determine what is best for you.

The greatest thing about being a modernization architect and helping customers re-architect their online applications to modern platforms is that from a technology perspective, you are dealing with a 'clean slate'. This 'clean slate' allows you to fully leverage the capabilities that modern products and technologies offer. From an application functionality and business process perspective, you have a lot of legacy to deal with. However, I see this as a benefit since you know what the system requirements are. The idea of building something better out of something that exists, using modern tools and technologies, is a very exciting activity.

Top Five Online Patterns

Just as with batch systems, smart legacy developers, architects, and managers found creative ways to accomplish business objectives using a variety of tools and technologies. Therefore, we will focus on five scenarios or patterns that we most commonly see in online legacy modernization projects.

COBOL/CICS Applications Accessing VSAM and DB2 Databases

This was by far the most common scenario as COBOL was the language of choice for most legacy systems. In fact, COBOL still remains one of the top three computer programming languages used today, the other two being Java and Visual Basic. Just as COBOL was the de facto standard for application logic, VSAM was the de facto standard for databases, and CICS for transaction processing.

COBOL and CICS

Both COBOL and CICS are well known entities, and their pervasiveness is without question, as this quote confirms; "COBOL/CICS applications account for 60 percent of all the applications that are currently in operation. Another estimate says that these applications process eighty-five percent of all the transactions that are processed" – Database and Network Journal.

DB2

DB2 on the mainframe is common, but usually not as core to the critical business processing on the mainframe as VSAM is. This is because DB2 is a relative newcomer on mainframe systems. We typically see DB2 data modernization as the first step taken by an organization when modernizing its legacy systems. This means that DB2 is still fed by VSAM or flat file databases, and functions as a reporting or business intelligence service. Since it is a relational database, it is fairly straight-forward to bring this forward into open systems running on an Oracle databases.

VSAM

VSAM is an indexed file that can be accessed by key field(s) as well as in the order the records are written. Records in indexed files can be fixed or variable. Indexed files are actually two physical files, one containing the data and the other containing the index. Indexed files will need to be converted to sequential files, before they can be imported into an Oracle database.

COBOL, IMS/DC, or IMS/TM Applications Accessing IMS/ DB Database

IMS database and transaction processing systems are known for their high throughput and performance. They can often be found in airline and financial services systems.

IMS/DC and IMS/TM

IMS/TM (IMS/Transaction Manager) or IMS/DC (IMS/Data Communication) are the two most common methods for running transactions against an IMS database (IMS/DB). IMS/DC is the old name for the IMS/TM product. CICS may also be used to access an IMS database. However, IMS/TM is considered to be more performant than CICS because, each IMS transaction runs in its' own address space and is therefore more tunable.

IMS/DB (IMS Database)

IMS/DB is a hierarchical database management system. It utilizes various access methods to store segments in a hierarchical sequence, which may be top-to-bottom, front-to-back, or left-to-right. The first segment is known as the root segment. For example, a payroll-based IMS database will typically have segments such as NAME, ADDRESS, and PAYROLL, just as a relational database would have tables with these names. In the case of IMS/DB, NAME is the root segment. Another IMS database would contain segments such as SKILL, NAME, EXPR (experience), and EDUC (education). SKILL is the root segment of this database. A single occurrence of a root and all of its dependents is known as a database record. The database record is the basis on which IMS stores the segments, and navigates the database as a whole. IMS uses the parent-child relationship to associate the segments. An example of a hierarchical data store in open systems is an LDAP directory server. XML also has a hierarchical data structure.

COBOL, CICS, Assembler Applications Talking to Datacom or IDMS Database

Assembler is mostly found in all these online patterns, but we wanted to keep the first two patterns fairly clean. As Assembler is closer to machine code, it is more difficult to read, and more difficult to re-architecture. In some cases, Assembler is modernized to COBOL. Modernization is relative, in the case of Assembler moving to COBOL, COBOL is considerably more modern.

Datacom

Datacom was originally architected as a navigational database. In navigational databases, objects in the database are found primarily by the following references from other objects. Navigational techniques use 'pointers' and 'paths' to navigate data records. Navigational techniques fell out of favor in the 1980s. However, object oriented (OO) programming and XML have rekindled an interest in navigational techniques. XML uses a navigational technique called XPATH (XML Path Language) to access nodes in an XML document. Navigating objects in Java is done through navigation of APIs that accept the Java object ID or the object name as parameters. Once again, "What's old is new again".

Datacom now supports communication through standard interfaces such as ODBC, JDBC, OLE/DB, ADO, and Common Gateway Interface (CGI). It also supports SQL access just like relational databases. Even more interesting is that it will run off the mainframe on Windows, Linux, and variations of Unix.

IDMS (Integrated Data Management System)

Like Datacom, it is also owned by Computer Associates (CA). Unlike Datacom, it does not have SQL support. However, third-party vendors, and CA offer ODBC drivers to access IDMS. In IDMS, the database key is directly related to the physical address of the record on disk. Records and sets are the main structuring concepts in this network model-based database. Records essentially consist of fields of different types. This allows complex internal structures such as repeating items, and repeating groups. IDMS was made popular by Cullinane Database Systems (later known as Cullinet). Cullinet is an important name in the IT industry as they were once one of the leading enterprise database vendors in the world.

Assembler

Assembly languages were first developed in the 1950s. Assembler is a very low-level programming language, and is really one step up from coding in binary (zeros and ones). It implements a symbolic representation of the numeric machine codes and other constants needed to program a specific hardware architecture. Therefore, Assembler is very hardware-specific, and not very portable.

PL/I and CICS Applications Making Use of VSAM and DB2 as Data Store

The goal of PL/I was to develop a single language usable for both business and scientific purposes. Business users mainly used COBOL, while scientific users used Fortran. PL/I supports recursion (which COBOL did not support) and is a structured programming language. PL/I is a very good business language as the syntax is English-like, and is suited for describing complex data formats with a wide set of functions available for verification and manipulation.

NATURAL and COBOL Applications Accessing an ADABAS Database

Somewhat similar to the IBM AS400/iSeries community, the NATURAL/ADABAS community has a 'cult-like' following. The people and organizations that run NATURAL/ADABAS really believe in their platforms.

ADABAS (Adaptable DAta BAse System)

Introduced in 1969 by Software AG, it was one of the first DBMSs for the mainframe. ADABAS is a navigational database similar to Datacom. ADABAS stores its data in tables (so it can be considered 'relational'), but also uses some non-relational techniques such as multiple values and periodic groups; much like what you would find in COBOL/VSAM applications. ADABAS is now available on a range of other systems including OpenVMS, Unix, and Windows servers. Software AG has extended support from ADABAS, so it can function in the new world of SQL, Web services, XML, Java, and .NET via a product offering from Software AG.

Natural

Natural, Software AG's development environment is a 4GL programming language that communicates with ADABAS, and the more recent Natural versions work with Oracle. Natural is designed specifically for building applications that combine flexibility and scalability. A number of the legacy mainframe 4GLs, Natural included, have separate of presentation, workflow, transaction processing, business logic, and database access. This separation of processing layers is much like modern OO languages, and unlike legacy COBOL and Assembler base systems where CICS, IMS/TM, 3270, database access, business rules, and IBM operating system environmental components are all intertwined. This makes these 4GL applications (like Natural) much easier to migrate to Java and SOA. Natural applications can also be deployed to all leading platforms including Windows, Unix, and other open systems platforms.

Obviously, there are other patterns that exist such as IDEAL/Datacom programming language and database, CLIST (command list) scripts, REXX (Restructured eXtended eXecutor) modules, Unisys DMS/DMS II databases, and Transaction Processing Facility (TPF). TPF is a high throughput transaction processer from IBM that is commonly found in the airline industry. As I mentioned at the start of this section, the variety and virtually endless combinations make it impossible to cover these and other legacy online architectures.

Technical View

Unlike the batch technical view, the online technical view will look the same for the five batch patterns discussed above, as well as for any online legacy application. The open systems technical architecture that you will move to will look like this:

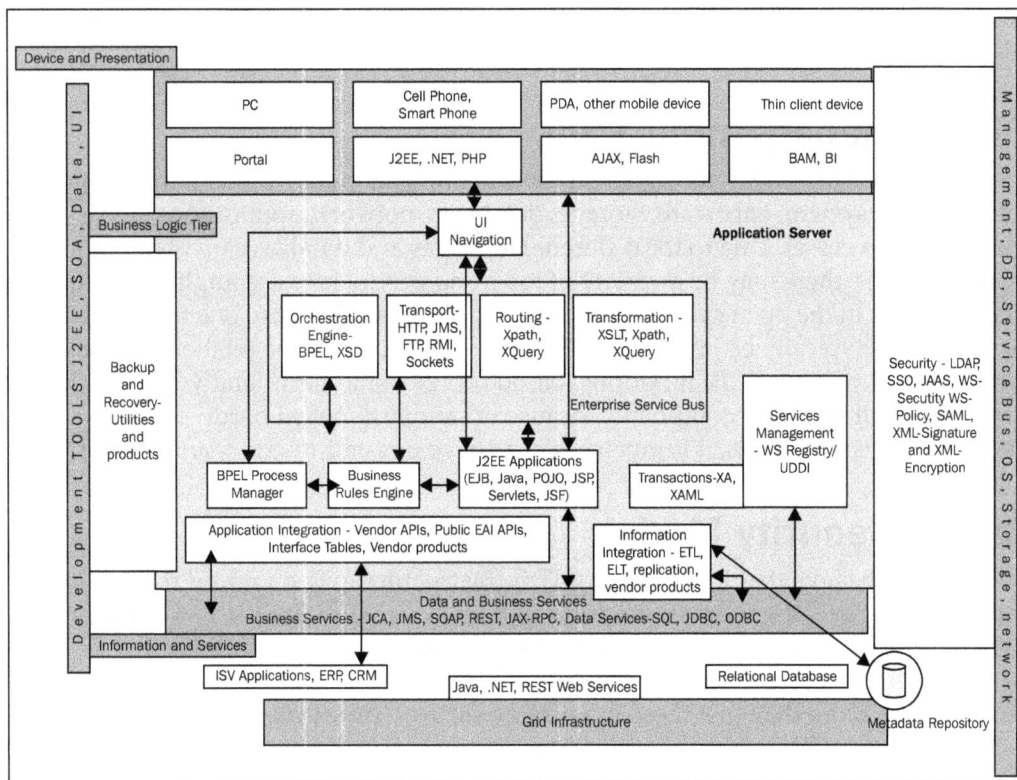

This should look very familiar to the Legacy SOA Integration chapters *Technical View* section. This is a great thing as it means we are practicing what we have been preaching. The architecture in the Legacy SOA Integration is the foundation of our modern open systems architecture. This is excellent for both IT and business organizations, because if you choose to start with Legacy SOA integration, you are not wasting your training dollars, software expenses, and time on products and activities that are not part of modernization via re-architecture.

Infrastructure Unique to Re-architecture

The technical view consists of the three same base layers we had in the functional view: device and presentation, business logic tier, and information and services. We already spent a significant amount of time talking about the presentation layer, BPEL, ESB, BAM, Web services management, portals, and transactions in Chapter 3. So, we will spend our time focusing on those infrastructure components that are new and/or different from the Legacy SOA Integration architecture.

Single Management Tool

We certainly have system management tools in our legacy environment to manage the operating system, hardware, storage, databases, network, applications, and transaction processer. Due to the different languages and databases involved in legacy systems, there may be a variety of tools and products to accomplish system management. In the open systems architecture, it is possible to use one tool, as the language will typically be Java/Java EE, and the database will be relational. Also, your network will use TCP/IP, storage based on open standards, and your security directories will be LDAP compliant. Because of standards based hardware, network, and software components, it is much easier to have one end-to-end management tool.

Single Security Model

Most people believe that in the current IT infrastructure, when viewed from a data center perspective, the security products in their system are limited to technologies such as Resource Access Control Facility (RACF) and Access Control Facility 2 (ACF2). What data center people may not realize, or avoid, all together is that they already have more than just these mainframe security products. They have Microsoft Active Directory, SSO servers, and various other security products.

LDAP directories in their organization. Re-architecturing your legacy systems presents a great opportunity to look at your security infrastructure. It is a great time to consolidate all these technologies into one security platform using modern security products such as federated identity, virtual directories, user provisioning, and certificate authority servers.

Development Tools

There are obviously many development tools on the mainframe for application development, batch JCL programming, and others. Development tools in open systems are focused on database and UML modeling, Portals, Java EE, ESB, BPEL, Web services, database access, UI navigation, and business rules. In the perfect world, all these components would be developed using one tool. Chances are that one tool will not do it all, but it may be possible to eliminate the number of development tools when re-architecting. The open source development tool Eclipse is the most widely used Java EE development tool. Most vendors, including Oracle, have specific plugins to Eclipse that allow you to do ESB, BPEL, Web services, database access, UI navigation, and Portal development in one tool.

Metadata Repositories

Chances are you will not be able to avoid having multiple repositories in open systems, much like you had in your legacy environment. The difference is that with standards like XMI (XML Metadata Interchange), it is much easier to share information among the repositories.

Enterprise Information Integration (EII)

An EII product provides you a comprehensive information integration platform that covers all enterprise information integration requirements—from high-volume, high-performance batches, to event-driven, trickle-feeds. EII products include pre-packaged legacy, messaging, database, FTP, file, COTS application, and other adapters. They also include capabilities for data replication and bi-directional change data capture (CDC).

Enterprise Application Integration (EAI)

We are intentionally discussing EAI separately from an ESB and Web services. ESBs and Web services are sometimes discussed as technologies that will cause the end of EAI products However, ESBs and Web services don't address vendor-specific APIs, adapters for content management, or message queues that may be required. For now, we have this as a separate entity. Perhaps as the COTS and technology vendors conform to common standards such as ESBs and Web services, we will, in the near future, not talk about EAI as a separate component.

Transactions

As mentioned in the functional view section, transactions now happen both on the middle-tier, and on the information layer in open systems. On mainframe systems, transactions are typically the domain of the middle-tier in the form of CICS and IMS/TM. This is because most legacy databases don't have built-in transaction management support as relational databases have; the exception is obviously mainframe DB2. All relational databases have transaction management support, and most client/server applications leverage the database transaction management engine. The advent of the Internet and middleware-tier application servers allow transactions processing and management to take place within the application server, and/or within the relational database. Both tiers offer industry standard transactions (XA based transactions), transaction scaling with caching, and clustering. As the application server is where business and transactions are processed, most architects choose the transactions to be managed on the middle-tier. This does not mean you will not have transactions happening in the relational database. It is just that the overall transaction management will be handled in the application server. The other reason for this is that high volume, or what is now known as **eXtreme Transaction Processing** (**XTP**), makes most sense to be in its own tier, as part of the application server. XTP can coordinate high volumes of transactions across databases, Web services, and external applications using caching and clustering of transactions.

Infrastructure Not Required for Legacy SOA Integration

The infrastructure components listed here were added from the Legacy SOA Integration technical architecture view, as they were not required because the application and data still resided on the legacy system.

UI Navigation

This is a separate framework or technology that is used to control the flow of screen navigation. Usually, when UI navigation is mentioned, the Struts framework is the first framework that is discussed. There are also UI navigation frameworks such as Java Server Faces (JSF) and Spring MVC. These frameworks are important as they make it easier to separate the presentation-tier from the application business logic and data access tiers. They also provide a graphical, model-based method of build screen flows.

Java EE Applications (EJB, Java, POJO, JSP, Servlets, JSF)

Java EE/Java applications are core to our re-architectured system. This is where the business processing that was in COBOL or other legacy languages will now reside. Although Java EE/Java is key to the modern architecture, we are not going into much detail here as there are already thousands of web sites and millions of web pages on Java EE/Java.

Relational Database

Well, we may not get to one relational database in your first or even fifth modernization project. However, you will at least have one database model, and that will be relational. The ultimate goal is to have a global instance of your relational database. Or at least, a global instance of your core business functionality such as accounting, inventory, sales, and supply chain, and then have other relational databases for operational data stores, data warehouses, and other departmental applications.

Grid Infrastructure (Grid Computing)

Grid computing is yet another type of distributed computing that takes advantage of the idle capacity of the computers on a network. Computing tasks are distributed to any idle computer on the network. The most well-known, and probably the most widely used, example of grid computing is the **SETI** (**Search for Extra-terrestrial Intelligence**) project. SETI is a scientific experiment that uses Internet-connected computers. You can participate by running a free program that downloads and analyzes radio telescope data. So rather than using an expensive supercomputer, SETI allows anyone to download a special 'screensaver' that becomes active when your PC is idle, and it is used to number crunch radio telescope data for SETI. This environment is a "grid computer" that has more CPUs than any actual computer system could ever have.

A grid infrastructure in its purest sense is physically dispersed and comprises of heterogeneous hardware (MAC, PCs, Unix servers, and even mainframes). Due to the complexities of managing large volumes of data in relational databases, and the business logic running on middle-tier, it is not possible to have a SETI type of grid computing in the business enterprise. Instead, hardware and software vendors offer enterprise grid architectures. The infrastructure needs to be in one enterprise data center, and all the hardware need to have the same processor. Grid is very real and alive in the business community. However, it is not the same grid that some of us have come to see, or use at home. The enterprise grid will most likely have an application, database, storage, and management grid.

Backup and Recovery

Backup and recovery in legacy systems and open systems until recently, was a manual process of doing full nightly backups with daily activity being written to log files that are achieved periodically during the day. This works to restore information in the event of human or IT-related error (deleting rows, incorrect data entry, updating a massive number of rows when only one should have been updated). However, it usually leads to minutes if not hours of downtime, as the latest nightly backup needs to be located, and the archive log files need to be re-applied one by one. In the end, your system has been down, and you have probably still lost information, as your latest archive log is not "up to the minute". You have also restored a lot of data that did not need to be restored, as the incorrect data was probably isolated to a single transaction, table, one column in a table, or a set of rows in a table.

Relational database technology and much cheaper hard disk storage have made it possible to make this traditional way of performing backup and recovery legacy in nature. It is now possible, to configure your database to do nightly backups directly to a disk and only back up information that has changed. You can make the log recovery process faster, less expensive, and more targeted by using relational database technologies that only recover specific transactions, or data in one table. The data lost can also be eliminated by using relational database features that have up to the second transactional log information on disk.

Technologies Not Necessary for Legacy SOA Integration

We were not as concerned with these technologies in Legacy SOA Integration because most business rules, data services, and business services stayed on the mainframe. For re-architecture, they become more essential to the architecture and take on a deeper meaning.

Business Rules

Business rules are seen as a must-have by IT organizations when re-architecting legacy systems. It is estimated that up to seventy percent of IT spending used to maintain legacy systems can be attributed to the fact that the business rules are not centralized, and that they reside in many different application languages (COBOL, Assembler, and even JCL). Now, you can see why a Business Rules Engine (BRE) is so important. It can help you reduce a majority of your application maintenance costs.

Data and Business Services

The focus in the Legacy SOA Integration chapter was on using Web services to access legacy artifacts (presentation, transactions, and data). Data and business Web services change focus (although you will still be using the Web services created in your Legacy SOA integration phase) so that for the most part, this layer functions as the data service tier to interface with the relational database. Recently, the idea of SOA-enabled data services has taken off in the IT industry. This is really not any different from the Legacy SOA integration using data as the legacy artifact and exposing it as a Web service. What is new is that the Business Logic Tier (BLT) can now view any database access service as a Web service. Business services in the re-architected platform are no longer just about legacy transaction, but include any piece of business functionality, or even messaging service, that is accessible internally or via the Internet.

Technical View Infrastructure Components

Many people think only about the application language and data migration when they are re-architecting a legacy application. In a simplified view of legacy re-architecture, once you move the application and the data, you are done. We all know this is not the case in the real world. In fact, infrastructure components can be more complicated to move not because of the technology, but because they typically involve culture and business process (for example business process re-engineering) changes, as well as, new ways of thinking and processing for the IT organization. The area of infrastructure is very broad and deep, so we cannot cover all the topics in depth in this book. We will, however, briefly mention infrastructure components that are typically found in legacy re-architecture projects.

Capacity Planning Tools

Capacity planning tools such as IBMs' Resource Measurement Facility (RMF) and CAs' Sysview are well established on mainframe platforms. All open system hardware, operating systems, application servers, storages, and database vendors offer capacity planning tools. However, the tools on the mainframe will typically give you a holistic capacity planning view. In open systems, the capacity planning tends to be more component-specific (OS, database, storage). Although more immature, we do see hardware companies like HP and Sun beginning to offer end-to-end capacity planning on open systems.

Chargeback and Accounting Solutions such as CA (JARS)

The open systems offering in this area are not nearly as mature. The mainframe model of computing which is similar to SaaS requires sophisticated chargeback and accounting solutions. As SaaS is relatively new, open systems chargeback offerings are still coming into the market place. One could also argue that chargeback and accounting are not nearly as critical because in the enterprise grid you can allocate specific grid nodes to a specific organization or company.

Application Development Tools

On the mainframe, application development tooling for source code change (such as IBM's ISPF), source code control (such as CA's Endeavor) and COBOL coding (Micro Focus Mainframe Express) are all mainframe based application development tools. The number of vendors and choice of application development tools is limited on the mainframe. There are many vendors and open source capabilities on open systems in the source code change, source code contorl, and coding areas. The tooling is also more graphical in nature, and will typically plug into the development framework that you decide to use.

Testing Tools

Application and system testing products such as Compuware's Expeditor, or AbendAid, exist on the mainframe. The vendor choices are limted on the mainframe. For open systems, this is an area where every major IT vendor has testing tools. There are also open source tools (Apache AnitUnit, Junit) available.

Reporting

Reporting infrastructures on the mainframe usually consist of custom COBOL modules, and Information Builders FOCUS and CA Easytrieve reports. Open systems reporting products are in the hundreds, if not thousands. Also, any PC-based product (Microsoft Excel is one example) that offers ODBC connectivity to a relational database can be used for reporting. This is not necessarily what your IT department likes to deal with, users creating ad hoc reports in MS Excel, but since it is possible it will probably happen.

High Speed Printing and Viewing

In theory, printing is an artifact from a bygone era. In reality, many people still like to have their 'hard copy'. Levi, Ray & Shoup (LRS) is a company that can give you both options in open systems by providing print management and online viewing of printed documents and reports.

Data Archiving

Storing information offline for government mandated purposes is not going away any time soon. Tape has been the traditional way to archive information. The possibility of using off-site, online storage using a database vendor standby database solution, and then moving the data to a MAID (massive array of idle disks) could open up new possibilities. Copan Systems is one such company that offers this as a potential solution. I am also confident that the other media types (long term DVD media, inexpensive memory cards) will emerge in the next decade.

Disaster Recovery

Legacy systems mostly used a combination of File Transfer Protocol (FTP) and off-site hardware. A scheduled batch, or a manually executed process is used to transfer data, via FTP, to the remote disaster recovery location. This is an expensive and human-driven process. Human intervention always adds the potential for more errors. Most open system application servers and relational database have built-in, automated features to keep an off-site location in sync with production.

Tape Management

I would argue that tape management has really evolved into the concept of Information Lifecycle Management (ILM). That is, managing information at every stage of its life cycle from real time to off-site storage. This way of thinking is more revolutionary than evolutionary. Whether your company can move from the idea of managing tapes to an ILM solution depends upon your company's culture and willingness to explore new concepts.

Human Error Recovery

This is why in the 'old days' you had log backup to disk and tape, and a manual recovery process. There are now built-in database features to 'rewind' an error made to a table, transactions, data column, or a set of rows.

Internationalization

Open systems products and technologies have internationalization 'out of the box' in the presentation tier (Portal products), business processing (Java), and relational database. This is provided via the universally adopted Unicode standard, and vendor localization, and globalization offerings.

Network Architecture/Protocol

Your company may be running IBM's **Systems Network Architecture (SNA)** or **Digital Equipment Corporation (DECnet)**. You will be making the move to TCP/IP which will affect your IT infrastructure, including how internal and external systems communicate with you. What we have found is that most corporation have already moved completely to TCP/IP or are in the process of moving.

Reliability, Availability, and Scalability

A discussion of IT infrastructure would not be complete without at least touching on RAS (Reliability, Availability. and Scalability). One of the first questions I invariably get is "Tom, How do I achieve RAS in my re-architectured system?", "My mainframe is very reliable, available, and scalable". Availability is the same or better in the open systems world, largely due to relational databases being used instead of legacy databases. Another reason for legacy systems lacking availability is that they were not architected to process online and batch at the same time. Reliability and scalability have been addressed in the last five years with the advent of enterprise grid computing at the application, database, and storage tiers with a combination of open systems hardware, operating system, database, application server, and storage vendors working together to deliver an end-to-end enterprise grid. RAS requirements should not be a road block when re-architecting your legacy system.

Keeping It Real: In reality, you will not have one database. You probably will not have one development, management tool, or even one application language (Java EE). The idea we are trying to impress upon is that you don't want to make the same mistakes that were made with your legacy 'accidental architecture': the many standalone systems, adding integration points in a tactical fashion, developers using the application language because this is what the know or like, and new reporting and BI tools popping up everywhere in the user community. You should attempt to minimize the number of languages, products, and technologies that make up your target architecture. You should also take a strategic approach to what tools and products you use instead of using a developers favorite tool, or a quick and dirty alternative.

Implementation Process—Online Systems

Unlike batch, where batch fundamentally stays batch, in online re-architecting, the entire design of the application changes. Although, we introduced object-oriented design concepts such as use cases and business objects along with SOA in the batch implementation section, we are using these concepts more, as we have a more significant presentation, business processing, and business rules layers. However, the overall implementation process for online re-architecture stays the same as batch re-architecture:

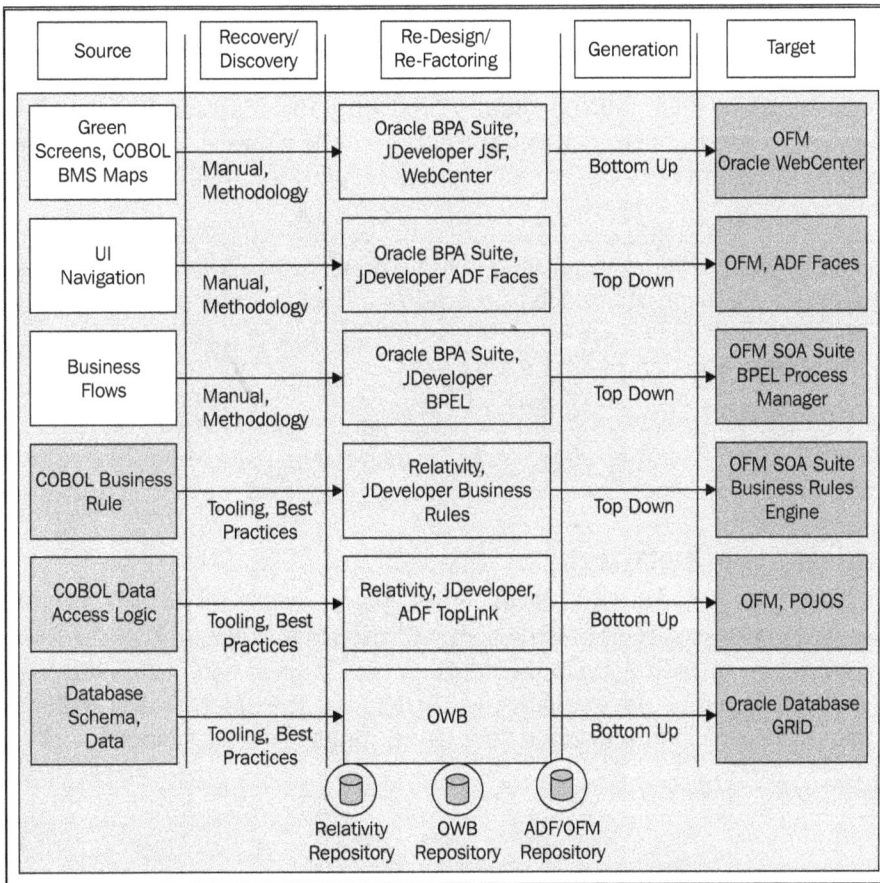

Source	Recovery/ Discovery	Re-Design/ Re-Factoring	Generation	Target
Green Screens, COBOL BMS Maps	Manual, Methodology	Oracle BPA Suite, JDeveloper JSF, WebCenter	Bottom Up	OFM Oracle WebCenter
UI Navigation	Manual, Methodology	Oracle BPA Suite, JDeveloper ADF Faces	Top Down	OFM, ADF Faces
Business Flows	Manual, Methodology	Oracle BPA Suite, JDeveloper BPEL	Top Down	OFM SOA Suite BPEL Process Manager
COBOL Business Rule	Tooling, Best Practices	Relativity, JDeveloper Business Rules	Top Down	OFM SOA Suite Business Rules Engine
COBOL Data Access Logic	Tooling, Best Practices	Relativity, JDeveloper, ADF TopLink	Bottom Up	OFM, POJOS
Database Schema, Data	Tooling, Best Practices	OWB	Bottom Up	Oracle Database GRID

Relativity Repository — OWB Repository — ADF/OFM Repository

We have already covered the implementation process for the four bottom layers. So we will focus on the 'green screens' and UI navigation.

Presentation/User Interface

This is different from the top layer ('green bar' reporting) in batch as Oracle JDeveloper ADF has the capability to easily bind the database access-tier objects to a JSF or a JSP page. So we are not doing top-down re-design like we did with 'green bar reporting'.

Recovery/Discovery

Many of the tools on the market today will analyze the user interface components of an existing system. This analysis often consists of enabling analysts to identify all user interactions. We can leverage the database schema we have created, and perform a bottom-up process to create the new presentation-tier.

These tools are very useful for deriving human process flow, but the limitations of these tools should be taken into consideration during the analysis process. These tools usually cannot derive screen values from runtime behavior. Those systems that rely on heavy program dynamics to generate user interfaces will not benefit much from these tools.

However, it is important not to rely too heavily on static analysis tools when deriving certain characteristics such as workflow. Typically, the user community doesn't always follow documented paths through the system, and has often discovered shortcuts in completing their tasks.

If it is important to carry forward the exact user interaction scenarios as part of the target requirements, then interviews with the user community should be carried out to identify all possible workflow scenarios.

Re-Design/ Re-Factor

Oracle ADF Faces uses a drag-and-drop UI based approach in JDeveloper to create JSF pages. Then using the bottom-up approach, you use the Oracle ADF TopLink mappings and bind these objects to the fields on the JSF page you just mocked up. If you prefer to have another layer of abstraction between the database access-tier and the JSF page, you can create JSR 227 ADF data bindings using JDeveloper.

UI Navigation

Online UI navigation processing is similar to the way a batch scheduler controls workflow in batch systems. Obviously, batch systems have limited user interaction and online systems are all about user interactions. UI navigation is very dynamic as there are a number of paths a user can take through the system. Batch systems, on the other hand, are very rigidly tied to a predefined workflow. As we did with the batch scheduler modernization, we will use a combination of Oracle BPA Suite and the Oracle development environment. In the case of the batch, we used the Oracle Batch Scheduler to help refactor the batch environment. For UI navigation, we will use Oracle JDeveloper ADF.

Recovery/Discovery

This involves using SMEs, interviews current documentation, and captures current business flows through **Joint Application Design (JAD)** sessions. The information discovered in these sessions are captured in BPA Suite models and use case, activity flow, state, interaction, and sequence UML diagrams.

Re-Design/ Re-Factor

The UML diagrams and BPA Suite models are used to guide you in the re-design of the screen navigation using JSF or Oracle ADF Faces. Oracle ADF has a drag-and-drop capability to create the web page flow once the JSF pages are created.

Oracle Implementation Tools and Source to Target Mapping

In this section, we will take a look at the Oracle implementation tools, and an example of legacy source system artifact count to Oracle target solution artifact count. The Oracle implementation tools table will give you a perspective of Oracle tools by process area. A process area can also be looked at as a high-level modernization implementation activity. For each process area or activity, we will show the Oracle tools that can be used to help expedite forward engineering, and development to the Oracle platform. The source to target mapping table will give you an example of the number of Oracle artifacts you can expect to have based upon the number of legacy artifacts. Remember, this is an example, so you may see different results. But we have found this example to be fairly indicative of most online re-architecture projects.

Summary of Tools and Frameworks

The first table we will look at views the tools used by processes area, and the Oracle product used. The following Oracle products for each process area are utilized for accelerating modeling/development in an online re-architect project:

Process Area	Oracle Tool
UML, Object Modeling, Class Modeling, Sequence Modeling, Use Case Modeling, Activity Modeling, Java Class Modeling	Oracle JDeveloper, Oracle BPA Suite
Data modeling, Schema generation, forward/reverse engineering	Oracle JDeveloper, Oracle Warehouse Builder
Model, compose and orchestrate Web service process flows	Oracle BPEL Process Manager
Business Rules Modeling	Oracle Business Rules
Developer IDE for accelerated development	Oracle JDeveloper
Modeling Java object-to-relational database persistence	Oracle TopLink
Service Oriented Development using Re-usable Business Services, Model View controller architecture, Rich set of standard 100+ components, Multiple Channel deployment - Browser, Mobile/PDA/Telnet	Oracle Application Development Framework (ADF)
Real-time operation dashboards with monitoring and alerting	Oracle Business Activity Monitoring
Application Discovery	Relativity - Oracle Modernization Alliance (OMA) Partner
Data Migration	Oracle Warehouse Builder

Development Life Cycle Support Tools

Another way to look at the tools and technologies used to accelerate online re-architecture is by the development life cycle support, and the tools used in each development life cycle activity:

Life Cycle Support	Accelerated development features	
Modeling	UML	
	Class Modeling	
	Sequence Modeling	
	Use Case Modeling	
	Activity Modeling	
	Java Class Modeling	
	Data Modeling	
	Forward/Reverse Engineer Java Classes	
Coding	WYSIWYG Editors	
	Visual Page Flow editor with drag-and-drop component palette.	
	EJB Visual Modeler and Dialog based EJB creation	
	Re-usable Business Services	
	Out-of-the-box design patterns	
	TopLink Visual Modeler	
	TopLink Persistence framework for Java Objects	
	Visual CSS editor	
	SQL Development	
	Ant build Integration	
	XDoclet Integration	
Testing	JUnit test creation	Refresh test suite
	Integrated test runner	Single method test
Debugging	Local and Remote Debugging	UI debugger
	Hot Swap Debugging	PL/SQL Debugger
	Memory Heap Examiner	
Tuning	Event Profiler	SQL Explain Plan
	Execution Profiler	Code Audit
	Memory Profilers	Code Metrics
	Code Coach	

Life Cycle Support	Accelerated development features
Deployment	Packaging wizards
	One Click Deploy
	Ant Integration
	Embedded Java EE container

All of the features listed in this table, are part of Oracle JDeveloper.

Source to Target Artifact Mapping

Just as we did with batch implementation, let's compare the source environment to the Oracle environment. This table compares the artifact difference for a re-architecture Proof of Concept (POC) when moving an online sysem from legacy to an Oracle/Java EE/SOA architecture:

Area	Legacy	Oracle
Presentation, Business and data access logic	500,000 Lines of COBOL code	A. Approx 15,000 lines of Java, JSP and XML. 95% generated by Oracle ADF
		B. Approx 14,000 lines of DB persistence and 'view objects'
		B. Stored procedures and triggers –2,300 lines
		C. + BPEL processes. 98% generated code
		D. Business Rules - 244
VSAM files	13 VSAM files • Average number of record type per file (in files with multiple record types) — 20 to 30 on average • Every file has occurs 200-300 occurs on average	126 database tables (almost 10:1 ratio)

The observation and explanation of the numbers in this table are as follows:

- Presentation, Business, and Data Access Logic: Once again, the significant reduction in code is not surprising.

- VSAM files/flat files: In the section on batch implementation, we covered the reasons for more tables than in the VSAM files. Another point on this is that relational databases like Oracle, store information in what is called a normalized format. This normalized format keeps related information in one entity (a database table). In legacy databases, information about an employee and the department they work for is stored in the same file. This means department information is repeated over and over again in all the records in this file. If something about the department changes, all records in that file have to be changed. In a normalized Oracle database, there are separate employee and department tables. Therefore, if a department name changes, it only needs to be changed once. Also, the same department information is not repeated multiple times in the employee table.

> **Keeping It Real**: Business rules extraction is one of the places where automated tools can greatly reduce the effort of a re-architecture project. Therefore, legacy rules extraction is a very prime area, and all the software and services vendors involved with modernization are investing heavily in this area. The next major innovation in the rules extraction arena is the ability to forward engineer these rules into a rules engine such as the Oracle Business Rules Engine (BRE).

Final Oracle On-line Architecture

This section will put everything we learned about legacy online systems, legacy online patterns, methodology and Oracle products into a real life scenario. The scenario selected is a classic COBOL/CICS system accessing VSAM and DB2 databases.

Scenario Details

The legacy system provides software and services that process applications for credit cards, debit cards, installment loans, mortgages, wireless services, and also supports a variety of commercial credit decisions. Through parameterized tables, clients are able to readily modify their processing structure in response to constant changes in credit policy, or market conditions. The system is a customized standalone service, capable of interfacing with a variety of receivables systems.

The system's applications have been in place for a considerable time. The system has continued to be highly profitable, but is under threat from new entrants, with more current technologies, in the market place. There has been little investment in either marketing the system to the global market place, or modernizing it to meet emerging threats, or to take advantage of new business opportunities.

The current applications architecture is based on COBOL, running under CICS, on an IBM Mainframe hosted data center. The applications also include a small number (8) of Assembler programs and some two hundred COBOL programs. Most of the applications data is stored in VSAM with a small amount in DB2. Each client that uses the system has its own set of programs, supported by a common base set.

The application's logical architecture view is as follows:

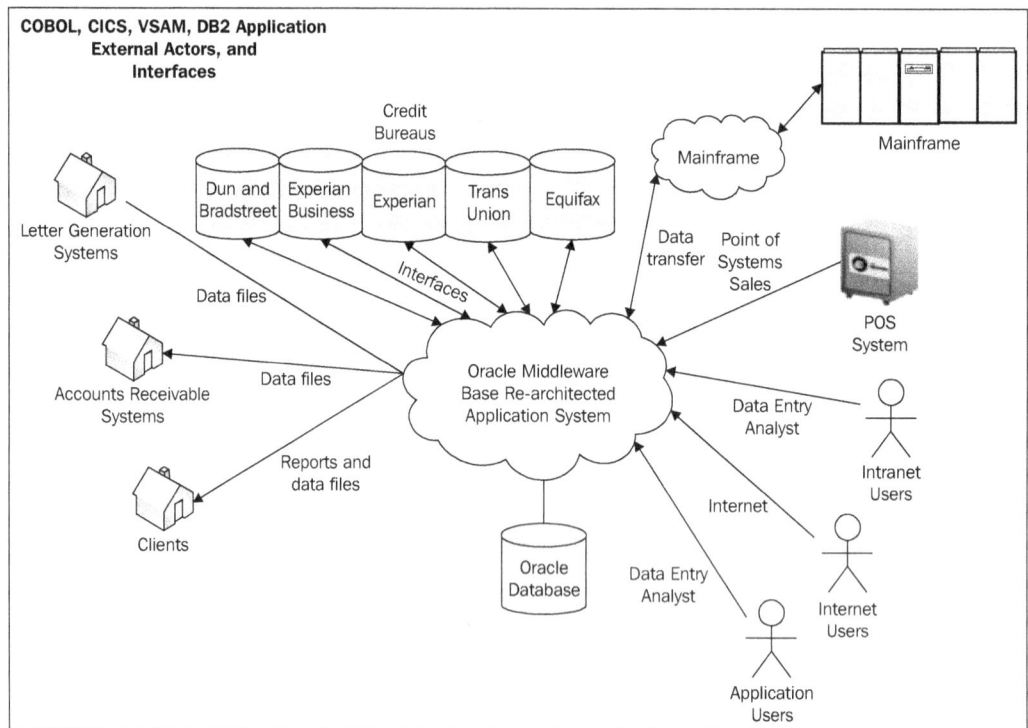

Description of processing shown in logical architectural view:

- Application Processing: The application processing subsystem handles the initial edits, duplicate checks, fraud checks, and business rules evaluation before sending the application to the credit report retrieval subsystem. After the credit report subsystem has returned the credit report, the application processing subsystem will summarize and score the data and then decide the fate of the application.

- Credit Report Retrieval: The credit report retrieval subsystem establishes a communication with the credit bureaus, sends the inquiry record, and returns the credit report data.

- Post Decision: The post decision subsystem controls the processing flow of the application after a decision has been made on the application. The subsystem allows the clients the ability to assign and track documents and stipulations required before a final booking can be made.

- Fraud Maintenance: The fraud maintenance subsystem allows the clients the ability to add known fraudulent information to the fraud files. The fraud files will be used during the fraud match process.

New Online Design Pattern in Oracle

We have talked about modern n-tier architectures and described the technologies associated with a re-architected online application. Now, we will put this architecture in the context of the Oracle product stack. We have already discussed many of these technologies in the Legacy SOA Integration chapter, and in Chapter 7.

Presentation

Remember the disposable presentation-tier we talked about earlier. Well, with the separation of the presentation-tier into a separate layer, and using open industry standards, we can achieve this disposable tier. The Oracle products are Oracle ADF Faces exposed in the Oracle WebCenter. Different presentation-tier technologies come and go on what seems to be a weekly basis. **Rich Internet Application (RIA)** development technologies such as Adobe Flex and the open source framework AJAX (Asynchronous JavaScript and XML) are the latest hot presentation tier RIAs.

UI Navigation

Oracle supports the use of JSF, Spring, or Struts as the navigation layer. Navigation layer technologies are very dynamic, and new ones come out every few years. Not quite as 'ever changing' as presentation-tier technologies, but they change enough that Oracle is most likely to continue supporting new ones as they emerge.

Application Server

This where your Java EE/Java server resides. The Oracle products that will run in this Java EE server include: Oracle Business Rules, Oracle BAM, Oracle BPEL, Oracle Web Services, Oracle WebCenter portlets, and Oracle BI Publisher.

Information Integration can be achieved using the Oracle Data Integrator. We will not utilize this product in this chapter, as we have already covered it in detail in Chapter 4.

Information and Business Services

Oracle TopLink which produces object to relational POJO components is used for **Service Data Objects (SDO)**.

The **Oracle Transparent Gateway** for IBM DRDA (**OTG**) can be used to submit Oracle changes back to the mainframe. Going back to Oracle from DB2 on the mainframe involves custom coding to read the DB2 logs, storing the logs in a temporary DB2 change table, reading the change table using OTG, and then applying the changes back to Oracle using Oracle Streams. This is a more custom coding approach to achieve the objective of running the open systems and mainframe systems in parallel. 'Out of the box' change data capture (CDC) for DB2 can be used from Oracle modernization partners such as GoldenGate, DataDirect, or Attunity.

Relational Database

The Oracle enterprise grid database is implemented using Oracle **Real Application Clusters (RAC)**.

The final Oracle technical view for this scenario appears as follows:

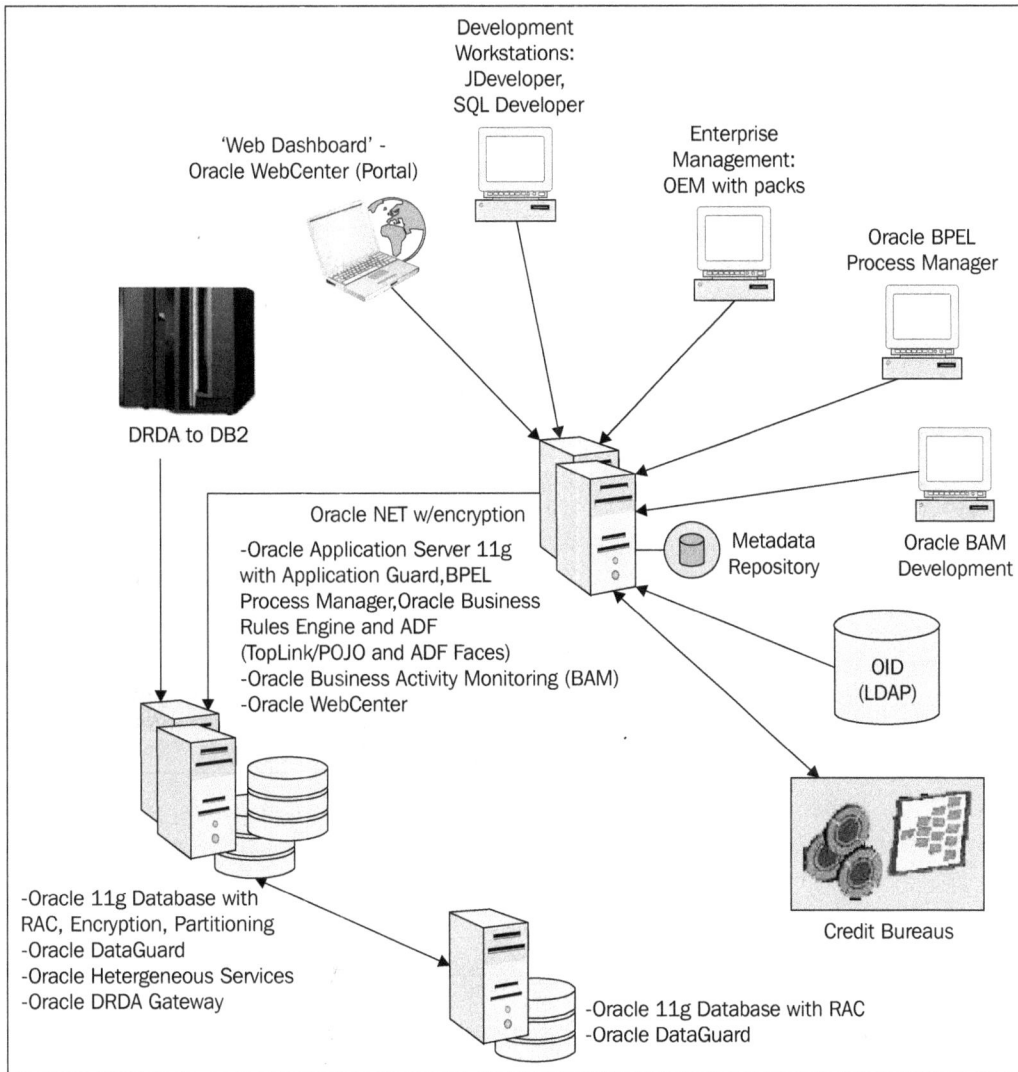

The following table describes each layer in the diagram above and the associated Oracle products depicted in the diagram:

Device/Presentation	Oracle Products
Applications received from multiple delivery channels including, but not limited to, the Internet, POS systems, third-party data entry service providers and telemarketing service providers Online, real-time data entry	Oracle JDeveloper/ADF Provides a presentation-tier that adheres to industry standard implementation patterns (JSF/ADF Faces) and cleanly separates business services implementation details from the user-interface.
Solicitation file processing that facilitates mass mailing campaigns, and reduces data entry by pre-filling application fields	Provides Web services interface to receive and process data from third-party applications.
Systematic assignment of account numbers and automatic update of approved applications to your receivables system	Modernize current "COBOL code-based" visual presentation to a declarative data transformation and rendering.
Cross-sell capabilities	Oracle WebCenter
Business KPI Real Time Dash boarding	Provides a presentation-tier with personalized visualization for campaigns and brand targeting. Oracle BAM Business Intelligence: Real-time interactive dashboard real-time Business Intelligence using Oracle BAM

Application Server	Oracle Products
Duplicate and fraud checks to prevent the opening of redundant accounts or accounts for known frauds	Oracle BPEL integrated with Business Rules Engine
Online communications with Equifax, Experian and Trans Union, as well as the Canadian offices of Equifax and Trans Union, and the Credit Reference Association of Australia, to provide immediate consumer credit reports	Provides a configurable orchestration model (Oracle BPEL) with Business Rules (Oracle Rules) Integration.
Automatic or manual decisions — After a loan application is entered and errors are corrected, the application obtains credit reports, makes system recommendations and decides the outcome of the loan without manual intervention	Oracle SOA Suite and Application Server Java EE and Modernize current "COBOL code-based" business logic to a configurable orchestration model for Duplicate and Fraud processing.
Processing flow tailored to your strategies as multiple credit products can be processed using different decision paths	
Workflow management capabilities that include online queues for holding applications with exception conditions	
Systematically fax decisions to branch and dealer location, and email notifications to consumers	

Information and Services	Oracle Products
Database Grid	Oracle Real Application Clusters
Fault tolerant database configuration	Oracle Dataguard
Communication with mainframe DB2 database	Oracle Hetergenous Services and Oracle Gateway for DRDA
SQL Development	Oracle SQL Developer

System Management	Oracle Products
Comprehensive web-based console for administration and real-time performance monitoring: - Manage and configure application components - Monitor server performance and application server logs - Deploy and monitor application - Maintain service level requirements - Maintain system and software configurations	Oracle Grid Control with Diagnostic, Tuning, Change Management and provisioning packs

> Keeping It Real: The key is an Oracle architecture that 'future-proofs' your application from business and technology changes. This means using Oracle products that separate your various architectural layers. It also means choosing the Oracle products that give you the biggest benefit up front, while keep your re-architecture time-to-market fast. Finally, it means avoiding using products and technologies just because they are the 'flavor of the day', or because your developers know them.

Summary

Online systems have moved from thin client hosted applications to client/server architectures with thick client PCs, and then to thin client Internet-hosted applications. Unlike hosted mainframe systems, these hosted new generation applications are based on open standards. They don't use specialized devices for the presentation-tier, have intuitive, easy to use interfaces, and are accessible on the Internet. We discussed the five most common online system patterns, and we focused on the COBOL/CICS accessing DB2 and VSAM pattern for our scenario technical deep dive. For this pattern, we covered the source to target approach, technology mapping from legacy to Oracle, and the final Oracle architecture, and why we selected the Oracle solution. We also covered some of the infrastructure requirements for reporting, disaster recovery, data archiving, high-speed print and print management, and capacity planning. All these are very important, and sometimes more important than the migration of the application code and data. In the next chapter, we will complete an end-to-end, hands-on example of a re-architecture of a simple mainframe, 'Order entry' application. The chapter will mine the business rules, interface and navigation-tiers from the COBOL/CICS VSAM based applications. These mined artifacts will then be forward engineered into a Java EE application that performs a two-phase commit across an Oracle database, and a mainframe VSAM data set.

9
Re-Architecture—Scenario in Detail

The purpose of the scenario is to reinforce that re-architecture is not "rip and replace", but leveraging existing mainframe artifacts and forward engineering these artifacts into an Oracle/Java EE architecture using Relativity, and Oracle tools and products. The focus in this example will be on Relativity tools. The most complex and important aspects of re-architecture are discovery, recovery, capture of legacy artifacts, and creation of a source model. Therefore, we will focus on these re-architecture activities in this detailed scenario.

We will also focus on these three architectural layers of the application:

- Presentation-tier/User Interface
- User Interface (UI) Navigation—The interactive business process flow
- Business rules

The other layers are the database (database schema and data migration), and the **Service Data Objects (SDO)** layer. Not to trivialize the activities involved in these layers, the activities are fairly straightforward as compared to the rest of the re-architecture. **Oracle Warehouse Builder** (OWB) can be used to import the schema definitions that are in the COBOL copybooks, and do a one-time data migration. Once the schema is in place, a bottom-up approach to developing the SDO layer using Oracle Toplink is performed. We will also show an example of using the free and ubiquitous Oracle SQL*Loader utility to unload data from the mainframe and to populate an Oracle database on open systems.

The re-architecture activities that we discussed in Chapter 8 that will be the bulk of this example are:

- Recovery/Discovery: The legacy artifacts are captured here by the Relativity tool, and stored in a source repository. These legacy artifacts, for this example, are the presentation-tier, UI navigation, and business rules. The business rules are key to the entire application.

- Re-design/Re-factor: This activity leverages the source model to create the Oracle target model and system. There is less focus here, but we will take a look at how to leverage legacy business rules by importing them into the Oracle Business Rules Engine. We will show how to import them manually using the web-based Oracle Rules Author, and also discuss the API that is available from Oracle.

Unlike the SOA example in Chapter 4, we cannot possibly demonstrate an end-to-end re-architecture example. There are too many application and infrastructure components that are impacted — everything from the presentation-tier to the security infrastructure. We also have online and batch to deal with. For this example, we will focus on online and concentrate on the application and database.

In the "real world", we would develop a Service Component Architecture during re-architecture. **Service Component Architecture (SCA)** is a set of specifications that describe a model for building applications and systems using a Service-Oriented Architecture. SCA emphasizes the decoupling of service implementation and service assembly from the details of infrastructure capabilities and the access methods used to invoke services. Oracle JDeveloper 11g release includes support for SCA through a composite assembly editor, as well as a unified service engine for all the Oracle SOA Suite components.

Keeping It Real: Having this chapter focus on JSF, TopLink, Oracle database, and other Oracle products will not be a good use of our time. Plenty of information available on this is available at `otn.oracle.com`. What is most valuable is an in-depth focus on presentation-tier, UI navigation, and business rules capture, discovery, recovery, and source model repository. Adding SOA technologies such as BAM, BPEL, ESB, and Oracle WebCenter will shift the focus. Therefore, they will not be included.

Oracle Software Required

The software required is referred to as the bill of materials. The bill of materials for this book scenario is listed below:

- Oracle SOA Suite with Oracle Application Server 10g Release 2—Version 10.1.3.1 `http://www.oracle.com/technology/software/tech/soa/index.html`

    ° The Oracle Business Rules Engine (BRE) component of the Oracle SOA Suite will be used to create and store the COBOL code rules discovered and captured by Relativity.

- Oracle JDeveloper—Version 10.1.3.3.0 `http://www.oracle.com/technology/software/products/jdev/index.html`

- Oracle Business Process Analysis Suite—Version 10.1.3.4 `http://www.oracle.com/technology/software/products/bpa/index.html`

Keeping It Real: Oracle is a very large software vendor, and has a software "trail version" model that is based upon "the honor system"– you download it, try it out, and license it when you decide it is right for you. Most modernization vendors such as Relativity, are much smaller and offer very unique products. Therefore, they typically have a much more restrictive, trail version software requirements.

UML and Screen Flow Diagrams

For a new application, UML diagrams are usually built by gleaning information from the user community that the application serves. There is a process in which the analyst starts by identifying the main concepts and categories and describes the high-level processes in need of automation. The initial high-level information is then analyzed, and new details are added until some concrete models emerge naturally. Functional and technical specifications are developed, and a mock application is created. If the models are clear and well-defined, some forward engineering helps them make the transition to the actual code of the application. We will use UML Deployment, Use Case and Activity Diagrams, as well as a screen flow diagram.

While for new applications, the top-down approach described above works very well, for existing applications, a new approach is warranted. The existing application already contains a large volume of information that should not be discarded. The paradigm is now different and involves two movements: bottom-up and top-down. In the bottom-up phase, the existing application is mined for specific information that would result in models at the appropriate levels of abstraction. These models can be refined to reflect new requirements or business conditions, and in the last phase, they are used for generating or building the new application.

What UML diagrams can we build based on information mined from the legacy code via static analysis tools? We will show you some of the possibilities here, from screen navigation to Use Case Diagrams.

First, let's start with a Deployment Diagram using Oracle BPA Suite just as we did in the Chapter 4:

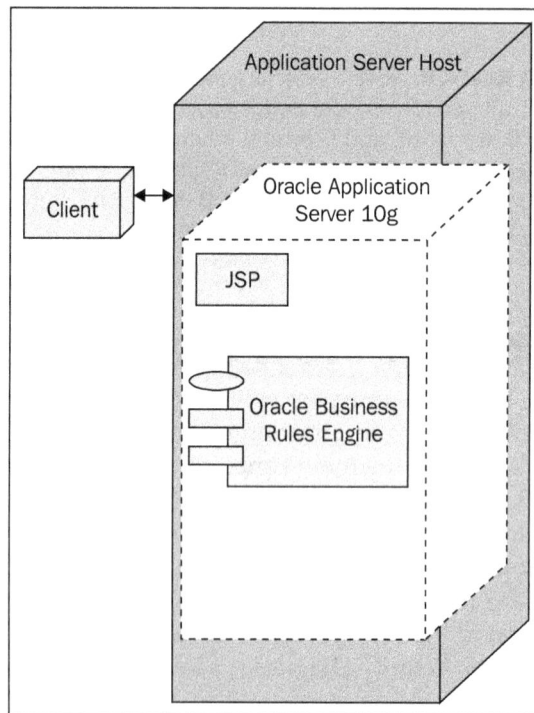

This is a very simple deployment diagram. There is no mainframe since we are re-architecting. In our example, we are not deploying to a database, so we do not need an Oracle Database. With no database, we have no data access-tier such as Oracle TopLink. We have the JSPs for the presentation and navigation-tiers, and the Oracle BRE for the business rules.

The Relativity's SOA Analyzer tool can extract screen navigation diagrams (see the following section on user interface and screen navigation). This screen navigation diagram shows the sample COBOL/CICS/VSAM customer, inventory, product, and order entry application we will be using for this example. We will discuss this application in more detail in the next section.

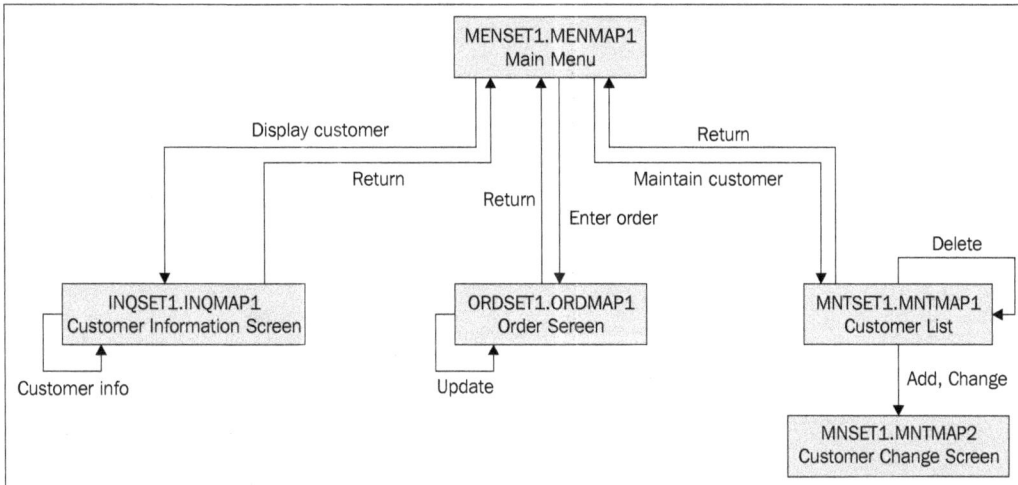

In this diagram, the boxes are screens (you can see both their technical and business names), and the edges are transitions between screens, which happen on certain events (say when pressing a Return key). The diagram gives us a lot of information about the use cases and the activities supported by the legacy application. We can notice, for instance, that the operator can register a customer in the system (via MNTMAP2 — Customer Change Screen), and can specify an order (via ORDMAP1 — Order Screen). From this, we can build a UML diagram, as shown in the following figure:

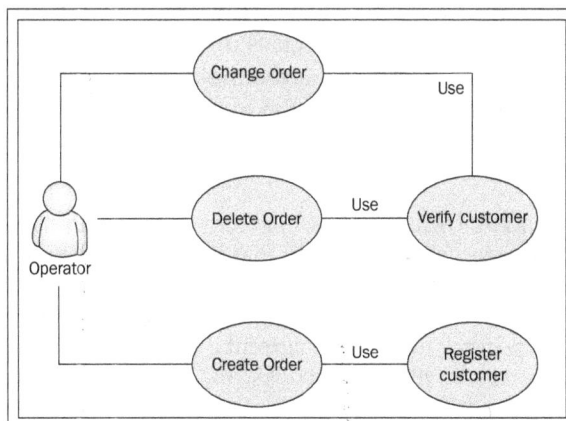

We can even specify an activity diagram, as shown in the following figure:

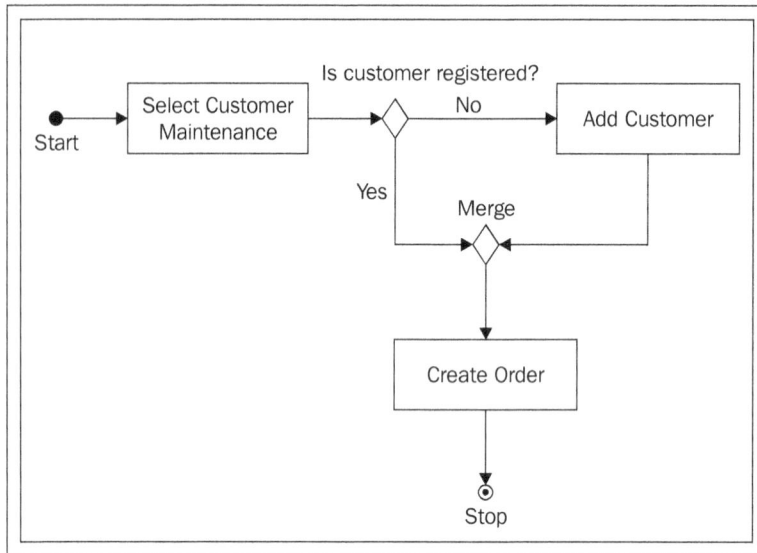

We have used some very simple and self-obvious cases here. In real life, legacy applications may contains tens or hundreds of screens with complex navigations between them. Deriving these diagrams from the actual screen navigation would ensure that all cases are accounted for, and no important aspects are left out.

As such UML diagrams are created from the analysis of the legacy application, they initially reflect the "as-is" state of the application. They can be the starting point for creating a "to-be" model, which will serve as the specification of the modernized application.

Another very useful UML diagram is the class diagram. At the core of this example, we have the business rules of the application. Since the business rules are in a business rules repository, this is really no class diagram to show the business rules. During implementation of the complete re-architecture project, there will be BPEL objects and/or Java EE code that executes the business rules. These objects can be represented in a UML class diagram.

Keeping It Real: UML and re-achitecture go "hand–in–hand" as we are dealing with a target environment that is based on an end-to-end Java EE, SOA, and Oracle relational database technologies. The development of the new system is accelerated by having functional and technical specifications in the form of the current database schema, application code, BMS maps, COBOL copybooks, and batch scripting languages.

Source Application

We will show a very classic legacy application that contains COBOL, CICS, VSAM, and batch JCL. From a business perspective, it is also a very classic application. It is a simple "Order entry" application that has CRUD CICS activity running against customer, inventory, product, and order VSAM data sets. The 3270 main menu "green screen" does the following:

1. Display customer information
2. Maintain customer information
3. Enter orders
4. *F3*=Exit *F12*=Cancel

A mainframe user will immediately recognize this main menu. Enter the numbers 1,2, or 3 to perform actions, or use the PF3 or PF12 keys.

The COBOL/CICS/VSAM application has a mix of the following legacy artifacts:

1. Five BMS maps
2. Three batch COBL modules with 620 lines of code
3. Twelve online CICS modules with 3,800 lines of code
4. Seven "supporting" COBOL modules with 468 lines of code containing business logic, navigation, and db access
5. Three JCL streams with seventy lines of JCL
6. One JCL Proc with eleven lines of JCL
7. Four CICS transactions
8. Fifteen COBOL copybooks, 1,500 lines of code, and working storage and file definitions
9. Four VSAM data files: Invoice, Inventory, Customer, and Product

This is not a large application by any means. However, this is sufficient and viable for our book example. We will only be working with the CICS/online piece, and won't have time to show an example of batch re-architecture.

[
Keeping It Real: The real world "accidental architecture" is much complex than this example. However, no matter how complex, the Relativity tool can still be used as the first step to modernization. Obviously, the length of time, and the skill required for the "accidental architecture" modernization will increase as the systems complexity increases.
]

Oracle Target Architecture

The target Oracle environment includes these Oracle products and Java EE technologies:

- Oracle database including the schema and data – Data persistence-tier.
- Oracle Toplink as persistence layer – Application database access objects-tier.
- Oracle Business Rules Engine (BRE) – Business logic/rules.
- JSF for presentation tier – User interface and screen navigation.

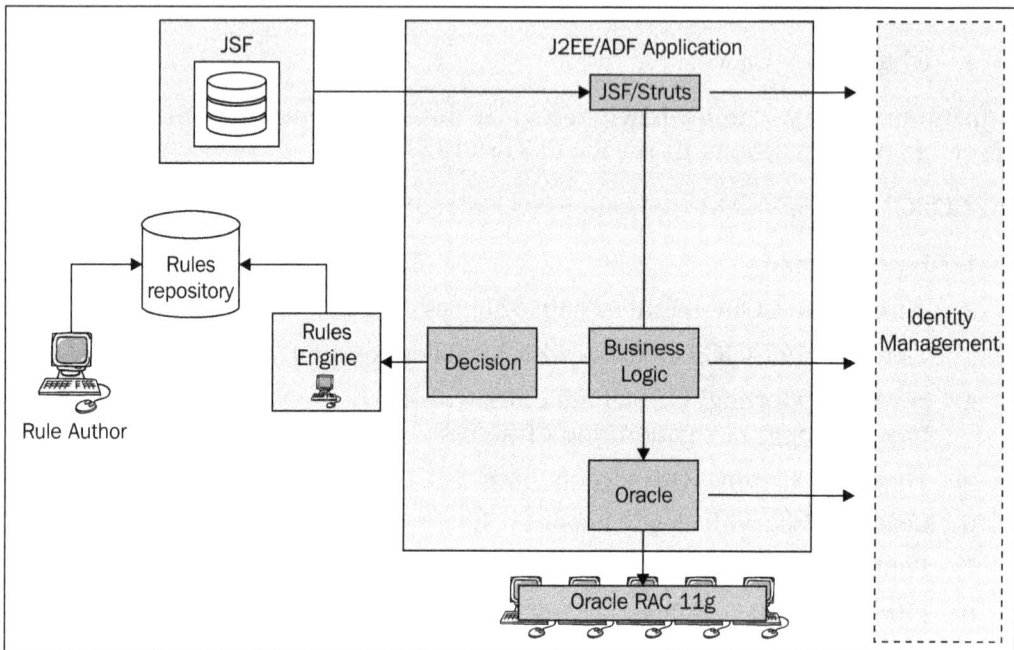

We do not have enough time or "print space" to show how to implement all the products in the above target architecture. Therefore, we will focus on:

- Business Logic-tier – Leveraging legacy artifacts and implementing them in the Oracle Business Rules Engine.
- Presentation and Navigation-tiers – However, for our example we will use JSPs.

We have intentionally left out some Oracle products in the above diagram, as they were covered in depth in the Legacy SOA Integration chapter:

- Web services
- BAM
- ESB
- BPEL

These are all very important to your new SOA Java EE re-architectured application. However, the first phase of your re-architecture project will probably not include these products. You may already have them in your IT infrastructure, as you used them in your Legacy SOA Integration modernization target architecture, or they are part of your core SOA Infrastructure.

Application Mining Using Relativity

This section will show you how the re-architecture approach is not just a "glorified green", or the dreaded "rip and replace". This is not a "rip and replace", as we have too many business requirements, and functional and technical specifications embedded in the legacy application. The mining and forward engineering of the legacy business requirements (business rules), and functional and technical specifications, embedded in the application code, makes this a re-architecture, and not a rewrite. We will use the application code to create new user interfaces, screen navigation, and business rules. This section will show how to go from COBOL code to business rules, and from 3270 to XML and HTML for the user interface and screen navigation. This is not a simple "run the tool and get a new application"; it requires some work, tool knowledge, and legacy application knowledge. The output of the process is not completely re-factored Java EE, but a great starting point. More importantly, it is a repository-based solution that can be queried and customized to fit your needs. In this section, we will learn how to perform application discovery, capture, and recovery into a source environment repository using Relativity.

Mining the User Interface and Navigation-Tiers

As we look at a legacy application, we may want to discover not only potential services, which form the flexible lower layer of a modern SOA architecture, but also the user interface and the screen navigation. If we can identify this "upper" layer and externalize it in a form that could be consumed by other modern tools, the road is open for re-implementation in a new environment.

The following table illustrates the ways in which the legacy artifacts are salvaged, and either reimplemented or used in a new architecture.

Layer	Legacy	Modern
Client facing	User interface (green screens) Navigation (via CICS or IMS transfer of control)	Browser or other user interfaces
Intermediate	Business rules imbedded in the code	Business Rules Engine
Data facing	Programs or program routines specialized in I/O operations	Database Access Objects (DAO), or Data Services as known in the SOA world

Relativity's SOA Analyzer gives us the tooling needed to address both the bottom layer and the top layer. In this section, we will explain how the user interfaces and the screen navigation could be harvested with the aid of the SOA Analyzer.

Tools needed:

- RMW Analyst (`http://www.relativity.com/pages/applicationanalyzer.asp`)
- RMW SOA Analyzer (`http://www.relativity.com/pages/soaanalyzer.asp`)

We have already used these tools for the Legacy SOA Integration example in Chapter 4. RMW Analyst is the basic tool used to parse the application code and store all the information in a repository for further access. The SOA Analyzer will be used to perform the actual user interface and navigation mining.

After we have registered the Order Entry application code to RMW and parsed the code, we can open the SOA Analyzer and immediately see the classification of the legacy artifacts into the proper layers. A more complete explanation of this classification was given in the Application Layers section of Chapter 4. For now, we'll pay attention mainly to the screens.

We notice that under the **User interface** node, we find:

- **Transaction** — These are the CICS transactions that the user can invoke in order to access various screens

- **Screens** are classified as follows:

    ○ **Screens without access to data** — These are most likely to be "menu" screens

    ○ **Screens with access to data** — Screens from which the user performs various operations against the persistent data of the application

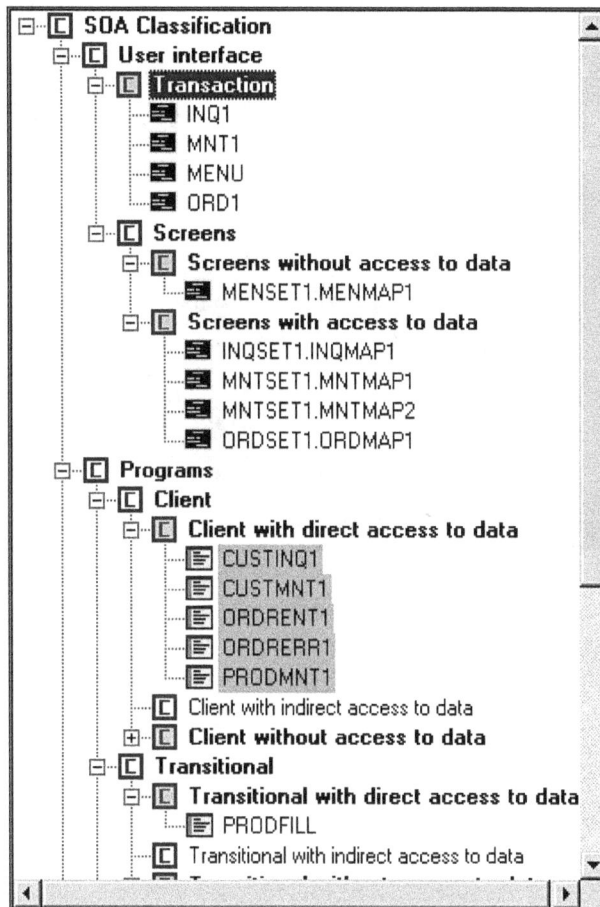

Now we can explore the position or role of the screen in the application. We can see the image of the screen itself, as well as a vertical slice and a horizontal slice through the application, both centered in the selected screen.

Capturing the Legacy User Interface

As we select the screen **ORDSET1.ORDMAP1**, we can look at its image, just as the user of the application would see it.

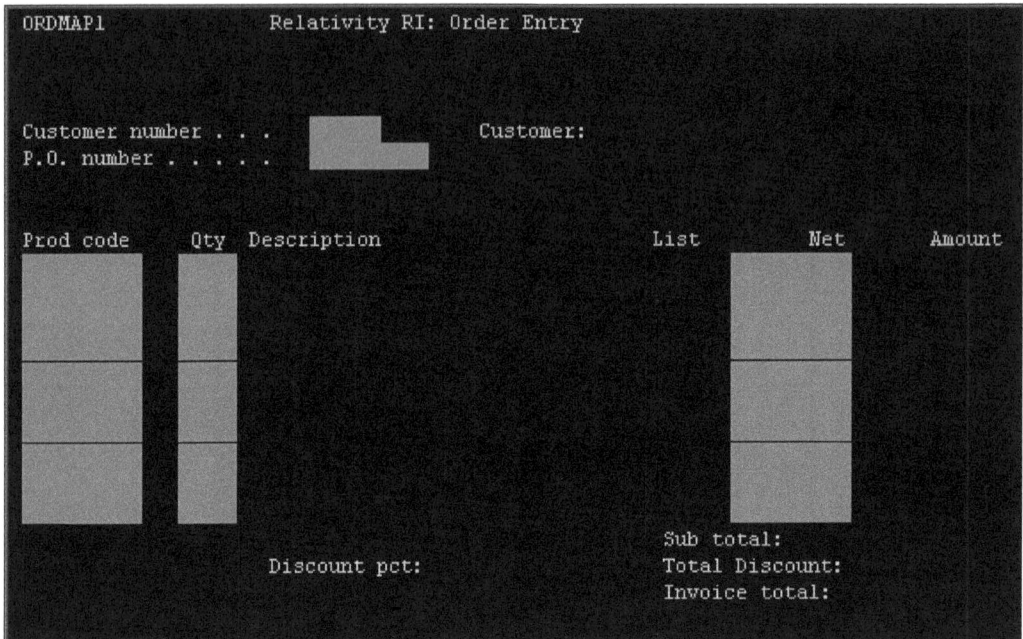

It is easy to understand that this is a screen on which an operator enters the details of a customer order. It is helpful for architects, analysts, and developers to view the legacy "green screens" without having to get access to, or to execute transactions on the mainframe.

Legacy User Interface Discovery

A vertical slice (more details on slicing can be found in Chapter 4) through the application architecture is represented in the following diagram:

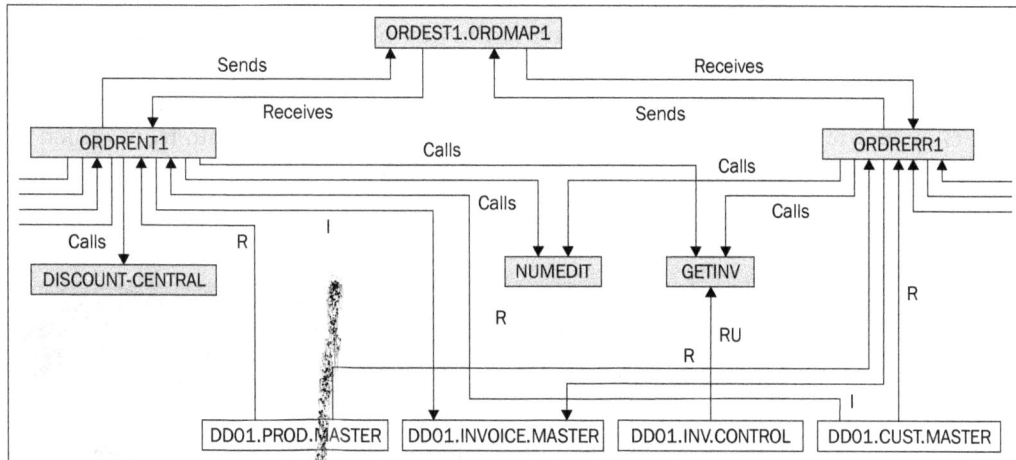

Some important facts about the legacy application can immediately be understood by studying this diagram:

- Screen ORDSET1.ORDMAP1 is accessed by two "client" programs, ORDENT1 and ORDERR1. The name of the last program suggests that it deals with exceptions from normal processing of an order.

- There are two "client" programs that access the screen and call other programs to fulfill some tasks.

- Some service programs such as NUMEDIT or GETINV. NUMEDIT are not accessing any persistent data. GETINV is reading and updating the DD01. INV.CONTROL file.

A horizontal slice of the same screen, ORDSET1.ORDEMAP1 will show navigation from and to other screens.

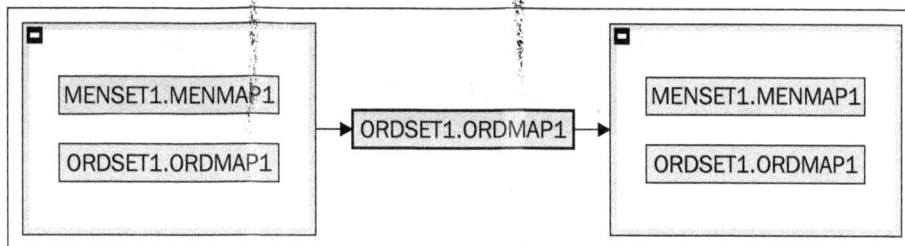

It indicates that one arrives to this screen from MENSET1.MENMAP1 and ORDSET1. ORDMAP1 (itself), and the user could navigate to the same screens.

Screen Navigation Discovery

Once we have this general understanding of the functional role of the screen as well as of its position in the overall architecture, we can move to the next steps, of which the first one is to specify the events that lead to these transitions between screens. A right-click on the node for the screen prompts us with a pop-up menu, from which we can select **Screen events**. This will lead us to a new window:

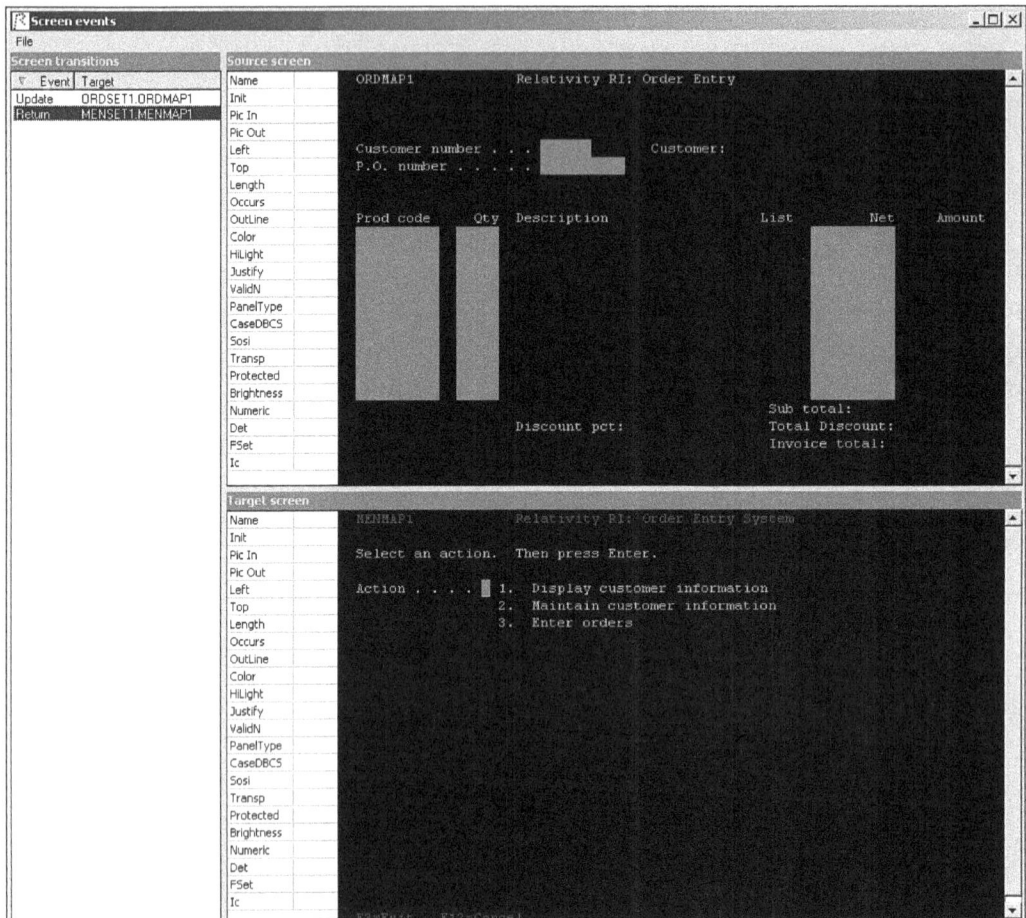

On the left pane, this window lists all possible transitions from this screen to other screens. If we select one of these transitions, for example, the transition to screen **MENSET1.MENMAP1**, the right pane displays the image of the source, and the target screens of a particular transition. On the left pane, next to the target screen, we can write the name of an event that leads to it. In this particular case, we specify an event named **Return** to indicate that, from the order entry screen, we return to the menu screen **MENSET1.MENMAP1**. For the transition between the screen and itself, we indicate the event **Update**, as an update request would place the order items in the file, and re-display the same screen. We can specify multiple events for the same transition. For example, it may be that from **MENSET1.MEMMAP1**, we can both update and insert new items for an order, in which case, we would specify the events separated by commas such as **Update,Add**.

We can repeat this event specification for each screen in the application, the same way as in this example. Once all the events are specified, we can select the **Tools | Screen** navigation menu of the SOA Analyzer in order to see a complete screen navigation diagram, as the one here:

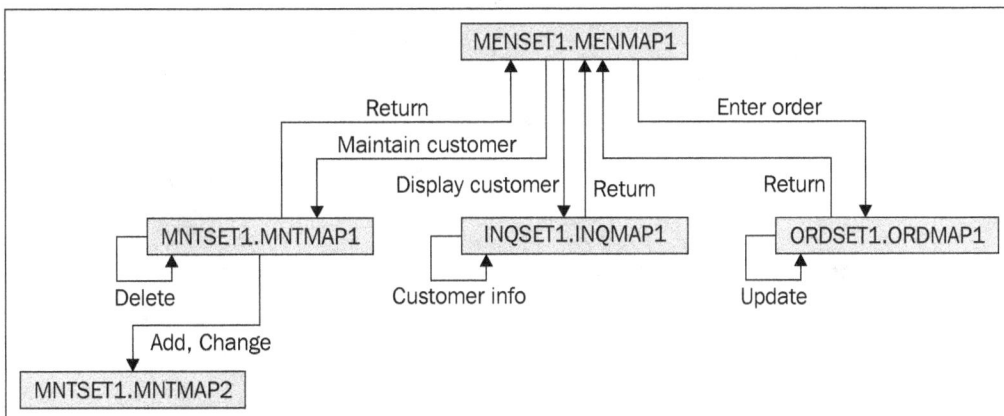

This diagram gives a complete picture of what the operator can do:

- From the "main menu" screen MENSET1.MENMAP, the operator can request to view or maintain customer information, or to enter a customer order.

- On the "customer inquiry" screen, INQSET1.INQMAP1, the operator may view the customer information.

- From the "customer maintenance" screen, MNTSET1.MNTMAP1, the operator can delete the customer, or move to the "customer data" screen MNTSET1.MNTMAP2, where the customer information may be added or changed.

Forward Engineering

At this point, we have a clear picture of the screen navigation and user interface, which can be exported in an XML format (using the **File | Export** navigation) menu. This will create an XML file that describes not only the layout of the screens, but also the events that control the navigation. This file can be used to generate the user interface and the navigation on another platform. Users of the SOA Analyst tool receive a sample XSLT file that defines a simple transformation from this file to an HTML format that renders the screens as exactly as they appear in their native environment. For example, the screen **ORDSET1.ORDMAP1**, which we have seen previously, will appear in an Internet browser as follows:

You may notice that the events that can be executed from this screen (**Update** and **Return**) appear at the bottom as buttons. This is necessary because some of the mainframe-specific events, such as those implemented through PF keys, are not available, or are assigned to other functions in the Internet browser.

The XSLT file used is shown here:

```
<?xml version="1.0" encoding="ISO-8859-1"?>
<xsl:stylesheet version = "1.0" xmlns:xsl =
                    "http://www.w3.org/1999/XSL/Transform">
    <xsl:template match = "/">
        <html>
            <body style = "background-color:black">
                <xsl:for-each select = "Screen/Fields/Field">
                    <xsl:choose>
                    <xsl:when test = "@Protected = 'No'">
                        <div>
                                <xsl:attribute name =
                                    "style">position:absolute;
                                            border:1p solid red;
                                            top:<xsl:value-of
                                            select = "25
                                            *@Line"/>;left:
                                            <xsl:value-of select
                                            = "15 *@Column"/>
                                </xsl:attribute>
                        <input>
                            <xsl:attribute name="type">
                                text</xsl:attribute>
                            <xsl:attribute name="size">
                            <xsl:value-of select="@Length"/>
                            </xsl:attribute>
                        </input>
                        </div>
                    </xsl:when>
                    <xsl:otherwise>
                        <div> <xsl:attribute name = "style">
                                color:green;font-weight:bold;
                                position:absolute;top:
                                <xsl:value-of select = "25
                                 *@Line"/>;left:
                                <xsl:value-of select
                                 = "15 *@Column"/>
                                </xsl:attribute>
                                <xsl:value-of select = "@name"/>
                                <xsl:value-of select = "@Value"/>
                        </div>
                    </xsl:otherwise>
                    </xsl:choose>
                </xsl:for-each>
                <center>
```

```
<div><xsl:attribute name = "style">
        position:absolute;top:625;
        left:0;width=1200</xsl:attribute>
<xsl:for-each select = "Screen/Events/Event">
        <input>
                <xsl:attribute name="type">
                 button</xsl:attribute>
                <xsl:attribute name="onclick">
                 window.location='<xsl:value-of
                 select="@TargetName"/>
                 .html'</xsl:attribute>
                <xsl:attribute name="value">
                 <xsl:value-of select="@Name"/>
                 </xsl:attribute>
                <xsl:attribute name="style">
                 background-color:while;
                 color:blue;border:
                 1px solid black
                 </xsl:attribute>
        </input>
</xsl:for-each>
</div>
</center>
</body>
</html>
</xsl:template>
</xsl:stylesheet>
```

This sample XSLT file is used to generate the HTML page for the XML file generated by Relativity. The XML file contains the fields and screen navigation. This XSLT file renders the XML file into an HTML page that can be displayed in a web browser. The XSLT may be modified to suit the needs of the new platform on which the UI is implemented.

We have covered a lot in this section. We went from capture and discovery of the legacy user interface and screen navigation to an HTML representation of these legacy artifacts.

Mining Business Rules

One of the major ways in which an application could be modernized is through the externalization of its business rules. In fact, once the business rules are identified and externalized, the development team has a spectrum of possibilities for the old code, starting with moving some of your business logic off the mainframe, and ending with a complete new Java EE application.

If we look at the actual code of an application, we may distinguish three distinct functional categories: process management, business rules, and mechanisms. Process management is often referred to as workflow, and more recently as business process execution.

The process management part is related to the order in which various tasks are performed. For instance, when processing a customer order, the application will perform certain activities, in the precise order: validating the request, checking the inventory, computing the prices, computing the taxes, computing the shipping costs, and sending a confirmation. There are portions of the program code that are involved with the control of these steps, and they are part of the process management. This may involve checking the success or failure of each step, screen navigation, and event processing.

The business rules code is that code which, as its name describes, controls and implements various restrictions or ways in which the enterprise business operates. Such rule may, for instance, state that a discount is offered for orders over $100 in value, or that the sales tax is computed in a particular way in a particular state.

Mechanisms refer to purely technical aspects that are incidental to a particular implementation. This may be the case when an area in memory is initialized, or when the length of a message is computed.

The three types of code can be easily identified in the case of a particular program. Let's consider, for example, three code segments:

Segment 1	```IF OPERATOR-REQUEST = "R" THEN PERFORM REMOVE-ITEM ELSE IF OPERATOR -REQUEST = "U' THEN PERFORM UPDATE-ITEM END-IF END-IF```
Segment 2	```IF TOTAL-PRICE > 100 THEN MULTIPLY TOTAL-PRICE BY DISCOUNT END IF```
Segment 3	```PERFORM VARYING IDX FROM 1 TO NUMBER-OF-ITEMS IF ITEM-NAME(IDX) = REQUESTED-NAME THEN REQUESTED-INDEX = IDX```

A simple look at these samples is enough to establish which category they belong to. Segment 1 reacts to an operator request, and therefore helps to control the process. Segment 2 expresses the rule that a discount is offered for orders over $100, while Segment 3 is a mechanism that simply performs a look-up to find an element in an array.

The three categories play separate roles in a modernization effort. Mechanisms are very much irrelevant, and may be changed only in order to improve the performance of the application. For instance, a look-up of an array could be improved by changing from a full array scan (as in the earlier example) to a binary search. However, if the application is reimplemented in a new environment, or using another technology, this is irrelevant, as new and modern development facilities already offer a large library of functions to take care of "mechanisms". In our case, this category will be re-factored into Java EE code.

On the other hand, the process management and business rules aspects remain relevant. The enterprise will prefer in most cases to preserve the way in which it does business, even if the implementation changes. For both cases, one would wish to first identify and then reimplement. Once identified, business processes may be implemented through the Oracle SOA using Oracle BPM and BPEL, while business rules may be implemented using Oracle Business Rules Engines. Users of Relativity Technologies tools may employ the SOA Analyzer to identify the processes and the services they use, and may employ the Business Rules Manager to identify the business rules.

We will take you now through a business rules mining scenario, to illustrate how the business rules identification may be accomplished in a practical way.

Prerequisites

Tools required:

- Relativity's RMW Application Analyzer is needed to register a legacy application, and parse its code in preparation for the business mining task.
- Relativity's Business Rule Manager is used for the actual identification of rules.

Besides tools and technologies, there are some other prerequisites for a successful business rule mining exercise. Perhaps the most important prerequisite is familiarity with the application. "Familiarity" may be a vague concept, but it is certainly enhanced by employing some analysis tools, for instance, Relativity's RMW Application Analyzer. Before the actual mining starts, we should first take a high-level view, so we can perceive the whole forest, not just trees (or even leaves). The static analysis of the application may help answer some important questions, as for instance:

- What are the application boundaries? We should make sure we look for all the code of the application, while avoiding the code that actually does not belong there. Most legacy applications contain modules that are no longer accessed. These modules are still in the source code control, and/or still in the production system. However, they never get "touched" by developers, or executed by the batch and online systems. Legacy applications also contain "dead code". This is code which belongs to a module that still runs in the production system, but which itself is never executed, as it can never be reached.

- Which are the main components? We may distinguish between environment components, such as batch and online, or between functional components such as client management, order processing and inventory.

- Which are the main processes? We may discover processes such as "adding a customer", "processing an order", or "updating an inventory item".

- Which programs tend to incorporate the main business rules? We may discover programs that incorporate only mechanisms (for instance, one that sends a report to the printer) and programs that are very rich in business rules (for instance, price calculation).

- Which are the main data elements of the application? They may be described by terms such as "invoice", or "order", or "shipping information".

- What is the size and complexity of the programs? This will help us estimate the size of the mining effort, and make some wise decisions on how to organize the project.

- How are various technical artifacts interrelated? It would be useful to create and hold for further reference some diagrams such as call maps and screen flow, and some reports such as the CRUD report that shows the interaction between programs and data.

As the definition (or understanding) of business rules may vary from person to person, we recommend that at the beginning of any mining project, the team involved sets a clear definition and objective. The problem with the "let's collect the business rules" objective is that one is never sure when the project is completed. For this reason, it is more useful to have an objective specified in a more concrete form. As an example, any combination of the following objectives will set a clear and achievable target for the mining project:

- Find all the validation rules for all the data that enters the application

- Find the ways in which a set of data elements is calculated (price, tax, premium)

- Find the criteria by which a client is qualified for a specific offer

It is only natural to assume that familiarity with the analysis and mining tools is a great plus. Finally, an application **Subject Matter Expert (SME)** is important as there is no substitute for some who knows the exact COBOL module name and paragraph for a specific business rule.

Identifying the Business Rules

Relativity's Business Rule Manager allows for three basic techniques for business rule identification: pattern search, validation rules search, and backward auto-detection. A combination of these could be employed from case to case. The immediate result of such searches will be the discovery of a number of "candidate rules", some of them of obvious interest, some nothing other than false positives. The mining process consists of a number of iterations in which the search criteria are constantly improved.

As candidate rules are discovered, there are always two questions to be answered:

1. Can we improve the search criteria in order to eliminate false positives?
2. Can we improve the search criteria to catch some candidate rules not discovered by the search?

Here are two concrete examples.

1. Example 1 – *Eliminating false positives*: Suppose that we establish a search criterion for finding the computation of the output fields displayed on a screen. After looking at the results, we discovered that we find more candidate rules than expected, because we captured the computation of all outputs, including the attributes of the output fields, which determine the color or display style of some data. As these attributes are not important, we can introduce more constraints so that we find only the computation of data from the screen, not its displayed attributes.

2. Example 2 – *Discovering more precise rules*: Suppose that we look for the error messages produced by an online program during input data validation. The result will be a number of code segments that look like this:

```
IF ERROR-CODE = 15 THEN
    MOVE "SHIPPING DATE IS TOO CLOSE" TO ERROR-MESSAGE.
```

This is not sufficient, as ERROR-CODE value 15 does not tell us anything about the real expectation on the shipping date. However, a new criterion may discover the code that produced ERROR-CODE 15. It may be:

```
MOVE INPUT-DATE TO DATE1
MOVE CURRENT-DATE TO DATE2
PERFORM DATE-INTERVAL-COMPUTATION
```

```
IF DATE-INTERVAL < 3 THEN
    MOVE 15 TO ERROR-CODE
```

This is more relevant, as it captures the fact that the shipping date cannot be less than three days from the current date.

Let's see now how the search criteria are built and used to discover rules.

Using Pattern Search

Relativity's Business Rule Manager allows you to search for patterns in the code, by using a facility called Clipper. With Clipper, you can create various queries based on the syntax of the language used by the application. Clipper will assist you in building correct queries, but you must know what you are after. As explained above, queries may be constantly refined in order to obtain more relevant results.

Let's suppose that with some knowledge of the application we know that somewhere in the code some computations are performed that depend on the state where the supplier of a product resides. That is enough to get started. The Clipper query will appear as follows:

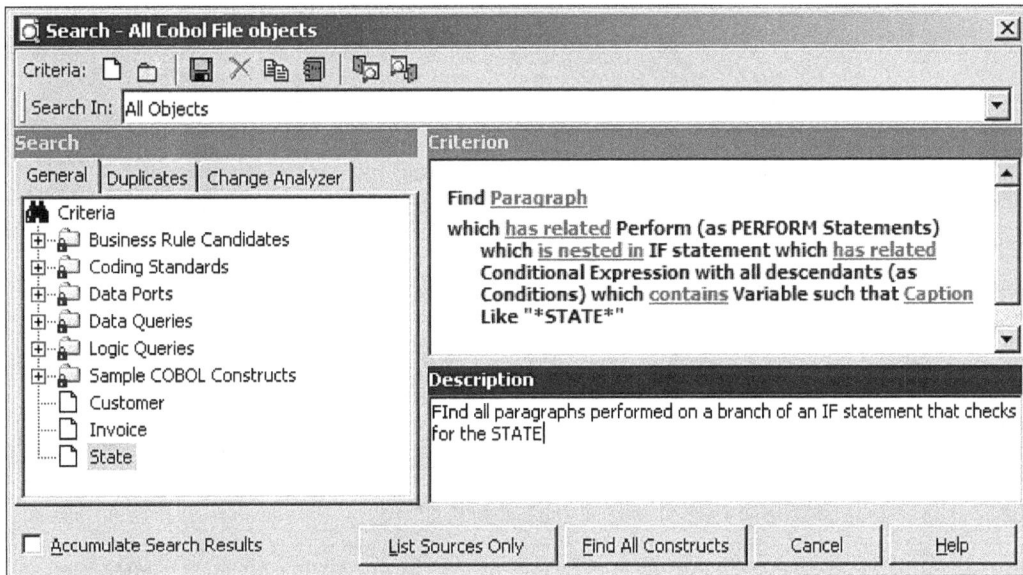

As you may notice on the left pane, Clipper comes with a number of predefined queries organized in various categories. However, in this case, we have created a new query, which we have named **States**. Clipper assists us by indicating at each point the types of objects or relationships that we may look for. We can click on any of the blue underlined words to make changes. We have also added a description on the bottom pane, which will help us remember what the query is doing in case we need it later.

As you can easily see, the query is for all paragraphs in the application that are performed on a branch of an `IF`, where we check for a variable with the name, say ***SUPP*** (for supplier). If we run the query by pressing the **Find All Constructs** button, we get the following result:

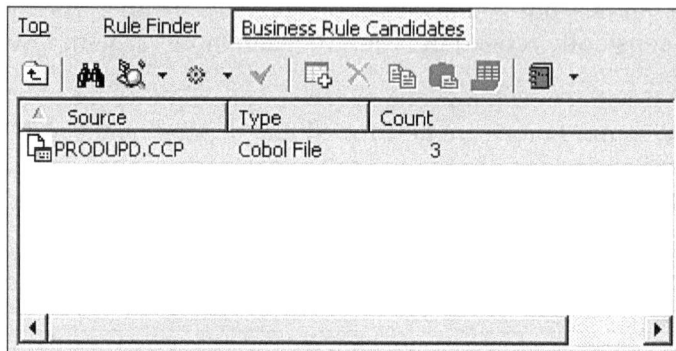

The result indicates that the pattern was found in just one of the programs (**PRODUPD.CCP**), in three instances. As we click on this line, we can see the individual instances and the associated source.

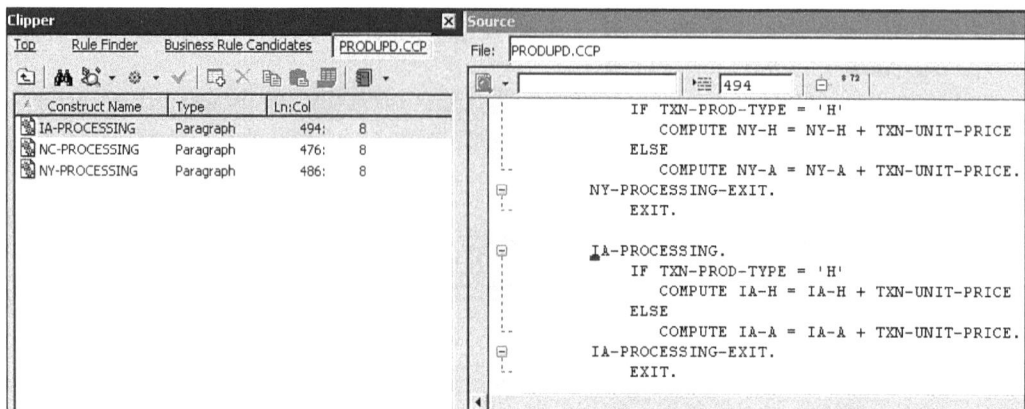

This particular instance refers to a supplier from the state of **IOWA (IA)**. At this point, if we are happy with the current finding, we can take all three instances of the code pattern and make them into "business rules". We use quotation marks because we do not yet have rules by the strict definition of the object. We have found implementations of rules, from which we will derive the rules.

As we request to create rules from these instances, we are prompted to enter the name of a Business Function and Rules Set to which they belong. The Business Function and Rule Set names are mere containers that help us to keep the business rules well organized. Later on, when we search the business rules, it is easier to find rules within specific Business Functions and Rule sets. Now, we can see the code instances captured as "business rules".

As you may see, we have given them names such as **Computation of inventory value for the state of NORTH CAROLINA**. You may also see that the Business Rule Manager has collected some additional information, for example, information about the use of some data elements in the rule. In the bottom right pane, you can see that the two of the variables are found to be both inputs and outputs, while the other three are just inputs. We have given each of them a **Business Name**, and we have also given a plain language description to each of the three rules.

Searching Validation Rules

Validation rules are of the highest importance in an application, as they describe restrictions on the data that comes from various input interfaces. Some validation rules are very simple ("Amount must be entered as a numeric value"), while some may be complex ("If the customer is in the state of Ohio, a valid address must be entered"). The Business Rule Manager can collect these rules automatically. The logic for finding such rules is simple; the tool finds all tests applied to data elements that get their values from an input on a screen.

To collect validation rules, in Business Rules Manager, we point to an input port in the source of a program (as for instance a `CICS RECEIVE` statement), and request the tool to produce a list of candidates. As a result, we will see the validation rules for the program. We may inspect them one by one, to eliminate false positives or rules that are of no interest. The tool may show, for example, rules that simply indicate that a particular field, such as the customer name, is mandatory. It is up to us to decide if this is a rule you want to keep, of if it is a "trivial" rule that can be removed.

Here is a validation rule discovered by the Business Rule Manager, which seems more significant:

```
Q ▾ rece              ▦ 652      ⊡ ⁺⁷²                              ▶
              COMPUTE CDACTUAL = (9 - REPCHECK-DIGIT).                ▲
              IF CDACTUAL = CHK-DIG
                  MOVE 'Y' TO VALID-CHECK-DIGIT-SW
              ELSE
                  MOVE 'N' TO VALID-CHECK-DIGIT-SW
                  STRING 'Invalid Product CheckDigit, Try ', CDACTUAL
                      DELIMITED BY SIZE INTO ORD-D-MESSAGE.
```

Inspecting the code, we can understand the meaning of this validation rule. It declares that when the operator enters a customer order on the screen, a "check-digit" validation is performed to make sure that all product numbers are correct. Understanding the meaning of the rule, we can now give it a more significant name and a description.

Using Backward Auto-Detection

We can employ this method when we try to answer the question "How is the value of a particular data element derived at a certain point in a particular program?" To find rules of interest, we should concentrate on the data elements that we know are calculated or derived, such as discount, total price, or insurance premium. Other data, such as customer name or address are of less interest, as they come from outside, instead of being determined by a program. The point of interest is usually around the place where the program either displays the results of the calculation (such as a screen or report), or records it in a permanent storage (table or file). It could be the output port itself, or a MOVE statement where the output data is constructed.

Here is an example. We know that a particular program computes the discount offered to a customer when the order has certain characteristics. The computation of the discount is complicated, as it takes into account parameters such as the state where the customer resides, the number of items ordered, and their value. To start the backward auto-detection, we point to the source of the statement where the discount is first set in the screen area and request the tool to find the rule.

Business Rule Manager will discover all the statements involved in the computation while ignoring everything else. Furthermore, the "backward" tracing of the discount calculation is not limited to one program, but can cross into other programs called to aid in the calculation. The result is a logic structure extracted from the program, which the Business Rule Manager displays in one of its panes as shown in the following screenshot:

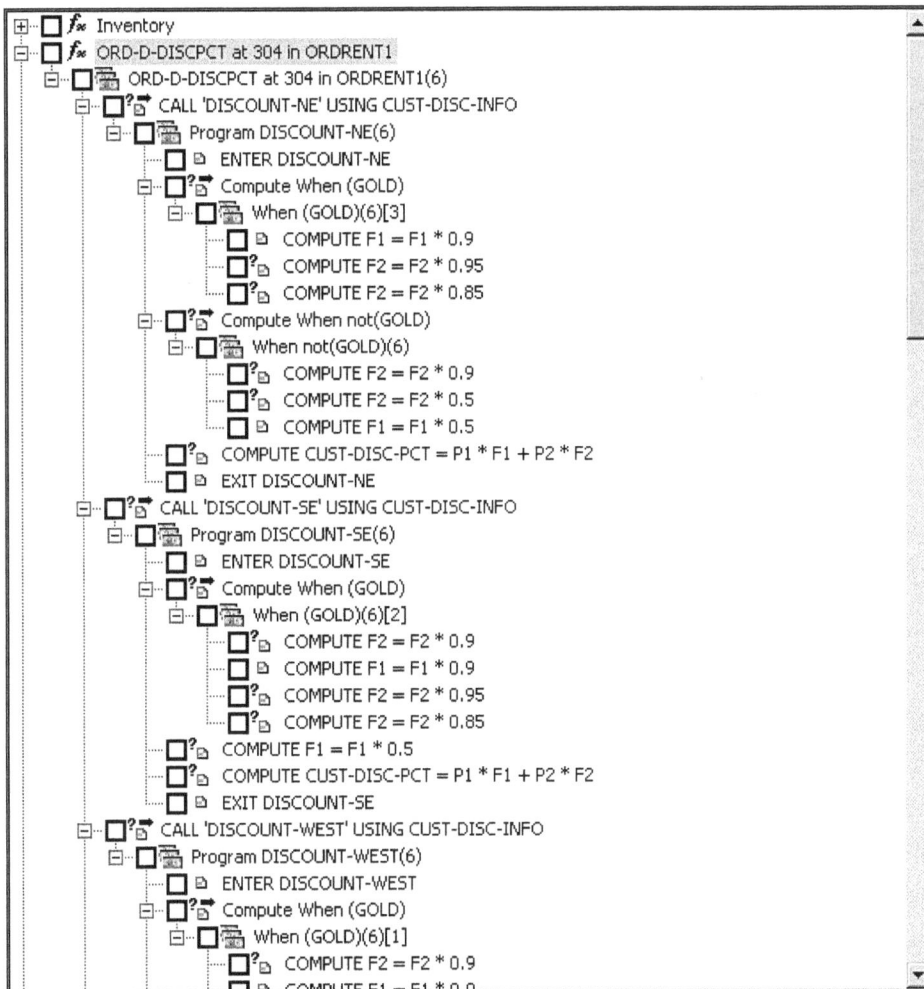

```
⊞ ☐ ƒx  Inventory
⊟ ☐ ƒx  ORD-D-DISCPCT at 304 in ORDRENT1
   ⊟ ☐   ORD-D-DISCPCT at 304 in ORDRENT1(6)
      ⊟ ☐?  CALL 'DISCOUNT-NE' USING CUST-DISC-INFO
         ⊟ ☐   Program DISCOUNT-NE(6)
            ─ ☐   ENTER DISCOUNT-NE
            ⊟ ☐?  Compute When (GOLD)
               ⊟ ☐   When (GOLD)(6)[3]
                  ─ ☐   COMPUTE F1 = F1 * 0.9
                  ─ ☐?  COMPUTE F2 = F2 * 0.95
                  ─ ☐?  COMPUTE F2 = F2 * 0.85
            ⊟ ☐?  Compute When not(GOLD)
               ⊟ ☐   When not(GOLD)(6)
                  ─ ☐?  COMPUTE F2 = F2 * 0.9
                  ─ ☐?  COMPUTE F2 = F2 * 0.5
                  ─ ☐   COMPUTE F1 = F1 * 0.5
            ─ ☐?  COMPUTE CUST-DISC-PCT = P1 * F1 + P2 * F2
            ─ ☐   EXIT DISCOUNT-NE
      ⊟ ☐?  CALL 'DISCOUNT-SE' USING CUST-DISC-INFO
         ⊟ ☐   Program DISCOUNT-SE(6)
            ─ ☐   ENTER DISCOUNT-SE
            ⊟ ☐?  Compute When (GOLD)
               ⊟ ☐   When (GOLD)(6)[2]
                  ─ ☐?  COMPUTE F2 = F2 * 0.9
                  ─ ☐   COMPUTE F1 = F1 * 0.9
                  ─ ☐?  COMPUTE F2 = F2 * 0.95
                  ─ ☐?  COMPUTE F2 = F2 * 0.85
            ─ ☐?  COMPUTE F1 = F1 * 0.5
            ─ ☐?  COMPUTE CUST-DISC-PCT = P1 * F1 + P2 * F2
            ─ ☐   EXIT DISCOUNT-SE
      ⊟ ☐?  CALL 'DISCOUNT-WEST' USING CUST-DISC-INFO
         ⊟ ☐   Program DISCOUNT-WEST(6)
            ─ ☐   ENTER DISCOUNT-WEST
            ⊟ ☐?  Compute When (GOLD)
               ⊟ ☐   When (GOLD)(6)[1]
                  ─ ☐?  COMPUTE F2 = F2 * 0.9
                  ─ ☐   COMPUTE F1 = F1 * 0.0
```

As with the other rule mining methods, at this point, we can assign significant names to the rules and give them a plain language description. The tool has calculated the input and the output fields of the rules, to which we can also give business names.

Putting it Together

Reviewing all the activities described so far, we can see the steps needed to perform a successful business rule mining project:

1. Register all sources into the RMW repository.
2. Verify (or parse) the sources.
3. Get a high-level understanding of the application with the aid of diagrams and reports. Supplement it with the help of an application SME.
4. Set clear objectives for the types of rules to be mined.
5. Use one of the three methods for rule detection: search patterns, search validations, and backward auto-detection.
6. Remove false positives.
7. Document the remaining significant rules.

These steps will result in a list of rules stored in the RMW repository. They can be reviewed at any time, and can be exported in XML format.

The discovered rules may be used in a variety of ways, starting with the simple documentation of the application, and ending with registration in a business rule engine, such as the one supplied by Oracle.

Keeping It Real: We must remember that re-architecture is not "green field" development. We are leveraging legacy artifacts and preparing them to be forward engineered into an Oracle, SOA, Java EE environment.

Forward Engineering into Oracle and Java EE

Let's take another look at the complete re-architecture scenario before we show you the actual process to move the user interface, screen navigation, and business rules to Oracle and Java EE:

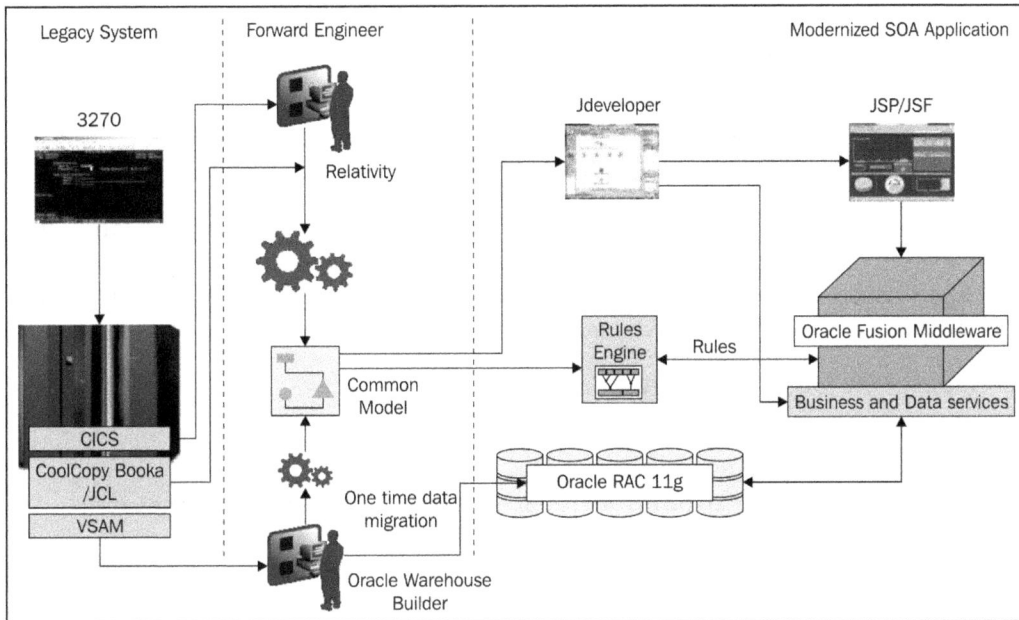

In this example, we will use JSPs for the user interface and navigation. We will not migrate data to the Oracle RAC Database using Oracle Warehouse Builder. We will demonstrate how to move captured business rules to the Oracle Business Rules Engine. We will not deploy a complete Business Rules application to Oracle Fusion Middleware. We will deploy a JSP application that has the user interface and screen navigation generated from Relativity's tools. We will also provide a "down and dirt" example of how to migrate the VSAM product master file from the mainframe to the Oracle Database using the Oracle SQL*Loader utility.

Producing the Target User Interface and Navigation

We already had a very good explanation of how the user interface and screen navigation is generated using the Relativity tools. These new artifacts were created for us from our legacy COBOL application and BMS maps:

- `ORDSET1.ORDMAP1.xml` – Screen representation in XML.

- `ScreenUIXSLT.xml` – XSLT style sheet to render the about XML screen representation.

- `ORDSET1.ORDMAP1.html` – Generated HTML page using the above two artifacts.

Next, we will do something simple that will prepare ourselves for an application that has a layered architecture. We will copy and rename the `ORDSET1.ORDMAP1.html` as the `NewOrderEntry.jsp`. Now, we have a JSP page that can call Java Bean façade objects that access the Oracle BRE and Oracle TopLink database access services.

A sample of the JSP looks like this:

```
<html>
    <body style="background-color:black">
        <div style="color:green;font-weight:bold;position:absolute;
                top:25;left:30">ORDMAP1</div>
        <div style="color:green;font-weight:bold;position:absolute;
                top:25;left:315">RELATIVITY RI: ORDER ENTRY</div>
        <div style="color:green;font-weight:bold;position:absolute;
                top:75;left:30"></div>
        <div style="color:green;font-weight:bold;position:absolute;
                top:125;left:30">CUSTOMER NUMBER . . .</div>
        <div style="position:absolute;border:1p solid red;
                top:125;left:360"><input type="text" size="6"></div>
        <div style="color:green;font-weight:bold;position:absolute;
                top:125;left:465"></div>
        <div style="color:green;font-weight:bold;position:absolute;
                top:125;left:555">CUSTOMER:</div>
        <div style="color:green;font-weight:bold;position:absolute;
                top:125;left:705"></div>
        <div style="color:green;font-weight:bold;position:absolute;
                top:150;left:30">P.O. NUMBER . . . . .</div>
        <div style="position:absolute;border:1p solid red;
                top:150;left:360"><input type="text" size="10"></div>
        <div style="color:green;font-weight:bold;position:absolute;
                top:150;left:525"></div>
```

```
<div style="color:green;font-weight:bold;position:absolute;
        top:150;left:705"></div>
<div style="color:green;font-weight:bold;position:absolute;
        top:175;left:705"></div>
<div style="color:green;font-weight:bold;position:absolute;
        top:200;left:705"></div>
<div style="color:green;font-weight:bold;position:absolute;
        top:200;left:1020"></div>
<div style="color:green;font-weight:bold;position:absolute;
        top:200;left:1065"></div>
```

More definitions for each of the fields...

```
<div style="color:green;font-weight:bold;position:absolute;
        top:550;left:765">INVOICE TOTAL:</div>
<div style="color:green;font-weight:bold;position:absolute;
        top:550;left:1005"></div>
<div style="color:green;font-weight:bold;position:absolute;
        top:575;left:30"></div>
<div style="color:green;font-weight:bold;position:absolute;
        top:600;left:30"></div>
<div style="color:green;font-weight:bold;position:absolute;
        top:600;left:1200"> </div>
<center>
    <div style="position:absolute;top:625;left:0;width=1200">
    <input type="button" onclick="window.location=
        'ORDSET1.ORDMAP1.html'" value="Update" style="background-
        color:while;color:blue;border:1px solid black">
    <input type="button" onclick="window.location=
        'MENSET1.MENMAP1.html'" value="Return" style="background-
        color:while;color:blue;border:1px solid black"></div>
</center>
</body>
</html>
```

The highlighted snippet contains the simple screen navigation.

Using JDeveloper, we deploy our application to the Oracle Application Server just as we did in Chapter 4.

Running the Presentation-Tier Mock-up in Oracle Application Server

In the Legacy SOA Integration application, we talked about the great new user interface that we produced. When we re-architect, often we find that the end users want the same look and feel for the initial release of the open system product. Therefore, our new application will look and act just as the 3270 "green screen".

Deploying to the Oracle Application Server

Please refer to Chapter 4. We will not go into detail here as this has already been shown in that chapter. There is also a very good example on OTN: `http://www.oracle.com/technology/obe/obe_as_1012/j2ee/deploy/deploytoappserver/lesson_deployment.htm`.

Running the Application

Test the application by accessing the web app at the URL: `http://localhost:8888/LegacyApp/LegacyRelativityScreenUIandNavigationArtifacts/NewOrderEntry.jsp`

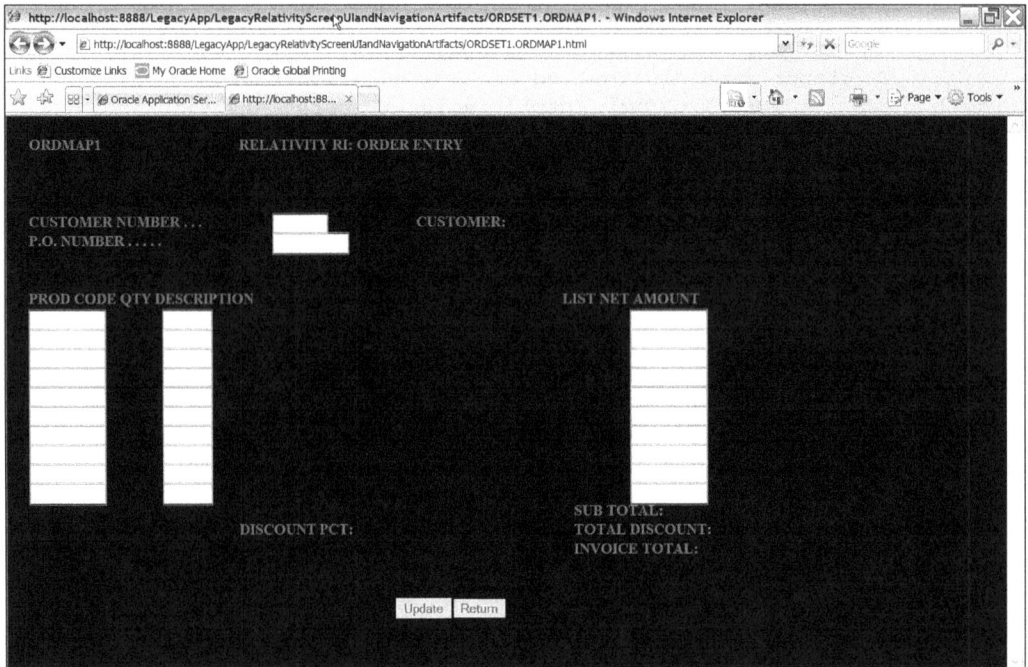

> **Keeping It Real**: Although our Java/JSP application is very simple, we hope you will find it impressive. We went from a COBOL and CICS application running on the mainframe to a screen that is running in the Oracle Application Server. Obviously, in order to make this user interface and screen navigation "industrial strength", and ready for production, we will need to do a fair amount of re-factoring, some modeling and a little bit of coding.

Producing the Target Business Rules

For our example, we will populate the Oracle Business Rules Engine (BRE) manually using the Oracle Rule Author web-base tool. There are a couple of reasons for doing this:

- It is a great way to introduce you to the Oracle Business Rules Engine.
- We don't have the time or space in this chapter to cover the Java API that Oracle provides to read an XML-based rules file and populate the Oracle Business Rules engine repository.

We are not going to start from scratch as we will be using the business rules generated by the Relativity Business Rule Manager. These rules are stored in an XML file. The structure (XSD) of this XML file is very similar to the structure used by the Oracle Business Rules Engine:

Rule Heirarchy	Relativity (Stored in or identified by)	Oracle (Stored in or identified by)
Repository	XML file generated from Relativity Oracle database repository	File or WebDav based repository
Dictionary	<Objects> tag	Dictionary in the Oracle web-base rule author
RuleSets - Groups of rules that are generally executed as one unit	<RULESET> tag	Ruleset in the Oracle web base rule author
Rules - Expressions on the facts	<RULE> tag	Rules in the Oracle web base rule author

A portion of the XML rules file generated by Relativity appears as follows:

```xml
<?xml version="1.0" encoding="ISO-8859-1"?>
<ERD BRMVersion = "2.1.02">
    <Repository>
        <Objects events = "false">
        <BUSINESSFUNC Name = "Inventory" BusinessArea = ""
            BusinessDescription = "" Classification = "Calculation"
            Audit = "Not Approved" Status = "Working"
            Transition = "Valid as is" Description = ""/>

                <RULESET Name = "Inventory by state" BusinessDescription
                                = "" Classification = "Calculation"
                    Audit = "Not Approved" Status = "Working"
                    Transition = "Valid as is" Description = ""
                    Created = "2008-06-12 10:02:12">
                        <Implements Entity = "BUSINESSFUNC"
                            Name = "Inventory" SeqNo = "0"/>

                <RULE
                    Name = "n39574.6723263889.3"
                    RuleName = "Computation of inventory value for the
                                state of NORTH CAROLINA"
                    BusinessDescription = ""
                    Model = "COBOL"
                    Program = "PRODUPD.CCP"
                    FileName = "SOURCES\COBOL\PRODUPD.CCP"
                    FromRow = "476"
                    ToRow = "482"
                    SourceText = "      NC-PROCESSING.&#xA;
            IF TXN-PROD-TYPE = 'H'&#xA;
        COMPUTE NC-H = (NC-H &#xA;
                    + (TXN-UNIT-PRICE * TXN-QUANTITY-ON-HAND))
                    &#xA;
            ELSE &#xA;
        COMPUTE NC-A = ( NC-A  &#xA;                         +
                (TXN-UNIT-PRICE * TXN-QUANTITY-ON-HAND)). &#xA;"
                    Validated = "2008-05-06 16:08:09"
                    Valid = "Valid"
                    AssignedTo = "MIKEO"
                    SeqNo = "100001"
                    Classification = "Calculation"
                    Audit = "Not Approved"
                    Status = "Working"
                    Transition = "Valid as is"
                    Description = "For each product type, add the value
                                computed by multiplying the unit price
                                with the quantity at hand.">
```

```
            <IsContainedIn Entity = "RULESET" Name = "Inventory
                                                     by state"/>
          </RULE>
        </Objects>
      </Repository>
      <Interface ReturnCode = "0"/>
    </ERD>
```

We will be working with the business rule shown above. The Relativity tool has identified the COBOL module that contains this rule as PRODUPD.CCP.

First, let's start with a quick primer on Oracle BRE (that applies to most Java rules engines). The Oracle Business Rules Engine is a Java library that applies rules to facts, and defines and processes rules. A fact is the data that the rule will evaluate. The rule enabled application passes the facts and rules to the Rules Engine (facts are asserted in the form of Java objects or XML documents). The Rules Engine runs in the rule enabled Java application, and uses the Rete algorithm to efficiently fire rules that match the facts.

Creating the Rules Repository and Dictionary

First, we need to create a repository and dictionary to store the business rules. Create the repository using the web-base Oracle Rule Author:

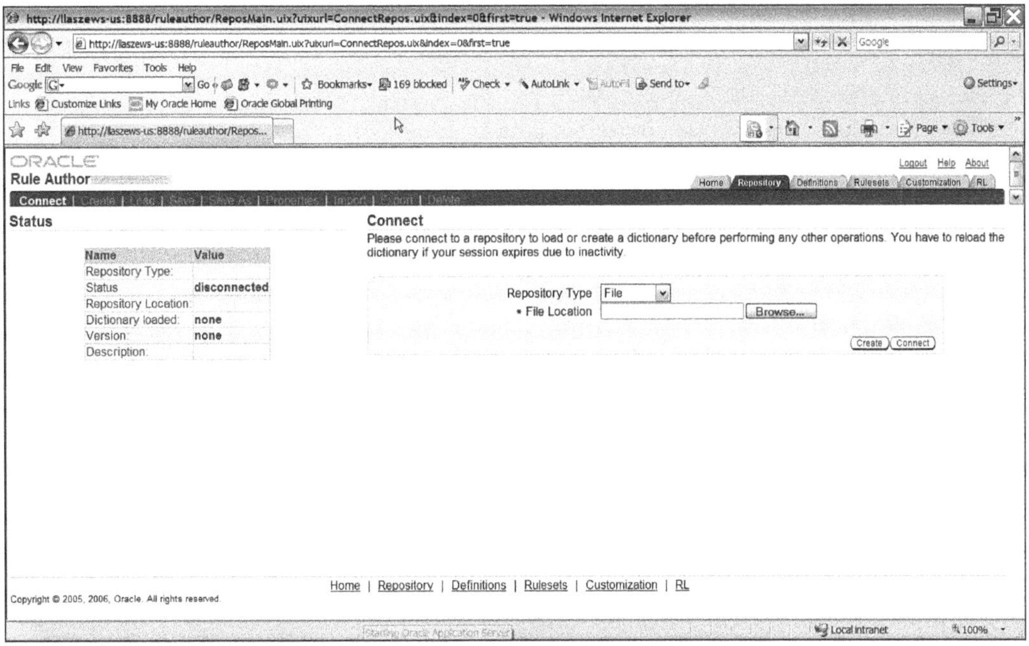

The Oracle Rule Author tool is accessed from the "SOA Launch Console". The repository we will create is called LegacyRearchRuleRepository. It is stored in the file system under the directory `d:\jdev10g\jdev\mywork\BookRearchitecture\ OrderEntryRearch\public_html\WEB-INF`.

Next, we will create the dictionary. The dictionary stores the rules and definitions of a rule enabled application. So, you usually create a dictionary for each application contained in your system. The dictionary is a set of XML files that stores the rules and the data models.

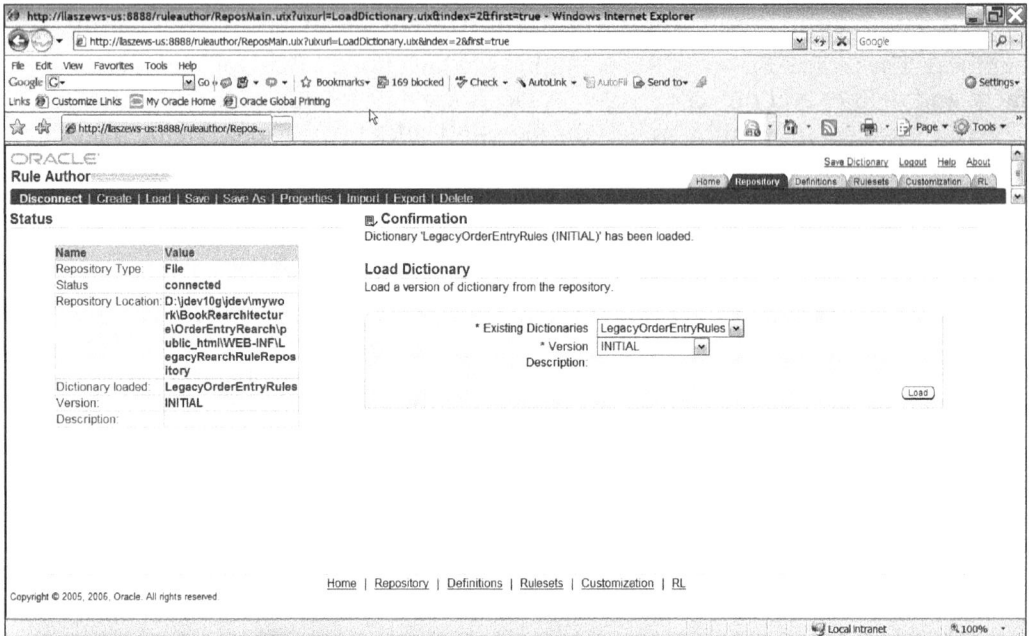

The dictionary to hold the business rules is called LegacyOrderEntryRules.

Creating Ruleset

Next, we define the ruleset in this repository (the file) and dictionary (the application):

A ruleset is a collection of rules that are intended to be evaluated together. The ruleset we are defining will contain all the Inventory State rules. So we will name it the **inventory_by_state** ruleset.

The corresponding Relativity ruleset is:

```
<RULESET Name = "Inventory by state" BusinessDescription = ""
        Classification = "Calculation" Audit = "Not Approved" Status
        = "Working" Transition = "Valid as is"
        Description = "" Created = "2008-06-12 10:02:12">
            <Implements Entity = "BUSINESSFUNC"
                        Name = "Inventory" SeqNo = "0"/>

        </RULESET>
```

Note that we used the same name as the Relativity tool did, but inserted underscores, since Oracle BRE does not allow spaces in the name.

Java Fact—Adding the Java Fact Class to the Rules Author

Before we can create a rule, we must first add a fact type in the Oracle Business Rules Engine. Fact types can be Java classes or XML documents. In this section, you only work with Java facts (called Java fact types). A Java fact type allows selected properties and methods of a Java class to be declared to the Oracle Business Rules Engine so that rules can access, create, modify, and delete instances of the Java class. Declaring a Java fact type allows the Oracle Business Rules Engine to access and use public attributes, public methods, and bean properties, and defines the Java fact. Basically, what you are doing in this step is to make the connection between your Java EE application and Oracle BRE. The rule we will create works on the transaction data that is part of the order entry process. Therefore, we will have Java class that defines the fields and methods associated with the order entry transaction object:

```java
package LegacyReachitecture;

import java.util.*;

public class TxnsRecord
{

    public double NC_A;
    public double NC_H;

    public TxnsRecord()
    {
        m_product_number = "";
        m_supplier_code = "";
        m_product_type = "";
        m_unit_price = 0.00;
        m_quantity_on_hand = 0;
        m_product_description = "";
    }

    public TxnsRecord ( String product_number,
                        String supplier_code,
                        String product_type,
                        double unit_price,
                        int quantity_on_hand,
                        String product_description)
    {
        m_product_number = product_number;
        m_supplier_code = supplier_code;
        m_product_type = product_type;
        m_unit_price = unit_price;
```

```
        m_quantity_on_hand = quantity_on_hand;
        m_product_description = product_description;
    }
    public String getProductNumber()
    {
        return m_product_number;
    }

    public void setProductNumber( String product_number )
    {
        String oldVal =  m_product_number;
        m_product_number = product_number;

    }
    public String getSupplierCode()
    {
        return m_supplier_code;
    }
    public void setSupplierCode( String supplier_code )
    {
        String oldVal =  m_supplier_code;

        m_supplier_code = supplier_code;

    }
    public String getProductType()
    {
        return m_product_type;
    }
    public void setProductType ( String product_type )
    {
        String oldVal =  m_product_type;
        m_product_type = product_type;

    }
    public double getUnitPrice()
    {
        return m_unit_price;
    }
    public void setUnitPrice ( double unit_price )
```

```
    {
        double oldVal = m_unit_price;

        m_unit_price = unit_price;

    }
    public int getQuantityOnHand()
    {
        return m_quantity_on_hand;
    }
    public void setQuantityOnHand( int quantity_on_hand )
    {
        int oldVal = m_quantity_on_hand;

        m_quantity_on_hand = quantity_on_hand;

    }
    public double getTotalValueofItemOnHand(double unit_price,
                                        int quantity_on_hand )
    {
        double totalValueOnHand;

        totalValueOnHand = (double) (quantity_on_hand * unit_price);

        return totalValueOnHand;

    }
    public String getProductDescription()
    {
        return m_product_description;
    }
    public void setProductDescription ( String product_description )
    {
        String oldVal = m_product_description;

        m_product_description = product_description;

    }
    static private final String UNKNOWN = "unknown";

    private String m_product_number;
    private String m_supplier_code;
    private String m_product_type;
    private double m_unit_price;
    private int m_quantity_on_hand;
    private String m_product_description;

}
```

This is a standard Java class with getter and setter methods. So nothing is out of the norm here. Since we are using Java facts, we must have a Java class that the Oracle Business Rules Engine can apply rules too. We know the fields that will make up the transaction Java class by examining the COBOL "01 level" in the program (PRODUPD. CCP) identified by Relativity in the XML rules definition:

```
01   TXN-REC.
       05   TXN-PROD-NUM              PIC X(10).
       05   TXN-SUPP-CODE             PIC XX.
       05   TXN-PROD-TYPE             PIC XX.
       05   TXN-UNIT-PRICE            PIC 9(7)v99.
       05   TXN-QUANTITY-ON-HAND      PIC 9(7).
       05   TXN-PROD-DESC             PIC X(20).
       05   filler                    PIC X(30).
```

Having a "filler" in this "01" working storage area is both normal and a point of interest. Most legacy-automated application migration tools would create Java variables and methods for this field, or even create a separate "filler" Java class for each instance of the filler it finds. Since we know that filler is not required in open systems, Java EE and relational database environment, we can simply ignore it. This is one of the advantages of re-architecture over legacy-automated application modernization; you have control over the resulting Java EE application.

We must make the Java class defined above available to the **Rule Author** before importing Java facts into a data model. To do this, use the **Rule Author** to specify the classpath that contains the Java classes (the Java JAR file). This is done under the **Definitions** tab and in the **JavaFact** folder:

Then import the **TxnsRecord** Java Bean we showed earlier:

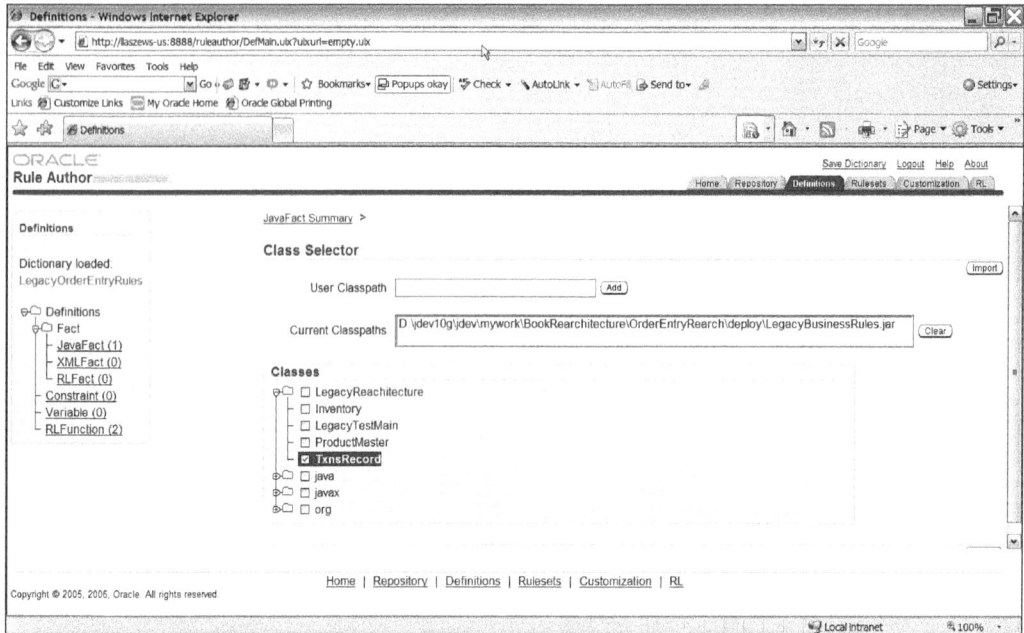

[
Keeping It Real: Business rules technology takes some time to ramp up. At first, it may seem easier to just leave the business logic in the application. However, once your business rules are in the BRE, you will find that your application maintenance and support costs are significantly lower.
]

Adding the Rule

Now that we have a repository, dictionary, ruleset, and a Java fact, we can create the rules associated with the ruleset. We will create one rule from the rules generated by Relativity. The rule in the Relativity XML format looks like this:

```
<RULE
            Name = "n39574.6723263889.3"
            RuleName = "Computation of inventory value for the
    state of NORTH CAROLINA"
            BusinessDescription = ""
            Model = "COBOL"
            Program = "PRODUPD.CCP"
            FileName = "SOURCES\COBOL\PRODUPD.CCP"
            FromRow = "476"
```

```
                    ToRow = "482"
                    SourceText = "          NC-PROCESSING.&#xA;          IF
TXN-PROD-TYPE = 'H'&#xA;               COMPUTE NC-H = (NC-H &#xA;
          + (TXN-UNIT-PRICE * TXN-QUANTITY-ON-HAND)) &#xA;
ELSE &#xA;               COMPUTE NC-A = ( NC-A  &#xA;
     + (TXN-UNIT-PRICE * TXN-QUANTITY-ON-HAND)). &#xA;"
                    Validated = "2008-05-06 16:08:09"
                    Valid = "Valid"
                    AssignedTo = "MIKEO"
                    SeqNo = "100001"
                    Classification = "Calculation"
                    Audit = "Not Approved"
                    Status = "Working"
                    Transition = "Valid as is"
                    Description = "For each product type, add the value
computed by multiplying the unit price with the quantity at hand.">
                    <IsContainedIn Entity = "RULESET" Name = "Inventory by
state"/>
              </RULE>
```

We will use the same rule name in the Oracle Rules Engine:
ComputationOfInventory ValueForTheStateOfNORTHCAROLINA. We need to
remove spaces since Oracle BRE does not allow spaces in the rules name. We will use
the identical description.

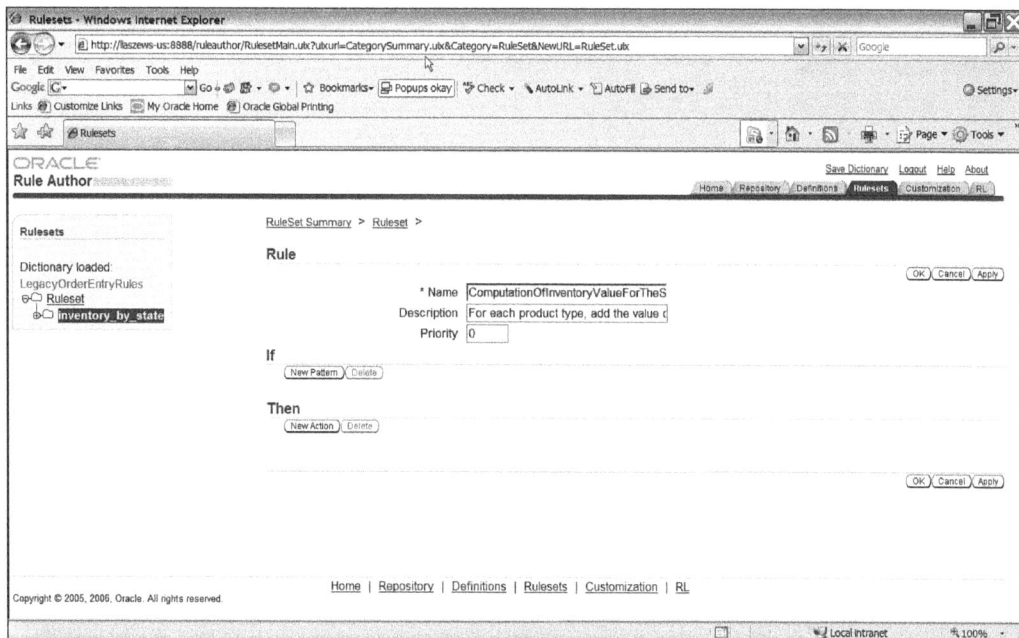

We must create a rule pattern before we can create the rule. This is the `if` statement for the rule, which will be identical to the `if` statement in the Relativity XML file:

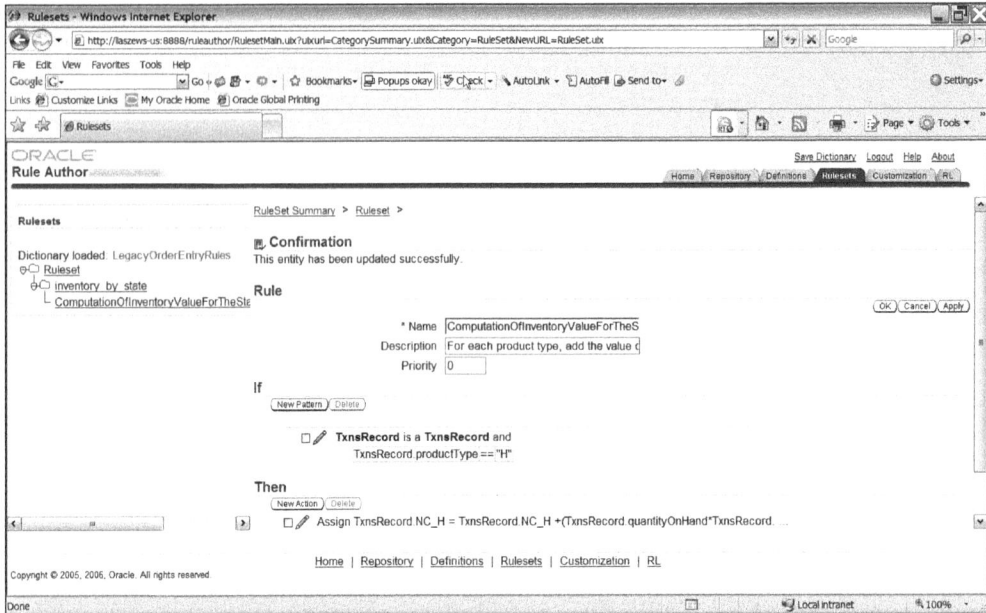

Lastly, we will create the rule for the `else` part of the `if` statement. We will call it **ComputationOfInventory ValueForTheStateOfNORTHCAROLINAElse**:

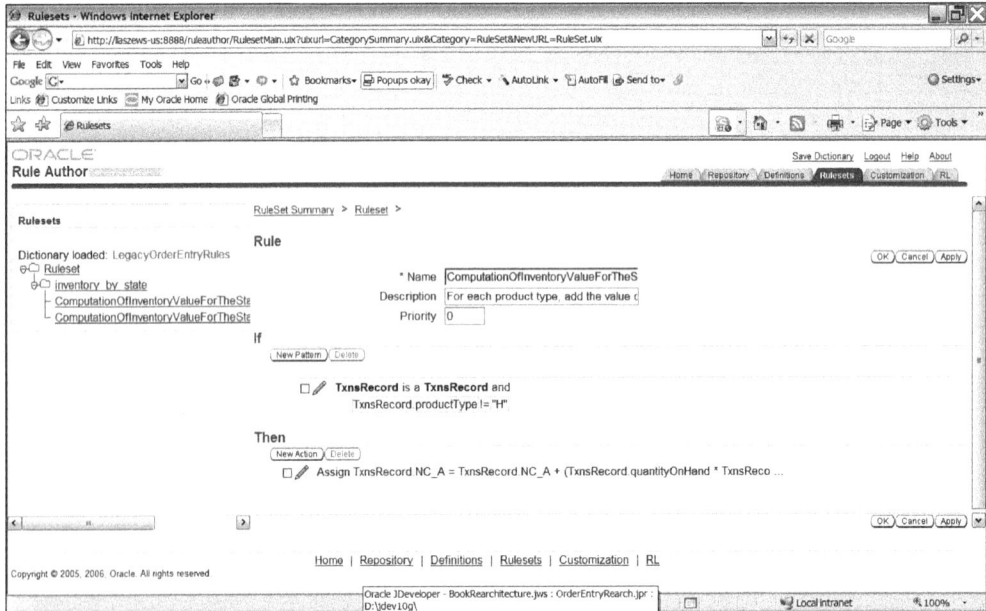

We have successfully created the ruleset and the rules that can now be asserted to, and from a Java EE application.

> **Keeping It Real**: There is no magic bullet here that can take you from COBOL/VSAM to Java EE/Oracle. However, as tools like Relativity advance in their level of Presentation-tier, UI navigation, and business rules understanding and extraction, forward engineering legacy systems into Java EE-based Oracle systems will become more automated. Oracle continues to work with Relativity and other vendors to make it easier to make the transition from source to target model an easier and seamless process.

Calling the Business Rules from Java EE and BPEL

Once you have your business rules defined, you can then call them from your Java application. Business rules can be called from a Java/Java EE application using an API. The best place to get more information on how to utilize the Oracle BRE API in your application is here:

```
http://download-east.oracle.com/docs/cd/B31017_01/web.1013/b28966/
toc.htm
```

A tutorial on how to call the Oracle BRE from Java/Java EE applications can be found here: `http://www.oracle.com/technology/products/ias/business_rules/files/how-to-rules-java.zip`.

For BPEL, it is simpler, and no coding is required. This is because Oracle has already done the integration between Oracle BPEL and Oracle BRE for you. A step-by-step presentation and introduction to calling Oracle Business Rules from BPEL can be found here: `http://www.oracle.com/technology/products/ias/bpel/pdf/bpelandbusinessrules.pdf`

When using BPEL, you will be creating and using XML-based rules (facts that are stored as XML documents). In Java EE, you will be executing Java facts, like we did in this chapter. A piece of sample code to call the rules repository and the ruleset we just created looks like this:

```java
package LegacyReachitecture;
import java.util.Date;
import oracle.rules.sdk.ruleset.RuleSet;
import oracle.rules.sdk.repository.RuleRepository;
import oracle.rules.sdk.repository.RepositoryManager;
import oracle.rules.sdk.repository.RepositoryType;
import oracle.rules.sdk.repository.RepositoryContext;
import oracle.rules.sdk.dictionary.RuleDictionary;
```

```java
import oracle.rules.sdk.exception.RepositoryException;

import oracle.rules.rl.RuleSession;

public class LegacyTestMain
{
    static final String fs = System.getProperty("file.separator");

    static public void main( String[] args )
    {
        try
        {
            //1.load dictionary
            String repoPath = "dict" + fs +
                              "LegacyRearchRuleRepository";

            RepositoryType jarType =
              RepositoryManager.getRegisteredRepositoryType
              ( oracle.rules.sdk.store.jar.Keys.CONNECTION );
            RuleRepository repo =
              RepositoryManager.createRuleRepositoryInstance
              ( jarType );

            //fill in init property values
            RepositoryContext jarCtx = new RepositoryContext();
            jarCtx.setProperty( oracle.rules.sdk.store.jar.Keys.PATH,
                                repoPath );

            //init the repository instance.  If the init is
            //successful,
            //we shall get a useable repository instance
            repo.init( jarCtx );
            RuleDictionary dict = repo.loadDictionary
              ( "LegacyOrderEntryRules", "INITIAL" );

            //init a rule session
            String rsname = "inventory_by_state";
            String dmrl = dict.dataModelRL();
            String rsrl;
            rsrl = dict.ruleSetRL( rsname );

            RuleSession session = new RuleSession();
            session.executeRuleset( dmrl );
            session.executeRuleset( rsrl );

            //assert facts

            //assert product Oracle Datbase
            TxnsRecord tr1 = new TxnsRecord( "OrclDB11g", "OO", "H",
              5000.00, 10, "Oracle Database11g with RAC" );

            //assert product Oracle Application Server
```

```
        TxnsRecord tr2 = new TxnsRecord( "OrclAS11g", "OO", "J",
           10000.00, 10, "Oracle Application Server 11g" );

        //assert product Oracle BEA
        TxnsRecord tr3 = new TxnsRecord( "OrclBEA", "OO", "K",
           10000.00, 9, "BEA Suite" );

        session.callFunctionWithArgument( "assert", tr1 );
        session.callFunctionWithArgument( "assert", tr2 );
        session.callFunctionWithArgument( "assert", tr3 );

        session.callFunctionWithArgument( "run", rsname );
    }
    catch( Throwable t )
    {
        t.printStackTrace();
    }
}


static public RuleRepository getWebDAVRepository( String urlPath,
  String user, String password ) throws RepositoryException
{

    RepositoryType webdavType =
       RepositoryManager.getRegisteredRepositoryType
       ( oracle.rules.sdk.store.webdav.Keys.CONNECTION );
    RuleRepository webdavInstance =
       RepositoryManager.createRuleRepositoryInstance
       ( webdavType );

    //fill in init property values ... we assume no proxy here
    RepositoryContext webdavCtx = new RepositoryContext();
    webdavCtx.setProperty
            ( oracle.rules.sdk.store.webdav.Keys.URL, urlPath );
      webdavCtx.setProperty( oracle.rules.sdk.store.webdav.Keys.
                            USER, user );
    webdavCtx.setProperty
       ( oracle.rules.sdk.store.webdav.Keys.PASSWORD, password );
    //init the repository instance.  If the init is successful,
    //we shall get a useable repository instance
    webdavInstance.init( webdavCtx );

    return webdavInstance;
}
}
```

Automatic Business Rules Generation Using Java Code

As the output produced by the Relativity tool is standard XML, you can use a number of XML parser options to read the file. The XML parser exposes the contents of an XML document through an API. A Java/Java EE application reads the XML document through this API. Java offers both DOM (Document Object Model) and SAX (Simple API for XML) styles of processing. These process APIs are used along with the Java API for XML Parsing (JAXP).

Once you have the input Relativity XML rules file in your Java application, you can then use the Oracle Rules SDK to create the rules in the Oracle BRE. The best example of using this SDK is found in the "Oracle How-To: Create Rules using the Rules SDK in a Java Application – create DataModel and Rules". The sample code can be downloaded here: `http://www.oracle.com/technology/products/ias/business_rules/files/how-to-sdk.zip`

You would then have your own application that can read, process, and generate Oracle Business Rules from the Relativity XML rules file generated from your COBOL applications.

> **Keeping It Real**: It is most likely that your legacy application has thousands of business rules. Therefore, it will be worthwhile to develop a utility to automatically populate the Oracle BRE repository from the Relativty XML file. As BRE repository standards progress, we can assume automatic repository population will be part of modernization vendors' product offerings.

Data Migration—A Quick, Easy, and a Cost-Effective Approach

Data migration by itself is a very broad and technology-deep area. We cannot provide a rich enough example to do justice to this topic. There are many different Oracle products and technologies that can used: **Oracle Warehouse Builder** (**OWB**), **Oracle Data Integrator** (**ODI**), Oracle DRDA Gateway, and SQL*Loader. For this chapter, we will use the data migration approach called "KISS (keep it simple stupid) legacy data migration". SQL*Loader is simple, as there is not much to install and configure. SQL*Loader is also very low-cost from a product perspective it is free. SQL*Loader is also flexible as it can run on or off the mainframe.

The following is a working sample to load the Oracle ProductMaster table from a VSAM file. Note, in this case, the mainframe file used as input came from an IDCAMS (using REPRO) unload provided for us. IDCAMS is an IBM utility that has many options, one of which is REPRO, which can be used to load and unload flat files to and from a VSAM file.

We have included some sample JCL using Oracle SQL*Loader, which shows how to load directly from the mainframe side of the fence across the network, in lieu of FTPing files. This, of course, would mean that sqlldr executable (SQL*LOADER) are available to you on z/OS, or you have installed it on the z/OS mainframe via **Oracle Universal Installer (OUI)**.

The running of any process that does bulk data movement, or processes large volumes of data has to be weighed against the availability of network resources. However, when done this way, SQL*Loader will automatically do the code page translation for you as well as handle things such as packed decimal, fixed, and floating point binary translation just like it would if you FTPed the files over (binary of course). The Oracle SQL Loader sqlldr control statements are the same as they would be on open systems with the exception of the INFILE, which needs to be amended to the file location of the input file.

We discovered that there are four VSAM data files: Invoice, Inventory, Customer, and Product. We will show a data migration SQL*Loader example for the Product VSAM file.

The JCL using SQL*Loader for loading a sample table on remote Oracle database:

```
========================================================================
//LEGACYREARCHDATAMIGRATIONLT JOB (0000,OR),'ORACLE INSTALL',CLASS=A,
//            MSGCLASS=X,PRTY=15,MSGLEVEL=(1,1),NOTIFY=TLASZEWS
//*
//*-----------------------------------------------------------*
//* Load table on remote Oracle instance
//*-----------------------------------------------------------*
//LOADTB    EXEC PGM=SQLLOAD,REGION=4M,
// PARM=('CONTROL=/DD/LDRCTL USERID=PSTR/PSTR@XE',
//       'LOG=/DD/LOGDD DIRECT=FALSE')
//STEPLIB   DD DSN=ORACLE.V10R2.CMDLOAD,DISP=SHR
//ORA$LIB   DD DSN=ORACLE.V10R2.MESG,DISP=SHR
//SYSOUT    DD SYSOUT=*,DCB=(LRECL=132,BLKSIZE=1320,RECFM=VB)
//SYSERR    DD SYSOUT=*,DCB=(LRECL=132,BLKSIZE=1320,RECFM=VB)
//ORAPRINT DD SYSOUT=*
//SYSIN     DD DUMMY
//TNSNAMES DD *
XE=
```

```
      (DESCRIPTION=
       (ADDRESS_LIST=
        (ADDRESS=(PROTOCOL=TCP)(HOST=138.1.123.87)
        (SSN=NT8Y)
        (PORT=1521))
        )
         (CONNECT_DATA = (SID = XE))
       )
//LDRCTL      DD DSN=LEGACYEXAMPLE.ORACLE.JCL(LOADCNTL),
//            DISP=SHR
//SYSREC00    DD DSN=LEGACYEXAMPLE.ORACLE.PRODUCT.DATA,
//            DISP=SHR
//LOGDD       DD SYSOUT=*
//BADDD       DD SYSOUT=*


Contents of LEGACYEXAMPLE.ORACLE.JCL(LOADCNTL)
=====================================
LOAD DATA
CHARACTERSET WE8EBCDIC500
INFILE /DD/SYSREC00
BADFILE /DD/BADDD
REPLACE LOG NO
INTO TABLE PSTR.PRODUCT-MASTER-RECORD
(PRM-PRODUCT-CODE                    POSITION (1:10)   CHAR
   ,PRM-PRODUCT-DESCRIPTION          POSITION (11:30) CHAR
   ,PRM-UNIT-PRICE                   POSITION (31:33) DECIMAL (7,2)
   ,PRM-QUANTITY-ON-HAND             POSITION (34:37) INTEGER
   )


Create Sample Table on Remote Oracle Instance
=============================================
//LEGACYREARCHDATAMIGRATIONCT JOB (0000,OR),'ORACLE INSTALL',CLASS=A,
//          MSGCLASS=X,PRTY=15,MSGLEVEL=(1,1),NOTIFY=TLASZEWS
//*
//*-------------------------------------------------------------*
//* Create table/index on remote Oracle instance
//*-------------------------------------------------------------*
//*
//CREATETB EXEC PGM=SQLPLUS,PARM='/NOLOG',REGION=4M
//STEPLIB  DD DSN=ORACLE.V10R2.CMDLOAD,DISP=SHR
//ORA$LIB  DD DSN=ORACLE.V10R2.MESG,DISP=SHR
//SPOOL    DD SYSOUT=*,DCB=(LRECL=132,BLKSIZE=1320,RECFM=VB)
//SYSOUT   DD SYSOUT=*,DCB=(LRECL=132,BLKSIZE=1320,RECFM=VB)
//SYSOUT2  DD SYSOUT=*,DCB=(LRECL=132,BLKSIZE=1320,RECFM=VB)
```

```
//SYSERR    DD SYSOUT=*,DCB=(LRECL=132,BLKSIZE?1320,RECFM=VB)
//*NS@NT8Y DD DUMMY
//TNSNAMES DD *
XE=
   (DESCRIPTION=
    (ADDRESS_LIST=
     (ADDRESS=(PROTOCOL=TCP)(HOST=138.1.123.87)
     (SSN=NT8Y)
     (PORT=1521))
     )
       (CONNECT_DATA = (SID = XE))
     )
//SQLLOGIN DD DUMMY
//ORAPRINT DD SYSOUT=*
//SYSIN    DD *
set echo on
set termout on
spool /DD/SPOOL
set concat |
define userid = PSTR
define pswd = PSTR

Rem ----------------------------------------------------------
Rem - Define where the tablespace (pageset) will reside
Rem ----------------------------------------------------------
define db_file_loc = '/u01/app/oracle_DB/oradata/db_01'


Rem ----------------------------------------------------------
Rem - Connect to the Remote Oracle Instance with Full Access (SYSADM)
Rem ----------------------------------------------------------
connect sys/dialtone@XE as sysdba;

Rem ----------------------------------------------------------
Rem - Drop prior schema (creator id)
Rem ----------------------------------------------------------
drop user &userid cascade;

Rem ----------------------------------------------------------
Rem - Create schema (create user and grant authorizations) Rem
----------------------------------------------------------
grant connect,resource,unlimited tablespace
to &userid identified by &pswd;

Rem ----------------------------------------------------------
Rem - Grant builtin Oracle role "dba"
Rem ----------------------------------------------------------
grant dba to &userid;
```

```
Rem ---------------------------------------------------------
Rem - Connect as that newly created user
Rem ---------------------------------------------------------
connect &userid/&pswd@XE;

Rem ---------------------------------------------------------
Rem - Define a substitution variable
Rem ---------------------------------------------------------
define table_name = ProductMaster

Rem ---------------------------------------------------------
Rem - Drop prior tablespace name
Rem ---------------------------------------------------------
drop tablespace &table_name|_ts including contents;

Rem ---------------------------------------------------------
Rem - Create tablespace name
Rem ---------------------------------------------------------
create tablespace &table_name|_ts
    datafile '&db_file_loc/&table_name|_ts.dbf' size 500k reuse
    autoextend on next 500k maxsize 10m;

Rem ---------------------------------------------------------
Rem - Create table
Rem ---------------------------------------------------------
create table ProductMaster
     (  product_code         CHAR    (10) DEFAULT ' '
       ,product_description   CHAR    (20) DEFAULT ' '
       ,unit_price            DECIMAL (9, 2)    NOT NULL
       ,quantity_on_hand      INTEGER           NOT NULL
     )
     tablespace &table_name|_ts;

Rem ---------------------------------------------------------
Rem - Create an Tablespace for an Index on the table
Rem ---------------------------------------------------------
drop tablespace &table_name|_ix including contents;

create tablespace &table_name|_ix
    datafile '&db_file_loc\&table_name|_ix.dbf' size 500k reuse
    autoextend on next 500k maxsize 1m;

Rem ---------------------------------------------------------
Rem - Create an index on the table
Rem ---------------------------------------------------------
create unique index &table_name$emplid_id on &table_name
      (  product_code
       )
     tablespace &table_name|_ix;
```

Keeping It Real: Most re-architecture projects also have an aspect of data modernization to them. Data modernization implies reconciling data duplication (data profiling), eliminating bad data (data quality), and master data management (MDM). Data modernization can also include planning an SOA data services architecture. Therefore, the data migration phase in a re-architecture project will mostly use an ETL/ELT tool such as Oracle Warehouse Builder (OWB), or Oracle Data Integrator (ODI). However, some clients like the zero-cost, hassle-free Oracle SQL*Loader.

Summary

Just as with Chapter 4 (*SOA Integration – Scenario in Detail*), we have covered significant ground in this chapter. As in Chapter 4, we started with a sample legacy COBOL/CICS/VSAM application. We then captured the legacy artifacts for the presentation-tier, screen navigation, and business rules using Relativity. These captured artifacts were mined to bring them forward into an Oracle, Java EE, and SOA architecture. We used Oracle JDeveloper to create the presentation and navigation-tiers. Oracle Rules Author was used to create the business rules. The application was deployed to the Oracle Application Server, and showed it running. We also provided a brief and simple introduction to migrating data off the mainframe. Now you have everything you need to get started with your own legacy re-architecture modernization pilot project. We say pilot project because we realize that moving applications, data, and most importantly infrastructure off the mainframe cannot possibly be shown in one chapter of a book.

Re-architecture is not the same as an application rewrite, or "rip and replace". We hope you are now able to come to the same conclusion that we have. Using products and technologies from Oracle and Relativity, it is possible to leverage all your legacy application code and use it as the foundation of you new application.

We have covered Legacy SOA Integration and re-architecture in great detail. We will now cover another legacy modernization option called re-host. The focus of this book was on SOA Integration and re-architecture. The main reason behind giving a brief introduction to re-host is that Oracle offers a re-host platform called Tuxedo.

10
Introduction to Re-Host based Modernization Using Tuxedo

In the previous chapters, we focused on two Modernization alternatives—SOA Enablement and Re-architecture—which force radically different scope of change on the application. SOA Enablement wraps key application interfaces in services, and integrates it into the SOA. This largely leaves the existing application logic intact, minimizing changes and adding risk only to those components that needed restructuring work to become SOA-ready. While the interfaces are modernized, without subjecting the core application components to a lot of change, the high costs and the various legacy risks associated with the mainframe platform remain. In addition, the performance and scalability of the new interfaces needs to be well-specified and tested, and the additional load they place on the system should be included in any planned capacity upgrades, potentially increasing the overall costs.

The re-architecture approach reduces the mainframe costs and legacy risks by migrating the application off the mainframe and re-structuring it using all the modern software tools and capabilities at our disposal. However, this very process of re-structuring the application, and essentially re-building it using knowledge and business rules mined from existing code, introduces certain risks. How can we ensure that the new application maintains functional equivalence, and operational characteristics of the original? Can we meet the performance and scalability requirements not only of the current environment, but future growth needs as well? Can we deliver the new application within the time and budget constraints agreed to at the beginning of the project? The older the application, the larger its scope and volume of code, and the fewer original developers available, the higher these risks may be.

This chapter takes a look at an alternative approach that attempts to balance these risks in a different way. Re-host-based modernization approach is focused on migrating the application off the mainframe to a compatible software stack on an open-systems platform, preserving the language and middleware services on which the application has been built. It protects legacy investment by relying on a mainframe-compatible software stack to minimize any changes in the core application, and preserve the application's business logic intact, while running it on an open-system platform using more flexible and less expensive system infrastructure. It keeps open the customer's options for SOA enablement and re-architecture, by using an SOA-ready middleware stack to support Web services and ESB interfaces for re-hosted components. And using an extensible platform with transparent integration to J2EE components, BPM-based processes, and other key tools of the re-architecture approach means you can start to re-architect selected components at will, without requiring changes to the re-hosted services running the remainder of the business logic.

Reducing or eliminating the legacy mainframe costs and risks via re-host based modernization also helps customers to fund SOA enablement, and the re-architecture phases of legacy modernization, and lay the groundwork for these steps. SOA-enabling a re-hosted application is a much easier process on an open-systems-based, SOA-ready software stack, and a more efficient one as well in terms of system resource utilization and cost. Re-architecting selected components of a re-hosted application based on specific business needs is a lower risk approach than re-architecting the entire applications en masse, and the risk can be further reduced by ensuring that target re-hosting stack provides rugged and transparent integration between re-hosted services and new components.

Keeping It Real: Selective re-architecture is all about maximizing ROI by focusing re-architecture investment in the areas with the best pay-off. Undertaking a change from one language or development paradigm to another shouldn't be undertaken lightly — the investment and risks need to be well understood and justified. It is the right investment for components that require frequent maintenance changes but are difficult to maintain, because of poor /structure and layered changes. The payback on re-architecture investment will come from reducing the cost of future maintenance. Similarly, components that need significant functional changes to meet new business requirements can benefit from substantial productivity increase after re-architecture to a more modern development framework with richer tools to support future changes. The payback comes from greater business agility and time-to-market improvements. On the other hand, well-structured and maintainable COBOL components that do not need extensive changes to meet business needs will have very little return to show for the significant re-architecture investment. Leaving them in COBOL on a modern, extensible platform saves significant re-architecture costs that can be invested elsewhere, reduces risk, and shortens payback time. These considerations can help to optimize ROI for medium-to-large modernization projects where components measure in hundreds or thousands and contain millions or tens of millions lines of code.

Re-Hosting Based Modernization

For many organizations, mainframe modernization has become a matter of 'how', and not 'if'. Numerous enterprises and public sector organizations choose re-hosting as the first tangible step in their legacy modernization program precisely because it delivers the best ROI in the fastest possible manner, and accelerates the move to SOA enablement and selective re-architecture. Oracle together with our services partners provides a comprehensive re-hosting-based modernization solution that many customers have leveraged for a successful migration of selected applications or complete mainframe environments ranging from a few hundred MIPS to well over 10,000 MIPS.

Two key pillars support successful re-hosting projects:

1. Optimal target environment that lowers the **Total Cost of Ownership** (TCO) by 50–80 percent and maintains mainframe-class Quality of Service (QoS) using open, extensible, SOA-ready, future-proof architecture

2. Predictable, efficient projects delivered by our SI partners with proven methodologies and automated tools

Optimal target environment provided by Oracle is powered by proven open systems software stack leveraging Oracle Database and Oracle Tuxedo for a rock-solid, mainframe-class transaction processing (TP) infrastructure closely matching mainframe requirements for online applications.

Mainframe-compatible Transaction Processing: Support for IBM CICS or IMS TM applications in native COBOL or C/C++ language containers with mainframe-compatible TP features.

RASP: Mainframe-class performance, reliability, and scalability provided by Oracle Real Application Clusters (RAC) and Tuxedo multi-node and multi-domain clustering for load-balancing and high availability despite failure of individual nodes or network links.

Workload and System Management: End-to-end transaction and service monitoring to support 24X7 operations management provided by Oracle's Enterprise Manager Grid Control and Tuxedo System and Application Monitor.

SOA Enablement and Integration : Extensibility with Web services using Oracle Services Architecture Leveraging Tuxedo (SALT), J2EE integration (using WebLogic-Tuxedo Connector (WTC), Enterprise Service Bus (ESB), Portal, and BPM technologies to enable easy integration of re-hosted applications into modern Service-Oriented Architectures (SOAs).

Scalable Platforms and Commodity Hardware: Scalable, Linux/UNIX-based open systems from HP, Dell, Sun, and IBM, providing:

- Performance on a par with mainframe systems for most workloads at significantly reduced TCO.

- Reliability and workload management similar to mainframe installations, including physical and logical partitioning.

- Robust clustering technologies for high availability and fail-over capabilities within a data center or across the world.

The diagram below shows conceptual mapping of mainframe environment to compatible open systems infrastructure:

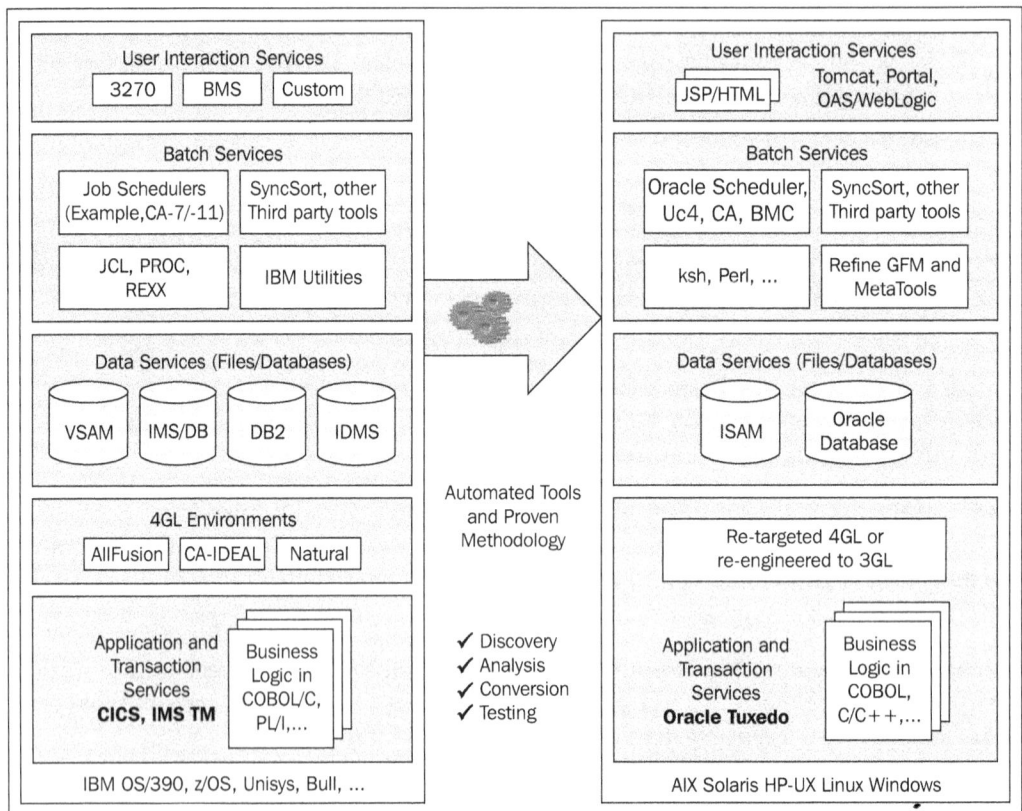

Predictable, efficient projects delivered by leading SIs and key modernization specialists use risk-mitigation methodologies, and automated tools honed over numerous projects to address a complete range of Online, Batch, and Data architectures, and the various technologies used in them. These project methodologies and automated tools that support them encompass all phases of a migration project:

- Preliminary Assessment Study
- Application Asset Discovery and Analysis
- Application and Data Conversion (pilot or entire application portfolio)
- System and Application Integration
- Test Engineering
- Regression and Performance Testing
- Education and Training
- Operations Migration
- Switch-Over

Combining a proven target architecture stack that is well-matched to the needs of mainframe applications with mature methodologies supported by automated tools has led to a large and growing number of successful re-hosting projects. There is a rising interest to leverage the re-hosting approach to mainframe application modernization, as a way to get off a mainframe fast, and with minimal risk, in a more predictable manner for large, business-critical applications evolved over a long term and multiple development teams. Re-hosting based modernization approach preserves an organizations long term investment in critical business logic and data without risking business operations or sacrificing the QoS, while enabling customers to:

- Reduce or eliminate mainframe maintenance costs, and/or defer upgrade costs, saving customers 50–80 percent of their annual maintenance and operations budget.
- Increase productivity and flexibility in IT development and operations, protecting long-term investment through application modernization.
- Speed up and simplify application integration via SOA, without losing transactional integrity and the high performance expected by the users.

The rest of this chapter explores the critical success factors and proven transformation architecture for re-hosting legacy applications and data, describes SOA integration options and considerations when SOA-enabling re-hosted applications, highlights key risk mitigation methodologies, and provides a foundation for the financial analysis and ROI model derived from over a hundred, mainframe re-hosting projects.

Critical Success Factors in Mainframe Re-hosting

Companies considering a re-hosting-based modernization strategy that involves migrating some applications off the mainframe have to address a range of concerns, which can be summarized by the following questions:

- How to preserve the business logic of these applications and their valuable data?

- How to ensure that migrated applications continue to meet performance requirements?

- How to maintain scalability, reliability, transactional integrity, and other QoS attributes in an open system environment?

- How to migrate in phases, maintaining robust integration links between migrated and mainframe applications?

- How to achieve predictable, cost-effective results and ensure a low-risk project?

Meeting these challenges requires a versatile and powerful application infrastructure—one that natively supports key mainframe languages and services, enables automated adaptation of application code, and delivers proven, mainframe-like QoS on open system platforms. For re-hosting to enable broader aspects of the modernization strategy, this infrastructure must also provide native Web services and ESB capabilities to rapidly integrate re-hosted applications as first-class services in an SOA.

Equally important is a proven, risk-mitigation methodology, automated tools, and project services specifically honed to address automated conversion and adaptation of application code and data, supported by cross-platform test engineering and execution methodology, strong system and application integration expertise, and deep experience with operations migration and switch-over.

Preserving Application Logic and Data

The re-hosting approach depends on a mainframe-compatible transaction processing and application services platform supporting common mainframe languages such as COBOL and C, which preserves the original business logic and data for the majority of mainframe applications and avoids the risks and uncertainties of a re-write. A complete re-hosting solution provides native support for TP and Batch programs, leveraging an application server-based platform that provides container-based support for COBOL and C/C++ application services, and TP APIs similar to IBM CICS, IMS TM, or other mainframe TP monitors.

Online Transaction Processing Environment

Oracle Tuxedo is the most popular TP platform for open systems, as well as leading re-hosting platform that can run most of mainframe COBOL and C applications unchanged in container-based framework that combines common application server features, including health monitoring, fail-over, service virtualization, and dynamic load balancing critical to large-scale OLTP applications together with standard TP features, including transaction management and reliable coordination of distributed transactions (a.k.a. Two-Phase Commit or XA standard). It provides the highest possible performance and scalability, and has been recently benchmarked against a mainframe at over 100,000 transactions per second, with sub-second response time.

Oracle Tuxedo supports common mainframe programming languages, that is, COBOL and C, and provides comprehensive TP features compatible with CICS and IMS TM, which makes it a preferred application platform choice for re-hosting CICS or IMS TM applications with minimal changes and risks. In the Tuxedo environment, COBOL or C business logic remains unchanged. The only adaptation required is automated mapping of CICS APIs (CICS EXEC calls) to equivalent Tuxedo API functions.

This mapping typically leverages a pre-processor and a mapping library implemented on Tuxedo platform, and using a full range of Tuxedo APIs. The automated nature of pre-processing and comprehensive coverage provided by the library ensures that most CICS COBOL or C programs are easily transformed into Tuxedo services. Unlike other solutions that embed this transformation in their compiler coupled with a proprietary emulation run-time, Tuxedo-based solution provides this mapping as a compiler-independent source module, which can be easily extended as needed. The resultant code uses Tuxedo API at native speed, allowing it to reach tens of thousands of transactions per second, while taking advantage of all Tuxedo facilities. In a re-hosted application CICS transactions become Tuxedo services, registered for processing by Tuxedo server processes. These services can be deployed in a single machine or across multiple machines in a Tuxedo domain (SYSPLEX-like cluster.). The services are called by front-end Java, .Net, or Tuxedo/WS clients, or UI components (tn3270 or web-based converted 3270/BMS screens), or by other services in case of transaction linking. Deferred transactions are handled by Tuxedo's/Q component, which provides in-memory and persistent queuing services.

The diagram below shows Oracle Tuxedo and its surrounding ecosystem of SOA, J2EE, ESB, CORBA, MQ, and Mainframe integration components:

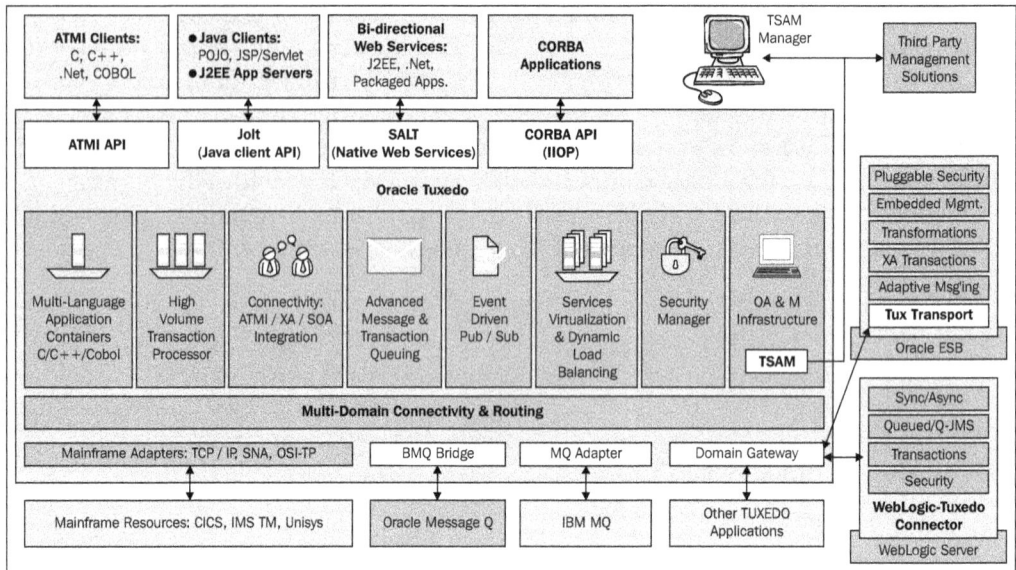

User Interface Migration

The UI elements in these programs are typically defined using CICS **Basic Mapping Support (BMS)** for 3270 "green screen" terminals. While it is possible to preserve these using tn3270 emulation, many customers in re-hosting projects choose to take advantage of automated conversion of BMS macros into JSP/HTML for Web UI. Supported by a specialized Javascript library, these Web screens mimic the appearance and the behavior of "green screens" in a web browser, including tab-based navigation and PF keys. These UI components can connect to re-hosted CICS transactions running as Tuxedo services using Oracle Jolt (Java client interface for Tuxedo), **Weblogic-Tuxedo Connector (WTC)**, or Tuxedo's Web services gateway provided by Oracle **Services Architecture Leveraging Tuxedo (SALT)** product.

The diagram on the next page depicts a target re-hosting architecture for a typical mainframe OLTP application. The architecture uses Tuxedo services to run re-hosted CICS programs and a web application server to run re-hosted BMS UI. The servlets or JSPs containing the HTML that defines the screens, connect with Tuxedo services via Oracle Jolt, WTC, or SALT.

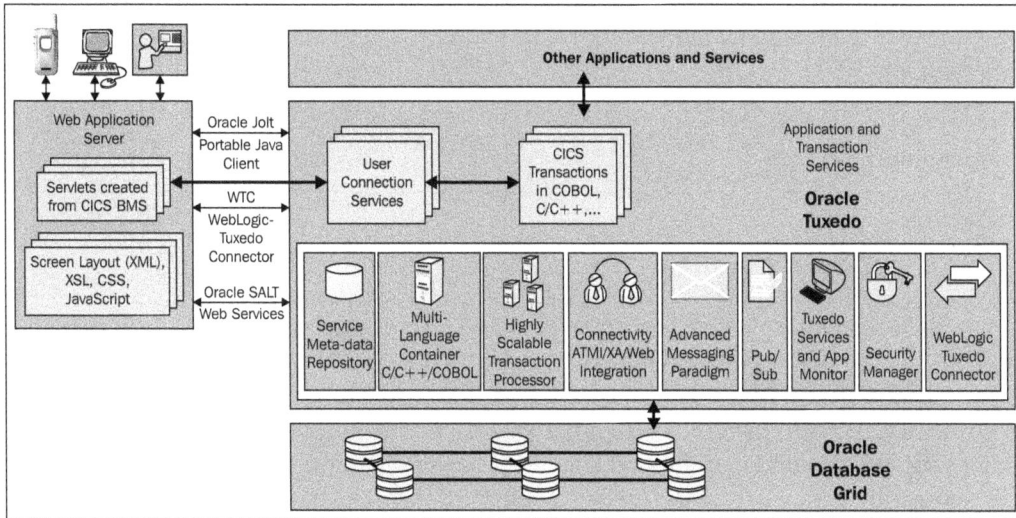

Customers using mainframe 4GLs or languages such as PL/I or Assembler frequently choose to convert these applications to COBOL or C/C++. The adaptation of CICS or IMS TM API calls is automated through a mapping layer, which minimizes overall changes for the development team and allows them to maintain the familiar applications. For more significant extensions and new capabilities, customers incrementally leverage Tuxedo's own APIs and facilities, or leverage a tightly-linked J2EE environment provided by the WebLogic Server, and even transparently make Web services calls. The optimal extensibility options depend on application needs, availability of Java or C/COBOL skills, and other factors.

The CICS calls in your application will, for the most part, map easily to the the Tuxedo API. The following table shows the most common CICS facilities and the Tuxedo API that provides the same functionality:

Feature or Action	CICS Verb	Tuxedo API
Communications Area	DFHCOMMAREA	Typed Buffer
Transaction Request	LINK	tpcall
Transaction Return	RETURN	tpreturn
Transfer Control	XCTL	tpforward
Allocate Storage	GETMAIN	tpalloc
Queues	READQ / WRITEQ TD,TS	/Q tpenqueue / tpdequeue

Feature or Action	CICS Verb	Tuxedo API
Begin new transaction	START TRANID	/Q and TMQFORWARD
Abort transaction	ISSUE ABEND	tpreturn TPFAIL
Commit or Rollback	SYNCPOINT / SYNCPOINT ROLLBACK	tpcommit / tpabort

Keeping it Real: For those familiar with CICS, this is a very short example of the CICS verbs. CICS has many functions, most of which either map natively to a similar Tuxedo API or are provided by migration specialists based on their extensive experience with such migrations.

In summary, Tuxedo provides a popular platform for deploying, executing, and managing COBOL and C re-hosted transactional applications requiring any of the following OLTP and infrastructure services:

- Native, compiler-independent support for COBOL, C, or C++.
- Rich set of infrastructure services for managing and scaling diverse workloads.
- Feature-set compatibility and inter-operability with IBM CICS and IMS/TM.
- Two-Phase Commit (2PC) for managing transactions across multiple application domains and XA-compliant resource managers (databases, message queues).
- Guaranteed inter-application messaging and transactional queuing.
- Transactional data access (using XA-compliant resource managers) with ACID qualities.
- Services virtualization and dynamic load balancing.
- Centralized management of multiple nodes in a domain, and across multiple domains.
- Communications gateways for multiple traditional and modern communication protocols.
- SOA Enablement through native Web services and ESB integration.

Workload Monitoring and Management

An important aspect of the mainframe environment is workload monitoring and management, which provides information for effective performance analysis and capabilities that enable mainframe systems to achieve better throughput and responsiveness. Oracle's **Tuxedo System and Application Monitor (TSAM)** provides similar capabilities too.

- Define monitoring policies and patterns based on application requests, services, system servers such as gateways, bridges, and XA-defined stages of a distributed transaction.

- Define SLA thresholds that can trigger a variety of events within Tuxedo event services including notifications, and instantiation of additional servers.

- Monitor transactions on an end-to-end basis from a client call through all services across all domains involved in a client request.

- Collect service statistics for all infrastructure components such as servers and gateways.

- Detail time spent on IPC queues, waiting on network links, and time spent on subordinate services.

TSAM provides a built-in, central, web-based management and monitoring console, and an open framework for integration with third-party performance management tools.

Batch Jobs

Mainframe batch jobs are a response to a human 24-hour clock on which many businesses run. It includes beginning-of-period or end-of-period (day, week, month, quarter) processing for batched updates, reconciliation, reporting, statement generation, and similar applications. In some industries, external events tied to a fixed schedule such as intra-day, opening or closing trade in a stock exchange, drive specific processing needs. Batch applications are an equally important asset, and often need to be preserved and migrated as well. The batch environment uses Job Control Language (JCL) jobs managed and monitored by JES2 or JES3 (Job Entry System), which invoke one or more programs, access and manipulate large datasets and databases using sort and other specialized utilities, and often run under the control of a job scheduler such as CA-7/CA-11.

JCL defines a series of job steps—a sequence of programs and utilities, specifies input and output files, and provides exception handling. Automated parsing and translation of JCL jobs to UNIX scripts such as Korn shell (ksh) or Perl, enables the overall structure of the job to remain the same, including job steps, classes, and exception handling. Standard shell processing is supplemented with required utilities such as SyncSort, and support for **Generation Data Group (GDG)** files. REXX/CLIST/PROC scripting environments on the mainframe are similarly converted to ksh or other scripting languages.

Integration with Oracle Scheduler, or other job schedulers running in UNIX/Linux or Windows provides a rich set of calendar and event-based scheduling capabilities as well as dependency management similar to mainframe schedulers. In some cases, reporting done via batch jobs can be replaced using standard reporting packages such as Oracle BI Publisher.

The diagram below shows a typical target re-hosting architecture for batch. It includes a scheduler to control and trigger batch jobs, scripting framework to support individual job scripts, and an application server execution framework for the batch COBOL or C programs. Unlike other solutions that run these programs directly as OS processes without the benefit of application server middleware, Oracle recommends using container-based middleware to provide higher reliability, availability, and monitoring to the batch programs.

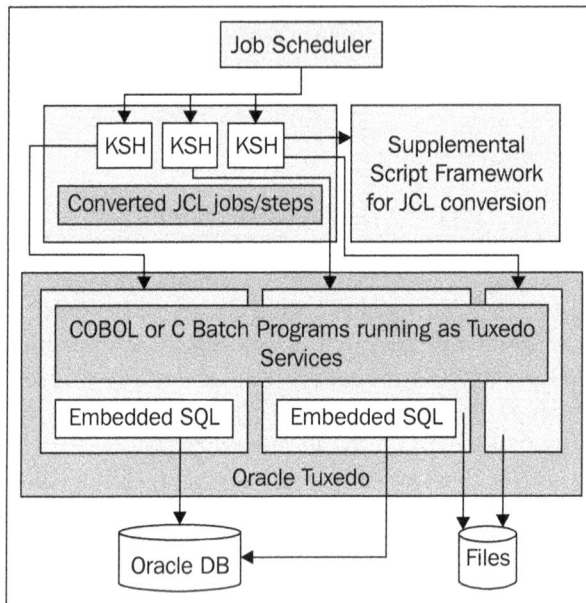

The target batch programs invoked by the scripts can also run directly as OS processes, but if mainframe-class management and monitoring similar to JES2 or JES3 environment is a requirement, these programs can run as services under Tuxedo, benefiting from the health monitoring, fail-over, load balancing, and other application server-like features it provides.

Files and Databases

As we have emphasized in other chapters, when moving platforms (mainframe to open systems), the application and data have to be moved together. Data schemas and data stores need to be moved in a re-hosted mainframe modernization project just as with a re-architecture. The approach taken depends on the source data store. DB2 is the most straightforward, since DB2 and Oracle are both relational databases. In addition to migrating the data, customers sometimes choose to perform data cleansing, field extensions, merge columns, or other data maintenance practices leveraging the automated tooling that synchronizes all data changes with changes to the application's data access code.

Mainframe DB2

DB2 is a predominant relational database on IBM mainframes. When migrating to Oracle Database, the migration approach is highly automated, and resolves all discrepancies between the two RDBMS in terms of field formats as well as error codes returned to applications, so as to maintain application behavior unchanged, including stored procedures if any.

IMS

IMS/DB (also known as DL/1) is a popular hierarchical database for older applications. Creating appropriate relational data schema for this data requires an understanding of the application access patterns so as to optimize the schema for best performance based on the most frequent access paths. To minimize code impact, a translation layer can be used at run-time to support IMS DB style data access from the application, and map it to appropriate SQL calls. This allows the applications to interface with the segments, now translated as DB2 UDB or ORACLE tables, without impacting application code and maintenance.

VSAM

VSAM files are used for keyed-sequential data access, and can be readily migrated to ISAM files or to Oracle Database tables wherever transactional integrity is required (XA features). Some customers also choose to migrate VSAM files to Oracle Database to provide accessibility from other distributed applications, or to simplify the re-engineering required to extend certain data fields or merge multiple data sources.

Meeting Performance and Other QoS Requirements

The mainframe's performance, reliability, scalability, manageability, and other QoS attributes have earned it pre-eminence for business-critical applications. How well do re-hosting solutions measure up against these characteristics? Earlier solutions based on IBM CICS emulators derived from development tools often did not measure up to the demands of mainframe workloads since they were never intended for true production environment and have not been exposed to large-scale applications. As a result, they have only been used for re-hosting small systems under 300 MIPS and not requiring any clustering or distributed workload handling.

Oracle Tuxedo was built to scale ground up, to support high performance telecommunications operations. It has the distinction of being the only non-mainframe TP solution recognized for its mainframe-like performance, reliability, and QoS characteristics. Most large enterprise customers requiring such capabilities in distributed systems have traditionally relied on Tuxedo. Consistently rated by IDC and Gartner as the market leader, and predominant in non-mainframe OLTP applications, it has also become the preferred COBOL/C application platform and transaction engine for re-hosted mainframe applications requiring high performance and/or mission-critical availability and reliability.

Reasons for the broad recognition of Tuxedo as the only mainframe-class application platform and transaction engine for distributed systems are based on mainframe-class performance, scalability, reliability, availability, and other QoS attributes proven in multiple customer deployments. The following table highlights some of these capabilities:

Reliability	Availability
Guaranteed messaging and transactional integrity	No single point of failure, 99.999% uptime with N+1/N+2 clusters
Hardened code from 25 years of use in the world's largest transaction applications	Application services upgradeable in operation
	Self-monitoring, automated fail-over, data-driven routing for super high availability
Transaction integrity across systems and domains through a two phase commit (XA) for all resources such as databases, queues, and so on.	Centralized monitoring and management with clustered domains; automated, lights-out operations
Proven in mainframe-to-mainframe transactions and messaging	

Workload Management	Performance and Scalability
Resource management and prioritization across Tuxedo services	Parallel processing to maximize resource utilization with low latency code paths that provide sub-second response at any load
Dynamic load balancing across domains based on load conditions	Horizontal and vertical scaling of system resources yields linear performance increases
Data-driven routing enables horizontally distributed database grids and differentiated QoS	Request multiplexing (synchronous and asynchronous) maximizes CPU utilization
End-to-end monitoring of Tuxedo system and application services enables SLA enforcement	Proven in credit card authorizations at over 13.5K tps, and in telco billing at over 56K tps.
Virtualization support enables spawning of Tuxedo servers on demand	Middleware of choice in HP, Fujitsu, Sun, IBM, and NEC TPC-C benchmarks

As it delivers mainframe-like performance, reliability, and scalability in most demanding environments, Tuxedo is used by some of the largest TP applications worldwide to deliver over tens of thousands of transactions per second in real-world production applications such as funds transfer, credit card authorizations, mobile billing, and reservations systems of major transportation vendors. It's no surprise that most of the large re-hosted mainframe applications in the 500 to 10,000-plus MIPS range are running on Tuxedo as well.

In larger deployments, Oracle Real Application Clustering is used to support the deployment of a single database across a cluster of servers, providing unbeatable fault tolerance, performance, and scalability with no need for application changes. Oracle RAC supports usage of multiple individual systems as one clustered, virtual database server. It provides transparent synchronization of read and write accesses to databases shared by all nodes in the cluster, dynamic distribution of database workload, and transparent protection against systems failures.

Oracle's key innovation is a RAC technology called cache fusion. Cache fusion enables nodes on a cluster to synchronize their memory caches efficiently using a high-speed cluster interconnect so that disk I/O is minimized. The key, though, is that cache fusion enables shared access to all the data on disk by all the nodes on the cluster. Data does not need to be partitioned among the nodes. Oracle RACs cache fusion technology provides the highest levels of availability and scalability. Oracle RAC dramatically reduces operational costs and provides new levels of flexibility so that systems become more adaptive, proactive, and agile. Dynamic provisioning of nodes, storage, CPUs, and memory allow service levels to be easily and efficiently maintained while lowering cost still further through improved utilization. Customers today run clusters that range from a few dual-CPU commodity servers, to an enterprise grid with dozens of small servers to clusters, where servers are large SMP systems with 32 or 64 CPUs each.

A further example of the benefit from integrated re-hosting architecture using Oracle Database, RAC, and Tuxedo is the **Fast Application Notification (FAN)** feature. FAN provides integration between the RAC database and Tuxedo. It allows Tuxedo to be aware of the current configuration of the cluster at any given time so that application connections are made only to instances that are currently able to respond to the application requests. The Oracle RAC HA framework posts a FAN event immediately when a state change occurs within the cluster. For example, for down events, Tuxedo can initiate transaction recovery.

In addition to delivering innovative and proven functionality in its own products, Oracle works closely with leading open-systems platform vendors to take full advantage of their highly scalable systems with massive processor, I/O, and memory scalability, a complete resource partitioning continuum, granular workload management, and sophisticated operating system and system management capabilities. Combining these systems with proven Oracle Database's RAC and built-in grid capabilities of Oracle Tuxedo and WebLogic Server enables robust clustering with high availability, fast failover, dynamic load balancing, and unlimited scalability at much lower TCO than the mainframe. Oracle customers running mission-critical applications in the open-systems environment experience a QoS as high as, and in many scenarios better than, the same applications provided on the mainframe. Customer benchmarks comparing re-hosted and original applications have repeatedly demonstrated equal or greater transaction throughput on Tuxedo running on leading UNIX systems as compared to the original application running on CICS or similar environments. In recent customer benchmarks of eXtreme Transaction Processing (XTP) applications comparing Tuxedo performance against the mainframe, Tuxedo has pushed the envelope beyond 100,000 transactions per second with application transactions that include computation and database I/O.

Phased Migration and Mainframe Integration

Some mainframe migrations are partial, often done to free up some needed mainframe capacity for other applications and avoid an expensive upgrade. And many full migrations are done in multiple phases. In both cases, integration with remaining mainframe applications and mainframe-resident data is a critical consideration. **Tuxedo Mainframe Adapters (TMA)** provides this capability in mainframe re-hosting projects as well as native Tuxedo applications, when Tuxedo is used to run distributed services, and co-ordinate access to mainframe applications and data for multiple front-end applications. TMA is available for TCP/IP, SNA, and OSI/TP networks (the latter used with Unisys mainframes) to deliver high-performance, bidirectional interoperability between applications running on Oracle Tuxedo and mainframe TP platforms such IBM CICS or IMS TM.

CICS uses a set of **InterSystem Communications (ISC)** protocols for distributed transaction execution across multiple CICS regions. Tuxedo supports CICS ISC, and supplies equivalent capabilities:

- Dynamic transaction routing that is data-driven, or based on load management policies.

- Asynchronous processing to allow transaction execution to be started asynchronously from an invoking transaction, leveraging in-memory and persistent queuing functions.

- CICS **Distributed Program Link (DPL)/Distributed Transaction Processing (DTP)** functions provided by TMA, which supports transparent, bidirectional integration, global transaction coordination between mainframe CICS and IMS/TM applications and re-hosted application on Tuxedo. This allows mainframe transactions to view Tuxedo as a remote CICS region virtually connected via APPC/LU6.2.

- Event-driven services infrastructure supporting a Publish/Subscribe model.

- DOMAINS functionality providing full bi-directional connectivity and programming model across multiple Tuxedo application domains (similar to CICS regions).

Tuxedo Mainframe Adaptors provide bidirectional connections with full buffer mapping, and propagate transaction context, including user ID for security. Support for CICS DPL (CICS EXEC Link) and DTP (CICS EXEC verbs for LU6.2/APPC commands) facilities makes Tuxedo domains appear as another CICS region. This integration is provided over TCP/IP stack, allowing TCP/IP network connections to the mainframe while locally using SNA LU6.2 to connect directly from Tuxedo's **Communications Resource Manager (CRM)** to CICS, or IMS TM. Additionally, support for SNA connections allows you to use TMA without installing any new components on the mainframe.

In certain cases of partial migrations, customers want to rely on a centralized security model using mainframe security solution even for components re-hosted to Tuxedo. This can be supported with mainframe security systems such as RACF, by using Tuxedo's LDAP-based authentication via z/OS LDAP server configured for native authentication using RACF or another security solution.

SOA Enabling Re-hosted Applications

To leverage and extend the value inherent in mainframe applications, re-hosting is often followed by service enablement for integration into an SOA framework. Integrating re-hosted applications into the SOA framework provides key benefits:

- Improves productivity, agility, and speed for both business and IT
- Allows IT to deliver services faster, and aligns closer with business
- Allows the business to respond quicker and deliver optimal user experience
- Masks the underlying technical complexity of the IT environment.

When business value of re-hosted applications motivates integration into a corporate SOA, the integration approach must maintain the applications' QoS attributes. Key considerations for integrating re-hosted mainframe applications into an SOA include:

- Defining expected response time, throughput, and scalability
- Understanding requirements for transactional integrity and reliability
- Ensuring end-to-end messaging security, including security policies and AAA
- Providing support for heterogeneous client connectivity
- Achieving appropriate services granularity
- Leveraging service orchestration and BPM integration
- Enabling SLA management and SOA governance.

Oracle offers strong SOA integration capabilities shown in the following table:

Integration Type	Oracle Product	Key Features	Benefits
Web services gateway for point-to-point integration	Oracle **SALT**	Inbound and Outbound WS: SOAP/HTTP(S)	Open standards-based integration
		Extensible XML Data Mapping	Faster time-to-market
		WS-Security	Lower integration cost
		WS-Addressing, WS-ReliableMessaging, MTOM	Avoids the need to re-write in Java or .Net
		WSDL Creation and Publishing via UDDI	

Integration Type	Oracle Product	Key Features	Benefits
Multi-protocol Service Bus for orchestrated services integration	**Oracle ESB**	Adaptive, heterogeneous messaging for Web services, EJB/RMI, JMS, Oracle Tuxedo, IBM MQ, SAP, SWIFT, FTP, etc.	Faster deployment and simpler management of shared services across the SOA
		Extensible message brokering	Rapid transformations
		Dynamic routing with multiple transports and transformations	SLA-based monitoring
		Transactional support (XA)	Service life cycle management and governance
		Embedded management with monitoring and reporting	
		Pluggable Security	
		Runtime policy enforcement	
Enterprise Repository for service discovery and life cycle governance	**Oracle Enterprise Repository**	Usage Tracking	Visibility, traceability of service assets
		Policy Management	SOA services governance
		Dependency Analysis	
		Metrics & Analytics	Greater re-use of re-hosted applications
		Interactive Navigation	Life cycle governance

The capabilities provided to re-hosted applications through Oracle SALT, Oracle Service Bus, and Oracle Enterprise Repository can be leveraged in phases, or as part of a single integrated initiative. Extending the re-hosted applications through SALT for Web services integration, or through Oracle Service Bus for heterogeneous service messaging is a simple initial step on the road to SOA enablement. Customers use SALT for its complete open-standards Web services capabilities that easily integrate with any Web services environment. This approach provides a powerful way to extend and integrate re-hosted applications with heterogeneous messaging beyond SOAP/HTTP, or if you require global transaction coordination with other XA-enabled components, or need strong transformation, orchestration, and management capabilities provided by Oracle Service Bus.

Following the initial integration steps, or in parallel with them, customers can leverage Oracle Enterprise Repository to provide a single meta-data repository populated with services information for governing the discovery, deployment, and full life cycle of these re-hosted application services, enabling greater leverage of these key assets throughout the enterprise.

A further step in SOA-enabling and modernization of the legacy applications is to begin leveraging re-hosted services in BPM-driven dynamic business processes. Re-using re-hosted legacy application services via BPM, such as Oracle BPEL Process Manager, unlocks the siloed logic, and puts it to use as a strategic enterprise asset. With services exposed via Oracle SALT or Oracle Service Bus, and services metadata published in Oracle Enterprise Repository, BPM design-time tools can easily discover the available services. Connecting to the service via Web service interface (provided by SALT), or an ESB proxy service (provided by Oracle Service Bus), provides run-time binding and access as depicted in the following diagram, which shows how re-hosted legacy services can be leveraged by a BPM framework, like Oracle BPEL Process Manager.

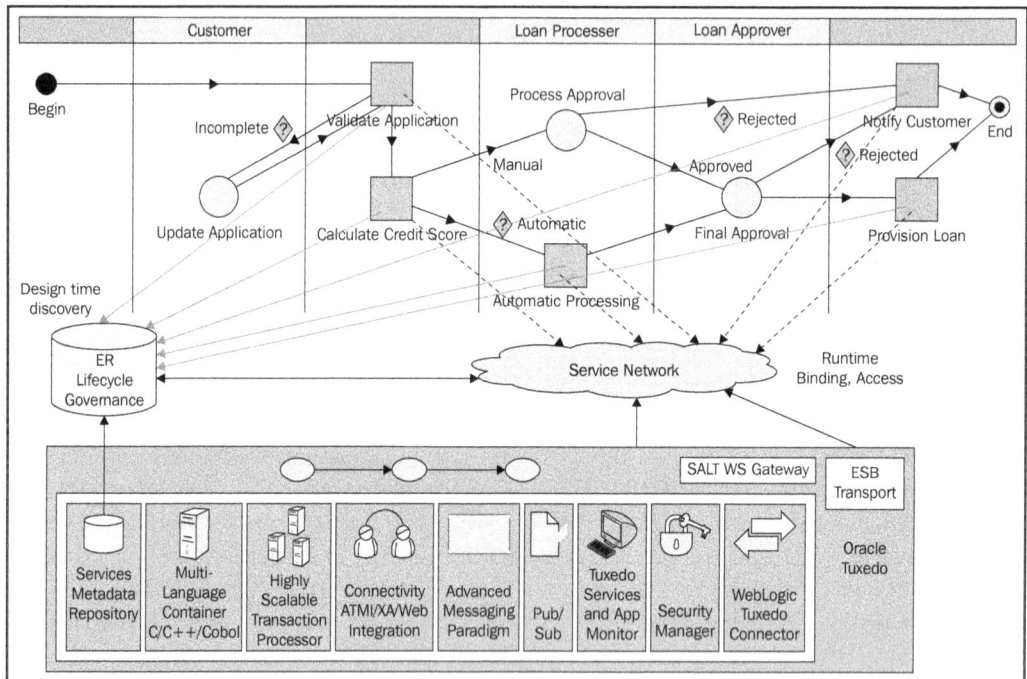

Further Re-architecture of Re-hosted Applications

Re-hosting application logic intact helps to preserve the investment in the code, and simplifies ongoing maintainability leveraging current resources. But what if the original code doesn't meet business needs or needs significant re-work because of poor maintainability? It's worthwhile to address these questions at the beginning of the project, and try to determine which components and modules have maintainability issues (leading APM tools can scan the code and derive various maintainability-related metrics) and/or face significant re-work driven by changing business requirements or external drivers such as compliance regulations.

In an SOA environment of Tuxedo application services, isolating individual components and replacing them with calls to re-architected Java services is pretty straightforward and transparent. This transparent integration between Tuxedo's COBOL, C, C++ services, and J2EE/Java services is provided through WebLogic-Tuxedo Connector (WTC), a Tuxedo Domain-based gateway that provides bidirectional transaction and security propagation. Additionally, Oracle SALTs Web services interfaces provide equally transparent interface to/from re-architected components, enabling transparent linkage to the re-architected components running outside of Tuxedo. In the chapters on re-architecture, we have already discussed the value of mining existing knowledge and business rules from existing components. Transparent integration between re-hosted and re-architected components further extends the the benefits from leveraging existing application assets.

Summary

Making the move off the mainframe via mainframe re-hosting has enabled numerous Oracle customers to lower costs, and helped IT deliver greater business impact due to flexibility of the open systems environment and greater agility of the application services re-hosted to an extensible, SOA-ready platform. Time and again, their success has been described in the following terms:

Mainframe Re-hosting Most-Often-Heard Customer Feedback	
Significant Cost Savings	Distributed computing TCO is a fraction of what customers are used to paying
	IT organizations have significantly lowered the cost of operations and annual IBM maintenance
Low Risk	Many customers have already migrated to open systems using Tuxedo
	Risk is low — application remains in its native language
	Tuxedo is a CICS-compatible, mainframe-class application platform
	Oracle and its SI partners have developed a proven migration strategy used in over 120 projects
	Oracle's many references in this area were compelling, and relevant to the customer's business
Higher Speed, Flexibility, and Business Impact	Re-hosted applications have become highly extensible to SOA
	IT Organizations are now faster, more flexible, and more involved in the overall business
	Enterprises don't have to remain locked-into with IBM anymore

Oracle's Re-hosting-based Modernization solution provides a proven, low risk, and highly efficient way for enterprises to migrate critical Online and Batch applications from the mainframe to lower-cost open systems environment powered by Oracle Database and Oracle Tuxedo. The key to a successful re-hosting project is the application platform that combines proven ability to run mainframe applications without requiring invasive changes with the required performance, availability, and reliability, while making it simpler to SOA–enable, and/or re-architect selected components following re-hosting. This approach can accelerate the cost savings, shorten the time to realize meaningful ROI, and substantially reduce legacy modernization risks. It balances the benefits of the powerful open-systems-based platform and software stack with the highly automated, low risk, noninvasive migration of the invaluable application logic and data. For many customers, this represented an optimal modernization approach—an approach that generated positive returns within two years, and put them on a solid financial and technological footing for further modernization investments.

11

Legacy Modernization— The Future

As with everything, change is a constant. Legacy modernization is no exception. We've seen a lot of maturity in this field over the past few years and we believe that the trend will accelerate as standards become more developed, tools mature, and hardware improves. Of course, I will not paint a picture of what the next ten years will look like, but let's examine a few things that we know are pushing the field forward. There are a few key fields that are developing, and are being used today, which will continue to trend into mainstream, and which will impact choices on the current mainframe legacy computing model. We'll will look at a few emerging trends which impact, how we compute, where we compute, and how we create the applications to do this.

Green Computing

With soaring energy costs, increasing data volumes and increasing demands for higher computing power, green computing is becoming more than just the politically correct way to spin a server product, as costs of energy soares, huge amounts of data increase, and the demand for higher computing power soar. Moreover, the environment will also benefit from green computing. So, what exactly is green computing? Green computing looks at increasing efficiencies, reducing the production of hazardous materials, and promoting re-cyclability.

There are several ways in which organizations are able to utilize the concept of green computing, including issues such as re-cyclability and, better power consumption. The following lists a few areas that the modern data center will move towards, to leverage this movement:

- Virtualization
- Materials re-cycling/less paper
- Power management
- Low power consuming chipsets

Managers are not very concerned with this, but there is an upward trend. In a survey of 400 IT Executives taken by the Standish Group in October 2007, only 1 percent of the respondents thought environmental considerations were 'extremely important' when considering hosting providers. So, though there is no overwhelming trend to buy green today, this will change, considering the environment also enables companies to save costs. In a report studying the US and World power consumption, power used to run a server was 0.6 percent of US energy consumption. But when the cooling and auxiliary infrastructure is factored, the figure rockets to 1.2 percent. The advances in chip design and hardware are leading to lower power consumption and heat dissipation, and lower cost. Combine this with soaring energy costs, green computingis certain to become a considerable metric with moving to a more modern technology platform.

Another practical example of how modernization is affecting green computing in a real and tangible way is the area of reporting. Legacy reports often generate reams of paper every day. There is an anicdotal story of a public sector agency who printed out 1,000 pages of paper every day just for the last page of the report. Further, it is not uncommon that these reports are totally obsolete. One of the huge upsides to modernization is in the area of business intelligence. Not only do we move away from static, old, hardcopy reports that are often 24 to 48 hours hold, but we can eliminate thousands of pounds of paper waste every year.

[ESTIMATING TOTAL POWER CONSUMPTION BY SERVERS IN THE U.S. AND THE WORLD, Jonathan G. Koomey, Ph.D `http://www.koomey.com`]

Standards Organizations

There are two organizations that are making significant efforts that have an impact on legacy modernization, and its future—The Object Management Group and the W3C. These organizations are made of key companies and industry leaders who come together to create standards for development design and information interchange.

Object Modeling Group (OMG)

The OMG is doing a significant amount of work as it pertains to Model-Driven Modernization(MDM), which is the application of Model-Driven Architecture(MDA) for legacy transformation. We will dive deeper into what MDA/MDM is and how it will impact this industry, but the premise is that developers can transform applications from a **Platform-Dependent Model (PDM)** to a **Platform Independent Model (PIM)**. If we can learn to derive any language, any business process or any data structure in terms of PIM, then we can begin to re-architect our new systems at a more abstract level. MDA is happening today. Many organizations use a PIM to design applications called UML. The trick is getting a legacy application into any given PIM in a highly automated fashion.

At the OGM, work is being done on defining the standard in which to exchange information about applications. According to the OMG, the **Knowledge Discovery Meta-Model (KDM)** "specifies a comprehensive set of common concepts required for understanding existing software systems in preparation for software assurance and modernization and provides infrastructure to support specialized definitions of domain-specific, application-specific, or implementation-specific knowledge". Now, if a modernization software tools vendor specialized in legacy understanding, they can parse the legacy code into a KDM compliant repository. This repository can then be leveraged by another System Integrator using JDeveloper or other MDA tools. So the transportability of knowledge will be much more mobile.

One problem with many of todays legacy modernization companies is that their technologies and repositories are proprietary. Most of these companies will say that they create modernization 'tools', but in the end, they are a services company because no one else has the expertise to understand or use the tools. With the growing adoption of standards put out by the OMG, companies can focus on increasing the capability of their tools whilst allowing experts in development and integration deliver.

The following code shows an example of how the KDM expresses information extracted from COBOL using the RecordTypes. The first snippet is actual COBOL code. The second is how we would express these in a generic model, based on the KDM, taken from the KDM specification.

Record Type (COBOL)

```
01 StudentDetails.
   02 StudentId        PIC 9(7).
   02 StudentName.
      03 FirstName      PIC X(10).
      03 MiddleInitial PIC X.
      03 Surname        PIC X(15).
   02 DateOfBirth.
      03 DayOfBirth     PIC 99.
      03 MonthOfBirth   PIC 99.
      03 YearOfBirth    PIC 9(4).
   02 CourseCode        PIC X(4).
MOVE "Doyle" To Surname
```

Above we have a simple Record Type in COBOL that stores information about a person. In the simple COBOL expression, we move `Doyle` to the last name, or `Surname` field.

We can express this record information and data option using a standard XML notation as shown next. It seems a bit complicated, but remember, we are aiming at a generic representation regardless of the source language, and we can use tools to automatically create these repositories. Once we have these repositories designed and populated, we can utilize modeling tools to manage change, create new function, and then generate to a new model.

```xml
<?xml version="1.0" encoding="UTF-8"?>
<kdm:Segment xmi:version="2.1"
  xmlns:xmi="http://schema.omg.org/spec/XMI/2.1"
  xmlns:action="http://schema.omg.org/spec/KDM/1.1/action"
  xmlns:code="http://schema.omg.org/spec/KDM/1.1/code"
  xmlns:kdm="http://schema.omg.org/spec/KDM/1.1/kdm"
        name="Record Example">
<model xmi:id="id.0" xmi:type="code:CodeModel">
  <codeElement xmi:id="id.1" xmi:type="code:CompilationUnit">
    <codeElement xmi:id="id.2" xmi:type="code:StorableUnit"
                 name="StudentDetails" type="id.3">
      <codeElement xmi:id="id.3" xmi:type="code:RecordType"
                   name="StudentDetails">
        <itemUnit xmi:id="id.4" name="StudentID" type="id.23"
                  ext="PIC 9(7)"/>
        <itemUnit xmi:id="id.5" name="StudentName" type="id.6">
          <codeElement xmi:id="id.6" xmi:type="code:RecordType"
                       name="StudentName">
            <itemUnit xmi:id="id.7" name="FirstName" type="id.24"
                      ext="PIC X(10)" size="10"/>
```

```
            <itemUnit xmi:id="id.8" name="MiddleName" type="id.24"
                      ext="PIC X" size="1"/>
            <itemUnit xmi:id="id.9" name="Surname" type="id.24"
                      ext="PIC X(15)" size="15"/>
          </codeElement>
        </itemUnit>
        <itemUnit xmi:id="id.10" name="DateOfBirth">
          <codeElement xmi:id="id.11" xmi:type="code:RecordType"
                        name="DateOfBirth">
            <itemUnit xmi:id="id.12" name="DayOfBirth" type="id.23"
                      ext="PIC 99" size="2"/>
            <itemUnit xmi:id="id.13" name="MonthOfBirth"
                      type="id.23" ext="PIC 99" size="2"/>
            <itemUnit xmi:id="id.14" name="YearOfBirth"
                      type="id.23" ext="PIC 9(4)" size="4"/>
          </codeElement>
        </itemUnit>
        <itemUnit xmi:id="id.15" name="CourseCode" type="id.24"
                  ext="PIC X(4)" size="4"/>
      </codeElement>
    </codeElement>
    <codeElement xmi:id="id.16" xmi:type="action:BlockUnit">
      <codeElement xmi:id="id.17" xmi:type="action:ActionElement">
        <codeElement xmi:id="id.18" xmi:type="code:Value"
                     name="&quot;Doyle&quot;" type="id.24"/>
        <actionRelation xmi:id="id.19" xmi:type="action:Addresses"
                        to="id.2" from="id.17"/>
        <actionRelation xmi:id="id.20" xmi:type="action:Reads"
                        to="id.18" from="id.17"/>
        <actionRelation xmi:id="id.21" xmi:type="action:Writes"
                        to="id.9" from="id.17"/>
      </codeElement>
    </codeElement>
  </codeElement>
  <codeElement xmi:id="id.22" xmi:type="code:LanguageUnit"
               name="Cobol common definitions">
    <codeElement xmi:id="id.23" xmi:type="code:DecimalType"/>
    <codeElement xmi:id="id.24" xmi:type="code:StringType"/>
  </codeElement>
  </model>
</kdm:Segment>
```

WC3

The WC3 is an international consortium with the mission of creating standards and guidelines to build consensus around Web technologies. At the time of writing this, they have published more than 110 standards. One of the projects that is currently underway, revolves around a business rule language called the Rules Interchange Format (RIF) Working Group.

The standardization of business rule language will free consumers from being locked into one particular business rule engine provider. Further, if you are in the business of deriving legacy business rules, then your target engine becomes less important. The major issue of the day is the question of what exactly is a business rule. Some think that pseudo code extracted from legacy Cobol isn't a business rule, but rather a 'candidate business rule' or a functional requirement. If you can't take a rule extracted from legacy code and import that into a business rule engine and execute it, then I would agree that these are not rules. So, what is a rule? This is why the standardization of business rules is so important.

The need for standardization in the market place arises from constant consolidation of technologies. As companies merge, products are absorbed, retired, or totally revamped. The consumer is then left with yet another legacy code base. So the future lies in open standard for rules interchange. This will be a great boon for legacy modernization.

Model Driven Architecture (MDA)

MDA is the elusive brass ring for legacy modernization. The OMG has defined the Model-Driven Architecture framework for software development. The core of the MDA approach is the application of models to describe systems and generate out the target code base. In Andrew Watson's book, *MDA Explained*, he outlines the traditional view of software development to the notion of MDA. Let's review quickly these concepts and then tie this back to legacy modernization.

Watson outlines the traditional software development lifecycle as illustrated in the following diagram:

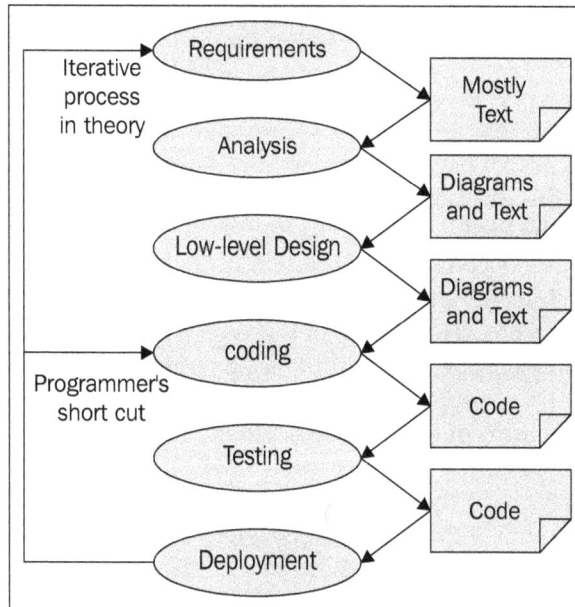

Challenges with the Traditional Approach

This methodology has many problems, which lend itself to the creation of why people want to migrate from legacy systems in the first place.

These system create challenges in:

- Portability
- Interoperability
- Maintenance
- Human Resource
- Agility

The MDA/MDM Approach

With Model-Driven Architecture (MDM) and Model-Driven Modernization (MDM), we can alleviate both the problems of traditional development and modernization of our legacy systems while capturing the value that is locked up inside.

In the MDM approach, we strive to define a PIM, which is a collection of processes or functions of a system that are not specifically tied to a particular language or operating system. In the MDA world, we would define our objects, models, and business function in this abstracted view. UML can be a particular PIM, and is commonly used, but the PIM is not restricted to UML. Further, when we want to generate our executable code, we can transit to the Platform-Specific Model, (PSM). The idea is that we let our development tools handle the automatic code generation of the PSM. The PSM will focus on a particular language and development framework. For example, a Java EE coding model using hibernation for data abstraction and spring would be an example of a PSM. The key here is that these transformations, from one model to another, are done via a transformation tool. Remember this point; this is where modernization of legacy applications can leverage automation more in the future. These tools that exist today are able to transform some PIM models to PSM models, when there is little shift in paradigms. So before we look into the where the MDM modernization is going, let's look at the difficulties with the traditional development model.

Let's examine another view of the traditional process, but in the context of working within MDM/MDA.

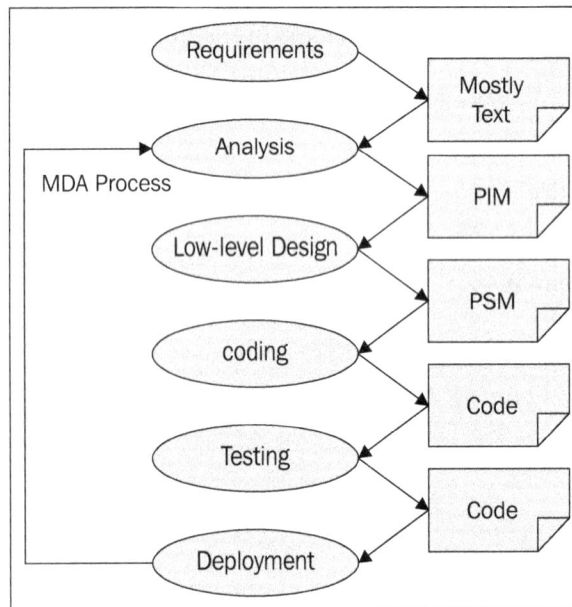

So, from the above model you can see that we work within the abstracted models and use transformation tools to navigate between PIMs and PSMs. These transformations are bi-directional. So, if coded applications can be reversed into the PSM, they can be brought back into the PIM and re-developed. Conceptually, there is a notion that COBOL on the mainframe would be considered a PSM. Theoretically, we would be able to create a PSM; and thus a PIM based on a legacy application. Any re-architecture, change in business process, and technology enhancements would be down within the PIM, and we would target a new PSM based off the mainframe, or off of the Legacy Cobol. Well, we are not quite there yet, but as the industry moves more towards open and portable standards as we've seen in business rules and code description portability, re-architecture will become a more reliable and cheaper form of legacy modernization.

Cloud Computing

According to Gartner, cloud computing is "a style of computing where massively scalable IT-related capabilities are provided 'as a service' across the Internet to multiple external customers". The notion of cloud computing is an emerging field with fluid and even debated definitions. So, for the sake of this book, we will take a fairly high level definition, and try to stay on the fray of the highly debated points. As we will see next, there are components which, in themselves aren't cloud computing, but make up components required for the cloud to exists.

Therefore, one can think of the cloud as a service, computing or storage, that exists somewhere else, and made accessible to a consumer over a well-defined protocol, usually via the Internet. As the agreement demands no human interference by the consumer, or by the provider. In fact, a key characteristic of the cloud is that if a consumer of the service needs to intervene in the management of the services (load balancing, provisions, request for increase storage), then that computing is not being done on a cloud. How this is stored or computed is irrelevant to the consumer.

Amazon Elastic Compute Cloud

A real world example of cloud computing can be found today in the Amazon Elastic Compute Cloud (Amazon EC2). This service provides resizable computing capacity for developers. The elastic characteristics of the service mean that you can increase capacity up or down in minutes automatically. In a typical data center computing environment, provisioning, or de-provisioning of computing power can take days or weeks. Another characteristic of this services is that the instances run at multiple locations with low latency connection which provide a high level of availability and reliability, again, without involving the consumer. These two are unique benefits of cloud computing.

Now that we have a bit of a definition, let us look at some of the components that enable cloud computing. It is important to note, however, that these components are standalone in their own right. They are highly utilized and valuable services that are emerging today. However, applied together they enable the notion of computing in the cloud.

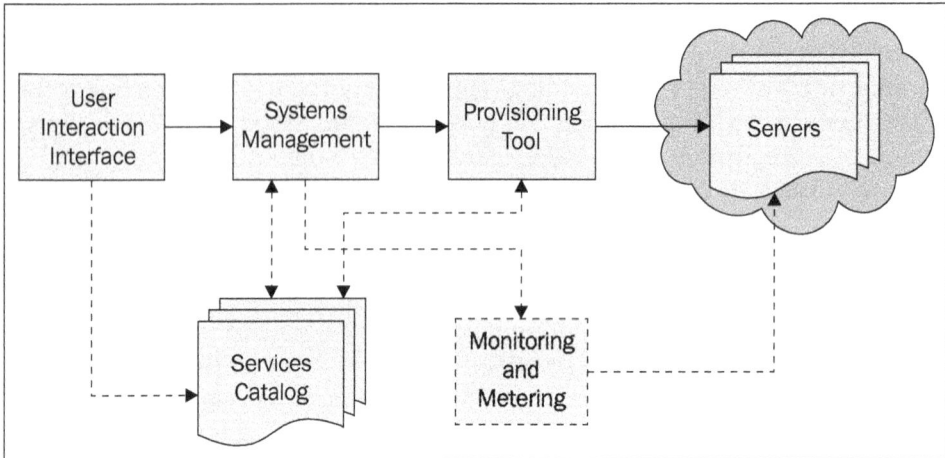

Grid Computing

Grid computing is sometimes called Utility Computing or On-demand Computing. The Grid offers storage of our computing resources from many resources dedicated to the application of a specific set of problems. The key here is that grid management software is used to apply the resources of heterogeneous resources in a synergistic way to solve a problem. This is different from a cluster of processors or databases, which run as a single homogeneous unit. The Grid offers a high degree of scalability and power as the resources can be spread across commodity-based processing, or storage, rather than a large, high horsepower server, or storage device. There is also power in the notion that these resources can be heterogeneous in nature. This can be applied to both computational power and storage.

The benefits of the grid, as you will see, meet the demands and needs of the business. We can articulate these benefits in three main points, which are important to accomplishing the mission of the organization:

- Lower Total Cost of Ownership (overprovision, virtualization)
- Agility in workload demands
- Predictable scalability

The strength of the grid is that it can be dispersed across a geographic region and each node of computing power on the grid can be built upon commodity hardware.

From an Oracle perspective, we can look at **Real Application Clusters (RAC)** as the core offering for grid computing. Oracle has pioneered this notion of grid computing from its early involvement in core component contributions, to the Open Source community, to enable clustering to middleware database grid with Coherence. We will explore more of these in the area of extreme processing.

Virtualization

The virtualized world is a concept that is fast becoming the norm for the modern data center. With virtualization, we abstract computer resources so that the specifics of a hardware platform or application are encapsulated to the end user. Users can create Virtual Machines that exist on the same platform, yet perform and behave like independent physical servers.

In the context of modernization, we are seeing this as a growing trend in the areas of server consolidation, disaster recovery, and application portability. Instead of running excess hardware because of multiple computing environments, we can leverage excess computing power or storage and bring all of these applications and operating systems under one roof. This creates a simpler operational environment, can provide lower operational costs, and increase performance by enabling grid computing across virtual clusters.

Application Fabrics

The concept of application fabrics is emerging from the junction of the commoditization of grid computing and the availability of high performance networks. Application fabrics is the next generation intersection of grid computing and virtualization. Whilst grid computing leverages high availability and portability of computing resources, and virtualization delivers a lower cost data center in a much more simplified environment application fabrics looks to bring these two concepts together.

The trend toward application fabrics was started mostly with companies like Google and Amazon, as we've seen with cloud computing. Application fabrics is the next step in their progression. Companies like Appistry (www.appistry.com) are pioneering this technology. According to Appistry, the future of application fabrics is based on the following principles:

- Time-critical applications require simultaneous scalability, dependability, manageability, and affordability. The next generation application infrastructure must eliminate the once-expected trade-offs among these requirements.

- The application is all that matters. Any infrastructure exists to serve the application, not the other way around.

- Physical infrastructure is an interchangeable commodity. Standards-based computing infrastructure has advanced to the point that organizations seeking to maximize dependability and minimize cost can purchase the most affordable hardware available.

- As physical infrastructure will inevitably fail, insulating the application is a must. Developers and administrators should worry as little as possible about physical infrastructure. Rather than trying to prevent failure at all costs (which is impossible), an application fabric accepts that failure will happen and deals with it by assigning application-level tasks to multiple nodes in the fabric.

Extreme Processing

Historically, within the mainframe world, traditional servers with RDBMS systems could not compete with the pure transactional power of the mainframe. Many managers are reluctant to migrate from their higher cost infrastructure because of this misperception in the open system environment. Not only does mainframe QoS(Quality of Service) dictate a high level of transactions, but the industry as a whole is moving in this direction. To create a high level of availability, we have put our database systems on a grid and clustered them for extreme availability. We now see that the next step in this demand is a high level of RAS which will introduce the ability for extreme processing. As computing demands expanding geographic regions, times zones, and support for the elastic nature of cloud computing, we will see a greater need for extreme processing. With extreme transactions processing we can leverage in-memory databases that can provide a mechanism for more than just a high level of availability, but also a huge level of transactions.

With Oracle's Coherence product, we are able to extend the power of grid database to the application. This is most often used for object level caching of databases in a heterogeneous environment. So, in the event of database failure, the clustering of the application server can maintain not just application availability to users, but also access the data stores and transactions which can continue until the underlying systems have been restored. Since the application is interacting with both data and transaction processing at the application level, it can be totally abstracted from the database.

Also, with extreme processing on Coherence the data is synchronously backed up onto at least one other server to make sure that it is not lost. This allows the transactions to run at in-memory speed without sacrificing the information in case of a server failure. The more the available, the higher the overall transaction rate, and that allows organizations to accomplish extreme transaction processing so our transactions processing power is not limited to just the bus size of the system. But as we are doing this at the memory level, the speed can be conducted at extreme rates.

Summary

What do these technologies have to do with legacy modernization? Great question! The difference between some of these emerging technologies, and say, advancements in processor clock speed or inexpensive disk space, is that it totally changes the paradigm of how we compute today. While SOA services are a logical steps in providing agility, cloud computing is a leap. We have gone from higher clock speed by making chips smaller and closer together, to increasing computing power whilst generating less energy, and harnessing computational power from the heterogeneous and geographically displaced locations. This is a true challenge to the monolithic monsters, at which throw more disk and energy towards to create more workload. Now,the promise of better, faster, cheaper can truly be realized.

A
Technology Glossary

Application Programming Interface (API) — The interface between an application's software and platform.

Application server — A program that handles all application operations between users, and an organization's back-end business applications or databases. Application servers are typically used for complex transaction-based applications.

Architecture — The style or method of design and construction that comprises the elements of an information system and defines the purpose and interrelationships of those elements.

Asynchronous Transfer Mode (ATM) — A type of packet switching that transmits fixed-length mode units of data. The recurrence of cells does not depend on the bit rate of the transmission system, only on the source requirements (Defining 1991).

Authentication — The process of verifying the identity of an end-user or process. Authentication may be accomplished using various methods such as user ID and password, digital signature, or biometrics devices.

Authorization — The process of determining whether the end-user's use of resources is permitted and of granting appropriate systems, network, or resource access. Authorization prevents unauthorized access and deters attempts to gain access.

Backbone — A network designed to interconnect lower speed channels (Defining 1991).

Bridge — A device that interconnects LANs using the bottom two OSI layers (Defining 1991).

Bus—A LAN topology in which all interconnected computers are aware of all transmissions, but each computer receives only those transmissions addressed to it (Defining 1991).

Business continuity—A process for maintaining practices and procedures to ensure that EDS and our clients receive continuous service (also known as disaster recovery plan). The **Business Continuity Action Team** (**BCAT**) has overall responsibility for the process.

Business process reengineering—The fundamental re-think and radical re-design of business processes to achieve dramatic improvements in critical, contemporary measures of performance such as cost, quality, service, and speed (M. Hammer and J. Champy 1993).

Cell—A fixed-length unit of data (Defining 1991).

Character-based interface—User interface that uses the character or text mode of the computer; typically refers to typing in a command.

Client/Server model of computing—Computer processing characterized by the division of an application into components processed on different networked computers. A client requests a service or information from a server; the server processes the request, performs the service, and returns the requested information to the client.

Cloud computing—A type of computing, comparable to grid computing, that relies on sharing computing resources rather than having local servers or personal devices to handle applications. The goal of cloud computing is to apply traditional supercomputing, or high-performance computing power, normally used by military and research facilities, to perform tens of trillions of computations per second, in consumer-oriented applications such as financial portfolios, or even to deliver personalized information, or power immersive computer games.

Collaborative authoring—The process of allowing a group of people to author a document together although they may be located in different places or working at different times. It also allows the comments of each person to be distinguishable.

Compact disk-interactive—A variant of the compact disk-read-only memory (CD/ROM) optical disk that supports sound and image as well as data. It is intended primarily for home and educational use (Illingsworth et al., 1990).

Compatibility — The capability of two or more systems or components to perform their required functions while sharing the same hardware or software environment (IEEE 1990).

Computer-Aided Systems Engineering (CASE) — The use of computers to aid in the software engineering process. It may include the application of software tools to software design, requirements tracing code production, testing, document generation, and other software engineering activities (IEEE 1990).

Continuously available systems — Fault-tolerant systems that eliminate all downtime, planned and unplanned. The hardware and software can be upgraded while the system is online.

CICS — Customer Information Control System, a TP monitor from IBM that was originally developed to provide transaction processing for IBM mainframes. It controls the interaction between applications and users, and lets programmers develop screen displays without detailed knowledge of the terminals being used.

De jure standards — Standards approved or sanctioned by local or national standards-setting organizations.

Digital audio tape (DAT) — A digital recording technology that uses a helical scan read/write head and 4mm magnetic tape. Although initially a CD-quality audio format, the **Digital Data Storage (DDS)** specification, developed by Sony Corporation and Hewlett-Packard Corporation in 1988, defined a format and quality level for DAT tapes so that they could be used by computers. DAT cassettes have capacities in the 2-4 GB range.

Downsizing — The re-deployment of current systems or applications to different and less expensive computing and network environments.

Electronic imaging — The capability to capture, store, retrieve, distribute, present, and manage documents in digital form.

Enterprise Application Integration (EAI) — A business computing term for plans, methods, and tools used to collaborate applications in an enterprise.

Ethernet — A contention-based networking scheme. See IEEE 802.3 for technical specifications.

Extensible Markup Language (XML) — Meta language for the creation of common information formats and sharing both the format and the data on the World Wide Web, intranets, and elsewhere. Unlike HTML, the markup symbols are unlimited and self-defining, which makes the language extensible.

Fault-resilient systems (or high-resiliency systems) — Systems with a component of hardware detection at the compute level. Although major elements of the computer can bring down the system or portions of it, minor components can fail without interruption. Failed components can be replaced without service downtime, power supplies, system fans, disk drives, and some input/output (I/O) controllers. The fault-resilient system is expected to cut downtime in half. The system averages less than five minutes downtime for recovery if the design and implementation are sound.

Fault-tolerant systems — Systems with redundant hardware components that continually check the veracity of each other. If one component is found to be in error, the system eliminates that component from the environment and notifies the operator that a failure has occurred. All failed component replacement occurs while the system is running. The component is restored to the environment with no penalty to the application. Recovery occurs in less than one second, and all unplanned downtime is eliminated.

Fiber Distributed Data Interface (FDDI) — ANSIs architecture for a MAN; a network based on the use of fiber-optic cable to transmit data (Defining 1991).

Fiber Distributed Data Interface II (FDDI II) — A variant of FDDI that supports isochronous traffic (Defining 1991).

Fiber-optic cable — Cable using tiny threads of glass or plastic; transmits large amounts of data at the speed of light (Darcy and Boston 1988).

Flexibility — The ease with which a system or component can be modified for use in applications or environments other than those for which it was specifically designed (IEEE 1990).

Frame relay — An upgrade of X.25 packet switching (Defining 1991).

Forward engineering — The transformation from a higher level of abstraction to a lower level.

Gateway — A device that interconnects dissimilar LANs employing different high-level protocols (Defining 1991).

Graphical User Interface (GUI) — Graphics-based user interface that incorporates icons, pull-down menus, and a mouse.

Grid computing — A form of networking. Unlike conventional networks that focus on communication among devices, grid computing harnesses unused processing cycles of all computers in a network for solving problems, too intensive for any standalone machine.

Groupware — Software that runs on a LAN and allows people on the network (typically a team) to participate in a joint (often complex) project (Newton 1993).

HELLO — The protocol used by a group of cooperative, trusting packet switches to allow them to discover minimal delay routes (Comer 1988).

High-availability systems — Systems designed around available technology used typically as general-purpose computers. These systems are usually clustered with a software monitor that acts like a traffic cop or switching mechanism. The monitor detects component failure, switches processing to another unit, and starts an automated procedure to rebuild data and ensure system integrity. Downtime averages from two to 20 minutes.

Host — A computer that is attached to a network and provides services rather than just acting as a store-and-forward processor or communication switch.

Human factors — The consideration of the human part of a system; it mostly refers to physical ergonomics, but also used sometimes in the context of computer systems.

Information technology — The merging of computing and high-speed communications links carrying data, sound, and video.

Infrastructure — Hardware, software, networks, services, and processes to support an organization.

Installed base — Current environment.

Intelligent Peripheral Interface (IPI) — A high-speed hard disk interface used with minis and mainframes transferring data in the 10-25 MBs range. IPI-2 and IPI-3 refer to differences in the command set that they execute.

Institute of Electrical and Electronics Engineers (IEEE) — Professional association that defines and promotes de jure standards for LANs. Developed standards are submitted to ANSI and possibly to ISO.

Integrated CASE (I-CASE) — Computer-aided systems engineering (CASE) software that automates the systems analysis, design, and programming necessary for systems development. I-CASE refers to environments that enforce the seamless integration of deliverables for all phases of the SLC.

Integrated Services Digital Network (ISDN) — An ITU-T-defined digital network.

Intelligent wiring hubs — Hubs that interconnect servers and route network traffic.

International Organization for Standardization (ISO) — An organization that develops standards for international and national data communications (Newton 1991). ANSI is the current U.S. voice in the ISO (Merkow 1990).

Internet — 1. A network that interconnects two or more other networks (Defining 1991). 2. An immense network of networks, connecting computers at universities, research labs, and commercial and military sites around the world (Downing and Covington 1992).

Internet Protocol (IP) — A standard describing software that tracks the Internetwork addresses of nodes, routes outgoing messages, and recognizes incoming messages (Newton 1991).

Internetwork Packet Exchange (IPX) — Novell's operating system (Defining 1991).

Interoperability — The capability of applications and computers from different suppliers to work together on a network, connecting, and sharing data and processes as appropriate.

Interprocess communication — Communication between two processes, whether residing on the same or different machines.

Isochronous — Equally timed. In data communications, timing information is transmitted on the channel along with data, sending asynchronous data by synchronous means. The method involves synchronously sending the asynchronous characters between each pair of start and stop bits (Defining 1991).

Kiosk — A station for delivering marketing or reference information, usually located in a common area. A typical kiosk consists of a microcomputer with a touch screen. Other attached input/output devices may include magnetic card readers and printers to enable user's transactions.

Legacy system — A functioning computer software application using conventional methodologies; usually a significant portion of the current installed base.

Local area network (LAN) — Typically, a high-speed network where all segments of the transmission are situated in an office, building, or campus environment (Defining 1991).

LPAR — Short for logical partitioning, a system of taking a computer's total resources — processors, memory, and storage — and splitting them into smaller units that each can be run with its own instance of the operating system and applications.

Magneto-optical (MO) — A high-density, rewriteable recording method that uses a combination of magnetic disk and optical methods.

Market-driven — Anticipating future requirements by developing timely product or service offerings to meet SU needs prior to client request.

Massively parallel systems — Tightly coupled multiprocessing computers that house 100 or more central processing units (CPUs), each with its own memory (Newton 1993).

Metropolitan Area Network (MAN) — A stretched LAN providing data communications over a distance of about 50 km, generally associated with the IEEE 802.6 MAN standard (Defining 1991).

Middleware — Software that provides a high-level programming interface meant to shield a distributed application developer from the complexities of the hardware, operating system, and network semantics. Middleware is frequently used as a mechanism for communication between distributed application processes.

Model — An abstract representation of a process, device, or system that accounts for all of its known properties.

NetPC — A low-end PC designed to be highly manageable and run all varieties of thin-client software along with conventional low-end PC applications.

Network — A collection of resources used to establish and switch communication paths between its terminals.

Network architecture — A set of design principles, including the organization of functions and services, used as the basis for design and implementation of a user application network.

Network computer — Processor-independent computers with prices starting at less than $1000. Initially envisioned to exclusively run Java applications downloaded from server, current versions are running terminal emulation and Windows applications through multiuser Windows software such as Citrix Systems WinFrame.

Non-Uniform Memory Access (NUMA) — Allows applications designed for the shared memory model of SMP machines to run on internal clusters of unlimited processors, creating a virtual MPP machine. The architecture's high-speed interconnect technology breaks up the address space of memory, while tricking the system into maintaining a contiguous memory view.

Object broker technology — Technology that allows application processes to communicate across a network using an object-oriented architecture.

Object-oriented systems—Systems composed of objects (conceptual or programmatic abstractions that include data and functionality encapsulated in a single unit) that communicate with one another using explicitly defined interfaces.

OMNIPoint (Open Management Interoperability Point)—A set of standards, implementation specifications, testing methods and tools, and object libraries that make possible the development of interoperable management systems and applications (Network Management Forum 1993).

Open Shortest Path First (OSPF)—A link-state-based routing protocol included in the TCP/IP protocol suite. It provides for the authentication of routing updates and uses IP multicast when sending or receiving updates.

Open systems—Any system in which the components conform to nonproprietary standards rather than to the standards of a specific supplier of hardware or software. According to X/Open, an open system is a supplier-independent computing environment consisting of commonly available products that have been designed and implemented in accordance with accepted standards.

Open Systems Architecture (OSA)—IBM's System 390 clustering technology.

Open Systems Interconnection (OSI)—ISO communications standard defining a seven-layer framework for implementing open systems rules and regulations.

Operating system—A collection of software, firmware, and hardware elements that control the execution of computer programs and provide such services as computer resource allocation, job control, input/output control, and file management in a computer system (IEEE 1990).

Optical fiber—Any filament or fiber made of dielectric materials and consisting of a core, which carries, for example, laser-generated light signals and a surrounding cladding that reflects the signal back into the core (Defining 1991).

Packet—A unit of data, consisting of binary digits including data and call-control signals, switched and transmitted as a composite whole (Defining 1991).

Packet switching—A data transmission technique where physical resources on a path are switched on a per packet basis, using control information in the header of each packet. It can operate in either a connection-oriented or connectionless mode (Defining 1991).

Portability—The ease with which a system or component can be transferred from one hardware or software environment to another (IEEE 1990). See binary portability and source portability.

Portable Operating System based on UNIX (POSIX) — The name of IEEE's 1003 committee and the standard that defines the portable operating system interfaces and functions (Rosen et al., 1990).

Premises distribution system — The transmission network inside a building or group of buildings that connects various types of voice and data communications devices, switching equipment, and other information management systems to each other as well as to outside communications networks (Newton 1993).

Primary Integrated Platform Environment (PIPE) — An EDS initiative to test key integration points for standard platforms and system elements such as databases and client tools.

Protocol — A set of conventions that govern the interaction of processes, devices, and other components within a system (IEEE 1990).

Quarter Inch Cartridge (QIC) — A backup technology that uses 1/4" wide (6.35mm) magnetic tape cartridges. It uses the serpentine recording method with cartridge capacities ranging from 40 MB to 13 GB.

Rearchitect — Mine business rules & component methods, reverse/refactor/forward engineer application, align application to business process, extend application reach and value.

Redundant Arrays of Independent Disks (RAID) — Technology that provides protection from data loss by providing a level of redundancy immediately within the array. The array contains removable disk drive modules that are automatically rebuilt in the event of a device failure, without causing the system to shut down.

Rehost — Move legacy applications to modern platforms and optimized architectures while preserving the value in the applications.

Relational database — A collection of related (usually through a common field) data files.

Relearn — Relearning applications is a discovery process that reverse engineers and captures the intellectual property investment that has been made in legacy applications over the years, and enables that investment to be preserved and carried forward to core modernization strategies to rehost, rearchitect and replace ageing legacy applications.

Remote Procedure Call (RPC) — A procedure call in which the actual execution of the body of the procedure takes place on a processor that is physically distinct from the one on which the procedure call takes place.

Repeater — An electronic device that amplifies or rebuilds an attenuated network signal.

Reverse engineering — The process of extracting, standardizing, and documenting data descriptions and program logic from an implementation-dependent form to an implementation-independent form, and then migrating that information to an I-CASE environment.

Rightsizing — The use of appropriate technology to deliver a system that is aligned with a client's business goals. Rightsizing can be any combination of Client /Server, open systems, and downsizing, depending on the tactical and strategic business objectives.

Router — A device that operates at the Network layer of the OSI model and links the data link layer and Physical layers of the OSI stack. Routers are used to interconnect multiple networks, potentially using different high-level protocols. Routers create many logically different subnetworks within Internetworks, maintain information about each network, and communicate with each other periodically to advertise their capability to reach other networks.

Routing Information Protocol (RIP) — The protocol used by Berkeley 4.3 BSD UNIX systems to exchange routing information among a (usually small) set of computers. Usually, all the participating machines are attached to a single LAN. Implemented by the UNIX program "routed". RIP is derived from an earlier protocol of the same name developed at Xerox (Comer 1988).

Rules Engine — Business rules describe and control the structure, operation and strategy of an organization. Often, they are captured in policy and procedure manuals, customer contracts, supplier agreements, marketing strategies, and as the expertise embodied in employees. They are dynamic, and likely to change with time, found in all manner of applications from the click-stream of a website to the numerous business rules codified as legalese in B2B trading partner contracts. Finance and insurance companies must enforce numerous internal policies and external regulatory policies. Separating the business rules, as shown in Figure 2, from application code and implementing them using a rule engine can make applications adaptable and maintainable. Since business rules are externalized from the application code, they can be changed independently without recompiling the application. When represented in a natural business language that business users understand, business users and analysts can actually write and maintain rules. Business logic isolated in this way doesn't impact the design of the application and can easily be adapted to existing software that would benefit from decreased maintenance costs and increased flexibility.

Scalability — The capability of a system to perform acceptably on a computer of any size, depending on the needs of the user. Implies minimal change to accommodate this variance.

Server — A network computer that provides services such as printing or e-mail to LAN users (Newton 1991).

Shielded twisted-pair (STP) wire — A type of wire that has a pair of wires twisted together and coated with an aluminum wrap for protection from external interference; depending on the intended use, STP can provide long-distance connections of up to 1,000 feet.

Software re-engineering — The transformation from one level of abstraction to another; a process based on a usual design methodology, proceeding from requirements to a final product.

Software reverse engineering — The process of extracting, standardizing, and documenting data descriptions and program logic from an implementation-dependent form to an implementation-independent form, and then migrating that information to an automated software engineering environment.

Structured Query Language (SQL) — A language used to query and process data in a relational database (Newton 1991).

SQL Access Group (SAG) — A consortium of 42 leading systems and suppliers that includes most suppliers in the relational database market. The group's mission is to solve the SQL RDBMS interoperability problems by developing a technical specification to enable multiple RDBMSs and application tools to work together.

Symmetric multiprocessing (SMP) — A type of multiprocessing in which all CPUs are identical, and in which any CPU can execute both user and kernel instructions.

Systems management — A set of processes that facilitates the use of, and change to technical resources that deliver information services. These processes are performed by a combination of manual procedures and automated tools.

Systems Network Architecture (SNA) — A network architecture developed by IBM for use with large mainframe computers.

Systems reengineering — Changing systems without changing functions; the process of modifying the internal mechanisms of a system or program or the data structures of a system or program without changing the functionality. See also process reengineering.

Third generation language (3GL) — A procedural programming language that offers a higher level of abstraction than the assembly language. Examples are COBOL, Fortran, C, C++, and Pascal.

Token-ring — A network using token-passing technology in a sequential manner, with each network workstation or terminal, passing the token to the station next to it (Freedman 1991).

Transmission Control Protocol/Internet Protocol (TCP/IP) — The reliable connection-oriented protocol used by the Defense Advanced Research Projects Agency (DARPA) for its Internetworking research.

Unified Modeling Language (UML) — An object-oriented design language that is the standard notation for the modeling of real-world objects. This notation unifies the popular methods into a single standard, including Grady Booch's work on describing a set of objects and relationships, Rumbaugh's Object Modeling Technique, and Ivar Jacobson's work on use cases.

Unshielded twisted-pair (UTP) wire — A type of wire that has an uncoated pair of wires twisted together. It is used for short-distance connections. Compare to shielded twisted-pair wire.

Upper Layer Protocol (ULP) — Layer above TCP.

Visual programming environment (VPE) — Software engineering environment that extends the productive capabilities of a 3GL or 4GL through the use of advanced graphical techniques. This environment provides visual methods for designing the characteristics of an application, and establishing a set of objects that can be easily associated with logic written in a programming language such as Smalltalk or Basic. The user interface is usually designed first, and then processing can be coded in the supported language and assigned to the interface objects.

Wide area network (WAN) — A data communication network that covers large geographical areas, generally implemented by linking several remote LANs through the use of gateways and bridges (Merkow 1990).

Windows-based terminal — A terminal that runs clients for WinFrame, and accesses Windows applications running on Windows NT server with application logic and data residing on the server, while the GUI runs on the client.

Workstation — An intelligent desktop device equipped with all the facilities required to perform a particular type of task.

X/Open — An international nonprofit organization that defines, promotes, and supplies open systems technology. It is owned by a consortium of the world's largest computer manufacturers.

X terminal — A terminal with built-in X Window software that provides graphical access to UNIX applications.

X.25 — An international standards document issued by ITU-T that defines the method of interworking between a client's equipment and a packet switching network when they are connected by a dedicated circuit (Illingsworth et al., 1990).

Common Legacy Acronyms

Acronyms and Initials

3-D	Three-dimensional
3GL	Third Generation Language
4GL	Fourth Generation Language
AAL	ATM Adaption Layers
ABC	Activity-based Costing
ABM	Activity-based Management
ACAS	Application Control Architecture Services
ACL	Access Control List
ACM	Association for Computing Machinery
ADE	Application Development Environment
ADSL	Asymmetric Digital Subscriber Line
ANI	American National Institute
ANSI	American National Standards Institute
API	Application Programming Interface
APPC	Advanced Program-to-Program Communication
APPN	Advanced Peer-to-Peer Networking
ATM	Asynchronous Transfer Mode; automated teller machine
B-ISDN	Broadband Integrated Services Digital Network
BGP	Border Gateway Protocol
BIP	Business Improvement Planning
BPEL	Business Process Engineering Language (Oracle Product)
CAD	Computer-Aided Design
CALS	Continuous Acquisition and Life cycle Support
CAM	Computer-Aided Manufacturing
CAN	Campus Area Network
CASE	Computer-Aided Systems Engineering

CD-ROM	Compact Disk-Read-Only Memory
CDE	Common Desktop Environment
CDS	Cell Directory Service
CHI	Computer Human Interaction
CICS	Customer Information Control System
CLI	Call Level Interface
CMC	Common Messaging Calls
CMM	Capability Maturity Model
COM	Component Object Model
CORBA	Common Object Request Broker Architecture
COTS	Commercial off the Shelf (Software package)
CPU	Central Processing Unit
CRA	Corporate Registration Authority
CSCW	Computer Supported Cooperative Work
CSTA	Computer Supported Telecommunications Applications
CSTS	Client/Server Technical Services
CT2	Cordless Telephone Second Generation
CTI	Comprehensive Tool Infrastructure; computer telephony integration
DAC	Discretionary Access Control
DAT	Digital Audio Tape
DBMS	Database Management System
DCE	Distributed Computing Environment
DDS	Digital Data Service
DES	Data Encryption Standard
DFS	Distributed File Services
DLT	Digital Linear Tape
DLSw	Data Link Switching
DMA	Document Management Alliance
DMI	Desktop Management Interface
DNS	Domain Name Service
DR	Disaster Recovery
DRDA	Distributed Relational Database Architecture
DSM	Distributed Systems Management
DSS	Decision Support System
DTP	Distributed Transaction Processing
DTS	Distributed Time Service

DVMRP	Distance Vector Multicast Routing Protocol
E-CASE	Enterprise Computer-Aided Systems Engineering
EAI	Enterprise Application Integration
ECTF	Enterprise Computer Telephony Forum
EDI	Electronic Data Interchange
EDV	Electronic Data Vaulting
EMA	Electronic Mail Association
EMSS	Electronic Meeting Support Systems
ESIOP	Environment-Specific Inter-ORB Protocol
FDDI	Fiber Distributed Data Interface
FTAM	File Transfer, Access, and Management
FTP	File Transfer Protocol
GDS	Global Directory Service
GDSS	Group Decision Support Systems
GIOP	General Inter-ORB Protocol
GSSAPI	Generic Security System Application Programming Interface
GUI	Graphical User Interface
HCI	Human Computer Interaction
HiPPI	High Performance Parallel Interface
HOOPS	Hierarchical Object-Oriented Programming System
HP	Hewlett-Packard Corporation
HSSI	High Speed Serial Interface
HTML	HyperText Markup Language
HTTP	HyperText Transport Protocol
I-CASE	Integrated Computer-Aided Systems Engineering
I/O	Input/Output
ICM	Implementing Change Methodology
IDL	Interface Definition Language
IEEE	Institute of Electrical and Electronics Engineers
IEF	Information Engineering Facility
IETF	Internet Engineering Task Force
IGRP	Interior Gateway Routing Protocol
IMS/TM	Information Management System/Transaction Monitor
IP	Internet Protocol
IPC	Interprocess Communication
IPI	Intelligent Peripheral Interface

IPX	Internetwork Packet Exchange
IS-IS	Intermediate System-Intermediate System
ISCG	Infrastructure Services Communication Group
ISDN	Integrated Services Digital Network
ISO	International Standards Organization
ISP	Internet service provider
IT	Information Technology
ITU	International Telecommunications Union
ITU-T	International Telecommunications Union-Telecommunications
JCL	Job Control Language (IBM)
JDBC	Java Database Connectivity
JES	Job Entry System (IBM)
JPEG	Joint Photographic Experts Group
KB	Kilobytes
LAN	Local Area Network
LU	Logical Unit
MAN	Metropolitan Area Network
MAPI	Messaging Application Programming Interface
Mbps	Megabits per second
MIME	Multipurpose Internet Mail Extensions
MO	Magneto-Optical
MOSPF	Multicast Extensions to Open Shortest Path First
MPEG	Motion Picture Experts Group
MPP	massively parallel processor
MVS	Multiple Virtual Storage
NC	Network Computer
NetBIOS	Network Basic Input/Output System
NFS	Network File System
NIC	Network Interface Card
NIST	National Institute of Standards and Technology
NIUF	North American ISDN Users' Forum
NMF	Network Management Forum
NNAM	Network Naming and Addressing Management
NNTP	Network News Transport Protocol
NSA	National Security Agency
NT	New Technology (refers to Microsoft's product)

NTP	Network Time Protocol
NUMA	Non-Uniform Memory Access
OC	Optical Carrier
OCE	Open Collaboration Environment
OCR	Optical Character Recognition
ODA	Open Document Architecture
ODBC	Open Database Connectivity
ODIF	Office Document Interchange Format
ODMG	Object Database Management Group
OMG	Object Management Group
ONC	Open Network Computing
OO	Object Oriented
OOA	Object-Oriented Analysis
OOA/D	Object-Oriented Analysis and Design
OOD	Object-Oriented Design
OODBMS	Object-Oriented Database Management System
OQL	Object Query Language
ORB	Object Request Broker
OSF	Open Software Foundation
OSI	Open Systems Interconnection
OSPF	Open Shortest Path First
OURS	Open User Recommended Solutions
PBX	Private Branch Exchange
PCI	Peripheral Connect Interface
PCI	Payment card Industry
PCMCIA	Personal Computer Memory Card International Association
PCS	Personal Communication Services
PDA	Personal Digital Assistant
PHIGS	Programmers' Hierarchical Interactive Graphics System
PIPE	Primary Integrated Platform Environment
PM 2	Project Management Version 2
PNNI	Private Network-to-Network Interface
POSIX	Portable Operating System based on UNIX
PRI	Primary Rate Interface
QIC	Quarter Inch SCartridge
QoS	Quality of Service

RAC	Remote Application Cluster (Oracle)
RAID	Redundant Arrays of Independent Disks
RAS	Reliability, Availability, and Serviceability
RDA	Remote Database Access
RDBMS	Relational Database Management System
RDP	Requirements Determination Process
RFC	Request for Comment
RIP	Routing Information Protocol
RISC	Reduced Instruction Set Computing
RPC	Remote Procedure Call
RSA	Rivest, Shamir, Adleman
RSVP	ReSerVation Protocol
S-HTTP	Secure HyperText Transport Protocol
SAG	SQL Access Group
SCM	Software Configuration Management
SCSI	Small Computer System Interface
SD DVD	Super Density Digital Video Disk
SDH	Synchronous Digital Hierarchy
SDSL	Single-line Digital Subscriber Line
SEI	Software Engineering Institute
SET	Secure Electronic Transaction
SFVN	Secure Fast Virtual LAN
SGML	Standard Generalized Markup Language
SIAM	Systems Impact Analysis Methodology
SLA	Service Level Agreement
SLC	Systems Life Cycle
SLC 3	Systems Life Cycle Version 3
SSL	Secure Socket Layer
SMCA	Systems Management Capabilities Architecture
SMD	Storage Module Drive
SMDS	Switched Multimegabit Data Services
SMP	Symmetric Multiprocessing
SMTP	Simple Mail Transfer Protocol
SNA	Systems Network Architecture
SNI	SNA Network Interconnection
SNMP	Simple Network Management Protocol

SOA	Service Oriented Architecture
SONET	Synchronous Optical Network
SPDL	Standard Page Description Language
SPELS	Software Performance Engineering for Legacy Systems
SPX	Sequenced Packet Exchange
SQL	Structured Query Language
SSL	Secure Sockets Layer
SSU	Strategic Support Unit
STP	Shielded Twisted Pair
STT	Secure Transaction Technology
SWDDS	Switched Digital Data Services
TAFIM	Technical Architecture Framework for Information Management
TCP/IP	Transmission Control Protocol/Internet Protocol
TDM	Time Division Multiplexing
TM	Transaction Manager
TOG	The Open Group
TOGAF	The Open Group Architectural Framework
TP	Transaction Processing
TPF	Transaction Processing Facility
TPI	Time Provider Interface
TSE	Technical Services Europe
UTC	Coordinated Universal Time
UML	Unified Modeling Language
ULP	Upper Layer Protocol
UTP	Unshielded Twisted Pair
VDSL	Very-high-bit-rate Digital Subscriber Line
VIC	Vendor-Independent Calendaring
VIM	Vendor-Independent Messaging
VLAN	Virtual Local Area Network
VM	Virtual Machine
VME	VersaModule Eurocard
VPE	Visual Programming Environment
VSAM	Virtual Storage Access Method (IBM)
WAN	Wide Area Network
WFW	Windows for Workgroups
WINS	Windows Internet Naming Service

WORM	Write Once, Read Many
WWW	World Wide Web
XAPIA	X.400 Application Programming Interface Association
XFN	X/Open Federated Naming
XML	Extensible Markup Language
XNS	Xerox Network Systems
XSM	X/Open Systems Management

PCI Security Standards

Many of the modernization activities today are in the Financial sectors. Modernized legacy systems must adhere to the PCI Data Security standards. So, we thought it would be helpful to include these in the appendix as a reference for modernizations in this field.

Build and Maintain a Secure Network

Requirement 1: Install and maintain a firewall configuration to protect data .

Requirement 2: Do not use vendor-supplied defaults for system passwords and other security parameters.

Protect Cardholder Data

Requirement 3: Protect stored data.

Requirement 4: Encrypt transmission of cardholder data and sensitive information across public networks.

Maintain a Vulnerability Management Program

Requirement 5: Use and regularly update antivirus software.

Requirement 6: Develop and maintain secure systems and applications.

Implement Strong Access Control Measures

Requirement 7: Restrict access to data by business need-to-know.

Requirement 8: Assign a unique ID to each person with computer access.

Requirement 9: Restrict physical access to cardholder data.

Regularly Monitor and Test Networks

Requirement 10: Track and monitor all access to network resources and cardholder data.

Requirement 11: Regularly test security systems and processes.

Maintain an Information Security Policy

Requirement 12: Maintain a policy that addresses information security

More information can be found:
`https://www.pcisecuritystandards.org/index.htm`

Index

B

backbone 377
BAM 27
Basic Mapping Support (BMS) 348
batch architecture, technical view
  about 230
  optional products 233
  process flow 231-233
batch design pattern, Oracle batch
        architecture
  about 250
  error handling 251
  Oracle ADF 251
  Oracle BPEL and business rules 250
  Oracle database grid 250
  Oracle enterprise manager 251
  Oracle scheduler 251
  Oracle warehouse builder 250
batch pattern. *See* batch system,
        requirements
batch system, implementation process
  about 236
  components, not present 237
  components, present 236
  legacy artifact group, re-designing 241
  legacy artifact group, re-factoring 241
  re-designing/re-factoring approach 239
  recovery/discovery approach 238
  repositories 240
batch system, requirements
  about 227, 228
  administrative batch 229
  error handling 229
  exception handling 229
  multi record type files 229
  third-party interfaces 230
  transaction processing 229
batch system, technical reasons 226, 227
BI 205
BOSS 84
BRE 204
bridge 377
bus 378
Business Activity Monitoring. *See* BAM
business community
  functional view 54, 55

functional view, components 56, 57
business continuity 378
Business Continuity Action Team (BCAT)
        378
Business Intelligence. *See* BI
business layer 41
Business Optimization Support System.
        See BOSS
business process reengineering 378
business rules, generating
  about 319-321
  dictionary, creating 322
  from J2EE and BPEL 331-333
  Java code used 334
  Java fact class, adding to rules author 324
  repository, creating 321, 322
  rule, adding 328-331
  ruleset, creating 323
business rules, mining
  about 304, 306
  backward auto-detection used 312-314
  identifying 308, 309
  merging 314
  pattern search used 309-311
  prerequisites 306-308
  validation rules, searching 312
Business Rules Engines. *See* BRE
Business Rules Manager. *See* business
        rules, mining

C

CCI 157
CDC 111
cell 378
Change Data Capture. *See* CDC
character-based interface 378
CICS
  about 379
  transaction gateway 99
client/server model of computing 378
cloud computing
  about 371, 378
  example, amazon elastic compute cloud
        (Amazon EC2) 371
collaborative authoring 378

Knowledge Discovery Meta-Model.
  See **KDM**
Knowledge Driven Modernization.
  See **KDM**
KPIs 27

L

layers. *See* **application layers**
legacy acronyms 389-396
legacy adapters, data modernization 27, 29
legacy artifact, exposing 112
legacy artifact group, batch system
  business flows, re-design/re-factor 243
  business flows, recovery/discovery 243
  COBOL business rules, re-design/re-factor
    244
  COBOL business rules, recovery/discovery
    243, 244
  COBOL data access logic, re-design/
    re-factor 245
  COBOL data access logic, recovery/
    discovery 244
  database and database schema, re-design/
    re-factor 246
  database and database schema, recovery/
    discovery 245
  green bar reports, re-design/re-factor 242
  green bar reports, recovery/discovery 242
  job scheduler, re-design/re-factor 242
  job scheduler, recovery/discovery 242
legacy artifacts
  about 57
  re-implementing, ways 296
legacy modernization
  benefits 30
  data modernization 26
  key factors 43, 44
  legacy understanding 11
  platform migration 21
  re-architecture 16-19
  replacement 29
  SOA integration 19
Legacy Service Bus. *See* **LSB**
Legacy Services Engine. *See* **LSE**
legacy SOA integration
  about 99

applicaton, running 165
applicaton, testing 165, 167
implementation lifecycle 78
legacy system 382
legacy understanding, legacy modernization
  about 11
  APA macro analysis 12, 13
  APA micro analysis 13, 15
  Application Portfolio Analysis (APA) 11
  Application Portfolio Management (APM)
    15
legacy VSAM file data access
  connection properties, setting 143, 144
  exposing 142
  Oracle connect adapter 149-153
  Oracle connect data source 145-149
  Oracle Connect on mainframe, connecting
    to 143, 144
  property settings 144
Local Area Network (LAN) 382
LPAR 382
LSB 56, 59
LSE
  about 56, 60, 106
  components 60
  run-time components 106
LSE components
  about 60
  connectivity and processing engine 60
LSE components, optional
  caching 65
  orchestration 64
  security 64
LSE development 65
LSE implementation/deployment
  about 66
  legacy artifacts 67, 68
  LSE server location 66
  metadata repositories 69

M

MAA 220
Magneto-optical (MO) 383
mainframe migration 356
mainframe modernization 343

Q

Quarter Inch Cartridge (QIC) 385

R

re-architect
  business drivers 219, 220
re-architecture
  about 16
  advanced development tools 176
  advantages 189-192
  approaches 209
  barriers 192
  characteristics 170, 171
  cons 185
  considerations 171
  drivers 171
  guidelines 208
  human factors 172
  in IBM view 173
  modernization life cycle, caveats 214
  need for 188
  phases 182, 215
  platform agility 172
  process 17, 19
  pros 185
  ripping and replacing 184
  technical considerations 177
  technical drivers 174
  versus re-host 178, 180
re-architecture, advantages
  application, maintenance 190
  architected for internet 190
  availability 191
  Enterprise Information Integration (EII)
      and Enterprise Application Integration
      (EAI) 190
  on demand reporting 191
  scalability 190
  security 192
  software options 191
re-architecture, approaches
  iterative-phased approaches (IPA) 209
re-architecture, barriers
  custom ETL 193
  custom integration applications 193
  custom workflow 193

re-architecture, functional view
  about 200-202
  components 203, 204
  software components 205
  technical perspective 202, 203
re-architecture, phases
  change-data-capture (CDC) 218
  design target architecture 215
  development iterations 217
  discovery/recovery 215
  legacy application, unplugging 218
  model target architecture 216
  performance scalability 217
  production roll out 217, 218
  re-factoring phase 183
  re-generation phase 183, 184
  re-specification phase 183
  recovery phase 182, 183
  user acceptance testing (UAT) 217
re-architecture implementation
  modernization factory used 218, 219
re-architecture modernization life cycle
  about 213
  lifecycle caveats 213, 214
re-design/re-factor 288
re-design/re-factor approach, batch system
  botto-down approach 240
  hybrid approach 240
  top-down approach 239
re-host strategy
  about 180
  summary, by Gartner report 181
  versus re-architecture 178-180
rearchitect 385
recovery/discovery 288
recovery/discovery approach, batch system
  best practices 239
  manual methodology 239
  tooling 239
Redundant Arrays of Independant Disks
      (RAID) 385
rehost 385
rehosting, platform migration
  about 23
  re-hosing based on modernization 24-26
relational database 385

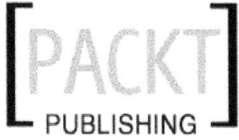

[PACKT] PUBLISHING

Thank you for buying

Oracle Modernization Solutions

About Packt Publishing

Packt, pronounced 'packed', published its first book "*Mastering phpMyAdmin for Effective MySQL Management*" in April 2004 and subsequently continued to specialize in publishing highly focused books on specific technologies and solutions.

Our books and publications share the experiences of your fellow IT professionals in adapting and customizing today's systems, applications, and frameworks. Our solution based books give you the knowledge and power to customize the software and technologies you're using to get the job done. Packt books are more specific and less general than the IT books you have seen in the past. Our unique business model allows us to bring you more focused information, giving you more of what you need to know, and less of what you don't.

Packt is a modern, yet unique publishing company, which focuses on producing quality, cutting-edge books for communities of developers, administrators, and newbies alike. For more information, please visit our website: www.packtpub.com.

Writing for Packt

We welcome all inquiries from people who are interested in authoring. Book proposals should be sent to author@packtpub.com. If your book idea is still at an early stage and you would like to discuss it first before writing a formal book proposal, contact us; one of our commissioning editors will get in touch with you.

We're not just looking for published authors; if you have strong technical skills but no writing experience, our experienced editors can help you develop a writing career, or simply get some additional reward for your expertise.

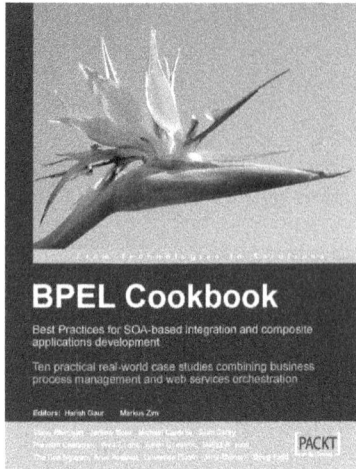

BPEL Cookbook

ISBN: 1-904811-33-7   Paperback: 188 pages

Ten practical real-world case studies combining business process management and web services orchestration

1. Real-world BPEL recipes for SOA integration and Composite Application development

2. Combining business process management and web services orchestration

3. Techniques and best practices with downloadable code samples from ten real-world case studies

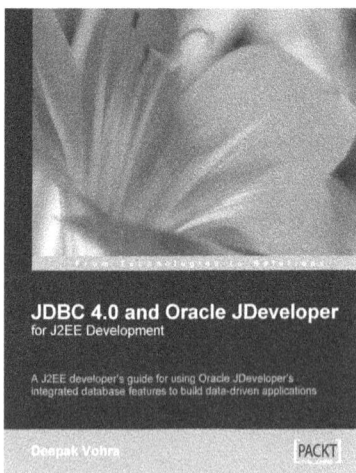

JDBC 4.0 and Oracle JDeveloper for J2EE Development

ISBN: 978-1-847194-30-5   Paperback: 431 pages

A J2EE developer's guide to using Oracle JDeveloper's integrated database features to build data-driven applications

1. Develop your Java applications using JDBC and Oracle JDeveloper

2. Explore the new features of JDBC 4.0

3. Use JDBC and the data tools in Oracle JDeveloper

4. Configure JDBC with various application servers

5. Build data-driven applications quickly and easily

Please check **www.PacktPub.com** for information on our titles

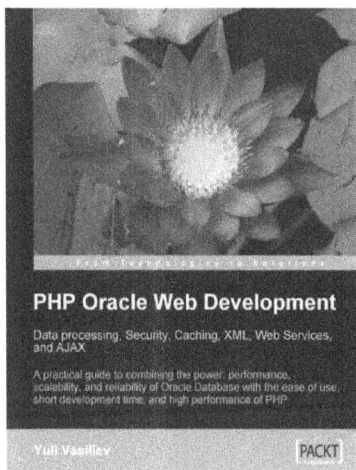

PHP Oracle Web Development

ISBN: 978-1-847193-63-6   Paperback: 350 pages

A practical guide to combining the power, performance, scalability, and reliability of the Oracle Database with the ease of use, short development time, and high performance of PHP

1. Program your own PHP/Oracle application

2. Move data processing inside the database

3. Distribute data processing between the web/PHP and Oracle database servers

4. Create reusable building blocks for PHP/Oracle solutions

5. Use up-to-date technologies, such as Ajax and web services, in PHP Oracle development

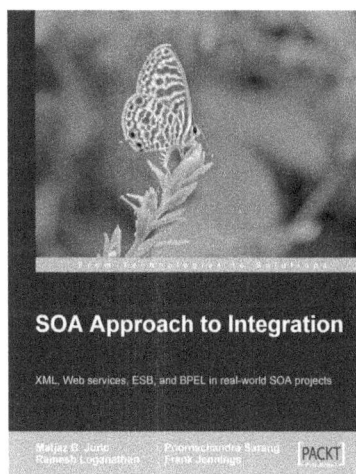

SOA Approach to Integration

ISBN: 978-1-904811-17-6   Paperback: 300 pages

XML, Web services, ESB, and BPEL in real-world SOA projects

1. Service-Oriented Architectures and SOA approach to integration

2. SOA architectural design and domain-specific models

3. Common Integration Patterns and how they can be best solved using Web services, BPEL and Enterprise Service Bus (ESB)

4. Concepts behind SOA standards, security, transactions, and how to efficiently work with XML